THE MAGNIFICENCE OF THE QUR'AN

Author by
PhD. Maḥmūd Ibn Aḥmad al Dosary

The Magnificence of the Qur'an

In the name of Allah, the Most Beneficent, the Most Merciful.
The original version of this book was a research thesis that was submitted to the Department of Islamic Studies in the National University of Yemen. The researcher of the thesis was a Master degree student who specialized in the Sciences of the Qur'an. The thesis was debated before a panel of professors on the following date: 25/11/1425 H.
By dint of his thesis, the researcher graduated with a Master Degree in the sciences of the Qur'an. His grade was "excellent" and he was additionally awarded with a special ranking of distinction. His thesis was summarized to an appropriate length so that it could benefit a wide audience of readers; the result of that summarization is the book you have before you now.

Introduction

Indeed, all praise is for Allah; we praise Him, repent to Him and seek His forgiveness and help. We seek refuge in Allah from the evil of our own selves and of our wicked deeds. Whomsoever Allah guides, none can lead astray; and whomsoever Allah leads astray, none can guide. And I bear witness that none has the right to be worshipped except Allah alone, and He has no partner; and I bear witness that our Prophet Muhammad is His slave and Messenger.

The importance of this book's subject
Of all the books in the entire world, there is only one that is free of errors and defects, and that book is none other than the Noble Qur'an. It is the soul of the Muslim nation, and it is by virtue of it that Muslims are raised in status and ranking above other peoples. Addressing His Messenger (s), Allah (sp) said:

وَكَذَٰلِكَ أَوْحَيْنَآ إِلَيْكَ رُوحًا مِّنْ أَمْرِنَا ۚ مَا كُنتَ تَدْرِى مَا ٱلْكِتَٰبُ وَلَا ٱلْإِيمَٰنُ وَلَٰكِن جَعَلْنَٰهُ نُورًا نَّهْدِى بِهِۦ مَن نَّشَآءُ مِنْ عِبَادِنَا ۚ

"And thus We have sent to you (O Muhammad) Ruhan (an inspiration and a mercy) of Our Command. You knew not what is the Book, nor what is Faith. But We have made it (this Book) a light wherewith We guide whosoever of Our slaves We will." (Qur'an: 42:52).

Without a doubt, a tremendous change occurred on earth when the Noble Qur'an was revealed. Those who followed its teachings were taken from darkness to light. They walked accompanied by a blessed light among men who were engulfed in darkness. And just as light will remain as long as this universe exists, the Qur'an will remain as long as there is life on earth; and its rays will continue to penetrate the different parts of earth until Allah (sp) inherits both the earth and its inhabitants. Allah (sp) said:

$$\text{أَوَمَن كَانَ مَيْتًا فَأَحْيَيْنَاهُ وَجَعَلْنَا لَهُ نُورًا يَمْشِي بِهِ فِي ٱلنَّاسِ كَمَن مَّثَلُهُ فِي ٱلظُّلُمَاتِ لَيْسَ بِخَارِجٍ مِّنْهَا}$$

"Is he who was dead (without Faith by ignorance and disbelief) and We gave him life (by knowledge and faith) and set for him a light (if belief) whereby he can walk amongst men, like him who is in the darkness (of disbelief, polytheism and hypocrisy) from which he can never come out?" (Qur'an 6:122). Jibreel (p) descended with the Noble Qur'an from the heavens above, taking it to the chief of all created beings, the most noble of all Prophets and Messengers (st) – our Prophet Muhammad (s). The Prophet (s) then conveyed the Noble Qur'an to the rest of mankind; additionally, he (s) explained the Qur'an through his actions and demeanour – by being a practical manifestation of its teachings and of the morals it contained. A new phase now began in the history of mankind, and a new and blessed and magnificent civilization was born. Every word of the Noble Qur'an had a profound effect on the hearts of believers. A gentle word, a promise of reward, or a reference to Allah's generosity brought a smile to their faces and hope to their hearts. Conversely, a threat of punishment caused their hearts to tremble with fear.

$$\text{إِنَّ هَٰذَا ٱلْقُرْءَانَ يَهْدِي لِلَّتِي هِيَ أَقْوَمُ وَيُبَشِّرُ ٱلْمُؤْمِنِينَ ٱلَّذِينَ يَعْمَلُونَ ٱلصَّالِحَاتِ أَنَّ لَهُمْ أَجْرًا كَبِيرًا (9) وَأَنَّ ٱلَّذِينَ لَا يُؤْمِنُونَ بِٱلْآخِرَةِ أَعْتَدْنَا لَهُمْ عَذَابًا أَلِيمًا}$$

"Verily this Qur'an guides to that which is most just and right and gives glad tidings to the believers (in the Oneness of Allah and His Messenger, Muhammad, etc.) who work deeds of righteousness that they shall have great reward. And that those who believe not in the Hereafter (i.e. they disbelieve that they will be recompensed for what they did in this world, good or bad etc.), for them We have prepared a painful torment." (Qur'an 17: 9, 10).

The Prophet (s) came with many miracles, as did the Prophets and Messengers, peace be upon them, who came before him; but each one of their miracles was momentary in nature; it occurred and then it came to an end. Or in other words, the number of people who actually witnessed a given miracle was limited to those who were present when it occurred. But not so regarding the Noble Qur'an: it is the only miracle that has been witnessed by generations of people and that will continue to be witnessed by people until Allah (sp) inherits the earth and all who are on it. Anyone who reads the Qur'an is able to appreciate its miraculous nature, and is thus able to appreciate the truthfulness of the Messenger of Allah (s).

Allah (sp) challenged all human beings and Jinns to produce anything that could be deemed similar to the noble Qur'an, but they failed to meet that challenge. Even if all human beings and Jinns were to work together and combine their efforts to produce something that is similar to the Qur'an, they would fail miserably in the attempt. Allah (sp) said:

$$\text{قُل لَّئِنِ ٱجْتَمَعَتِ ٱلْإِنسُ وَٱلْجِنُّ عَلَىٰ أَن يَأْتُوا بِمِثْلِ هَٰذَا ٱلْقُرْءَانِ لَا يَأْتُونَ بِمِثْلِهِ وَلَوْ كَانَ بَعْضُهُمْ لِبَعْضٍ ظَهِيرًا}$$

"Say: 'If the mankind and the Jinns were together to produce the like of this Qur'an, they could not produce the like thereof, even if they helped one another.'" (17:88).

In these trying times, Muslims are in dire need of the Qur'an, for without it, they will not be able to meet the challenges of today's problems. By adhering to the Noble Qur'an, they will achieve worldly success, victory against their enemies, and the ultimate success of the Hereafter. In the following

Verses, Allah (sp) established a clear link between following the guidance of the Qur'an and achieving success:

$$\text{فَإِمَّا يَأْتِيَنَّكُم مِّنِّى هُدًى فَمَنِ ٱتَّبَعَ هُدَاىَ فَلَا يَضِلُّ وَلَا يَشْقَىٰ}$$

$$\text{وَمَنْ أَعْرَضَ عَن ذِكْرِى فَإِنَّ لَهُ مَعِيشَةً ضَنكًا وَنَحْشُرُهُ يَوْمَ ٱلْقِيَـٰمَةِ أَعْمَىٰ}$$

"Then if there comes to you guidance from me, then whoever follows My guidance shall neither go astray, nor fall into distress and misery. But whosoever turns away from My Reminder (i.e. the Qur'an), verily for him is a life of hardship, and We shall raise him up blind on the Day of Resurrection." (20: 123,124).

Why I chose this subject matter

In choosing this subject matter for my Master thesis, I was motivated by a number of goals and considerations, the most important of them being as follows:

1. I wanted to serve the Noble Qur'an, to extract its treasures, to deduce its rulings – and to reveal to readers certain aspects of its greatness and magnificence. I hope to thus perhaps be able to contribute to the knowledge we have concerning the sciences of the Qur'an.
2. I hoped to show readers that Allah (sp) bestowed a great favour upon the Prophet (s) and the people of his nation by giving them the best and most magnificent of all divinely revealed books.
3. I wanted to warn Muslims not to become heedless of the Noble Qur'an. For it is every Muslim's duty not just to recite the Qur'an, but also to understand it, to reflect upon its meanings and to implement its rulings and teachings.
4. I was convinced that the subject matter of this book – describing and illustrating the magnificence of the Noble Qur'an – has not been dealt with justly in any of the books that I have come across. Yes, the topic is discussed in certain pages of books that have been written concerning the Sciences of the Noble Qur'an; but it has not been dealt with as the entire subject matter of a written work.
5. In the times we live in, great masses of people are ignorant of the greatness and magnificence of the Noble Qur'an; hence the dire need of books that deal specifically with the subject-matter of this work.
6. The enemies of Islam have, with great creativity, dedication and energy, striven to promote false beliefs and divinely-revealed books that have been distorted to the point that they contain a mix of falsehood and the truth. Should it not then be befitting of Muslims to strive equally hard to promote their Book, especially considering the facts that it has not been distorted, that it has remained preserved and unchanged over the centuries, and that it contains in it the Speech of the Lord of all that exists?
7. Finally, I wanted to correct some of the more dangerous misconceptions that people have regarding the Noble Qur'an.

My methodology in writing this research paper

Following is an outline of the methodology I adhered to in authoring this work:

1. As the reader will see, Allah willing, I relied heavily on Verses of the Qur'an, sayings of the Prophet (s) and sayings of the people of knowledge; therefore, through this work my primary aim is not to give my view of things, if you will, but to present in an organized manner revealed texts and sayings of prominent scholars that deal with the subject matter of this work. This is not to say, however, that that is the extent of this work, for in addition to presenting texts, I have endeavoured to analyze, infer, and deduce the meanings of those texts.
2. Whenever possible, I quoted texts from older references, since source material is contained in them. Only when I was unable to find specific information in older texts did I cite information from more recent or modern-day works. I should point out that each of the following falls underneath the category of modern-day works: research papers, scholarly magazines and information shared during conferences and the meetings of legal bodies and organizations.
3. I referenced each Qur'anic text by mentioning both Verse number and Chapter title (Surah).
4. I also mentioned the source of every Hadeeth that is cited in this work; additionally – or at least whenever possible – I mentioned what the people of knowledge have said regarding the level of their authenticity; however, I abstained from doing so whenever a Hadeeth was related by both Bukharee and Muslim or at least by one of them.

In authoring *The Magnificence of the Noble Qur'an*, I do not claim to have written the perfect book. It goes without saying that deficiency and flaws are part of the nature of man and that perfection is a quality that can be attributed to Allah (sp) alone. It is, however, enough for me to know that I have tried my utmost to give justice to the subject matter of this work.

It certainly behooves me to thank everyone who helped me complete this project; I appreciate all of the energy and time they sacrificed to aid me in this scholarly pursuit. May Allah reward those who provided me with either advice or important reference material. Guidance is from Allah alone; upon Him do I place my trust, and to Him do I repent. And all praise is for Allah by whose favor good works are accomplished.

Written by:
Mahmood bin Ahmad Ad-Dausaree
A *da'wah* worker in the Ministry of Islamic Affairs,
Endowments, Propagation of Islam and Guidance,
Kingdom of Saudi Arabia
Dosary33@hotmail.com
Ad-Damaam, P.O. box: 2779, R.B.: 31461
Written on 15/8/1426 H.

INTRODUCTION

First topic: The meaning of the word "Qur'an" in Islam.

Second topic: The meaning of "the Magnificence of the Qur'an".

First topic:
The meaning of the word "Qur'an" in Islam.

The meaning of the Word "Qur'an" is obvious to all Muslims; it is the final book of divine revelation which Allah (sp) revealed to the Seal of all Prophets, Muhammad (s). Nonetheless, given the importance of the Noble Qur'an, scholars have endeavored to give a more precise and scholarly definition of the "Qur'an". It is as follows: "Allah's Speech, as revealed to His Prophet Muhammad (s); its wording is miraculous in nature; to recite it is an act of worship; it is that which is written in *al-Masaahif* (written copies of the Qur'an) and is related in *Mutawaatir* form."[1]

In general, the purpose of mentioning so many clauses in the definition is to exclude everything that is not the Qur'an. Let us take a look at each individual clause so that we can better appreciate its importance to the overall definition:

1. "Allah's Speech": Based on this clause, all speech of men, Jinns and angels is excluded.
2. "As revealed": This clause eliminates from the definition any of Allah's Speech that was not revealed, or that He imparted to the angels without instructing them to descend with it to a human being. Allah did not reveal to human beings everything He said; some of what He has said is known exclusively to Him, or to certain angels as well. Allah (sp) said:

قُل لَّوْ كَانَ ٱلْبَحْرُ مِدَادًا لِّكَلِمَٰتِ رَبِّى لَنَفِدَ ٱلْبَحْرُ قَبْلَ أَن تَنفَدَ كَلِمَٰتُ رَبِّى وَلَوْ جِئْنَا بِمِثْلِهِ مَدَدًا

   "Say (O Muhammad to mankind), 'If the sea were ink for (writing) the Words of my Lord, surely, the sea would be exhausted before the Words of my Lord would be finished, even if We brought (another sea) like it for its aid." (Qur'an 18: 109).

3. "To His Prophet Muhammad" (s): This clause eliminates everything that Allah (sp) revealed to other Prophets, peace be upon them, such as the Torah, which was revealed to Moosa (p) (Moses); the Injeel, which was revealed to 'Iesa (p) (Jesus) ; the Zaboor, which was revealed to Dawood (p), or As-Suhuf ("The Scrolls"), which were revealed to Ibraaheem (p).
4. "Its wording is miraculous in nature": This clause eliminates the category of Allah's Speech that is not meant to be miraculous in nature, such as Qudsee Ahaadeeth, which are Allah's Sayings, but because they are not meant to be miraculous like the Qur'an, the Prophet (s) would sometime re-word those sayings when he would relate them to his Companions (rp). Similarly, this clause eliminates previously revealed books, since, unlike the Qur'an, Allah (sp) did not challenge human beings to produce the equivalent of them.
5. "To recite it is an act of worship": This eliminates Qudsee Ahaadeeth as well as recitations of specific Verses that were related by individual narrators; such recitations are known as "*Shaadh*", or "strange".

---
[1] *Mabaahith Fee 'Uloom al-Qur'an'* p. 20.

6. "It is that which is written in *Al-Masaahif* (written copies of the Qur'an)": This eliminates Allah's Sayings that are not written down in copies of the Qur'an; therefore, by dint of this clause, we know that it is incorrect to use the term "Qur'an" to describe Verses that had been a part of the Qur'an but were then not only abrogated in meaning, but actually removed from the Qur'an.
7. "And is related in *Mutawaatir* form": Something that is related in *Mutawaatir* form is related by so many people at each level of a narration that it is impossible for them to all have colluded in the act of fabricating a lie. Therefore, this clause eliminates recitations that were related not in *Mutawaatir* form, but by individual narrators – or in other words, recitations that are "*Shaadh*" or "strange".

Second topic:
The meaning of "the Magnificence of the Qur'an"

Upon reading the title of this work, the reader might be tempted to ask a question, "What specifically does the author mean by the phrase, 'The Magnificence of the Qur'an?'". Well, the word 'magnificent' is a loose translation of the word that is used in the title of the original Arabic version of this book: '*Adhama*'. '*Adhama*' conveys many similar meanings, such as magnificence, grandeur, greatness, exaltedness and splendor (these words, so as to create a sense of variety, will often be used interchangeably throughout this work). More specifically, the phrase "The Magnificence of the Qur'an" refers to the following qualities of the Qur'an:

1. Its lofty meanings and its perfect and flawless style.
2. The perfect justness of its teachings.
3. The comprehensiveness of its rulings, in that the solution to every problem in life can be found in the Qur'an.
4. The wonderful and upright nature of its teachings and aims.
5. The sense of awe and sanctity that Allah (sp) instilled in the heart of every person or entity that listens to it or recites it – be he man or jinn, believer or disbeliever, inanimate object or animal.
6. The honor that is achieved by every person who believes in it and applies its teachings.
7. Its miraculous nature – in terms of its tone, flow, eloquence, profound meanings, etc. – because of which the disbelievers have been unable to produce anything that is similar or comparable to it.

CHAPTER 1
The Magnificence of its Meanings, Aims and Powerful Influence

This chapter consists of three parts:

Part one: The Magnificence of the Qur'an's Meanings

Part two: The magnificence of the Qur'an's tone and aims.

Part three: The powerful influence of the Noble Qur'an.

Part one: The Magnificence of the Qur'an's Meanings.

This part consists of four topics:
Topic one: The magnificence of the Noble Qur'an as clarified by its Verses.
Topic two: Manifestations of the Qur'an's magnificence.
Topic three: Proofs of the Qur'an magnificence.
Topic four: The grandeur of the names and attributes of the Qur'an.

Topic one: The Magnificence of the Noble Qur'an as clarified by its Verses

This topic consists of six distinct sections:
Section one: Allah's praise of His Book.
Section two: The Superiority of the One who Descended with the Qur'an.
Section three: The Qur'an is a Revelation from the Lord of All that Exists.
Section four: The Qur'an is Upright and Contains in it no Crookedness.
Section five: The Humbling and Fear of Mountains.
Section six: Mankind and Jinns are Challenged to Produce Something that is Comparable to the Noble Qur'an.

Section one:

Allah's Praise of His Book.

In the title of this work, I used the word *'Adhama* (magnificence) to describe the Noble Qur'an. To be sure, this was no innovation on my part, for Allah (sp) Himself used one of the noun-forms of *'Adhama* – *''Adheem* – to describe the Qur'an. He (sp) said:

وَلَقَدْ ءَاتَيْنَٰكَ سَبْعًا مِّنَ ٱلْمَثَانِى وَٱلْقُرْءَانَ ٱلْعَظِيمَ

"And indeed, We have bestowed upon you seven of al-Mathani (seven repeatedly recited Verses, namely the Fatiha) and the Grand Qur'an." (Qur'an: 15:87).
In another Verse, Allah (sp) used the word 'perfected' to describe the Qur'an:

$$\text{الر كِتَابٌ أُحْكِمَتْ ءَايَاتُهُ ثُمَّ فُصِّلَتْ مِن لَّدُنْ حَكِيمٍ خَبِيرٍ}$$

"Alif-Lam-Ra. (This is) a Book, the Verses whereof are perfected and then explained in detail from One Who is All-Wise and Well-Acquainted (with all things)." (Qur'an: 11:1).

And in yet another Verse, Allah (sp) said that the Qur'an is a witness over previous scriptures:

$$\text{وَأَنزَلْنَا إِلَيْكَ الْكِتَابَ بِالْحَقِّ مُصَدِّقًا لِّمَا بَيْنَ يَدَيْهِ مِنَ الْكِتَابِ وَمُهَيْمِنًا عَلَيْهِ}$$

"And We have sent down to you (O Muhammad) the Book (this Qur'an) in truth, confirming the Scripture that came before it and Muhayminan (trustworthy in highness and a witness) over it." (Qur'an: 5:48).

In this Verse, Allah (sp) said that the Qur'an was *Muhayminan* over previous scriptures. What this means is that it contains in preserved form the aims and teachings of previously revealed Books – such as the Torah and Injeel (Gospel); furthermore, it is a witness over them, confirming what is correct in them (for they have been distorted by the hands of men), and correcting the mistakes that they contain (mistakes which of course are not from Allah, but from the people who distorted the Books He revealed).

Also, Allah (sp) informs us that, in the Mother of the Book (i.e. *Al-Lauh Al-Mahfuz*), He (sp) described the Qur'an as being "exalted, full of wisdom":

$$\text{وَإِنَّهُ فِى أُمِّ الْكِتَابِ لَدَيْنَا لَعَلِىٌّ حَكِيمٌ}$$

"And verily, it (the Qur'an) is in the Mother of the Book (i.e. Al-Lauh Al-Mahfuz), before Us, indeed exalted, full of wisdom." (Qur'an: 43:3).

Without a doubt, the Noble Qur'an is exalted above all other Books that Allah (sp) revealed to previous Prophets, peace be upon them; it is after all, a miracle that will remain manifest on earth until the end of time.[2] The Qur'an is also *hakeem*, which is loosely translated as meaning 'full of wisdom'. Although 'full of wisdom' is meant by the word *hakeem* in the above-mentioned Verse, other meanings are implied as well, such as the fact that the Qur'an is put together in a perfect manner, or that it is completely free of all defects, or that none of its rulings run contrary to the ideals of wisdom and justice.[3]

And finally, in four separate Verses, Allah (sp) described the Qur'an as being a Blessed Book.[4]

Section two:
The Superiority of the One Who Descended with The Qur'an.

Within various Verses of the Qur'an, Allah (sp) spoke highly of the one who descended with the Qur'an to our Messenger Muhammad (s). I am referring here to none other than Jibreel (p), the angel that was entrusted with the task of conveying divine revelation to the Prophet (s). Allah (sp) praised Jibreel (p) for his superior qualities in a number of Verses, such as the following from Surah *An-Nahl*:

---

[2] *At-Tafseer al-Kabeer* (27/167).
[3] *Tafseer as-Sa'dee* (4/437).
[4] *Al-An'aam* : 92, 155 ; *Al-anbiyaa* : 5 ; *Saad* : 29.

$$\text{قُلْ نَزَّلَهُ رُوحُ ٱلْقُدُسِ مِن رَّبِّكَ بِٱلْحَقِّ لِيُثَبِّتَ ٱلَّذِينَ ءَامَنُوا۟ وَهُدًى وَبُشْرَىٰ لِلْمُسْلِمِينَ}$$

"Say (O Muhammad) Ruh-ul-Qudus (Jibreel, Gabriel) has brought it (the Qur'an) down from your Lord with truth, that it may make firm and strengthen (the Faith of) those who believe and as a guidance and glad tidings to those who have submitted (to Allah)." (Qur'an: 16: 102).

The word *Ruh* means soul or spirit, but in the context of the above-mentioned Verse it refers to Jibreel (p), and *Qudus* connotes the meanings of purity and virtue. Allah (sp) used the word *Ruh* to describe Jibreel in another Verse as well:

$$\text{فَأَرْسَلْنَآ إِلَيْهَا رُوحَنَا}$$

"Then We sent to her Our Ruh (angel Jibreel/Gabriel)". (Qur'an: 19: 17).

And in another Verse, Allah (sp) said:

$$\text{وَإِنَّهُ لَتَنزِيلُ رَبِّ ٱلْعَٰلَمِينَ}$$
$$\text{نَزَلَ بِهِ ٱلرُّوحُ ٱلْأَمِينُ}$$
$$\text{عَلَىٰ قَلْبِكَ لِتَكُونَ مِنَ ٱلْمُنذِرِينَ}$$

"And truly, this (the Qur'an) is a revelation from the Lord of Worlds. Which the trustworthy Ruh (Jibreel) has brought down. Upon your heart (O Muhammad) that you may be (one) of the warners." (Qur'an: 26: 192-194).

We know that *Ruh* means spirit or soul, so why was Jibreel (p) given the name *Ar-Ruh*? Scholars have answered this question with various explanations, such as these ones:

1. Jibreel (p) is in fact a pure and virtuous soul, and so Allah (sp) named him thus as a way of honoring him and proclaiming his lofty status.
2. The religion of Islam is alive through Jibreel, just as a body of a person is alive through his soul. This makes sense since Jibreel (p) was charged with the duty of bringing down revelation not just to Prophet Muhammad (s) but to previous Prophets (st) as well.
3. Spirituality is one of the dominant qualities of all angels, but to a greater degree with Jibreel (p) than with any other angel.[5]

Allah (sp) said:

$$\text{إِنَّهُ لَقَوْلُ رَسُولٍ كَرِيمٍ}$$
$$\text{ذِى قُوَّةٍ عِندَ ذِى ٱلْعَرْشِ مَكِينٍ}$$
$$\text{مُّطَاعٍ ثَمَّ أَمِينٍ}$$

"Verily, this is the Word (this Qur'an brought by) a most honorable Messenger (Jibreel, from Allah to the Prophet Muhammad). Owner of power, and high rank with (Allah) the Lord of the Throne, Obeyed (by the angels), trustworthy there (in the heavens)." (Qur'an 81: 19-21).

In this Verse, Allah (sp) described Jibreel (p) with five qualities:

1. He is 'most honorable'.
2. He is an owner of power.
3. He enjoys a high-ranking with Allah (sp).
4. He is obeyed in the heavens.

---

[5] *At-Tahreer wat-Tanweer* (1/581), (13/229).

5. He is trustworthy.

Upon contemplating this Verse and all of the above-mentioned Verses, one is made to appreciate and to stand in awe of the chain of the Noble Qur'an. "Chain" in this context refers to a chain of a narration; every Hadeeth, for instance, has a chain: so-and-so related from so-and-so, who related from so-and-so, who related from such-and-such Companion (r) that the Messenger of Allah (s). Upon studying the chains of the most authentic of aHadeeth, one finds the names of many eminent scholars of Hadeeth from various generations, the likes of Abu Hurayra, 'Abdullah bin Mas'ood, Sufyaan Ath-Thauree, Maalik bin Anas, Sa'eed, Al-Hassan, and so on (rp). Now consider the lofty and awe-inspiring chain of the Noble Qur'an: the Messenger of Allah (s) related from the angel Jibreel (p), who related directly from the Lord of all that exists, Allah (sp).

Section three:
The Qur'an is a Revelation from the Lord of All that Exists.

Allah (sp) said:

وَإِنَّهُ لَتَنزِيلُ رَبِّ ٱلْعَٰلَمِينَ
نَزَلَ بِهِ ٱلرُّوحُ ٱلْأَمِينُ

"And truly, this (the Qur'an) is a revelation from the Lord of Worlds. Which the trustworthy Ruh (Jibreel) has brought down." (Qur'an: 26: 192-193).

Allah (sp) has ascribed the revelation of the Qur'an to Himself in more than 50 Verses of the Qur'an. This is a clear indication of how the Qur'an has been especially blessed with divine help and care. As for any person who recites the Qur'an, his awe and veneration of the Qur'an continues to increase in his heart while he is being constantly reminded that it came from Allah (sp), the Lord of all that exists. After all, the greater the author of a work, the better that work will be – and Allah (sp) is the Greatest, the All-Mighty, the Most-Just, the All-Wise, so consider how great the Qur'an then is.[6]

In another Verse, Allah (sp) used the pronoun "We" to ascribe the Qur'an to Himself:

إِنَّآ أَنزَلْنَٰهُ فِى لَيْلَةِ ٱلْقَدْرِ

"Verily! We have sent it (the Qur'an) down in the night of Destiny/Decree." (97:1).

On this note, the Qur'an has been blessed with six special qualities:

1. It was revealed from Allah alone, and from no one else, for the purpose of benefiting and guiding mankind.
2. It is the best of all divinely revealed books.
3. It was revealed through the best of angels and the strongest among them, the one who was entrusted with revelation from Allah (sp).

---

[6] 'Inaayatullah wa 'inaayatu-rasoolihi bil-Qur'an al-kareem, Dr. Abu Saree' Muhammad (p. 10) ; this work was a research paper that was presented during a conference in the Faculty of Sharee'a, in the University of Kuwait.

4. It descended upon the best of all created beings, Muhammad (s).
5. It was revealed to the best nation that has ever been sent to mankind.
6. It was revealed in the best, most comprehensive, and most eloquent of all languages: Arabic.[7]

Section four:
The Qur'an is Upright and Contains in it no Crookedness.

Allah (sp) said:

$$\text{ٱلۡحَمۡدُ لِلَّهِ ٱلَّذِىٓ أَنزَلَ عَلَىٰ عَبۡدِهِ ٱلۡكِتَٰبَ وَلَمۡ يَجۡعَل لَّهُۥ عِوَجَاۜ (١) قَيِّمٗا}$$

"All the praises and thanks be to Allah, Who has sent down to His slave (Muhammad) the Book, and has not placed therein any crookedness. (He has made it) Straight". (Qur'an: 18: 1,2).

In this Verse, Allah (sp) informs us that one of the reasons why He is deserving of praise is that He has sent down the Noble Qur'an – as if to point out that the Qur'an is the greatest of His blessings to mankind (and to Jinns as well).

In the above-mentioned Verse, Allah (sp) said that the Qur'an contains in it no crookedness. In explaining this Verse, scholars of the Arabic language have pointed out that, although crookedness ('*iwaj* in Arabic) is traditionally meant for tangible things – such as a crooked nose, crooked leg, or crooked lamp-stand – it can also be used in a figurative sense. Therefore, the fact that the Qur'an contains in it no crookedness implies the following qualities: first, there is no contradiction between the various Verses of the Qur'an. Allah (sp) said:

$$\text{وَلَوۡ كَانَ مِنۡ عِندِ غَيۡرِ ٱللَّهِ لَوَجَدُواْ فِيهِ ٱخۡتِلَٰفٗا كَثِيرٗا}$$

"Had it been from other than Allah, they would surely have found therein many contradictions." (Qur'an: 4: 82).

And second, everything that Allah (sp) said in the Qur'an – in regard to Islamic Monotheism, Prophethood, rulings, laws, legislations, morals, history lessons, etc. – is the absolute truth; there is not even an iota of a mistake in any of its Verses.[8]

In another Verse, Allah (sp) again mentioned that the Qur'an contains in it no crookedness, or in other words, it contains no contradictions, errors, or defects:

$$\text{قُرۡءَانًا عَرَبِيًّا غَيۡرَ ذِى عِوَجٖ}$$

"An Arabic Qur'an, without any crookedness (therein)." (Qur'an: 39: 28).

Section five:
The Humbling and Fear of Mountains

---

[7] *Tafseer as-Sa'dee* (3/485).
[8] *At-Tafseer al-Kabeer*, ar-Razee (21/64).

The Qur'an is so glorious and its effect is so powerful that, were it to descend upon any mountain, and were that mountain to be given a mind and a soul, it, despite being hard and firm, would have humbled itself and rendered itself asunder because of its fear of Allah (sp). Allah (sp) said:

$$\text{لَوْ أَنزَلْنَا هَٰذَا ٱلْقُرْءَانَ عَلَىٰ جَبَلٍ لَّرَأَيْتَهُۥ خَٰشِعًا مُّتَصَدِّعًا مِّنْ خَشْيَةِ ٱللَّهِ}$$

"Had We sent down this Qur'an on a mountain, you would surely have seen it humbling itself and rendering asunder by the fear of Allah." (Qur'an: 59:21).

When one gives a physical display of humbling oneself, one lowers one's head and bows down; the meaning of a mountain humbling itself in this Verse is that its higher parts would fall down to the ground. And "rendering asunder" means to split apart; in the above-mentioned Verse, it means that the mountain would shake and split apart as a result of its fear of Allah (sp).

The moral of the above-mentioned Verse is this: If a mountain were to understand the Qur'an as you do, O people of this world, it would have, in spite of its hardness and firmness, humbled itself and rendered itself asunder as a result of its fear of Allah. So is it not befitting for you, O people of this world, to humble yourselves and to make your hearts soft as a result of your fear of Allah (sp), especially considering the fact that you have been blessed with the abilities of understanding Allah's commands and of contemplating the meanings of His Book?[9]

In short, the above-mentioned Verse emphasizes and draws attention to the greatness and magnificence of the Qur'an; it furthermore encourages us to honor the Qur'an and contemplate its profound meanings, all the while implying a stern warning for those who neither honor the Qur'an nor implement its teachings.

Section six:

Mankind and Jinns are Challenged to Produce Something that is Comparable to the Noble Qur'an.

So as to emphasize the true magnificence of the Noble Qur'an, Allah (sp) challenged all human beings and Jinns to produce something that is comparable to it; or at least to produce ten chapters that are similar to ten of its chapters; or even still to produce something that is comparable to only one of its chapters. Allah (sp) said:

$$\text{قُل لَّئِنِ ٱجْتَمَعَتِ ٱلْإِنسُ وَٱلْجِنُّ عَلَىٰٓ أَن يَأْتُواْ بِمِثْلِ هَٰذَا ٱلْقُرْءَانِ لَا يَأْتُونَ بِمِثْلِهِۦ وَلَوْ كَانَ بَعْضُهُمْ لِبَعْضٍ ظَهِيرًا}$$

"Say: 'If the mankind and the Jinns were together to produce the like of this Qur'an, they could not produce the like thereof, even if they helped one another.'" (Qur'an: 17: 88).[10]

In this Verse, Allah (sp) gave the command, "Say", as if to make it clear to Prophet Muhammad (s) that it was not a private challenge, but instead one that the Prophet (s) was to proclaim before all people; the challenge, therefore, was not for a specific tribe or group of people, but for all of mankind.[11]

---

[9] *Tafseer Ibn Katheer* (4/343, 344).
[10] The reader would do well to contemplate other Verses that also contain in them challenges: Chapter *at-Toor*, Verse 34; Chapter *Hood*, Verse 13; Chapter *Yoonus*, Verse 38 and *al-Baqara*, Verse 23.
[11] *Tafseer ash-Sha'rawee* (14/8727).

In Chapter *Hood*, Allah (s) said:

$$\text{أَمْ يَقُولُونَ ٱفْتَرَىٰهُ ۖ قُلْ فَأْتُوا۟ بِعَشْرِ سُوَرٍ مِّثْلِهِۦ مُفْتَرَيَٰتٍ وَٱدْعُوا۟ مَنِ ٱسْتَطَعْتُم مِّن دُونِ ٱللَّهِ إِن كُنتُمْ صَٰدِقِينَ}$$

$$\text{فَإِلَّمْ يَسْتَجِيبُوا۟ لَكُمْ فَٱعْلَمُوٓا۟ أَنَّمَآ أُنزِلَ بِعِلْمِ ٱللَّهِ وَأَن لَّآ إِلَٰهَ إِلَّا هُوَ ۖ فَهَلْ أَنتُم مُّسْلِمُونَ}$$

"Or they say, 'He (Prophet Muhammad (s)) forged it (the Qur'an). Say: 'Bring you then ten forged Surah (chapters) like unto it, and call whomsoever you can, other than Allah (to your help), if you speak the truth!' If then they answer you not, know then that the Revelation (this Qur'an) is sent down with the Knowledge of Allah and that La ilaha illa Huwa: (none has the right to be worshipped but He)! Will you then be Muslims (those who submit to Islam)?" (Qur'an 11: 13, 14).

Even though the polytheists knew that they could not answer the challenge, and even though they were fully aware of the greatness and magnificence of the Qur'an, they still did not return to their senses. Allah (sp) then gave them a final challenge: that they should produce something that could be deemed comparable to even a single Chapter of the Qur'an. Allah (sp) said:

$$\text{أَمْ يَقُولُونَ ٱفْتَرَىٰهُ ۖ قُلْ فَأْتُوا۟ بِسُورَةٍ مِّثْلِهِۦ وَٱدْعُوا۟ مَنِ ٱسْتَطَعْتُم مِّن دُونِ ٱللَّهِ إِن كُنتُمْ صَٰدِقِينَ}$$

"Or do they say: 'He (Muhammad (s) has forged it?' Say: 'Bring then a Surah (Chapter) like unto it, and call upon whomsoever you can, besides Allah, if you are truthful!'" (Qur'an: 10: 38).

Not being able to meet even this challenge, the polytheists fell into a state of confusion and disarray; and yet they still refused to submit to the truth. At times, like deranged people, they said mockingly:

$$\text{وَ نَشَآءُ لَقُلْنَا مِثْلَ هَٰذَآ إِنْ هَٰذَآ إِلَّآ أَسَٰطِيرُ ٱلْأَوَّلِينَ}$$

"We have heard this (the Qur'an); if we wish we can say the like of this. This is nothing but the tales of the ancients." (Qur'an 8: 31).

Not to make an exact comparison – since to Allah (sp) belongs the highest example – but what they said is akin to a person of average intelligence saying, "If I wanted to, I could have matched Einstein's achievements in science!" And at other times, they would, just to pass time, say:

$$\text{ٱئْتِ بِقُرْءَانٍ غَيْرِ هَٰذَآ أَوْ بَدِّلْهُ}$$

"Bring us a Qur'an other than this, or change it." (Qur'an 10: 15).

In spite of such remarks on the part of the disbelievers, the fact of the matter is this: Allah (sp) challenged all of mankind to produce something similar to the Qur'an, knowing fully-well that they would fail to meet His challenge; and fail they most miserably did. Allah (sp) said:

$$\text{قُل لَّئِنِ ٱجْتَمَعَتِ ٱلْإِنسُ وَٱلْجِنُّ عَلَىٰٓ أَن يَأْتُوا۟ بِمِثْلِ هَٰذَا ٱلْقُرْءَانِ لَا يَأْتُونَ بِمِثْلِهِۦ وَلَوْ كَانَ بَعْضُهُمْ لِبَعْضٍ ظَهِيرًا}$$

"Say: 'If the mankind and the Jinns were together to produce the like of this Qur'an, they could not produce the like thereof, even if they helped one another.'" (Qur'an: 17: 88).

Topic 2:
Manifestations of the Qur'an's Magnificence

This topic consists of six sections:
Section one: The Qur'an was revealed during the best of times.
Section two: The Qur'an was revealed in the best and most comprehensive of languages.
Section three: The ease with which the Qur'an can be understood by all people.
Section four: Allah (sp) preserved the Qur'an.
Section five: The universal message of the Qur'an.
Section six: The Qur'an is a witness over previously revealed books.

Introduction

Allah's favors upon mankind are at once varied and numerous; but of all of His favors, the Noble Qur'an is the greatest and the most important. Allah (sp) highlighted this fact when He (sp) mentioned the favor of the Qur'an before mentioning the favor of creating human beings in the first place. Allah (sp) said:

ٱلرَّحْمَـٰنُ (١) عَلَّمَ ٱلْقُرْءَانَ (٢) خَلَقَ ٱلْإِنسَـٰنَ (٣) عَلَّمَهُ ٱلْبَيَانَ (٤)

"The Most Beneficent (Allah)! Has taught (you mankind) the Qur'an (by His Mercy). He created man. He taught him eloquent speech." (Qur'an 55: 1 – 4).

One who contemplates the Qur'an is sure to notice the great frequency with which Allah (sp) discusses or points to the greatness and magnificence of the Qur'an; this is especially the case in the beginnings and endings of Makki chapters (Surahs) of the Qur'an. In pointing to the magnificence of the Qur'an, Allah (sp) gave it many names and attributes; revealed it in the best of times and in the best of languages; made it easy for human beings to understand; made it a witness over the rest of His revealed books; and guaranteed to preserve it until the end of time. And all of these facts – which we will discuss in more detail in this section – are indications or manifestations, if you will, of the lofty status and greatness of the Qur'an.

Section one:
The Qur'an was revealed during the best of times

Allah (sp) said:

شَهْرُ رَمَضَانَ ٱلَّذِىٓ أُنزِلَ فِيهِ ٱلْقُرْءَانُ هُدًى لِّلنَّاسِ وَبَيِّنَـٰتٍ مِّنَ ٱلْهُدَىٰ وَٱلْفُرْقَانِ

"The month of Ramadan in which was revealed the Qur'an, a guidance for mankind and clear proofs for the guidance and the criterion (between right and wrong)." (Qur'an 2: 185).

To be sure, Ramadan is the best and most blessed of months; but what is more, the Qur'an was revealed on the most blessed of Ramadan's nights:

إِنَّآ أَنزَلْنَـٰهُ فِى لَيْلَةٍ مُّبَـٰرَكَةٍ إِنَّا كُنَّا مُنذِرِينَ

$$\text{فِيهَا يُفْرَقُ كُلُّ أَمْرٍ حَكِيمٍ}$$

"We sent it (this Qur'an) down on a blessed night (i.e. night of al-Qadr, in the month of Ramadan, the 9th month of the Islamic calendar). Verily, We are ever warning. Therein (that night) is decreed every matter of ordainments." (Qur'an 44: 3 – 4).

The blessed night referred in this Verse is the Night of al-Qadr, regarding which Allah (sp) has said:

$$\text{إِنَّا أَنزَلْنَاهُ فِى لَيْلَةِ ٱلْقَدْرِ (١) وَمَا أَدْرَاكَ مَا لَيْلَةُ ٱلْقَدْرِ (٢) لَيْلَةُ ٱلْقَدْرِ خَيْرٌ مِّنْ أَلْفِ شَهْرٍ (٣)}$$

"Verily! We have sent it (this Qur'an) down in the night of Al-Qadr (Decree). And what will make you know what the night of Al-Qadr (Decree) is? The night of Al-Qadr (Decree) is better than a thousand months (i.e. worshipping Allah in that night is better than worshipping Him a thousand months, i.e. 83 years and 4 months)." (Qur'an 97: 1 – 3).

It should be noted that the Night of al-Qadr is not special by dint of its timing; after all, every portion of time is the same as that which came before it, and that which comes after it. So the Night of al-Qadr is special not because of its timing, but because of what happened during it: The Noble Qur'an was revealed. This principle is general in its application: no portion of time is special in and of itself; if it is special or superior to other portions of time, it is because of the events that occurred during it. So while it is true that the Qur'an was given special status because it was revealed on the best of nights, it is equally true that the best of nights, the Night of al-Qadr, achieved its special status because of the events that occurred during it, one of them being the revelation of the Noble Qur'an.[12]

Section two:

The Qur'an was Revealed in the Best and Most Comprehensive of Languages

Allah (sp) chose to reveal the last of His books in the Arabic language. This choice can be traced back to the superiority of the Arabic language and to certain of its wonderful qualities, qualities that, though they may be found in some degree in other languages, are complete and whole only in the Arabic language. It would require at least an entire volume to describe in detail the superior qualities of the Arabic language, and so, given the scope of this work, I will suffice here with a brief discussion of the topic.

Even during the pre-Islamic days of ignorance, language played an important role in the lives of Arabs. Eloquence was to Arabs what advanced technological and scientific knowledge is in today's modern world – a mark of prestige and distinction. Eloquence defined a person's level of refinement, and poets were honored throughout society. Poetry competitions were held, and the winner's poetry was inscribed and hung up on the Kaaba. By the time the Prophet (s) was born, Arabic was a highly developed language.

Without a doubt, Arabic is a very flexible language; it did not need to borrow words from other languages, but instead was able to produce derivatives of previous Arabic words to accommodate new meanings. In this sense, Arabic is a very independent language: it is the norm in Arabic, and not the exception, that many words can be derived from a single root word. This makes Arabic a very enjoyable language to study. In English, for instance, one has to trace the root of a word back to Latin, Greek, French, or even Arabic. But in Arabic, each word is traced back to an Arabic root word, thus making Arabic a very independent and self-sustaining language. By the same token, Arabic is a very comprehensive language: not only are there ample words to describe any given concept, but also there

---

[12] *At-Tafseer al-Kabeer*, ar-Raazee (27/203,204).

are often tens of words to describe a similar meaning, and each of those words has a specific nuance to distinguish it from the others; or in other words, though twenty Arabic words may be synonyms, they are each unique in that they convey an additional shade of meaning that is not found in the other nineteen words.

Unless he has a bias against Islam or Arabs, a scholar of world languages cannot help but to declare Arabic as the most eloquent and comprehensive of languages. One of the main features of the Arabic language – a feature that was needed for the purpose of the Noble Qur'an – is that one is able to express many meanings in very few words; other languages might feature the same quality, but certainly to a lesser degree.

Additionally, because of the nature of Arabic, clarity is promoted. What I mean by this is that certain languages, especially modern day languages such as English, by dint of their formation and development and historical usage actually promote obfuscation and what has become known as doublespeak; one can say much without saying anything at all. But the development of the Arabic language as well as its historical use, on the other hand, promoted precision and clarity in speech.

In many Verses of the Noble Qur'an, Allah (sp) mentioned the blessing of revealing the Qur'an in the Arabic language. For example, in Chapter *az-Zukhruf*, Allah (sp) said:

إِنَّا جَعَلْنَٰهُ قُرْءَٰنًا عَرَبِيًّا لَّعَلَّكُمْ تَعْقِلُونَ

"We verily, have made it a Qur'an in Arabic, that you may be able to understand (its meanings and its admonitions)." (Qur'an 43: 3).

In Chapter *Yusuf*, Allah (sp) said:

إِنَّآ أَنزَلْنَٰهُ قُرْءَٰنًا عَرَبِيًّا لَّعَلَّكُمْ تَعْقِلُونَ

"Verily, We have sent it down as an Arabic Qur'an in order that you may understand." (Qur'an: 12: 2)[13]

The Qur'an needed to be revealed in a language that could handle its demands and accommodate its lofty meaning, and Arabic was probably the only language that fulfilled these conditions. Arabic is meant to be spoken in an eloquent manner; its rules, sentence structures, and grammatical forms do not promote anything less than eloquent speech. And so it was only natural that figurative speech – which is the highest form of speech and the one most employed by poets of all languages - should have been a prominent feature of the Arabic language. Simile, metaphor, personification, apostrophe, metonymy, symbol, allegory, paradox, overstatement, understatement, irony - each of these instances of figurative language was well developed by Arab poets even prior to the advent of Islam. And they were certainly needed to accommodate or bear, if you will, the eloquence of the Noble Qur'an.

As developed as Arabic was as a language, the Noble Qur'an took it to its peak; a peak that could not be reached by any Arab poet, no matter how eloquent he was. This was a fact that was acknowledged by the most eloquent of poets, regardless of whether they submitted and embraced Islam – such as Labeed bin Rabee'ah, Ka'ab bin Zuhair, and An-Naabighah Al-Ja'dee – or those who stubbornly and intransigently rejected the truth and remained disbelievers – such as Al-Waleed bin Al-Mugheerah.

One particularly wonderful feature of the Arabic language has to do with onomatopoeia, which involves using words that sound like what they mean, such as bang and snap. Although there are some onomatopoetic words in every language, Arabic far surpasses all other languages in the number of onomatopoetic words it contains, which, to be sure, makes it a wonderful language to listen to.

To summarize, any linguistic device that could be used to further enhance the eloquence of speech - such as imagery; what, in poetry, is known as 'musical devices', or the music of language; alliteration, assonance, and consonance; and so on - is more developed in Arabic than in any other language. Though it is true that other languages feature the same qualities that are mentioned above, they are found in Arabic to a greater degree. Ibn Faaris, may Allah have mercy on him, said, "No one is able to translate the Qur'an to another language and do it justice, as opposed to the Injeel (Gospel) which was

---

[13] Refer to examples of similar Verses : 13 : 37; 16: 103; 20:113; 26: 192-195; 39: 27, 27; 41: 3; 42: 7; 46: 12.

translated ... and the Torah, the Zaboor and the rest of Allah's divinely revealed books, which were translated (with justice done to the originals). This is because, in eloquence and the use of figurative language, no language is able to accommodate the meanings that are easily accommodated in the flexible, vast, precise, and comprehensive language of the Qur'an, Arabic."[14]

Section Three:

The Ease with which the Qur'an can be Understood by all People

Upon hearing the phrase 'an eloquent speech', one probably does not associate with it the idea of an easily understood speech, or one that can be understood by all kinds of audiences. And yet that is precisely one of the things that makes the Qur'an so magnificent: It is both eloquent - in fact no speech of man can come even near to its eloquence - and easily accessible to all audiences; or in other words, Allah (sp) made it easy for people to not only recite it, but to understand its meanings as well. This is so that men cannot put forward the excuse that they do not understand the Qur'an's Message. Allah (sp) said:

وَلَقَدْ يَسَّرْنَا ٱلْقُرْءَانَ لِلذِّكْرِ فَهَلْ مِن مُّدَّكِرٍ

"And We have indeed made the Qur'an easy to understand and remember, then is there any that will remember (or receive admonition)?" (Qur'an 54: 17)

In another Verse, Allah (sp) said:

فَإِنَّمَا يَسَّرْنَـٰهُ بِلِسَانِكَ لِتُبَشِّرَ بِهِ ٱلْمُتَّقِينَ وَتُنذِرَ بِهِ قَوْمًا لُّدًّا

"So We have made this (the Qur'an) easy in your own tongue (0 Muhammad), only that you may give glad tidings to the Muttaqun (pious and righteous persons who fear Allah much (abstain from all kinds of sins and evil deeds which He has forbidden), and love Allah much (perform all kinds of good deeds which He has ordained)), and warn with it the Ludda (most quarrelsome) people." (Qur'an 19: 97).

That Allah (sp) made the Qur'an easy is intended to have the twofold effect of encouraging believers to study the Qur'an in more depth and of extending an invitation to disbelievers, so that perhaps they change their ways and listen to the Qur'an with open minds and hearts. It is in this vein that Allah (sp) said, *"Then is there any that will remember (or receive admonition)?"*

The reader would do well to ask the question: what does making the Qur'an easy actually mean? Basically it means that one can understand its meanings without a great deal of difficulty. So clarity is one component of the Qur'an being easy to understand; another is that, if one reads it with an open heart and mind, one will not only understand the basic meaning of what he is reading, but also one will, with each cycle of contemplation, be open to new meanings that branch off from the original. And that is the beauty of contemplating the Qur'an: the more one contemplates its Verses, the more one learns and appreciates finer nuances of meaning.

The Qur'an has been made easy in another sense as well: Its words have been joined together

---

[14] *As-Sahaabee* (p.26).

in such a perfect manner and with such a beautiful flow that it is easy to memorize.
In his Tafseer of Allah's Saying, "And We have indeed made the Qur'an easy to understand and remember", Ar-Raazee (m) pointed out the following:
> Allah (sp) has made the Qur'an easy to memorize; it should be duly noted that of all of the Books that Allah (sp) has revealed to Prophets (st), it is only the Qur'an that is memorized and stored, in its entirety, in the hearts of men.
>
> Allah (sp) made it easy not only to understand the Qur'an, but also to learn lessons from its teachings, which is not surprising considering the fact that it contains in it all wisdom.
>
> Allah (sp) made the hearts of men become attached to the Noble Qur'an. Normally, if one reads something many times over, one will become bored, and one will tire of reading the same thing over and over again, not finding anything to gain from an additional reading. But such is not true of the Qur'an: A Muslim's heart becomes so attached to the Qur'an that, the more he reads it and contemplates its meanings, the more pleasure he derives and the more knowledge he gains.[15]

Yes, the Qur'an is certainly easy; of this, there is no doubt. But as Muslims we need to then ask the question: Where are those who remember it, study it, and receive admonition from it? There lies the problem for our nation.

Section Four:

Allah (sp) Preserved the Qur'an

Allah (sp) preserved the Qur'an before revealing it to the Prophet (s), during the process of revelation, and after the Qur'an was completely revealed. Prior to revealing the Noble Qur'an, Allah (sp) kept it in "Records held (greatly) in honor", or in other words, in the *Al-Lauh Al-Mahfuz*. These Records remain purified and in the hands of honorable and obedient angels. Allah (sp) said:

كَلَّا إِنَّهَا تَذْكِرَةٌ (١١) فَمَن شَاءَ ذَكَرَهُ (١٢) فِى صُحُفٍ مُّكَرَّمَةٍ (١٣) مَّرْفُوعَةٍ مُّطَهَّرَةٍ (١٤) بِأَيْدِى سَفَرَةٍ (١٥) كِرَامٍ بَرَرَةٍ (١٦)

"Nay, (do not do like this); indeed it (this Qur'an) is an admonition. So, whoever wills, let him pay attention to it. (It is) in Records held (greatly) in honour (Al-Lauh Al-Mahfuz), Exalted (in dignity), purified, in the hands of scribes (angels), honorable and obedient." (Qur'an 80: 11-16)

Such was the preservation of the Qur'an prior to its revelation. It was also preserved and guarded over while it was actually being revealed, as is indicated by the following two Verses:

وَبِٱلْحَقِّ أَنزَلْنَٰهُ وَبِٱلْحَقِّ نَزَلَ

"And with truth We have sent it down (i.e. the Qur'an), and with truth it has descended." (Qur'an 17: 105).

عَٰلِمُ ٱلْغَيْبِ فَلَا يُظْهِرُ عَلَىٰ غَيْبِهِۦٓ أَحَدًا (٢٦) إِلَّا مَنِ ٱرْتَضَىٰ مِن رَّسُولٍ فَإِنَّهُۥ يَسْلُكُ مِنۢ بَيْنِ يَدَيْهِ وَمِنْ خَلْفِهِۦ رَصَدًا (٢٧)

---

[15] *At-Tafseer al-Kabeer* (29/38, 39).

$$\text{سْلُكُ مِنْ بَيْنِ يَدَيْهِ وَمِنْ خَلْفِهِ رَصَدًا}$$

"(He Alone) the All-Knower of the Ghaib (unseen), and He reveals to none His Ghaib (unseen). Except to a Messenger (from mankind) whom He has chosen (He informs him of unseen as much as He likes), and then He makes a band of watching guards (angels) to march before him and behind him." (Qur'an 72: 26, 27).

And we know that Allah (sp) preserved the Qur'an after it was revealed and that He (sp) will continue to preserve it until the end of time based on this Verse:

$$\text{إِنَّا نَحْنُ نَزَّلْنَا ٱلذِّكْرَ وَإِنَّا لَهُ لَحَٰفِظُونَ}$$

"Verily We: It is We Who have sent down the Dhikr (i.e. the Qur'an) and surely, We will guard it (from corruption)." (Qur'an 15: 9).

Basically, this Verse makes it clear that the Qur'an will remain in its pristine state until the end of time and that any attempt to distort or corrupt it will end in complete failure. More than fourteen centuries have gone by, and by Allah's permission, and in spite of attempts made by Islam's enemies, the Qur'an remains unchanged and in its original form, written down in thousands of copies of the Qur'an and stored in the hearts of thousands of Muslims. Allah (sp) said:

$$\text{إِنَّ ٱلَّذِينَ كَفَرُواْ بِٱلذِّكْرِ لَمَّا جَآءَهُمْۖ وَإِنَّهُۥ لَكِتَٰبٌ عَزِيزٌ (٤١) لَّا يَأْتِيهِ ٱلْبَٰطِلُ مِنۢ بَيْنِ يَدَيْهِ وَلَا مِنْ خَلْفِهِۦۖ تَنزِيلٌ مِّنْ حَكِيمٍ حَمِيدٍ (٤٢)}$$

"Verily, those who disbelieved in the Reminder (i.e. the Qur'an) when it came to them (shall receive the punishment). And verily, it is an honorable respected Book (because it is Allah's Speech, and He has protected it from corruption, etc.). Falsehood cannot come to it from before it or behind it (it is) sent down by the All-Wise, Worthy of all praise (Allah)." (Qur'an 41: 41, 42)

In the heavens, the Qur'an is recorded in a well-guarded Book that is with Allah - the *Al-Lauh Al-Mahfuz*. That Book can be touched only by pure angels; such is the importance that Allah (sp) has attached to the Noble Qur'an. Allah (sp) said:

$$\text{إِنَّهُۥ لَقُرْءَانٌ كَرِيمٌ (٧٧) فِى كِتَٰبٍ مَّكْنُونٍ (٧٨) لَّا يَمَسُّهُۥٓ إِلَّا ٱلْمُطَهَّرُونَ (٧٩)}$$

"That (this) is indeed an honorable recital (the Noble Qur'an). In a Book well-guarded (with Allah in the heaven i.e. Al-Lauh Al-Mahfuz). Which (that Book with Allah) none can touch but who are pure from sins (i.e. the angels)." (Qur'an 56: 77-79)

What the preservation and guarding of the Qur'an precisely means is that Allah (sp) protects it from being lost and from being distorted - from words being added, changed, or removed. Additionally, Allah (sp) has decreed that the necessary steps are taken to ensure the preservation of the Qur'an; thus, from the time of the Prophet (s) onwards, the Qur'an has been related by so many people from each generation that it is impossible for them to have colluded in the act of fabricating Verses. Also, from the time of the Prophet (s) until this very day, a great many people from each generation have committed the Qur'an to memory.

All of this begs the question: How was it that previously revealed books were distorted, and yet the Qur'an has remained unchanged throughout time? The answer to this question is simple: Whereas Allah (sp) entrusted priests and rabbis to protect previously revealed Books, He (sp) took it upon Himself to protect and guard the Noble Qur'an. The former we know from this Verse:

$$\bigl(\text{بِمَا ٱسْتُحْفِظُوا۟ مِن كِتَـٰبِ ٱللَّهِ}\bigr)$$

"For to them was entrusted the protection of Allah's Book." (Qur'an 5: 44)
And the latter fact is confirmed in the following Verse:

$$\bigl(\text{إِنَّا نَحْنُ نَزَّلْنَا ٱلذِّكْرَ وَإِنَّا لَهُۥ لَحَـٰفِظُونَ}\bigr)$$

"Verily We: It is We Who have sent down the Dhikr (i.e. the Qur'an) and surely, We will guard it (from corruption)." (Qur'an 15: 9).

We know of at least one incident in which people, resorting to a most devious plan, have tried to distort the Qur'an; in the end, of course, their plan ended in failure. The deviousness of their plan revolved around the idea of trying to add words that are very dear to each and every Muslim: "May the peace and salutations of Allah be upon him" (i.e., upon the Prophet (s)). They inserted this phrase after, "The Messenger of Allah", in the following Verse:

$$\bigl(\text{مُّحَمَّدٌ رَّسُولُ ٱللَّهِ وَٱلَّذِينَ مَعَهُۥٓ أَشِدَّآءُ عَلَى ٱلْكُفَّارِ رُحَمَآءُ بَيْنَهُمْ}\bigr)$$

"Muhammad is the Messenger of Allah, and those who are with him are severe against disbelievers and merciful among themselves." (Qur'an 48: 29)

Muslims are commanded to say, "May the peace and salutations of Allah be upon him", every time they hear the Prophet (s) being mentioned; nonetheless, that phrase is not a part of the above-mentioned Verse, so it may not be added to it. The culprits behind the said plot printed copies of the Qur'an that contained the additional phrase, hoping to get away with their crime by appealing to the emotions of Muslims - for what Muslim is against sending prayers and salutations upon Prophet Muhammad (s). But the people of knowledge grasped the implications of what they were doing, and they ordered for all of the copies that were printed with the additional phrase to be destroyed. Certain people of knowledge reportedly said, "It contains an addition". The person who was responsible for printing the corrupted copies said, "Yes, but it is an addition that is to your liking". The scholars retorted, "We refuse to recite and print the Qur'an except in the exact form that it was revealed".[16]

What was Done to Ensure the Preservation of the Qur'an

Contrary to the events that affected previously revealed Books, Allah (sp) brought about circumstances that ensured the preservation of the Noble Qur'an; some of those circumstances are as follows:

1) Allah (sp) revealed the Qur'an to a people who were blessed with powerful memories. Even prior to the advent of Islam, Arabs were a people who prided themselves in communicating oral traditions and poems to one another. They were an illiterate people, in that they were not able to read or write, and so they were forced to memorize all of their traditions and poems. No matter how long a poem was, as long as it was good, Arabs were prepared to memorize it. Thus, over the centuries they developed very powerful memories, to the degree that it is related about certain Arabs that it would take them only a single hearing to memorize even a long poem. In literate societies, a people's literature is recorded in books and stored in libraries; but among Arabs, their literature and poetry was stored in their minds. It is not surprising, therefore, that certain Companions (rp) memorized not only the entire Qur'an, but thousands of AHadeeth as well.

---

[16] Ash-Sha'raawee (12/7653).

2) Allah (sp) made the Qur'an easy to memorize. Even though the Qur'an is more than 600 pages long (in the copy that is printed by the King Fahd Printing Press), thousands of people across the globe have committed all of it to memory. Allah (sp) said:

$$\text{وَلَقَدْ يَسَّرْنَا ٱلْقُرْءَانَ لِلذِّكْرِ فَهَلْ مِن مُّدَّكِرٍ}$$

"And We have indeed made the Qur'an easy to understand and remember, then is there any that will remember (or receive admonition)" (Qur'an 54; 17)

3) Once a year, the Prophet (s) would revise every Verse he memorized with Jibreel (p) then, in the final year of his blessed life, he revised the entire Qur'an with Jibreel (p) twice.

4) The Companions (rp) would memorize the Qur'an under the direct supervision of the Prophet (s), then it was only after they had a Verse clearly and firmly committed to memory that they would record it in writing. No opportunity was ever given to anyone to distort the Qur'an. Those who had the Qur'an memorized inspected each copy of the Qur'an that was written down, going through each Verse one word at a time in order to make sure that the copy contained no mistake whatsoever. Even today, there are committees of eminent scholars that inspect printed copies of the Qur'an to make sure that no mistakes are made. It is through such steps that Allah (sp) has fulfilled, and continues to fulfill, the promise He (sp) made in this Verse:

$$\text{إِنَّا نَحْنُ نَزَّلْنَا ٱلذِّكْرَ وَإِنَّا لَهُ لَحَافِظُونَ}$$

"Verily We: It is We Who have sent down the Dhikr (i.e., the Qur'an) and surely, We will guard it (from corruption)" (Qur'an 15: 9)

This guarantee, as well as the abovementioned circumstances that have been created to ensure the preservation of the Qur'an, has had a twofold effect: On the one hand, it removes hope from all evildoers who might consider the idea of trying to distort the Qur'an, and on the other hand, it instills a sense of complete trust in Muslims, it removes all doubt from their hearts, and it reminds them of the great blessing of having the Qur'an in its original, pristine form, without containing any distortion whatsoever.

Section five:
The Universal Message of the Qur'an

That the message of the Qur'an is universal means that it is not specific to one group of people or to one particular era. We know that many previously revealed scriptures were intended for a limited audience: The Children of Israel. The enemies of Islam claim that the same holds true for the Qur'an: That it has already served its purpose and is no longer needed, in that it was suitable to the needs of Arabs fourteen centuries ago, but is no longer applicable to today's modern world; furthermore, they claim that the message of Islam was not intended for all of mankind. As Muslims, we know the opposite to be true: The Message of the Noble Qur'an is universal: it is at once valid and necessary among all peoples of all generations. In the Noble Qur'an, Allah (sp) addressed all of mankind until the Day of Resurrection. The Message of the Qur'an is truly universal: It applies to all times, all places, both sexes, the young and the old, and to all members of society; in fact, it is intended not just for mankind, but for jinns as well. Every person, no matter what race he belongs to, no matter what his age or sex is, no matter what century he lives in, is in dire need of learning from the Noble Qur'an correct beliefs, noble manners, divine wisdom, and all of the divinely revealed laws he needs to lead an upright life.

There are countless revealed texts from the Qur'an and Sunnah that point to the universality of the Qur'an; the scope and purpose of this work, however, do not permit me to list them all here.[17] Nonetheless, it is interesting to note that some scholars have said, "There are more than 350 Verses that point to the universality of the Qur'an."[18]

And there are four Verses in particular, each containing the same wording, which explicitly state that the Noble Qur'an is a reminder for all created beings:

إِنْ هُوَ إِلَّا ذِكْرٌ لِّلْعَٰلَمِينَ

"It (this Qur'an) is only a Reminder for the Alamin (mankind and jinns)" (Qur'an 12: 104; 38: 87; 81:27)

Short as this Verse is, it points to the universality of the Qur'an in more than one way. First, the wording of the Verse emphasizes the point that is being made. What I mean by this is, instead of saying that the Qur'an is a reminder for all created beings, Allah (sp) said that it is nothing more than a Reminder for all created beings, as if to say: The sole purpose of the Qur'an is to be a reminder for all human beings and all jinns until the Day of Resurrection. Second, Allah (sp) makes it clear that He is addressing all human beings. The word *Alamin* is the plural of *Alam*; the latter means everything that is in the universe and the former means all beings that are endowed with a mind – human beings and jinns. And so the very word *Alamin* indicates that the Qur'an is a reminder for all human beings and jinns not just of one era or place, but of every era and every place. And third, the definitive 'Al' that precedes *Alamin* gives a further indication that, instead of only some human beings and some jinns, all human beings and all jinns are being addressed.

Following are some Verses that explicitly point to the universality of the Noble Qur'an:

1) Allah (sp) said:

تَبَارَكَ ٱلَّذِى نَزَّلَ ٱلْفُرْقَانَ عَلَىٰ عَبْدِهِۦ لِيَكُونَ لِلْعَٰلَمِينَ نَذِيرًا

"Blessed be He Who sent down the criterion (of right and wrong, i.e. this Qur'an) to His slave (Muhammad(s)) that he may be a warner to the Alamin (mankind and jinns)." (Qur'an 25: 1)

2) Allah (sp) said:

وَمَآ أَرْسَلْنَٰكَ إِلَّا رَحْمَةً لِّلْعَٰلَمِينَ

"And We have sent you (O Muhammad (s)) not but as a mercy for the Alamin (mankind, jinns and all that exists)." (Qur'an 21: 107)

3) Allah (sp) said:

وَلَقَدْ صَرَّفْنَا لِلنَّاسِ فِى هَٰذَا ٱلْقُرْءَانِ مِن كُلِّ مَثَلٍ فَأَبَىٰٓ أَكْثَرُ ٱلنَّاسِ إِلَّا كُفُورًا

---

[17] The following are just examples of Verses that point to the universality of the Noble Qur'an: (*Al-Baqarah*: 185), (*An-Nisaa*. 1, 79, 170, 174).

[18] *Dilaalah Asmaa Suwar Al-Qur'an Al-Kareem Min Mandhoor Hadaaree* by Dr. Muhammad Khaleel Jeejak (pg. 132).

"And indeed We have fully explained to mankind, in this Qur'an, every kind of similitude, but most mankind refuse (the truth and accept nothing) but disbelief." (Qur'an 17:89)

4) Allah (sp) said:

وَلَقَدْ ضَرَبْنَا لِلنَّاسِ فِى هَٰذَا ٱلْقُرْءَانِ مِن كُلِّ مَثَلٍ لَّعَلَّهُمْ يَتَذَكَّرُونَ

"And indeed We have put forth for men, in this Qur'an every kind of similitude in order that they may remember." (Qur'an 39: 27)

5) Allah (sp) said:

إِنَّآ أَنزَلْنَا عَلَيْكَ ٱلْكِتَٰبَ لِلنَّاسِ بِٱلْحَقِّ فَمَنِ ٱهْتَدَىٰ فَلِنَفْسِهِۦ وَمَن ضَلَّ فَإِنَّمَا يَضِلُّ عَلَيْهَا وَمَآ أَنتَ عَلَيْهِم بِوَكِيلٍ

"Verily, We have sent down to you (O Muhammad (s)) the Book for mankind in truth. So whosoever accepts guidance, it is only for his ownself, and whosoever goes astray, he goes only for his (own) loss. And you (O Muhammad (s)) are not a Wakil (trustee or disposer of affairs, or keeper) over them." (Qur'an 39: 41)

Consider this Verse:

وَمَآ أَرْسَلْنَٰكَ إِلَّا رَحْمَةً لِّلْعَٰلَمِينَ

"And We have sent you (O Muhammad (s)) not but as a mercy for the Alamin (mankind, jinns and all that exists)." (Qur'an 21: 107)

Having contemplated this Verse, the reader might be tempted to ask the questions, "How could Prophet Muhammad (s) have been a mercy to all of mankind? Wasn't he a mercy for Muslims only, for it is they alone who benefited from his message, and it is they alone who will enter Paradise as a result of his having been sent." In his *Tafseer* of the abovementioned Verse, Ibn Al-Qayyim (m) gave a wonderful answer to these questions. He pointed out that the Verse should be understood based on its literal wording, in that the Prophet (s) was truly a mercy for all of mankind (and for all jinns as well). What this means is that every group of human beings – Muslims, polytheists, hypocrites, etc. – benefited in some way from him being sent with the message of Islam. Let us go through the various categories of human beings one by one and see how the members of each category benefited from the sending of Prophet Muhammad (s):

1) The Prophet's followers: Obviously they benefited the most, by achieving honor both in this world and in the Hereafter.

2) Enemies of Islam who fought against the Prophet (s): The polytheists who died in battle actually benefited from an early death. Had they lived longer, they would have perpetrated more sins, and they would have received an even greater punishment in the Hereafter. This follows from the general principle that a longer life is beneficial for the believer – since he can perform more good deeds and then reap the rewards of those deeds in the Hereafter – and harmful for the disbeliever. Misery has been decreed for disbelievers, but there are degrees of misery. A disbeliever who lives a long life and is thus enabled to perpetrate more sins becomes deserving of a greater punishment than the one he would have deserved had he died, say, halfway through his life – since he would have had fewer sins to be punished for.

3) Non-Muslims who lived peacefully as citizens in Muslim lands. In this world, they lived under a treaty that they had agreed upon with Muslims. Thus they benefited from a guarantee of safety and protection. It should be noted that these disbelievers are certainly less evil than the ones who openly waged war against Islam.

4) Hypocrites: By openly displaying Faith, they benefited by having their blood spared, by being respected in this world, by knowing that their wealth and families would not be harmed, and so on from the rights that were enjoyed by all Muslim citizens.

5) Peoples who lived far away from Al-Madeenah, and who did not even hear about Islam: Had the Prophet (s) not been sent, disbelief would have been the common trait of all people on earth, and so a universal and comprehensive punishment would have been in order for all of earth's inhabitants. By sending the Prophet (s), Allah (sp) spared the inhabitants of earth of that punishment. Therefore, not being destroyed was the benefit that was enjoyed by the peoples of distant lands.

Imam Ibn Al-Qayyim (m) mentioned a second possible interpretation of the abovementioned Verse: That, yes, the Prophet (s) was a mercy for every single human being, but it was only the Muslims who accepted that mercy and benefited from it both in this world and in the Hereafter, as for the disbelievers, they rejected it. Even though they rejected it, it was there for the taking, and could therefore still be described as being "a mercy for all that exists." After all, a gift is a gift, regardless of whether a proposed recipient accepts it or not; by the same token, a cure for a disease is still its cure, even if a person afflicted with that disease refuses to take it. Similarly, therefore, the Prophet (s) was a mercy for all of mankind, and every single human being had the opportunity to accept the 'mercy' that he was.

When Allah (sp) addresses human beings in the Qur'an, He makes it clear that the Noble Qur'an is a universal Message, one that is meant for all places and all peoples. Often, the words, "O people", or, "O mankind" are used, thus indicating that Allah (s) is addressing every human being of every era. And even when Allah (sp) chooses to be more specific, He uses words that are general in meaning and that are comprehensive of many categories of people; or in other words, when addressing people, He (sp) rarely specifies the names of places, times, or persons. So when Allah (sp) does not address mankind with the words, "O people" or, "O mankind", He uses such words as, "believers", or "disbelievers", or "hypocrites", or "righteous ones" or "heedless ones". These words are not specific to a tribe or generation of people; Allah (sp) does not say, "O believers of Makkah," or, "O believers of Al-Madeenah", or "O believers of the first century of Islam." "Believers," therefore, is a term that, though seemingly specific in meaning, comprehensively refers to all believers of all places and of all generations. The same is the case for all of the other aforementioned descriptive words: disbelievers, hypocrites, righteous ones, heedless ones, etc.

Consider, for instance, the story of how Aishah (rh) was falsely accused of wrongdoing; its details are mentioned in the Noble Qur'an. One should notice, while reading the Verses that describe the details of her story, that specific names or tribes are not mentioned. This indicates that the lessons of her story are universal in that they are intended for all people who falsely accuse an innocent person of perpetrating wicked deeds. Based on those Verses, as well as other Verses that deal with specific incidents that occurred during the Prophet's lifetime, scholars have derived an important principle that is often used in interpreting Verses of the Qur'an: "What matters is the general wording (and the overall lesson that is applicable to all people who have a similar experience), and not the specific occurrence that prompted the revelation of the Verse."

Section Six:

The Qur'an is a witness over Previously Revealed Books

The discussion of this section is based on the following Verse:

وَأَنزَلْنَآ إِلَيْكَ ٱلْكِتَٰبَ بِٱلْحَقِّ مُصَدِّقًا لِّمَا بَيْنَ يَدَيْهِ مِنَ ٱلْكِتَٰبِ وَمُهَيْمِنًا عَلَيْهِ

"And We have sent down to you (O Muhammad) the Book (this Qur'an) in truth, confirming the Scripture that came before it and Mohayminan (trustworthy in highness and a witness) over it (old Scriptures)." (Qur'an 5: 48).

We learn from this Verse that the Qur'an is related to previously revealed scriptures in two important ways: It confirms them, and it is *"Mohayminan* (trustworthy in highness and a witness) over them." This English translation of *Musaddiqan* (confirming) and of *Mohayminan* (trustworthy and a witness over previously revealed scriptures) does not, as is often the case regarding translations of Verses of the Qur'an, do justice to their true meanings. This is because both words, in the abovementioned Verse, encompass a variety of meanings. As for *Mohayminan*, it conveys all of the following:

1) The Qur'an is a judge over previously revealed Books. Those Books were tampered with by priests and rabbis; consequently, they contain not only true revelation, but falsehood and exaggerations that were written down by the hands of corrupt men. Then, when the Qur'an was revealed, it acted as a judge over those Books, pointing out both the truth and the falsehood they contained. So, for instance, after Christians exaggerated the qualities of 'Iesa (Jesus) (p) and his mother (sh), ascribing to them divine attributes, Allah (sp) revealed this Verse:

مَّا ٱلْمَسِيحُ ٱبْنُ مَرْيَمَ إِلَّا رَسُولٌ قَدْ خَلَتْ مِن قَبْلِهِ ٱلرُّسُلُ وَأُمُّهُ صِدِّيقَةٌ كَانَا يَأْكُلَانِ ٱلطَّعَامَ ٱنظُرْ كَيْفَ نُبَيِّنُ لَهُمُ ٱلْآيَٰتِ ثُمَّ ٱنظُرْ أَنَّىٰ يُؤْفَكُونَ

"The Messiah (Jesus), son of Mary, was no more than a Messenger, many were the Messengers that passed away before him. His mother (Mary) was a Siddiqah (i.e. she believed in the Words of Allah and His Books (See V. 66:12)). They both used to eat food (as any other human being, while Allah does not eat). Look how We make the Ayat (proofs, evidences, Verses, lessons, signs, revelations, etc.) clear to them, yet look how they are deluded away (from the truth)." (Qur'an 5:75)

The People of the Book corrupted the *Injeel* (Gospel) in another way as well, placing therein the false claim that Jesus was crucified. Allah (sp) then refuted their claim by revealing this Verse:

وَمَا قَتَلُوهُ وَمَا صَلَبُوهُ وَلَٰكِن شُبِّهَ لَهُمْ

"But they killed him not, nor crucified him, but the resemblance of Jesus was put over another man (and they killed that man.)" (Qur'an 4: 157)

Allah (sp) informs us in this Verse that the claim that Jesus (p) was crucified is not something that was revealed to Jesus (p) in the form of a divinely revealed Book; instead, it is a lie that Christians introduced into their corrupted version of the *Injeel* (the Gospel).

2) The Qur'an bears witness to previously revealed Books. What this means is that the Qur'an confirms that, even though the Gospel, for instance, contains falsehood and fabrications that came about as a result of human tampering, the original version of the Gospel (which is no longer extant) was revealed by Allah (sp) and it contained in it true and correct teachings.

3) The Qur'an proves the validity of previously revealed Books. How so? Well, those books foretell the coming of Prophet Muhammad (s) and provide a detailed description both of him and of the people of his nation. In order for it to be proven that those Books were truly from Allah (sp) what they foretold had to occur. Therefore, that the Prophet (s) was sent on earth (with the Noble Qur'an) was proof of the validity and the divine source of previously revealed Books. So it is because of the

Qur'an that we know for certain that the Torah, the Injeel (The Gospel), and the Zaboor were books that were revealed by Allah (sp).[19]

That the Qur'an acts as a confirmation of previously revealed Books conveys the following meanings (note: Some are similar to the ones hitherto discussed):

1) The Qur'an confirms that previous scriptures were in fact revealed by Allah (sp); for example, Allah (sp) said:

$$إِنَّآ أَوْحَيْنَآ إِلَيْكَ كَمَآ أَوْحَيْنَآ إِلَىٰ نُوحٍ وَٱلنَّبِيِّۦنَ مِنۢ بَعْدِهِۦ$$

"Verily, We have inspired you (O Muhammad) as We inspired Noah and the Prophets after him." (Qur'an 4: 163)

And in another Verse, Allah (sp) said:

$$نَزَّلَ عَلَيْكَ ٱلْكِتَٰبَ بِٱلْحَقِّ مُصَدِّقًا لِّمَا بَيْنَ يَدَيْهِ$$

"It is He Who has sent down the Book (the Qur'an) to you (O Muhammad) with truth, confirming what came before it." (Qur'an 3:3)

2) The Qur'an confirms the description that was given of it in previously revealed Books. For in those Books, a description of Prophet Muhammad (s) was given, and it was mentioned that he was to come with a Book from Allah (sp). That the Prophet (s) came with such a Book confirms the validity of those revealed Books.

3) The Noble Qur'an is in agreement with previously revealed Books regarding the fundamentals of Religion, for all divinely revealed Books share in common these qualities:

– Each of them invites people to believe in Allah (sp), His Books, His Messengers (st), the Last Day, and other similar beliefs that pertain to the perfect attributes of Allah (sp).

– Each of them promotes qualities that are universally recognized as being noble and good, and denounces forms of evildoing that are widely recognized as being wicked and repulsive. Hence every divinely revealed Book promotes justice, truthfulness, patience, trustworthiness, mercy, and other similar qualities. Conversely, every divinely revealed Book forbids oppression, lying, treachery, stealing, tyranny, and so on.

— Each of them promotes the same fundamental acts of worship: prayer, fasting, Zakat, etc. Allah (sp) informed us that, just as He ordered us to perform such acts of worship, He (sp) commanded previous nations to do the same; for instance, Allah (sp) said:

$$يَٰٓأَيُّهَا ٱلَّذِينَ ءَامَنُوا۟ كُتِبَ عَلَيْكُمُ ٱلصِّيَامُ كَمَا كُتِبَ عَلَى ٱلَّذِينَ مِن قَبْلِكُمْ لَعَلَّكُمْ تَتَّقُونَ$$

"O you who believe! Fasting is prescribed to you as it was prescribed for those before you, that you may become Al-Muttaqun (the pious)." (Qur'an 2: 183)
And in regard to prayer and Zakat, Allah (sp) said:

---

[19] Refer to the following Verses, for each of them points to how the Qur'an confirms, corrects, and bears witness to previously revealed Books: (*Al-Baqarah:* 41, 89, 91), (*Aal-Imraan:* 3), (*An-Nisaa:* 47), (*Al-Maaidah:* 48), (*Al-Anaam:* 92), (*Yunus:* 37), (*Yousuf:* 111), (*TaHa.* 133), (*Ash-Shuaraa,* 196), (*Faatir: 31*), (*Al-Ahqaaf. 12, 30).*

$$\text{وَإِذْ أَخَذْنَا مِيثَاقَ بَنِىٓ إِسْرَٰٓءِيلَ لَا تَعْبُدُونَ إِلَّا ٱللَّهَ وَبِٱلْوَٰلِدَيْنِ إِحْسَانًا وَذِى ٱلْقُرْبَىٰ وَٱلْيَتَٰمَىٰ وَٱلْمَسَٰكِينِ وَقُولُوا۟ لِلنَّاسِ حُسْنًا وَأَقِيمُوا۟ ٱلصَّلَوٰةَ وَءَاتُوا۟ ٱلزَّكَوٰةَ}$$

"And (remember) when We took a covenant from the Children of Israel, (saying): Worship none but Allah (Alone) and be dutiful and good to parents, and to kindred, and to orphans and the poor who beg, and speak good to people (i.e. enjoin righteousness and forbid evil, and say the truth about Muhammad), and offer the prayers, and give Zakat." (Qur'an 2: 83)

That the most basic acts of worship are common in all divinely revealed Books is further confirmed in the saying of Allah (sp):

$$\text{شَرَعَ لَكُم مِّنَ ٱلدِّينِ مَا وَصَّىٰ بِهِۦ نُوحًا وَٱلَّذِىٓ أَوْحَيْنَآ إِلَيْكَ وَمَا وَصَّيْنَا بِهِۦٓ إِبْرَٰهِيمَ وَمُوسَىٰ وَعِيسَىٰٓ أَنْ أَقِيمُوا۟ ٱلدِّينَ وَلَا تَتَفَرَّقُوا۟ فِيهِ}$$

"He (Allah) has ordained for you the same religion (Islam) which He ordained for Noah, and that which We have inspired in you (O Muhammad), and that which We ordained for Abraham, Moses and Jesus saying you should establish religion (i.e. to do what it orders you to do practically), and make no divisions in it (religion) (i.e. various sects in religion)". (Qur'an 42:13)

As for the detailed aspects of legislations, laws, acts of worship (but not beliefs), they may differ from one divinely revealed book to another. Certain legislations were appropriate for the Children of Israel, because of their situation and the era during which they lived, but those very legislations might not appropriate for the nation of Muhammad (s). Allah (sp) said:

$$\text{لِكُلٍّ جَعَلْنَا مِنكُمْ شِرْعَةً وَمِنْهَاجًا}$$

"To each among you, We have prescribed a law and a clear way." (Qur'an 5: 48)

The Relationship Between "Confirmation" and "Mohayminan"
Allah (sp) said:

$$\text{وَأَنزَلْنَآ إِلَيْكَ ٱلْكِتَٰبَ بِٱلْحَقِّ مُصَدِّقًا لِّمَا بَيْنَ يَدَيْهِ مِنَ ٱلْكِتَٰبِ وَمُهَيْمِنًا عَلَيْهِ}$$

"And We have sent down to you (O Muhammad) the Book (this Qur'an) in truth, confirming the Scripture that came before it and Mohayminan (trustworthy in highness and a witness) over it (old Scriptures)." (Qur'an 5: 48)

We have hitherto discussed the meaning of both "confirming the Scripture that came before it", and "*Mohayminan* over it (old scriptures)". In its relation to previously revealed scriptures, the Qur'an plays two primary functions: It confirms the revealed Books that came before it, and it is *Mohayminan* over them (trustworthy in highness and a witness over them). We have defined the term *Mohayminan*, and explained its meaning with examples, so by now the term should be clear to the reader. What might not be fully clear to the reader is the difference between *Mohayminan* and the term "confirming". Any confusion regarding this matter probably stems from the fact that the meanings of both terms overlap: Both terms indicate that the Qur'an bears witness to previously revealed Books, confirming the facts that they were revealed by Allah (sp) and that, in their pristine form, they contain in them true and correct teachings. So that is where the terms *Mohayminan* and "confirming" meet; where they differ is in the fact that *Mohayminan* denotes additional meanings: That the Qur'an is a judge over previously revealed Books, not only bearing witness to the truth that they contain, but also exposing the falsehood and distortions that were introduced into them by the hands of corrupt priests and rabbis. Thus it should be clear that, in the abovementioned Verse, the meaning of *Mohayminan* is more comprehensive than that of "confirming".

Ways in which The Qur'an is *Mohayminan* Over Previously Revealed Scriptures

That the Qur'an is *Mohayminan* over previously revealed scriptures is manifested in the following ways:

1) It Points out the Distortions that can be Found in Previously Revealed Scriptures

The preservation of previously revealed Books, such as the Gospel and the Torah, was not an important issue for many priests and rabbis; to the contrary, their primary aim was to mold and change those books based on their desires, whims, false interpretations, or the dictates of their greedy ambitions. In fact, Allah (sp) informs us that they rewrote revealed Scriptures with their own hands and then had the audacity to falsely ascribe their finished product to Allah (sp).
Allah (sp) said:

$$\text{فَوَيْلٌ لِّلَّذِينَ يَكْتُبُونَ ٱلْكِتَبَ بِأَيْدِيهِمْ ثُمَّ يَقُولُونَ هَذَا مِنْ عِندِ ٱللَّهِ لِيَشْتَرُواْ بِهِ ثَمَنًا قَلِيلًا فَوَيْلٌ لَّهُم مِّمَّا كَتَبَتْ أَيْدِيهِمْ وَوَيْلٌ لَّهُم مِّمَّا يَكْسِبُونَ}$$

"Then woe to those who write the Book with their own hands and then say, 'This is from Allah', to purchase with it a little price! Woe to them for what their hands have written and woe to them for that they earn thereby." (Qur'an 2: 79)

2) It Mentions Important Issues Regarding which Previously Revealed Books Contain False Information

In terms of beliefs, for instance, the Qur'an exposes the lie that Jesus (p) was killed on the cross, for it is a lie that is promulgated in the distorted version of the Gospel. Allah (sp) said:

$$\text{وَمَا قَتَلُوهُ وَمَا صَلَبُوهُ وَلَكِن شُبِّهَ لَهُمْ}$$

"But they killed him not, nor crucified him, but the resemblance of Jesus was put over another man (and they killed that man.)" (Qur'an 4: 157)
In the same way, Allah (sp) declared that, because of their beliefs in the trinity and in the divinity of Jesus (p), Christians are guilty of disbelief:

$$\text{لَقَدْ كَفَرَ ٱلَّذِينَ قَالُوٓاْ إِنَّ ٱللَّهَ هُوَ ٱلْمَسِيحُ ٱبْنُ مَرْيَمَ وَقَالَ ٱلْمَسِيحُ يَبَنِىٓ إِسْرَٰٓءِيلَ ٱعْبُدُواْ ٱللَّهَ رَبِّى وَرَبَّكُمْ إِنَّهُۥ مَن يُشْرِكْ بِٱللَّهِ فَقَدْ حَرَّمَ ٱللَّهُ عَلَيْهِ ٱلْجَنَّةَ وَمَأْوَىٰهُ ٱلنَّارُ وَمَا لِلظَّٰلِمِينَ مِنْ أَنصَارٍ (٧٢) لَّقَدْ كَفَرَ ٱلَّذِينَ قَالُوٓاْ إِنَّ ٱللَّهَ ثَالِثُ ثَلَٰثَةٍ وَمَا مِنْ إِلَٰهٍ إِلَّآ إِلَٰهٌ وَٰحِدٌ وَإِن لَّمْ يَنتَهُواْ عَمَّا يَقُولُونَ لَيَمَسَّنَّ ٱلَّذِينَ كَفَرُواْ مِنْهُمْ عَذَابٌ أَلِيمٌ}$$

"Surely, they have disbelieved who say: 'Allah is the Messiah (Jesus), son of Mary'. But the Messiah (Jesus) said: 'O Children of Israel! Worship Allah, my Lord and your Lord'. Verily, whosoever sets up partners in worship with Allah, then Allah has forbidden Paradise for him, and the Fire will be his abode. And for the Zalimun (polytheists and wrong-doers) there are no helpers. Surely, disbelievers are those who said: 'Allah is the third of the three (in a Trinity).' But there is no Ilah (god) (none who has the right to be worshipped) but One Ilah (God - Allah). And if they cease not from what they say, verily, a painful torment will befall the disbelievers among them." (Qur'an 5:72, 73)

As for the distorted version of the Torah, it ascribes many faults to Allah (sp). The Torah that was in circulation during the lifetime of the Prophet (s) ascribed a son to Allah (sp), and the Jews that were contemporaries of the Prophet (s) described Allah (sp) as being poor and miserly. In the Noble Qur'an, Allah (sp) refuted such lies; for instance, Allah (sp) said:

$$\text{وَقَالَتِ ٱلْيَهُودُ عُزَيْرٌ ٱبْنُ ٱللَّهِ وَقَالَتِ ٱلنَّصَـٰرَى ٱلْمَسِيحُ ٱبْنُ ٱللَّهِ ۖ ذَٰلِكَ قَوْلُهُم بِأَفْوَٰهِهِمْ ۖ يُضَـٰهِـُٔونَ قَوْلَ ٱلَّذِينَ كَفَرُوا۟ مِن قَبْلُ ۚ قَـٰتَلَهُمُ ٱللَّهُ ۚ أَنَّىٰ يُؤْفَكُونَ}$$

"And the Jews say: Ezra is the son of Allah, and Christians say: Messiah is the son of Allah. That is a saying from their mouths. They imitate the saying of the disbelievers of the old. Allah's Curse be on them, how they are deluded away from the truth" (Qur'an 9:30)

In another Verse, Allah (sp) said:

$$\text{لَّقَدْ سَمِعَ ٱللَّهُ قَوْلَ ٱلَّذِينَ قَالُوٓا۟ إِنَّ ٱللَّهَ فَقِيرٌ وَنَحْنُ أَغْنِيَآءُ ۘ سَنَكْتُبُ مَا قَالُوا۟ وَقَتْلَهُمُ ٱلْأَنۢبِيَآءَ بِغَيْرِ حَقٍّ وَنَقُولُ ذُوقُوا۟ عَذَابَ ٱلْحَرِيقِ}$$

Indeed, Allah has heard the statement of those (Jews) who Say: 'Truly, Allah is poor and we are rich!' We shall record what they have said and their killing of the Prophets unjustly, and We shall say: 'Taste you the torment of the burning (Fire)' (Qur'an 3:181).

And in yet another Verse, Allah (sp) said:

$$\text{وَقَالَتِ ٱلْيَهُودُ يَدُ ٱللَّهِ مَغْلُولَةٌ ۚ غُلَّتْ أَيْدِيهِمْ وَلُعِنُوا۟ بِمَا قَالُوا۟ ۘ بَلْ يَدَاهُ مَبْسُوطَتَانِ يُنفِقُ كَيْفَ يَشَآءُ}$$

"The Jews say: 'Allah's hand is tied up (i.e. He does not give and spend of His bounty).' Be their hands tied up and be they accursed for what they uttered. Nay, both His Hands are widely outstretched. He spends (of His bounty) as He wills." (Qur'an 5:64).

3) The Qur'an Brought out into the Open Issues that the Corrupters of Previously Revealed Scriptures Tried to Keep Hidden

One who studies the Old Testament finds that it contains no mention of the Hereafter – neither of the Bliss of Paradise nor of the punishment of the Hellfire. The Hereafter is therefore a topic that Jewish rabbis tried to keep hidden. By the same token, they tried to hide all information that pertained to the seal of all Prophets – his description, his qualities, the timing of his coming on earth, etc. We know that such information was a part of the original scriptures because, in certain Verses of the Qur'an, Allah (sp) informs us that that was the case. And based on the following Verse, we know that, in general, the People of the Book tried to hide certain aspects of their religion by removing any mention of those aspects from their revealed Books:

$$\text{يَـٰٓأَهْلَ ٱلْكِتَـٰبِ قَدْ جَآءَكُمْ رَسُولُنَا يُبَيِّنُ لَكُمْ كَثِيرًا مِّمَّا كُنتُمْ تُخْفُونَ مِنَ ٱلْكِتَـٰبِ وَيَعْفُوا۟ عَن كَثِيرٍ ۚ قَدْ جَآءَكُم مِّنَ ٱللَّهِ نُورٌ وَكِتَـٰبٌ مُّبِينٌ}$$

"O people of the Scripture (Jews and Christians)! Now has come to you much of that which you used to hide from the Scripture and passing over (i.e. leaving out without explaining) much. Indeed, there has come to you from Allah a light (Prophet Muhammad (s)) and a plain Book (this Qur'an.)" (Qur'an 5:15)

4) The Qur'an Made it Unnecessary and Outright Forbidden to Apply the Laws of All Previously Revealed Books

Every previously revealed Book was meant for a specific group of people. So, for instance, it was the duty of the People of the Book to follow the pristine teachings of the Torah and the Gospel. But that duty came to an end when the Messenger of Allah (s) was sent with the Qur'an. The Qur'an, in effect, rendered invalid all previously revealed Books, since it was meant not for a specific group of people, but for all of mankind. The universality of the Qur'an was the main reason why previously revealed

Books were rendered invalid; another was the fact that, through the corrupt actions of certain priests and rabbis, they contained distortions and falsehood, and thus were not suitable to serve the purpose of guiding mankind.

Given that it is forbidden to apply the teachings of previously revealed Books, one might ask the question, "Since the Qur'an affirmed many teachings that are contained in previously revealed Books – for instance, a call to such virtues as honesty, chastity, and trustworthiness – does it not follow, then, that we can still apply certain parts of previously revealed Books?" The answer to this question is a resounding, no. If a given legislation is common both to the Qur'an and to previously revealed Books, we follow it only because it is found in the Qur'an. Regarding any law or legislation, it does not really matter for us whether or not something is mentioned about it in previously revealed Books. Ultimately, we are not required to follow those Books, but only the Noble Qur'an. Therefore, it might be nice to know that a certain law was legislated for the People of the Book in the Torah, but that knowledge has no real impact on our lives. If we apply the same law, we apply it only because we are ordered to do so in the Noble Qur'an.

There are many laws which are found in previously revealed Scriptures that are confirmed in the Noble Qur'an; others have been outright abrogated. The point here is that the laws of previously revealed Books have been rendered invalid; if any of them are still applied, it is because they have been legislated anew in the Qur'an. Incidentally, I should point out that application is one thing, and belief is another: Although we don't apply the laws of previously revealed Books, we believe that those Books were revealed by Allah and that they contain, in their pristine form, the same beliefs and core acts of worship that are found in the Noble Qur'an.

Topic Three:

Proofs of the Qur'an's Magnificence

One of the clearest proofs of the Qur'an's magnificence, which I will focus on in this section, is the fact that so many of Islam's enemies, throughout history, have bore witness to the greatness of the Qur'an. For in an ancient Arab saying it is said, "The truth is that which is attested to by one's enemies." From the very onset of the Prophet's mission, many of Islam's enemies could not help but to listen to the Qur'an and to admire its divine eloquence. Those who persecuted Islam the most from among Makkah's chieftains were most prone to secretly listening to the Prophet (s) recite the Qur'an. While it is true that the complete magnificence of the Qur'an can be appreciated in Arabic only, many historians, scholars, philosophers, and statesmen have become impressed simply by reading accurate translations of the Qur'an's meanings. Among the educated and literate members of Western societies, the Qur'an is admired for its beauty and magnificence. Some do so in secret, others openly. Upon hearing a Western non-Muslim praise the Qur'an, one almost concludes that one is listening to a Muslim, even though such is not the case. Harold Bloom, for instance (perhaps the most eminent literary critic of today), wrote: "(Muhammad's) shattering spiritual and imaginative originality cannot be doubted. No one else in human religious history has given us a text in which God alone is the speaker. Audacity, a crucial characteristic of Muhammad in every way, marks the Quran's achievement of a literary effect unlike any other. We can never relax as we read it, or when we recite it, alone or with others."[20]

The Westerner's fascination with the Qur'an depends on his perspective, background, and initial impressions. Some Western scholars of literature are impressed with the language, eloquence, and flow of the Qur'an. Scientists are amazed at how the Qur'an is in complete harmony with modern

---

[20] *Genius* by Harold Bloom (pg. 144).

scientific knowledge, we know, for instance, that Dr. Keith Moore of the University of Toronto introduced into his book on Embryology an entire chapter on the Qur'an's description of an embryo's growth in a mother's womb. He did this after he realized that that description was in exact accordance with modern scientific knowledge. As for the layman who has no particular interest in science or literature, he is taken aback by the unified Message of the Qur'an; everything else he comes across contains contradictions, but not the Qur'an: It consistently, and without any contradiction whatsoever, calls to the worship of the One True God, Allah (s).

In this section, I will cite some of the sayings of Western philosophers, statesmen, and scholars regarding their impressions of the Noble Qur'an.[21]

1) The French Philosopher Alex Lawazon wrote, "Muhammad left to the world a Book that is a miracle of eloquence; it is a holy Book that is a repository of lofty manners and teachings. Nothing that has been discovered in modern day knowledge contradicts the fundamental teachings of Islam; in fact, there is complete harmony between the teachings of the Qur'an and the laws of nature."[22]

2) Commenting on how the Qur'an has brought the peoples of many lands together by endowing them with a common language and shared beliefs, Louis Saydayyo said, "It is important to point out that, despite the many languages that are spoken by the peoples of Asia...and of Africa, there is a Book that they all understand and that unites them in spite of their different natures; and that Book is the Qur'an."[23]

3) Golad Sutton, acting as Minister of the British Colonies, once said while addressing the British Parliament, "As long as the Qur'an is in the hands of the Muslims, we will not be able to rule over them. Therefore, we have no choice but either to wipe it out of existence or to turn Muslims away from it." Bad as conditions are for today Muslims, Sutton failed miserably in achieving either of those goals. Today, the Qur'an is recited by more than a billion Muslims; it is memorized by thousands; its recitation is broadcast on radio and on television all over the world; and it can be found in virtually every Muslim household. And though Muslims, as a group, do not apply its teachings to the degree that is required of them, they have not – as the abovementioned facts indicate – completely turned away from it, but are rather extremely attached to it. And all praise is for Allah, the Lord of all that exists.[24]

4) Dr. Shoombas, a German Orientalist, said, "Perhaps you will be amazed to hear this confession from a European such as myself. But I cannot help myself. I have studied the Qur'an and have found in it great eloquence and profoundly wise teachings, such as I have never come across throughout my entire life. One line from the Qur'an is worth volumes. Without a doubt, therefore, the Qur'an is the greatest miracle that Muhammad (s) came with from his Lord."[25]

5) The French scholar Count Henry D. Castaray wrote, "It boggles the mind to contemplate how those Verses (of the Qur'an) could have come from an illiterate man. The entire population of the East agrees that the human mind is incapable of producing Verses that can match either its wordings or meanings."[26]

6) James Matchins said, "Perhaps no book is read more widely throughout the world than the Qur'an; at any rate, it is surely the easiest to memorize, and has more of an impact than any other book on the day-to-day lives of those who believe in it. It is not long like the Old Testament; furthermore, it is written in an elevated style, one that is closer to Verse than to

---

[21] Translator's note. In the original Arabic version of this book, the author writes their names in Arabic only. The author arabized, if you will, their names to the degree that it was very difficult to get a clear picture of what their actual names are in English — he even used letters in Arabic (such as the Ghain) which have no equivalent in English. Furthermore, upon quoting them, he refers the reader to Arabic works and not to original publications in English, French, or German. Thus I was left with no choice but to arrive at as clear an approximation of their names as possible.

[22] *Bil-Qur'an Aslama Haaulaa* by AbdulAzeez Sayyid Al-Ghazzaawee (pgs. 47, 48).

[23] *Taareekh Al-Arab Al-'Aam* (pg. 458).

[24] *Aalamiyyatu-l-Qur'an Al-Kareem* by Dr. Wahbah AzZuhailee (pgs. 14, 15).

[25] *Bi-l-Qur'an Aslama Haaulau* (pg. 49).

[26] *Al-Qur'an Al-Kareem Min Mandhoor Gharbee* by Dr. Imaadud-Deen Khaleel (pg. 18).

prose. Among its qualities is that no sooner do its Verses come into contact with man's heart than he feels a sense of spirituality, a sense that is accompanied by an increase of Faith."[27]

7) Nasree Salhab, an Arab Christian scholar, said about the Prophet (s), "He could neither read nor write, and yet he left as a gift for mankind the most complete written work that mankind could dream of."[28] Nasree further confessed, "It is impossible for either a non-Arab or one who is not proficient in the Arabic language to fully appreciate the beauty of the Qur'an." Moving on to the topic of the universal message of the Qur'an, Nasree said, "The Qur'an does not address Muslims alone, nor does it deal solely with their affairs; rather, it addresses all of mankind and deals with all of their affairs. Were human beings to embrace the Qur'an and to both accept and apply its teachings, mankind would be in a much better state than it is in right now." Finally, Nasree had this to say about the Qur'an's influence on Arabic poetry: "We take much delight in Arab poetry; this holds true for the people of Beirut, Damascus, Cairo, Baghdad, Tunis, and every other Arab land. And the credit for that (pride in the Arabic canon of poetry) goes to the Qur'an - to nothing but the Qur'an."[29]

8) The Orientalist Sail said, "The style of the Qur'an is truly beautiful...especially when it discusses the Greatness and Majesty of Allah (sp). One of the most amazing qualities of the Qur'an is that it enraptures the heart of any person who listens to it being recited, regardless of whether that person believes in it or rejects it."[30]

9) Kopeland said, "It is the Qur'an that enabled Arabs to conquer the world and allowed them to establish an Empire that surpassed – in its size, population, strength, and level of civilization – both the Empire of Greater Alexandria and the Roman Empire."[31]

10) Dr. Laura Fishya wrote, "The greatness of Islam is found in the Qur'an. One of the clearest proofs of the Qur'an having a divine source is the fact that the text of the Qur'an remains in its pristine form from the day it was revealed until this very day, it has not been corrupted or distorted in the least. This Book, which is recited throughout the Muslim world, does not cause even the slightest degree of boredom in the hearts of believers; to the contrary, the more believers recite it, the more beloved it becomes to them. Even today, when faith (in religion) is at a low (throughout the world), thousands of people are able to recite the entire Qur'an from memory. In a single town you will find more people who have memorized the entire Qur'an than there are in all of Europe who have memorized the entire Bible."[32] She also said, "The fact is that Islam spread with lightning-like speed not through strength or the efforts of proselytizers, but rather as a result of the Book that Muslims presented to conquered peoples."

11) While delivering a speech in the British Parliament, Mr. Birk said, "Indeed the teachings of the Qur'an are more merciful, wiser, and more logical than any other set of laws throughout all of history".[33]

12) Harl Sheffield said, "In its eloquence, wording, and power to convince the Qur'an has no equal. It deserves full credit for the flourishing of knowledge throughout all parts of the Islamic world."[34]

13) The famous Lebanese Christian Dr. George Hanna said, "One must admit that, beyond being a Book of religion and of laws, the Qur'an is also a Book of pure and eloquent Arabic. It is because of the Qur'an that the Arabic language has flourished. Throughout the centuries, scholars of the Arabic Language have recognized the Qur'an as being their primary reference book for understanding the connotations and denotations of words. And here I am referring to both Muslim and Christian scholars of language. As for the former, they believe that the correctness of the Qur'an's Arabic is a direct result of it having been revealed by Allah; or in other words, it is because of its divine source that it is free of defects and mistakes. As for Christian scholars of the Arabic language, they too acknowledge the correctness of the

---

[27] *Al-Qur'an Al-Kareem Min Mandhoor Gharbee* by Dr. Imaadud-Deen Khaleel (pg. 18).
[28] *Fee Khutta Muhammad* (pg. 94).
[29] *Fee Khutta Muhammad* (pg. 344).
[30] *Al-Qur'an Al-Kareem Min Mandhoor Gharbee* by Dr. Imaadud-Deen Khaleel (pg. 61).
[31] *Al-Bahth Anillah* (pg. 51).
[32] *Difaa Anil-Islam* (pgs. 30-32).
[33] *Difaa Anil-Islam* (pg. 63).
[34] *At-Tarbiyyah Fee Kitaabillah* by Mahmood AbdulWahhaab (pgs. 52, 53).

Qur'an's Arabic, and they do so without regard to the belief that it was revealed (by Allah (sp)). So regardless of his religious learning, a scholar of the Arabic language, whenever faced with a difficult language issue, refers to the Qur'an in order to arrive at a correct answer."[35]

14) William Geoffrey Balkraaf said, "It is only when the Qur'an disappears from earth, and when the city of Makkah disappears from Arab lands that we can hope to see Arabs embrace the ways of Western civilization."[36]

15) Marking the 100th anniversary of the occupation of Algeria, the man who served as France's viceroy of Algeria delivered a speech in which he said, "Verily, we will not defeat the Algerians as long as they recite the Qur'an and speak Arabic. Therefore, we must wipe out the Qur'an from existence and take away from them the Arabic language."[37]

16) Having failed to make Algerians French in their character, manners, and beliefs, Lacoste, the Minister of French Colonies, said, "What can I do when the Qur'an is more powerful than France?"[38]

These are just a few of many praises that the enemies of Islam have lavished on the Qur'an. As can be seen from the aforementioned quotes, such praises are generally made by three categories of people:

1) Those that see the Qur'an as being a barrier between them and their aim of converting Muslims to Christianity. In a moment of resignation, such people realize that, because of the magnificence of the Qur'an and the powerful influence it has over people, their efforts to proselytize Muslims are doomed to failure.
2) Those non-Muslims who want to point out to their people the Secret behind the strength of Muslims.
3) Those who don't believe in Islam but are still sincere and just enough to recognize the greatness of the Qur'an and to openly express their admiration of its profoundly wise teachings.

If many non-Muslims acknowledge the grandeur of the Noble Qur'an, is it not then befitting for Muslims to honor it, and to do justice to it by seeking guidance from it and living life according to its laws and precepts?

Topic 4

The Grandeur of the Names and Attributes of the Qur'an

First: The Grandeur of the Qur'an's Names

Second: The Grandeur of the Qur'an's Attributes

---

[35] Refer to *Qissatul-Insaan* (pgs. 79, 80).
[36] *Khasadis Al-Qur'an Al-Kareem (pg. 217)*, and *Judhoor Al-Balaa by* Abdullah AtTall (pg. 201).
[37] *Majallah Al-Manaar (1962)*.
[38] *QaadatulGharb Yaqooloon* by Jalaal Al-Aalam (pg. 51); also, refer to *Jareedah Al-Ayyaam (7780), (1962)*.

Introduction

Human beings can do their best to describe the magnificence of the Qur'an in their own words; but as much as they try to be eloquent and pithy in their description, Allah's description of the Qur'an is better and more fitting. This is only natural since none is more acquainted with His speech than He is. Allah (sp) described the Qur'an in two important ways: First, He (sp) gave it different names. It is a well-known feature of the Arabic language that, the more names a thing has, the more significance is attached to it. This applies to everything: people, beings, events, things. The Day of Judgment, for instance, has been given many names because of its importance and because of the terrifying and awful things that will take place during it. Also, the Prophet (s) has more than a few names; he was given those names to honor him and to show his importance among mankind. The examples of things or people or beings that have many names in Arabic due to their importance are many – and as we will see in this section, the Qur'an is no exception. And second, Allah (sp) gave a description of the various qualities, features, and attributes of the Qur'an (which will be the topic of the next section *In Sha Allah* – Allah willing).

As we listen to or read the Qur'an, we should contemplate the meanings of the names that Allah (sp) has given to the Qur'an. In this section, I will endeavor to explain the meanings and significance of those names.

First: The Grandeur of the Qur'an's Names

First: *Al-Furqaan*
Second: *Al-Burhaan*
Third: *Al-Haqq*
Fourth: *An-Naba Al-'Adheem*
Fifth: *Al-Balaagh*
Sixth: *Ar-Rooh*
Seventh: *Al-Mau'idhah*
Eighth: *Ash-Shifaa*
Ninth: *Ahsanul-Hadeeth*

First:

Al-Furqaan

Allah (sp) gave the Qur'an the name *Al-Furqaan* in the following four Verses:
 1) Allah (sp) said:

تَبَارَكَ ٱلَّذِى نَزَّلَ ٱلْفُرْقَانَ عَلَىٰ عَبْدِهِۦ لِيَكُونَ لِلْعَٰلَمِينَ نَذِيرًا

"Blessed be He Who sent down the criterion (of right and wrong, i.e. this Qur'an) to His slave (Muhammad) that he may be a warner to the 'Alamin (mankind and jinns)." (Qur'an 25: 1)

 2) Allah (sp) said:

وَأَنزَلَ ٱلْفُرْقَانَ

"And He sent down the criterion (of judgment between right and wrong (this Qur'an)." (Qur'an 3:4)

3) Allah (sp) said:

شَهْرُ رَمَضَانَ ٱلَّذِىٓ أُنزِلَ فِيهِ ٱلْقُرْءَانُ هُدًى لِّلنَّاسِ وَبَيِّنَـٰتٍ مِّنَ ٱلْهُدَىٰ وَٱلْفُرْقَانِ

"The month of Ramadan in which was revealed the Qur'an, a guidance for mankind and clear proofs for the guidance and the criterion (between wrong and right)." (Qur'an 2:185)

4) Allah (sp) said:

وَقُرْءَانًا فَرَقْنَـٰهُ لِتَقْرَأَهُۥ عَلَى ٱلنَّاسِ عَلَىٰ مُكْثٍ وَنَزَّلْنَـٰهُ تَنزِيلًا

"And (it is) a Qur'an which We have divided (into parts), in order that you might recite it to men at intervals. And We have revealed it by stages." (Qur'an 17: 106)

Before going into the meaning of the word *Al-Furqaan*, I should point out that the translation of it in the abovementioned Verses – the criterion – will not do for the purpose of this discussion. A single word such as 'criterion' does not sufficiently explain why Allah (sp) named the Qur'an *Al-Furqaan*.

The first step in understanding the meaning of *Al-Furqaan* is to explain its various connotations in the Arabic language, and to study its root word. The three-letter root word of *Al-Furqaan* is *Faraqa*, which means to separate, part, or divide. *Faariq*, which is derived from *Faraqa*, means something that distinguishes, or it means that which makes something distinctive, a meaning that is similar to that of the word 'criterion'. For criterion can mean a standard or test by which a thing is identified. These definitions will suffice for the purpose of this discussion.

In the last of the aforementioned Verses, *Al-Furqaan* is mentioned in its verb form: *Farraqnaahu*. Based on how the Verse was recited by Alee (r), Ibn Abbaas (r2), Ibn Masood (r), Ubai bin Kaab (r), Qataadah (r), and Ash-Shabee – they recited the word with two letter *Rahs*, whereas the majority of scholars recited it with one letter *Rah* – *Farraqnaahu* means that the Qur'an was divided into parts; or in other words, it was revealed in parts, and not all at once. And according to how the Verse was recited by the majority of scholars, *Faraqnaahu* means either, "We have made clear the Qur'an," or, "In it, We have distinguished between truth and falsehood."

As for *Al-Furqaan* in the first three Verses, scholars disagree about its meaning. In all, there are three scholarly opinions of why the Qur'an is named *Al-Furqaan*:

1) It is named *Al-Furqaan* because it was revealed in parts over a period of more than twenty years; remember that the root word of Al-Furqaan, *Faraqa*, means to separate, part, or divide. The Qur'an is unique in this sense, since every other divinely revealed Book was revealed all at once.

   This interpretation of *Al-Furqaan* is corroborated by how Alee (r), Ibn Abbaas (r), bin Masood (r), Ubai bin Kaab (r), Qataadah (r), and Ash-Shabee recited the Verse:

   وَقُرْءَانًا فَرَقْنَـٰهُ لِتَقْرَأَهُۥ عَلَى ٱلنَّاسِ عَلَىٰ مُكْثٍ وَنَزَّلْنَـٰهُ تَنزِيلًا

   "And (it is) a Qur'an which We have divided (into parts), in order that you might recite it to men at intervals. And We have revealed it by stages." (Qur'an 17: 106)

They recited the verb form of *Al-Furqaan* with two of the letter *Rahs*, which conveys the meaning of dividing into parts.

2) The Qur'an is called *Al-Furqaan* because it distinguishes truth from falsehood, the lawful from the forbidden, good from evil, guidance from misguidance, happiness from misery, believers from disbelievers, and justice from tyranny. Remember that *Faariq*, which is derived from *Faraqa*, means something that distinguishes, or that which makes something distinctive. For the same reason, Umar (r) was called *Al-Faarooq*, which like *Al-Furqaan*, is derived from the root *Faraqa*. Umar (r) was called *Al-Faarooq* because, through him and his actions, truth could be distinguished from falsehood. Or in other words, he was so clearly upon the truth that he acted as a standard by which the truth could be identified.

Ibn Aashoor (may Allah have mercy on him) said, "The Qur'an is named *Al-Furqaan* because, with more frequency than any other divinely revealed book, it clarifies the difference between truth and falsehood... A sufficient example in this regard is the fact that the Qur'an is more comprehensive in its explanation of *Tawheed* (Islamic Monotheism) than are the *Torah* and the *Injeel*. Verses such as,

$$\text{لَيْسَ كَمِثْلِهِ شَيْءٌ}$$

"There is nothing like unto Him" (Qur'an 42: 11); illustrate this point."[39]

Scholars have pointed out that, just as the Qur'an distinguishes truth from falsehood, so too does it act as a dividing line between different eras. For with the revelation of the Qur'an, the era of tangible miracles (the Prophet (s) and previous Prophets came with many tangible miracles, such as the splitting of the moon, the healing of blindness, etc.) came to an end. Similarly, the era of regional divinely revealed messages came to an end, and was replaced by an era of a universal divinely revealed message; in the former, Prophets (peace be upon them) were sent to specific groups of people, and in the latter, Prophet Muhammad (s) was sent to all of mankind."[40]

3) The famous scholars Ikrimah and As-Suddee proclaimed that the meaning of *Al-Furqaan* is safety or salvation. Theirs is an interpretation that has nothing to do with the linguistic meaning of the word *Furqaan* or of its root word. They explained that the Qur'an was named *Al-Furqaan* because mankind, which was in a state of darkness and misguidance, found safety and salvation in the Qur'an. Based on this interpretation of Al-Furqaan, some scholars of *Tafseer* maintain that criterion in the following Verse actually means safety and salvation:

$$\text{وَإِذْ ءَاتَيْنَا مُوسَى ٱلْكِتَٰبَ وَٱلْفُرْقَانَ لَعَلَّكُمْ تَهْتَدُونَ}$$

"And (remember) We gave Moses the Scripture (the Torah) and the criterion (of right and wrong) so that you may be guided aright." (Qur'an 2:53)

It might be that there is no contradiction between the said opinions; perhaps, therefore, *Al-Furqaan* denotes all three of the aforementioned meanings: 1) The Qur'an is *Al-Furqaan* because, unlike other revealed books, it was revealed in parts and not all at once; 2) The Qur'an is *Al-Furqaan* because it distinguishes truth from falsehood; and 3) the Qur'an is *Al-Furqaan* because it contains in it salvation from darkness and misguidance. It is possible that the Qur'an was named *Al-Furqaan* for only one of the said meanings; nonetheless, the other meanings are true as well. The point here is that, when something is given a name that conveys a variety of meanings, it often points to the importance of that thing; such is certainly the case regarding the Qur'an, regardless of the actual reason why it was named *Al-Furqaan*.

---

[39] *At-Tahreer Wat-Tanweer* (1/71).
[40] *Fee Dhilaal Al-Qur'an* (5/2547).

Second:

Al-Burhaan

Again, it will be of use to the reader to consider the meaning of the word *Burhaan* in the Arabic language before attempting to understand why it was chosen as a name for the Qur'an. The word *Burhaan* is often given the same translation as the word *Hujjah*, which means proof or evidence. But the fact is that *Burhaan* conveys a deeper meaning; not just any proof, but clear and decisive proof – proof that is conclusive, convincing, and irrefutable.

Allah (sp) used *Burhaan* as a name for the Qur'an in only one Verse of His Noble Book:

يَـٰٓأَيُّهَا ٱلنَّاسُ قَدْ جَآءَكُم بُرْهَـٰنٌ مِّن رَّبِّكُمْ

"O mankind! Verily, there has come to you a convincing proof from your Lord." (Qur'an 4:174).

By giving the Qur'an the name *Burhaan*, Allah (sp) was directing His speech to Jews, Christians, and all other disbelievers – notice that Allah (sp) began the Verse with, "O mankind." In the abovementioned Verse, Allah (sp) warned all non-Muslims that the Qur'an was clear and convincing proof against the falsehood they followed. As the following Verse indicates, Allah (sp) provided disbelievers with many signs and proofs:

سَنُرِيهِمْ ءَايَـٰتِنَا فِى ٱلْءَافَاقِ وَفِىٓ أَنفُسِهِمْ حَتَّىٰ يَتَبَيَّنَ لَهُمْ أَنَّهُ ٱلْحَقُّ

"We will show them Our Signs in the universe, and in their own selves, until it becomes manifest to them that this (the Qur'an) is the truth." (Qur'an, 41:53).

But in the aforementioned Verse from Chapter *An-Nisaa*, it is as if Allah (sp) is informing disbelievers that, all by itself, the Qur'an is conclusive evidence of the truthfulness of the Messenger of Allah (s) and of the message he came with.[41]

Third:

Al-Haqq

The word *Haqq* has one primary meaning: truth. Used as a name for the Qur'an, *Haqq* is preceded by Al (the), so that *Al-Haqq*, as a name for the Qur'an, means not only truth, but the absolute truth. It is as if, by naming the Qur'an *Al-Haqq* (the absolute truth), Allah (sp) is alluding to previously revealed Books. If that is the case, the message Allah (sp) is sending the People of the Book is that, whereas the Qur'an consists purely of the absolute truth, previously revealed Books, as a result of human tampering, consist of a mix of truth and falsehood.

Allah (sp) called the Qur'an *Al-Haqq* in many Verses of the Qur'an; here are some examples:

1) Allah (sp) said:

وَإِنَّهُ لَحَقُّ ٱلْيَقِينِ

---

[41] *Fathul-Qadeer* (1/542), *Adwaa Al-Bayaan* (7/79, 80), and *Tafseer As-Sa'dee* (1/217).

"And verily, it (this Qur'an) is an absolute truth with certainty." (Qur'an 69:51)

2) Allah (sp) said:

$$\text{بَلْ نَقْذِفُ بِٱلْحَقِّ عَلَى ٱلْبَٰطِلِ فَيَدْمَغُهُ فَإِذَا هُوَ زَاهِقٌ}$$

"Nay, We fling (send down) the truth (this Qur'an) against the falsehood (disbelief), so it destroys it, and behold, it (falsehood) is vanished." (Qur'an 21:18)
It is stated in this Verse that the truth, or the Qur'an, is cast down against falsehood and destroys it. "Destroys it" is a translation of *Yadmaghuhu*." One should appreciate the imagery of this wording, because the original meaning of *Yadmaghu* in the Arabic language is to pierce a person's head and skull and to reach inside of his brain. So, with the wording of the Verse, we get a sense, or picture, of how the Qur'an easily penetrates, and thus destroys, falsehood.

3) Allah (sp) said:

$$\text{وَكَذَّبَ بِهِ قَوْمُكَ وَهُوَ ٱلْحَقُّ قُل لَّسْتُ عَلَيْكُم بِوَكِيلٍ}$$

"But your people (O Muhammad) have denied it (the Qur'an) though it is the truth. Say: I am not responsible for your affairs." (Qur'an 6: 66)

4) Allah (sp) said:

$$\text{وَمَن يَكْفُرْ بِهِ مِنَ ٱلْأَحْزَابِ فَٱلنَّارُ مَوْعِدُهُ فَلَا تَكُ فِى مِرْيَةٍ مِّنْهُ إِنَّهُ ٱلْحَقُّ مِن رَّبِّكَ وَلَٰكِنَّ أَكْثَرَ ٱلنَّاسِ لَا يُؤْمِنُونَ}$$

"But those of the sects (Jews, Christians and all the other non Muslim nations) that reject it (the Qur'an, the Fire will be their promised meeting place. So be not in doubt about it (i.e. those who denied Prophet Muhammad and also denied all that which he brought from Allah, surely, they will enter Hell). Verily, it is the truth from your Lord, but most of the mankind believe not." (Qur'an 11:17)
That the Qur'an is the absolute truth from Allah (sp) implies that no one should have any doubts about the truthfulness of the Qur'an. In this Verse, Allah (sp) states this point explicitly: "So be not in doubt about it." In the translation of the abovementioned Verse, the explanation of "so be not in doubt about it" is given in parentheses: "(i.e. those who denied Prophet Muhammad (s) and also denied all that which he brought from Allah, surely, they will enter Hell)". Nonetheless, in his *Tafseer*, Abu As-Sa'ood said that "so be not in doubt about it" means: So be not in doubt about the Qur'an and about the fact that it has come down from Allah (sp).[42] That there can be no doubt about the fact that the Qur'an was sent down by Allah (sp), the Lord of all that exists, is explicitly stated in other Verses of the Qur'an, such as in the Saying of Allah (sp):

$$\text{الٓمٓ (١) تَنزِيلُ ٱلْكِتَٰبِ لَا رَيْبَ فِيهِ مِن رَّبِّ ٱلْعَٰلَمِينَ}$$

"Alif-Lam-Mim, (These letters are one of the miracles of the Qur'an, and none but Allah (Alone) knows their meanings). The revelation of the Book (this Qur'an) is from the Lord of the 'Alamin (mankind, jinns and all that exits) in which there is no doubt" (Qur'an 32: 1, 2)
Or in the Saying of Allah (sp):

$$\text{الٓمٓ (١) ذَٰلِكَ ٱلْكِتَٰبُ لَا رَيْبَ فِيهِ هُدًى لِّلْمُتَّقِينَ}$$

---

[42] *Tafseer as-Sa'ood* (4/195).

"Alif-Lam-Mim. (These letters are one of the miracles of the Qur'an, and none but Allah (Alone) knows their meanings). This is the Book (the Qur'an), whereof there is no doubt." (Qur'an 2: 1, 2)

5) Allah (sp) said:

قُلْ إِنَّ رَبِّى يَقْذِفُ بِٱلْحَقِّ عَلَّـٰمُ ٱلْغُيُوبِ (٤٨) قُلْ جَآءَ ٱلْحَقُّ وَمَا يُبْدِئُ ٱلْبَـٰطِلُ وَمَا يُعِيدُ

"Say (O Muhammad): 'Verily! My Lord sends down Inspiration and makes apparent the truth (i.e. this Revelation that had come to me), the All-Knower of the Ghaib (unseen)'. Say (O Muhammad): 'The truth (the Qur'an and Allah's inspiration) has come, and Al-Batil (falsehood – Iblis) can neither create anything nor resurrect (anything).'" (Qur'an 34:48, 49)

Fourth:

An-Naba Al-'Adheem

Allah (sp) called the Qur'an *An-Naba Al-'Adheem* twice in the Noble Qur'an: In Chapter *Saad*, and in Chapter *An-Naba*. This name consists of two words: *An-Naba*, which means news or information or tidings, and *Al-'Adheem*, which means great. To be sure, the name is apt: the Qur'an is indeed great news. It is great in its style; its awe-inspiring Verses; its profound meanings; its important message; its laws and legislation; its parables and stories; and so on.

And it certainly does contain a great deal of information - hence the appropriateness of *An-Naba*, in *An-Naba Al-'Adheem*. The Qur'an gives us crucial information about the most important questions of life: Who is our creator? What are His attributes? What is the purpose of life? Allah (sp) answers all of these questions, informing us about His greatness, about our duty to worship Him without associating partners with Him, about the laws by which we are to live on earth, and about everything we as human beings need to know about regarding both religious and worldly affairs. Furthermore, the Qur'an informs us about the histories of past nations. In terms of history, the Qur'an informs us about what happened in the beginning – the creation of Adam (p) – and what will happen in the end – with some people entering Paradise, and others, the Hellfire – as well as many matters in between. So it is based on all of these reasons that Allah (sp) named the Qur'an *An-Naba Al-'Adheem*. Allah (sp) said:

قُلْ هُوَ نَبَؤٌاْ عَظِيمٌ (٦٧) أَنتُمْ عَنْهُ مُعْرِضُونَ

"Say: 'That (this Qur'an) is great news. From which you turn away'" (Qur'an 38: 67, 68)

The news that is contained in the Qur'an was intended just as much for all of mankind in general as it was for the Quraish and Arabs in particular. So, just as the Qur'an was great news for the Quraish, it is the same for Muslims of today. What is frightening about this comparison is that today's Muslims have, at least in some ways, reacted similarly to the reaction of the Quraish more than fourteen centuries ago: Many Muslims today, though they proclaim the Testimony of Faith, do not appreciate the magnificence of the Qur'an, and do not contemplate the truth that it contains.

Fifth:

Al-Balaagh

In the Arabic language, *Al-Balaagh* can convey a variety of meanings. The root verb of *Al-Balaagh*, *Balagha*, means to reach or to ripen. *Ablagha*, a verb form derived from *Balagha*, means to inform.

Taballagha (with something), another verb that is derived from *Balagha*, means to deem something to be sufficient; it can also mean to use something as a means of reaching a specific goal. *Bulghah*, a noun that is derived from *Balaghah*, means something that is sufficient for ones needs. Given the interrelated nature of Arabic words that share the same root letters, *Balaagh* as a name can potentially convey any of the aforementioned meanings.

Allah (sp) called the Qur'an *Al-Balaagh* in Chapter *Ibraaheem*:

هَٰذَا بَلَٰغٌ لِّلنَّاسِ وَلِيُنذَرُوا۟ بِهِۦ

"This (Qur'an) is a Message for mankind (and a clear proof against them, in order that they may be warned thereby." (Qur'an 14:52)

In his famous *Tafseer*, As-Sa'dee (may Allah have mercy on him) said that the Qur'an has been given the name *Balagh* because "It is used as a means of reaching the highest of rankings (in Paradise)."[43]

In *Al-Itqaan Fee 'Uloom Al-Qur'an*, As-Suyootee (may Allah have mercy on him) said that the Qur'an is called *Al-Balaagh* because "it conveys to people that which they are commanded to do, as well as that which they have been forbidden from doing." As-Suyootee (m) then said, "Perhaps, however, it is called *Al-Balaagh* because it stands alone and is sufficient, with it, one does not need anything else (i.e., any other book to act as a guide)." So the Qur'an is completely sufficient for us; we must rely on it alone, and not on manmade laws or previously revealed books that have been tampered with. The reader should note that both As-Suyootee's and As-Sa'dee's interpretations of *Al-Balaagh* are based on one of the linguistic meanings either of *Al-Balaagh* or of one of its related words – which are mentioned above.

Sixth:

Ar-Rooh

Allah (sp) named the Qur'an *Ar-Rooh* in this Verse:

وَكَذَٰلِكَ أَوْحَيْنَآ إِلَيْكَ رُوحًا مِّنْ أَمْرِنَا ۚ مَا كُنتَ تَدْرِى مَا ٱلْكِتَٰبُ وَلَا ٱلْإِيمَٰنُ وَلَٰكِن جَعَلْنَٰهُ نُورًا نَّهْدِى بِهِۦ مَن نَّشَآءُ مِنْ عِبَادِنَا

"And thus we have sent to you (O Muhammad) Ruhan (an Inspiration, and a Mercy) of Our Command. You knew not what is the Book, nor what is Faith? But We have made it (this Quran) a light wherewith We guide whosoever of Our slaves We will." (Qur'an 42:52)

In the Arabic language, *Ar-Rooh* means soul, spirit, or essence. In his *Tafseer*, Abu As-Sa'ood (may Allah have mercy on him) said that the Qur'an has been named *Ar-Rooh* because it is to the heart of man what the spirit is to his body: The spirit infuses man's body with life, and the Qur'an infuses man's heart with life.[44]

It follows, therefore, that, bereft of the Qur'an; a person is not alive but dead. Ignorance, pride, disbelief – these and similar vices destroy a man, rendering him dead, even if outwardly he seems to be alive. So from the greatness of the Qur'an is that it infuses the hearts of men with life, and it thus distinguishes between the living and the dead. Allah (sp) said:

إِنَّكَ لَا تُسْمِعُ ٱلْمَوْتَىٰ وَلَا تُسْمِعُ ٱلصُّمَّ ٱلدُّعَآءَ إِذَا وَلَّوْا۟ مُدْبِرِينَ ۝ وَمَآ أَنتَ بِهَٰدِى ٱلْعُمْىِ عَن ضَلَٰلَتِهِمْ ۖ إِن تُسْمِعُ إِلَّا مَن يُؤْمِنُ بِـَٔايَٰتِنَا فَهُم مُّسْلِمُونَ

---

[43] *Tafseer As-Sa'dee* (1/428).
[44] *Tafseer Abu As-Sa'ood* (8/38).

"Verily, you cannot make the dead to hear (i.e. benefit them and similarly the disbelievers), nor can you make the deaf to hear the call, when they flee, turning their backs. Nor can you lead the blind out of their error, you can only make to hear those who believe in Our Ayat (proofs, evidences, Verses, lessons, signs, revelations, etc.), and who have submitted (themselves to Allah in Islam as Muslims)." (Qur'an 27: 80, 81)

Seventh:
Al-Mau'idhah

Allah (sp) said:

يَٰٓأَيُّهَا ٱلنَّاسُ قَدْ جَآءَتْكُم مَّوْعِظَةٌ مِّن رَّبِّكُمْ

"O Mankind! There has come to you a good advice from your Lord (i.e. the Qur'an, ordering all that is good and forbidding all that is evil." (Qur'an 10:57)
In the Arabic language, *Mau'idhah* means a sermon or a reminder. During the course of a sermon, a preacher promotes virtue, repudiates vice, softens the hearts of his audience, and promises rewards for good-doers and punishment for evildoers. Each of these tasks is performed by the Noble Qur'an, which explains why Allah (sp) named it *Al-Mau'idhah*. The main difference, however, is that the preachers of sermons are human beings, whereas the Qur'an is from Allah (sp).[45] It is as if Allah (sp) is saying in the abovementioned Verse: O people! What has come to you is a Book that is full of practical wisdom; a book that informs you about both evil and good, and then exhorts you to follow what is good, and to repudiate what is evil. This Book that has come to you consists of comprehensive reminders and advice; and it guides you to the truth and to the Straight Path that leads to ultimate happiness both in this world and in the Hereafter.[46]
At the end of the aforementioned Verse, Allah (sp) informs us that *Al-Mau'idhah* (the Qur'an) is "from your Lord". This brings home the significance of the Qur'an being compared to a sermon or reminder; it is the ultimate sermon and reminder and all human beings are in dire need of it because it comes not from human beings, but from the Lord of all human beings and of all that exists. Can there be a sermon that is of greater value, that penetrates more deeply the hearts of men, or that is more profound in its wisdom than one that comes from our Creator and Lord, Allah (sp)? Even if all of mankind and all jinns were to work together to produce something that is similar to the reminder we are given in the Qur'an, they would not even come close to achieving their goal. For every sermon there are generally two groups of people in the audience: Those who do not benefit from it – either they don't listen to it, or they forget it when they get home, or they decide to act contrary to what was said during it – and those who listen to it and benefit from it. In the following Verse, we learn that those who benefit from the sermon and reminder of the Qur'an are those who are pious and fear Allah (sp) - and we ask Allah (sp) to make each of us one of them:

هَٰذَا بَيَانٌ لِّلنَّاسِ وَهُدًى وَمَوْعِظَةٌ لِّلْمُتَّقِينَ

"This (the Qur'an) is a plain statement for mankind, a guidance and instruction to those who are Al-Muttaqun (the pious)." (Qur'an 3: 138)

---

[45] *Tafseer Ath-Tha'aalabee* (2/181).
[46] *Tafseer Al-Baidaawee* (3/204), and to *At-Tafseer Al-Muneer Fi-l-'Aqeedah Wa sh-Sharee'ah Wal-Manhaj* by Dr. Wahbah Az-Zuhailee (6/213).

Eighth:

Ash-Shifaa

The meaning of *Shifaa* in Arabic is simple: a cure or a remedy from an ailment. Allah (sp) called the Qur'an *Shifaa* in three Verses of His Noble Book:

1) Allah (sp) said:

$$\text{يَٰٓأَيُّهَا ٱلنَّاسُ قَدْ جَآءَتْكُم مَّوْعِظَةٌ مِّن رَّبِّكُمْ وَشِفَآءٌ لِّمَا فِى ٱلصُّدُورِ}$$

"O Mankind! There has come to you a good advice from your Lord (i.e. the Qur'an, ordering all that is good and forbidding all that is evil, and a healing for that (disease of ignorance, doubt, hypocrisy and differences, etc.) in your breasts." (Qur'an 10:57)

Thus the Qur'an is a cure for the diseases that afflict the hearts of men; one should be aware that those diseases – such as doubt in ones faith, hypocrisy, jealousy, malice, etc. – are ultimately more harmful than any disease that afflicts a person's body.

2) Allah (sp) said:

$$\text{وَنُنَزِّلُ مِنَ ٱلْقُرْءَانِ مَا هُوَ شِفَآءٌ وَرَحْمَةٌ لِّلْمُؤْمِنِينَ}$$

"And We send down from the Qur'an that which is a healing and a mercy to those who believe (in Islamic Monotheism and act on it." (Qur'an 17: 82)

This Verse means that the Qur'an, in its entirety, is both a cure and a mercy for believers. In Verses wherein the Qur'an is described as being a cure, we are correct in concluding that those Verses are referring to diseases of the heart. But even though the Qur'an is a cure for diseases of the heart, it can be a cure for physical diseases as well. Scholars say that, in the aforementioned Verse, the Qur'an is described as being a cure both to spiritual and physical diseases. Their interpretation is corroborated by authentic *Ahaadeeth* in which it is mentioned that reciting certain Verses of the Qur'an can have the effect of curing certain physical ailments.[47]

3) Allah (sp) said:

$$\text{قُلْ هُوَ لِلَّذِينَ ءَامَنُوا۟ هُدًى وَشِفَآءٌ}$$

"Say: It is for those who believe, guide and a healing." (Qur'an 41:44)

A good explanation of how the Qur'an acts as a cure was given by Fakhrur-Raazee in his *Tafseer*: "First, be clear on the point that the Qur'an is a cure for both spiritual diseases and for physical ailments. How the Qur'an acts as a cure for spiritual diseases is clear. Spiritual diseases are of two kinds: 1) False beliefs, and 2) vile acts and manners. As for the former, the worst form of false beliefs involves having incorrect beliefs regarding Allah (sp), the Prophets, resurrection, or Divine Preordainment. The Qur'an contains in it the truth regarding all of these issues; furthermore, it refutes those who hold false beliefs regarding them. As for the latter, the Qur'an lists vile deeds and manners, points out why they are vile, and guides mankind to their opposites: to good deeds and noble manners. (Thus it is clear how the Qur'an, through information and reminders and commands, acts as a cure for spiritual diseases.) How, then, does the Qur'an act as a cure for physical ailments? The answer to this question is simple: If one seeks blessings from it when one recites it, then that has the effect of warding off diseases and ailments."[48]

Ar-Raazee widened the scope of the meaning of *Ash-Shifaa* in the abovementioned Verses. We should widen the scope of its meaning even further and agree that, just as the Qur'an is a cure for diseases of the heart, soul, and body, it is also a cure for ailments that are causing our societies to decay in this day

---

[47] *At-Tahreer Wat-Tanweer* (14/150).

[48] *At-Tafseer al-Kabeer* (21/29).

and age. Such ailments can, among other things, be political, economic, or societal in nature. We, as a society, are afflicted with many diseases, and we should look to the Qur'an to cure all of our woes, and not just a headache, stomachache, or other similar ailments.[49] One of the ways in which the Qur'an is magnificent and great is that it contains in it a panacea for all of our woes on earth - for false beliefs, base manners, physical diseases, as well as all forms of societal problems.

Ninth:

Ahsanul-Hadeeth

Ahsanul-Hadeeth literally means the best of speech.
Allah (sp) said:

ٱللَّهُ نَزَّلَ أَحْسَنَ ٱلْحَدِيثِ

"Allah has sent down the best statement." (Qur'an 39:23).
According to the author of *Tafseer As-Samarqandee*, Ahsanul-Hadeeth in this Verse means the most perfect of speech.[50] Here, Allah (sp) is praising the Book He (sp) revealed to Prophet Muhammad (s), describing it as being categorically, and without exception, the very best speech. The abovementioned Verse, therefore, clearly proves that the Qur'an is superior to all of the other books that Allah (sp) sent down to earth, such as the Torah or the Injeel (the Gospel); upon this point scholars from the early generations of Islam are in agreement, for not a single one of them made the claim that, since all divinely revealed Books are from Allah (sp), they are all equal in status.[51] That the Qur'an is the best speech signifies, among other things, that it is the most eloquent of all speech and that the meanings it conveys are more profound and wise than those that are conveyed by any other speech.
According to the author of *Fathul-Qadeer*, the Qur'an is called "*Hadeeth* (speech)" because the Prophet (s) related it verbally to his people, informing them through speech the Verses that were being revealed to him.[52] In fact, Allah (sp) named the Qur'an *Hadeeth* not just in the abovementioned Verse, but in a number of other Verses as well; here are four examples:

فَبِأَيِّ حَدِيثٍ بَعْدَهُ يُؤْمِنُونَ

"In what message after this will they then believe" (Qur'an 7: 185)

فَلَعَلَّكَ بَاخِعٌ نَّفْسَكَ عَلَىٰ ءَاثَـٰرِهِمْ إِن لَّمْ يُؤْمِنُوا۟ بِهَـٰذَا ٱلْحَدِيثِ أَسَفًا

"Perhaps, you, would kill yourself (O Muhammad) in grief over their footsteps (for their turning away from you, because they believe not in this narration (the Qur'an)." (Qur'an 18: 6)

أَفَمِنْ هَـٰذَا ٱلْحَدِيثِ تَعْجَبُونَ

"Do you then wonder at this recital (the Qur'an)" (Qur'an 53: 59)

---

[49] *Mafaateeh Lit-Ta'aamul ma'al-Qur'an* (pgs. 34, 35).
[50] *Tafseer As-Samarqandee* (3/174).
[51] *Kutub WaRasaail Wa Fataawa Ibn Taymiyyah Fit-Tafseer* (11/17).
[52] *Fathul-Qadeer* (4/458).

$$\text{فَذَرْنِي وَمَن يُكَذِّبُ بِهَٰذَا ٱلْحَدِيثِ}$$

"*Then leave Me Alone with such as belie this Qur'an.*" (Qur'an 68:44)

Second: The Greatness of the Qur'an's Attributes

First: *Al-Hakeem*

Second: *Al-Azeez*

Third: *Al-Kareem*

Fourth: *Al-Majeed*

Fifth: *Al-'Adheem*

Sixth: *Al-Basheer Wan-Nadheer*
Seventh: *Laa Ya'tihi Al-Baatil Min Baini Yadaihi Walaa Min Khalfihi* (Falsehood cannot come to it from before it or behind it)

First:

Al-Hakeem

Al-Hakeem is another Arabic word that carries many shades of meaning; so again, it will be of use to the reader to become acquainted with the family of words that have in common with *Al-Hakeem* the root word *Hakama*. One of the meanings of *Hakama* is to judge. *Ahkama*, which is derived from *Hakama*, can mean to perfect something. And *Hikmah*, which is also derived from *Hakama*, means wisdom. These definitions should help the reader understand why Allah (sp) described the Qur'an as being *Al-Hakeem*. Of the many Verses in which Allah (sp) described the Qur'an as being *Al-Hakeem*, I will focus on two only:

1) Allah (sp) said:

$$\text{تِلْكَ ءَايَٰتُ ٱلْكِتَٰبِ ٱلْحَكِيمِ}$$

"*These are the Verses of the Book (the Qur'an) Al-Hakim*" (showing lawful and unlawful things, explaining Allah's (Divine) Laws for mankind, leading them to eternal happiness by ordering them to follow the true Islamic Monotheism, - worshipping none but Allah Alone – that will guide them to Paradise and save them from Hell) (Qur'an 10:1, 31: 2)

Based on the various shades of meanings of the word *Hakama* and the family of words that are derived from it, *Al-Hakeem* in this Verse can be interpreted in more than one way:

- In the Qur'an all laws and legislations are perfected. This interpretation is corroborated by the Verse:

كِتَابٌ أُحْكِمَتْ ءَايَتُهُ

"*(This is) a Book, the Verses whereof are perfected* (in every sphere of knowledge, etc.)" (Qur'an 11:1)

- The Qur'an acts as a judge, issuing rulings that inform us about what is lawful, and about what is forbidden; also, the Qur'an judges among men by the truth. This interpretation is corroborated by the Verse:

وَأَنزَلَ مَعَهُمُ ٱلْكِتَٰبَ بِٱلْحَقِّ لِيَحْكُمَ بَيْنَ ٱلنَّاسِ فِيمَا ٱخْتَلَفُواْ فِيهِ

"*And with them He sent the Scripture in truth to judge between people in matters wherein they differed.*" (2:213).
It appears as if the translator of the abovementioned Verse from Chapters *Younus* and *Luqmaan* based his translation on this interpretation of the word *Al-Hakeem*. And Allah (sp) knows best.
- The Qur'an contains in it important judgments. So, for instance, in the Qur'an Allah (sp) judged that Paradise will be the reward for those who obey Him and that the Hellfire will be the punishment for those who disobey Him.
- The Qur'an is perfect and contains in it neither falsehood nor contradictions; this was the interpretation of the eminent scholar Muqaatil. In his Tafseer of the aforementioned Verse from Chapters *Younus* and *Luqmaan*, As-Sa'dee (m) listed a variety of ways in which the Qur'an has been perfected:

a. It is worded in the best of ways, and its wording points to the most important and lofty of meanings.
b. It is safe from human tampering. We recite the exact same Qur'an that was recited by the Prophet (s) and his Companions (rp). And it will, by the guarantee of Allah (sp), remain in its pristine form. So unlike previously revealed Books, it will not undergo changes at the hands of corrupt men.
c. All of the information it contains – about previous nations, about the unseen world, about natural phenomenon in the universe, etc. – corresponds exactly to reality. Even after the advent of modern science, there is no new knowledge we have that contradicts any part of the Qur'an.
d. Everything it orders us to do is either purely good or the overriding good. And anything it forbids us from doing is either purely evil or the overriding evil. Incidentally, it is often the case that Allah (sp) juxtaposes a command with the wisdom and benefits of following it; likewise, He (sp) frequently forbids something and then explains the wisdom behind its prohibition.
e. The Qur'an consists of a perfect balance between giving people hope of rewards if they obey Allah (sp), and terrifying them with the prospect of punishment if they disobey Him.
f. Various aspects of stories, legislations, and commands are repeated throughout the Qur'an. Yet, in spite of all of that repetition, there is never any contradiction between one Verse of the Qur'an and another.[53]

---

[53] *Tafseer As-Sa'dee* (4/101).

2. Allah (sp) said:

$$\text{وَٱلْقُرْءَانِ ٱلْحَكِيمِ}$$

"By the Qur'an, full of wisdom (i.e. full of laws, evidences, and proofs)" (Qur'an 36: 2)
In this Verse, *Al-Hakeem* is interpreted as meaning full of wisdom; nonetheless, it is important to note that, regardless of what the actual meaning of *Al-Hakeem* is, each of the aforementioned interpretations conveys a true meaning and points to the magnificence and greatness of the Qur'an.

Second:

Al-'Azeez

Describing the Qur'an, Allah (sp) said:

$$\text{وَإِنَّهُ لَكِتَابٌ عَزِيزٌ}$$

"And verily, it is an honorable respected Book" (because it is Allah's speech, and He has protected it from corruption, etc.)" (Qur'an 41:41)
The translator of this Verse based his translation on one of the meanings of *'Azeez*; something that is honored and revered. *'Azeez* has other meanings as well; for instance, it can mean something that is precious and valuable. And *'Azeez* is derived from *'Izzah*, which means unassailable, invincible, impregnable, or something that is defended in such a way that it cannot be defeated. The relationship between the two stated meanings is that, if something is valuable and precious, those that own it will defend and protect it. *'Azeez* can also mean something that always triumphs and is never defeated; this meaning of *'Azeez* applies to the clear and irrefutable proofs of the Noble Qur'an.[54] Allah (sp) described the Qur'an as being *'Azeez* because, by virtue of the absolute truth it contains, it is unassailable: It is protected by Allah and it is impossible to find mistakes in it.[55]
In summary, the scholars of Tafseer have given various interpretations for why Allah (sp) has described the Qur'an as being *'Azeez*. The reader would do well to notice that each of the following interpretations is based on one of the abovementioned meanings of *'Azeez*:

1) The Qur'an is safeguarded from the *Shaitaan* (the Devil, who can find no way to distort or corrupt it in any way whatsoever.
2) The Qur'an is deemed honorable by Allah (sp) (hence the abovementioned translation of *'Azeez* in Verse 41 of Chapter 41 *Fussilat*; therefore, it is our duty to honor and revere the Qur'an.
3) It is impregnable in that it is inaccessible to and well fortified against falsehood.
4) The Qur'an will always remain triumphant: People cannot say anything that is similar to or better than it.
5) It is an honorable Book because it is Allah's speech, and, as such, is not something that has been created.

Again, regardless of what the exact intended meaning of *'Azeez* is in Chapter 41 *Fussilat*, each of the abovementioned interpretations says something true about the Qur'an. It is a well-known fact that, in

---

[54] *At-Tahreer Wat-Tanweer* (25/71).
[55] *Tafseer Ibn Atiyyah* (5/19).

the sciences of Tafseer, there are generally two kinds of opposing interpretations: 1) When two different interpretations are in conflict with one another; in such instances, one interpretation is correct and the other is false; and 2) When two different interpretations are not in conflict with one another, but instead convey different aspects of the truth. To better understand this principle, consider three People's description of a garden: One of them says it is beautiful; another says it is green; and the third person says its fruits are ripe. Who is telling the truth? Well, it is possible that all three of them are telling the truth: The garden is beautiful and green, and its fruits are ripe. Similarly, in the Noble Qur'an, it often occurs that one scholar of Tafseer gives one interpretation of a Verse, while a second scholar gives another, and both of them are correct. Each of them is describing one aspect of the Verse's overall meaning. This is part of the beauty of the Qur'an: A single Verse can convey many meanings. This principle applies at least most of the time to the names and attributes of the Qur'an: A single attribute can be interpreted in three, four, or five (or more) different ways, and each interpretation is correct. In regard to the word 'Azeez, it is interesting to note that Allah (sp) used it to describe the Qur'an, the Prophet (s), and the nation of Muslims. As for the Qur'an, Allah (sp) said:

وَإِنَّهُ لَكِتَابٌ عَزِيزٌ

"And verily, it is an honorable respected Book" (because it is Allah's speech, and He has protected it from corruption, etc.) (Qur'an 41:41).

Describing the Prophet (s), Allah (sp) said:

لَقَدْ جَاءَكُمْ رَسُولٌ مِّنْ أَنفُسِكُمْ عَزِيزٌ

"Verily, there has come unto you a Messenger (Muhammad) from amongst yourselves (i.e. whom you know well). It grieves him ('Azeez 'Alaihi) that you should receive any injury or difficulty." (Qur'an 9: 128)

And in regard to the nation of Muslims, Allah (sp) said:

وَلِلَّهِ ٱلْعِزَّةُ وَلِرَسُولِهِ وَلِلْمُؤْمِنِينَ

"But honor, power and glory belong to Allah, His Messenger (Muhammad), and to the believers." (Qur'an 63: 8)

Third:

Al-Kareem

The word *Kareem* means honorable or noble. Describing the Noble Qur'an, Allah (sp) said:

فَلَا أُقْسِمُ بِمَوَاقِعِ ٱلنُّجُومِ (٧٥) وَإِنَّهُ لَقَسَمٌ لَّوْ تَعْلَمُونَ عَظِيمٌ (٧٦) إِنَّهُ لَقُرْءَانٌ كَرِيمٌ (٧٧)

"I swear by Mawaqi' (setting or the mansions etc.) of the stars (they traverse). And verily, that is indeed a great oath, if you but know. That (this) is indeed an honorable recital (the Noble Qur'an)." (Qur'an 56: 75-77)

Allah (sp) has conferred honor upon the Qur'an, raising it in status above all other divinely revealed Books. That Allah (sp) honored the Qur'an also means that it is above being a fabrication or a product of magic.[56]

Allah (sp) conferred honor upon the Qur'an in the very Verses wherein He (sp) described the Qur'an as being "an honorable recital". He (sp) didn't immediately state the fact that the Qur'an is an honorable recital; no, He (sp) preceded that statement with an oath: "I swear by Mawaqi (setting or the mansions, etc.) of the stars." Then Allah (sp) made it clear that He (sp) was making an important oath: "That is indeed a great oath, if you were but to know." In the following Verse, Allah (sp) stated what that great oath was about: It was about affirming the lofty status of the Qur'an.

So it was as if Allah (sp) was saying: I swear by the setting of the stars that this Qur'an is an honorable recital; it is the product of neither magic nor soothsaying; nor does it contain any lies; rather, it is an honorable and praiseworthy recital, which Allah (sp) as has made a miracle for His Prophet (s). The Qur'an is revered by believers because it is the speech of their Lord, and because it is a cure for the spiritual diseases from which they suffer. And the Qur'an is revered by the inhabitants of the heavens because it is revelation from their Lord.

There is one interpretation of *Kareem* that is not based on its meaning in the Arabic language; some scholars say that *Kareem* means that the Qur'an is not created. Other interpretations do take into consideration the original meanings of *Kareem* in Arabic; according to one interpretation, for instance, the Qur'an is described as being *Kareem* because it contains honorable teachings and invites mankind to adopt noble manners. And finally, it has been said that the Qur'an is described as being Kareem because honor is gained by those who memorize it, as well as by those who recite it.[57]

Kareem, it is interesting to note, is an adjective that applies to many: Allah (sp) is *Al-Kareem* (the All-Generous, Most Munificent, etc.; one of the meanings of *Kareem* is generous). He (sp) sent down a Book that is *Kareem* (honorable). The one who descended with it was a *Kareem* (honorable) angel, and he took it down to a *Kareem* (honorable) Prophet (s), for the sake of a *Kareem* nation. And if the people of that nation adhere closely to it and follow its teachings, they will gain a *Kareem* (generous, since it is one of the meanings of *Kareem*) reward. Allah (sp) said:

إِنَّمَا تُنذِرُ مَنِ ٱتَّبَعَ ٱلذِّكْرَ وَخَشِيَ ٱلرَّحْمَٰنَ بِٱلْغَيْبِ ۖ فَبَشِّرْهُ بِمَغْفِرَةٍ وَأَجْرٍ كَرِيمٍ

"You can only warn him who follows the Reminder (the Qur'an), and fears the Most Beneficent (Allah) unseen. Bear you to such one the glad tidings of forgiveness, and a generous reward (i.e., Paradise)." (Qur'an 36:11).

Fourth:

Al-Majeed

Majeed means glorious and exalted. Allah (sp) said:

بَلْ هُوَ قُرْءَانٌ مَّجِيدٌ
فِى لَوْحٍ مَّحْفُوظٍ

"Nay! This is a Glorious Qur'an, (Inscribed) in Al-Lauh Al-Mahfuz (the Preserved Tablet)" (Qur'an 85: 21, 22)

---

[56] *Fathul-Qadeer* (5/160).

[57] *Tafseer Al-Qurtubee* (17/216).

This Verse means: In spite of what those who disbelieve say, this Qur'an is exalted in its wording and style, to the degree that it is a miracle. And it reaches the utmost levels of honor, nobility, and blessings. Contrary to what the disbelievers say, it is not poetry or the product of magic or soothsaying; instead, it is the speech of Allah (sp), which is protected from all forms of tampering or corruption. And it is inscribed with Allah (sp) in *Al-Lauh Al-Mahfuz* (the Preserved Tablet). One interpretation of *Majeed* in the aforementioned Verse is that the Qur'an is exalted above all other books – even above all previously revealed Books.[58] According to another interpretation, that the Qur'an is *Majeed* refers to the exalted nature of its message and to the fact that it only takes a few of its words to convey a wide variety of meanings.

Fifth:

Al-'Adheem

This attribute was used as the title of this work. And as I have hitherto pointed out, *Al-'Adheem* connotes greatness, magnificence, and grandeur. Allah (sp) said:

وَلَقَدْ ءَاتَيْنَٰكَ سَبْعًا مِّنَ ٱلْمَثَانِى وَٱلْقُرْءَانَ ٱلْعَظِيمَ
لَا تَمُدَّنَّ عَيْنَيْكَ إِلَىٰ مَا مَتَّعْنَا بِهِۦٓ أَزْوَٰجًا مِّنْهُمْ

"*And indeed, We have bestowed upon you seven of Al-Mathani (seven repeatedly recited Verses), (i.e. Surat Al-Fatiha) and the Grand Qur'an. Look not with your eyes ambitiously at what We have bestowed on certain classes of them (the disbelievers).*" (Qur'an 15: 87, 88).
In these Verses, Allah (sp) says to His Prophet (s): "Yes, I have bestowed on certain classes of the disbelievers many worldly things. But do not look ambitiously at what I have bestowed upon them, nor upon the world and its temptations, for I have given you that which is sufficient for you: The Grand Qur'an. Since you have the Qur'an, you need nothing else. For the Qur'an is the greatest of all blessings. Every other blessing, no matter how great it is, is small and insignificant when compared with the blessing of the Qur'an."[59]

Sixth:

Al-Basheer Wan-Nadheer

Simply put, a *Basheer* is a bearer of glad tidings, and a *Nadheer* is a warner (of impending doom or disaster). In the second of the following Verses, Allah (sp) uses both *Basheer* and *Nadheer* to describe the Noble Qur'an:

كِتَٰبٌ فُصِّلَتْ ءَايَٰتُهُۥ قُرْءَانًا عَرَبِيًّا لِّقَوْمٍ يَعْلَمُونَ
بَشِيرًا وَنَذِيرًا

---

[58] *Tafseer Abu As-Sa'ood* (9/139), *Tafseer As-Samarqandee* (3/545), and *Tafseer Al-Qaasimee* (6/316).
[59] *Al-Kashshaaf* by *Az-Zamakhsharee* (2/549) and *Tafseer Ath-Tha'aalabee* (2/300).

"A Book whereof the Verses are explained in detail; – a Qur'an in Arabic for people who know. Giving glad tidings (of Paradise to the one who believes in the Oneness of Allah (i.e. Islamic Monotheism) and fears Allah much (abstains from all kinds of sins and evil deeds) and loves Allah much (performing all kinds of good deeds which He has ordained)), and warning (of punishment in the Hell Fire to the one who disbelieves in the Oneness of Allah)." (Qur'an 41: 3, 4)

The reason why the Qur'an is described with these two attributes is fairly obvious. It gives glad tidings to those who believe, informing them that their reward will be Paradise; and it warns those who disbelieve that, if they continue in their evil ways, their final destination will be the Hellfire.[60]

Given that two of the main functions of the Qur'an, as per the meaning of the abovementioned Verse, are to bring glad tidings and to warn about impending doom, human beings must strive to understand the implications of both the glad tidings and the warning of impending doom; after all, their ultimate fate is at stake. Human beings work hard to learn about the things that will benefit them in the short term: how to gain wealth and enjoy pleasures in this life. It is only logical, therefore, that they should learn about the path that leads to eternal bliss as well as the path that leads to eternal punishment in the Hellfire.[61]

The qualities of being a bearer of glad tidings and a warner of impending doom are common to the Noble Qur'an and to Prophets, peace be upon them. For in describing the function and duty of Prophets, Allah (sp) said:

فَبَعَثَ ٱللَّهُ ٱلنَّبِيِّـۧنَ مُبَشِّرِينَ وَمُنذِرِينَ

"And Allah sent Prophets with glad tidings and warnings." (Qur'an, 2: 213).

And Allah (sp) gave this description of Prophet Muhammad (s):

إِنَّآ أَرْسَلْنَـٰكَ شَـٰهِدًا وَمُبَشِّرًا وَنَذِيرًا

"Verily, We have sent you (O Muhammad) as a witness, as a bearer of glad tidings, and as a warner." (Qur'an 48:8).

Without a doubt, spiritual development requires the emphasis of both the positive and the negative. Allah (sp), with His infinite wisdom, knows that a purely positive message – positive in the sense of promising rewards without warning about impending doom – stunts spiritual growth in human beings. When human beings focus only on the promise of salvation and rewards, they fall into a state of wishful thinking: They perpetrate evil deeds with impunity, and focus not on action or the performance of good deeds, but on a sense of entitlement, the idea that Paradise is their guaranteed destination. Similarly, a purely negative message – one that warns about impeding punishment without promising rewards - also stunts the spiritual development of human beings. A person who focuses only on the Hellfire lacks an understanding of Islam, is ignorant of Allah's Mercy, is (because of his unbalanced understanding of Islam) likely to follow a deviant set of beliefs and acts of worship, and will end up losing hope in Allah (sp).

The only way to spiritual development is to strike a balance between hope and fear, hope for rewards from Allah (sp), and fear of Allah's punishment. That is why the Qur'an is both *Basheer* and *Nadheer*, containing doses of both glad tidings and warnings. The dual function of the Qur'an - of being a bearer of glad tidings and a warner – is again emphasized in this Verse:

لِّيُنذِرَ بَأْسًا شَدِيدًا مِّن لَّدُنْهُ وَيُبَشِّرَ ٱلْمُؤْمِنِينَ ٱلَّذِينَ يَعْمَلُونَ ٱلصَّـٰلِحَـٰتِ أَنَّ لَهُمْ أَجْرًا حَسَنًا

"to give warning (to the disbelievers) of a severe punishment from Him, and to give glad tidings to the believers (in the Oneness of Allah – Islamic Monotheism), who work righteous deeds, that they shall have a fair reward (i.e. Paradise)." (Qur'an 18: 2)

---

[60] *Tafseer Ibn 'Atiyyah* (5/4).
[61] *Tafseer As-Sa'dee* (1/7644) and *At-Tafseer Al-Kabeer* (27/82).

The wise person is he who benefits from the Qur'an's warnings – by casting off false beliefs and avoiding evil deeds – and rejoices upon reading the glad tidings of the Qur'an, and he does the latter by performing more good deeds.[62]

Seventh:

Laa Ya'tihi Al-Baatil Min Baini Yadaihi Walaa Min Khalfihi (Falsehood cannot come to it from before it or behind it)

This quality of the Qur'an is described not with a word or two, but with an entire phrase. Allah (sp) said:

$$\text{لَّا يَأْتِيهِ ٱلْبَٰطِلُ مِنۢ بَيْنِ يَدَيْهِ وَلَا مِنْ خَلْفِهِۦ}$$

"Falsehood cannot come to it from before it or behind it." (Qur'an, 41: 42).
In translating this Verse, the translator gave one interpretation of its meaning, but there are others as well. That there are various interpretations of this Verse can be attributed to two main reasons: First, the word *Baatil* (falsehood) can convey more than one meaning: falsehood in general, or a specific kind of falsehood. And second, 'cannot come to it from before it or behind it', can be intended to convey either a literal or a figurative meaning. If one understands this phrase literally, the concepts of 'before', 'behind', or 'after' will appear in one's interpretation.
Ar-Raazee, may Allah have mercy on him, enumerated various possible interpretations of the abovementioned Verse. It should be noted that each one of them is plausible in that it says something true about the Qur'an.
1. The Books that came before the Qur'an - such as the Torah, Injeel, and Zaboor – do not contradict it; and there will not come any book after it that will disprove it.
2. Whatever the Qur'an declares to be true does not then become false, and whatever the Qur'an declares to be false does not then become true.
3. *Baatil* in this Verse means changes to the Qur'an - additions or the removing of passages. Therefore, the meaning of this Verse is as follows: The Qur'an is protected from having any of its passages removed and from having any foreign statements or words added to it; it is thus completely safe from having falsehood come to it either from before it or from behind it. This interpretation is supported by the saying of Allah (sp):

$$\text{إِنَّا نَحْنُ نَزَّلْنَا ٱلذِّكْرَ وَإِنَّا لَهُۥ لَحَٰفِظُونَ}$$

"Verily We: It is We Who have sent down the Dhikr (i.e. the Qur'an) and surely, We will guard it (from corruption)." (Qur'an, 15: 9)
4. Before and behind (or after) are to be taken figuratively. Therefore, the Verse simply means that, regardless of the direction it comes from, falsehood cannot reach the Qur'an, touch it, or find a way into it. The author of *Al-Kashshaaf* was a proponent of this interpretation.[63]
5. *Baatil* in this Verse refers to any devil. Therefore, this Verse means that no devil - whether he be a jinn or a human being - can successfully tamper with the Qur'an by adding to it, or by removing something from it. It is, and will remain, in its pristine form, the form in which it was revealed; that it will always remain as such is guaranteed by Allah (sp).[64]

---

[62] *Yu'allimuhumul-Kitaab* by Muhammad Ash-Sha'aal (pg. 20).
[63] *Al-Kashshaaf* by Az-Zamakhsharee (4/207).
[64] *Tafseer As-Sa'dee* (4/402).

One might say that if falsehood cannot touch the Qur'an, then what about those who have attacked the Qur'an or interpreted it falsely? The answer to this question is, yes, people have made false interpretations of the Qur'an, but Allah (sp), through His infinite wisdom, has protected it in such a way that falsehood cannot cling to it. What I mean by this is that Allah (sp) has blessed this nation with noble scholars in every era and country, so that no sooner does someone ascribe a false meaning to the Qur'an, than a scholar of *Ahlu-Sunnah* refutes him, leaving him - and his false interpretation - without a foot to stand on. Any false statement about the Qur'an is sure to be destroyed by clear proofs. And that is partly the meaning of Allah's Saying:

إِنَّا نَحْنُ نَزَّلْنَا ٱلذِّكْرَ وَإِنَّا لَهُ لَحَافِظُونَ

"*Verily We: It is We Who have sent down the Dhikr (i.e. the Qur'an) and surely, We will guard it (from corruption).*" (Qur'an, 15: 9)

All praise is for Allah (sp) Who has made it impossible for falsehood to touch His Noble Book. About that Noble Book, Allah (sp) said:

وَلَوْ كَانَ مِنْ عِندِ غَيْرِ ٱللَّهِ لَوَجَدُوا۟ فِيهِ ٱخْتِلَٰفًا كَثِيرًا

"*Had it been from other than Allah, they would surely have found therein much contradictions.*" (Qur'an 4: 82)

And in another Verse, Allah (sp) said:

وَمَا كَانَ هَٰذَا ٱلْقُرْءَانُ أَن يُفْتَرَىٰ مِن دُونِ ٱللَّهِ وَلَٰكِن تَصْدِيقَ ٱلَّذِى بَيْنَ يَدَيْهِ وَتَفْصِيلَ ٱلْكِتَٰبِ لَا رَيْبَ فِيهِ مِن رَّبِّ ٱلْعَٰلَمِينَ

"*And this Qur'an is not such as could ever be produced by other than Allah (Lord of the heavens and the earth, but it is a confirmation of (the revelation) which was before it (i.e. the Torah, and the Gospel, etc.), and a full explanation of the Book (i.e. laws and orders, etc, decreed for mankind) – wherein there is no doubt from the Lord of the 'Alamin (mankind, jinns and all that exists).*" (Qur'an 10: 37)

CHAPTER 2

The Magnificence of the Qur'an's Aims, Legislations, and Stories

This Chapter Consists of Three Parts:

Part One: The Magnificence of the Qur'an's Aims
Part Two: The Magnificence of the Qur'an's Legislations
Part Three: The Magnificence of the Qur'an's Stories

PART 1

The Magnificence of the Qur'an's Aims

This Part Consists of Five Sections:

Section One: Correcting People's Beliefs and Outlook on Life
Section Two: Removing Difficulties from People's Lives
Section Three: Confirming the Dignity of Man and the Sanctity of Human Rights
Section Four: Promoting Strong Family Morals, and Doing Justice to Women
Section Five: Bringing Happiness to Human Beings in Both this World and the Hereafter

Introduction

Every book has one or more aims; for instance, one can say that the aims of a diet book are to teach people how to lose weight and to make people feel better about themselves. Without a doubt, the Noble Qur'an has aims. The aims of the Qur'an are not literally enumerated in any single part of the Qur'an, but they are clearly discussed in several of its chapters (*Soorahs*). Simply put, the aims of the Qur'an are the things it intends to achieve, realize, or bring about.

One might ask, if the Qur'an's aims are not listed anywhere in the Qur'an, how do we know them? The answer to this question is simple: We know them because, even though they are not listed in the Qur'an, they are clear to anyone who contemplates and reflects on the meanings of the Qur'an. Therefore, a good student of the Qur'an knows, for instance, that one of the aims of the Qur'an is to teach man how to achieve ultimate happiness in both this world and the Hereafter; and that another one of its aims is to establish, through its legislations and laws, justice on earth. In this section, I will focus on five important aims of the Qur'an.

Section one:

Correcting people's beliefs and outlook on life

Without a Book to guide them, people will not necessarily develop correct beliefs about their Creator or their purpose in life. The Qur'an was therefore revealed in order to correct people's false beliefs and to inform them about what their beliefs should be. In regard to beliefs, the Qur'an strove to educate people about three issues in particular:

1) *At-Tawheed* **(Islamic Monotheism)**

From its beginning until its end, the Qur'an repudiates polytheism and invites people to worship the One True God: Allah (sp). Having promoted the message of Islamic Monotheism — or True Monotheism – the Qur'an distinguishes between the final destinations of Islamic Monotheists and of polytheists, with the former going to Paradise, and the latter, to the Hellfire. The topics of Monotheism and polytheism are the dominant themes of the Qur'an; that should not be surprising, since the Qur'an considers polytheism to be the greatest crime that any human being can commit. Allah (sp) said:

$$\text{إِنَّ ٱللَّهَ لَا يَغْفِرُ أَن يُشْرَكَ بِهِۦ وَيَغْفِرُ مَا دُونَ ذَٰلِكَ لِمَن يَشَآءُ}$$

"Verily, Allah forgives not that partners should be set up with Him in worship, but He forgives except that (anything else) to whom He pleases." (Qur'an 4: 48)

What polytheism truly means is a fall by man from a station of divinely appointed mastery over the world to a station of slavery and servitude to created beings – whether it be to inanimate objects, plants, animals, people, stone idols, or otherwise. Allah (sp) said:

$$\text{فَٱجْتَنِبُوا۟ ٱلرِّجْسَ مِنَ ٱلْأَوْثَٰنِ وَٱجْتَنِبُوا۟ قَوْلَ ٱلزُّورِ حُنَفَآءَ لِلَّهِ غَيْرَ مُشْرِكِينَ بِهِۦ وَمَن يُشْرِكْ بِٱللَّهِ فَكَأَنَّمَا خَرَّ مِنَ ٱلسَّمَآءِ فَتَخْطَفُهُ ٱلطَّيْرُ أَوْ تَهْوِى بِهِ ٱلرِّيحُ فِى مَكَانٍ سَحِيقٍ}$$

"So shun the abomination (worshipping) of idol, and shun lying speech (false statements) – Hunafa lillah (i.e. to worship none but Allah), not associating partners (in worship etc.) unto Him and whoever assigns partners to Allah, it is as if he had fallen from the sky, and the birds had snatched him, or the wind had thrown him to a far off place." (Qur'an 22: 30, 31)

The call to Tawheed (Islamic Monotheism) is the most important common feature of the messages of all Prophets, peace be upon them, for every single Prophet that was sent to mankind called upon his people to:

$$\text{ٱعْبُدُوا۟ ٱللَّهَ مَا لَكُم مِّنْ إِلَٰهٍ غَيْرُهُۥ}$$

"Worship Allah! You have no other Ilah (God) but Him." (La ilaha ill Allah: none has the right to be worshipped but Allah). (Qur'an 7:59)

The Qur'an also pointed out that the relationship between man and the One True God is direct; or in other words, every individual must invoke and pray to his Lord directly, without going through any intermediaries. Allah (sp) said:

$$\text{وَإِذَا سَأَلَكَ عِبَادِى عَنِّى فَإِنِّى قَرِيبٌ}$$

"And when My slaves ask you (O Muhammad) concerning Me, then (answer them), I am indeed near (to them by My Knowledge)." (Qur'an 2:186)

He (sp) also said:

$$\text{وَقَالَ رَبُّكُمُ ٱدْعُونِىٓ أَسْتَجِبْ لَكُمْ}$$

"And your Lord said: 'Invoke Me, (i.e. believe in My Oneness (Islamic Monotheism)) (and ask Me for anything) I will respond to your (invocation).'" (Qur'an 40: 60)

2) Correcting Beliefs about Prophethood

First, the Qur'an made it clear that human beings need Prophets and Messengers (st) in order to learn about and follow the truth:

$$\text{كَانَ ٱلنَّاسُ أُمَّةً وَٰحِدَةً فَبَعَثَ ٱللَّهُ ٱلنَّبِيِّۦنَ مُبَشِّرِينَ وَمُنذِرِينَ وَأَنزَلَ مَعَهُمُ ٱلْكِتَٰبَ بِٱلْحَقِّ لِيَحْكُمَ بَيْنَ ٱلنَّاسِ فِيمَا ٱخْتَلَفُوا۟ فِيهِ}$$

"Mankind were one community and Allah sent Prophets with glad tidings and warnings, and with them He sent the Scripture in truth to judge between people in matters wherein they differed." (Qur'an 2: 213)

Second, Allah (sp) pointed out the main duties of Prophets (st):

$$رُسُلاً مُبَشِّرِينَ وَمُنذِرِينَ$$

"Messengers as bearers of good news as well as of warnings" (4: 165).
The Qur'an is clear about the role of Prophets and Messengers leaving no room for doubt about their status in the universe: They are neither gods nor the sons of gods, but are simply human beings that are the recipients of divine revelation. Allah (sp) said:

$$قُلْ إِنَّمَا أَنَا بَشَرٌ مِّثْلُكُمْ يُوحَىٰ إِلَيَّ أَنَّمَا إِلَـٰهُكُمْ إِلَـٰهٌ وَاحِدٌ$$

"Say (O Muhammad): I am only a man like you. It has been inspired to me that your Ilah (God) is One Ilah (God - i.e., Allah)." (Qur'an 18: 110)
And because they are human beings and not gods, Prophets do not have the power to guide the hearts of men; their duty is simply to convey their message, and then the power to guide or misguide is in the hands of Allah (sp) alone. Allah (sp) said:

$$فَذَكِّرْ إِنَّمَا أَنتَ مُذَكِّرٌ$$
$$لَّسْتَ عَلَيْهِم بِمُصَيْطِرٍ$$

"So remind them (O Muhammad), you are only one who reminds, You are not a dictator over them." (Qur'an 88: 21, 22)
In regard to the misconceptions people have about Prophets (st), Allah (sp) first quoted some of the doubts that were raised by polytheists and then refuted them. For instance, Allah (sp) related that the disbelievers of past nations said:

$$إِنْ أَنتُمْ إِلَّا بَشَرٌ مِّثْلُنَا$$

"You are no more than human beings like us" (Qur'an 14:10) Then Allah (sp) refuted that claim by saying:

$$قَالَتْ لَهُمْ رُسُلُهُمْ إِن نَّحْنُ إِلَّا بَشَرٌ مِّثْلُكُمْ وَلَـٰكِنَّ ٱللَّهَ يَمُنُّ عَلَىٰ مَن يَشَاءُ مِنْ عِبَادِهِ$$

"Their Messengers said to them: "We are no more than human beings like you, but Allah bestows His Grace to whom He wills of His slaves." (Qur'an 14:11)
In another example, Allah (sp) related that the disbelievers said:

$$وَلَوْ شَاءَ ٱللَّهُ لَأَنزَلَ مَلَـٰئِكَةً$$

"Had Allah willed, He surely could have sent down angels." (Qur'an 23:24)
Yes, if angels inhabited the earth, Allah (sp) would have sent down to them an angel as a Messenger; but because human beings inhabit the earth, it is only fitting that a human Messenger should be sent to them. Allah (sp) said:

$$قُل لَّوْ كَانَ فِي ٱلْأَرْضِ مَلَـٰئِكَةٌ يَمْشُونَ مُطْمَئِنِّينَ لَنَزَّلْنَا عَلَيْهِم مِّنَ ٱلسَّمَاءِ مَلَكًا رَّسُولاً$$

"Say: If there were on the earth, angels walking about in peace and security, We should certainly have sent down for them from the heaven an angel as a Messenger." (Qur'an 17: 95)

3) Correcting Beliefs about Faith in the Hereafter

Just as they were misguided about issues that pertained to True Monotheism, almost all people who were alive when the Prophet (s) was sent to mankind had false beliefs regarding the Hereafter. The People of the Book, having distorted the books that were revealed to their Prophets (st), had misguided notions about the Hereafter; for instance, the Jews felt that, among mankind, they alone would enter Paradise; or that, even if they would be punished for a day, they would then enter Paradise. As for the polytheists of Arabia, they did not even believe in resurrection after death.

Because of the many false notions people held about the Hereafter, the Qur'an relied on various approaches to establish in people's hearts true beliefs about what happens after we depart from this world.

Since the people of the Quraish disbelieved in resurrection after death altogether, Allah (sp) presented various proofs to establish both the possibility and the inevitability of life after death; for instance, Allah (sp) said:

وَهُوَ ٱلَّذِى يَبْدَؤُاْ ٱلْخَلْقَ ثُمَّ يُعِيدُهُۥ وَهُوَ أَهْوَنُ عَلَيْهِ

"And He it is Who originates the creation, then will repeat it (after it has been perished), and this is easier for Him." (Qur'an 30: 27)

Allah (sp) pointed out to disbelievers that, if there would be no resurrection after death, life on earth would be futile and the creation of man would have been lacking in purpose – both of which are contrary to the infinite wisdom of Allah (sp). There is a purpose to life; evildoers and good-doers cannot be treated equally with death and no ultimate justice. Another world must exist in which every man — both the evildoer and the good-doer – will be rewarded for his actions. Allah (sp) said:

أَفَحَسِبْتُمْ أَنَّمَا خَلَقْنَٰكُمْ عَبَثًا وَأَنَّكُمْ إِلَيْنَا لَا تُرْجَعُونَ

"Did you think that We had created you in play (without any purpose), and that you would not be brought back to Us?" (Qur'an 23:115) And in another Verse, Allah (sp) said:

وَمَا خَلَقْنَا ٱلسَّمَآءَ وَٱلْأَرْضَ وَمَا بَيْنَهُمَا بَٰطِلًا ذَٰلِكَ ظَنُّ ٱلَّذِينَ كَفَرُواْ فَوَيْلٌ لِّلَّذِينَ كَفَرُواْ مِنَ ٱلنَّارِ
أَمْ نَجْعَلُ ٱلَّذِينَ ءَامَنُواْ وَعَمِلُواْ ٱلصَّٰلِحَٰتِ كَٱلْمُفْسِدِينَ فِى ٱلْأَرْضِ أَمْ نَجْعَلُ ٱلْمُتَّقِينَ كَٱلْفُجَّارِ

"And We created not the heaven and the earth and all that is between them without purpose! That is the consideration of those who disbelieve. Then woe to those who disbelieve (in Islamic Monotheism) from the Fire! Shall We treat those who believe (in the Oneness of Allah – Islamic Monotheism) and do righteous good deeds, as Mufsidun (those who associate partners in worship with Allah and commit crimes) on earth? Or shall We treat the Muttaqun (the pious ones) as the Fujjar (criminals, disbelievers, wicked, etc.)" (Qur'an 38: 27, 28)

There is much discussion in the Qur'an about the Hereafter: about the Day of Resurrection and its terrors; about the book of each man, which contains in it every single one of his deeds, be it small or large; about the scale that weighs the deeds of men; about the period of accountability, during which no man shall be wronged in the least, and during which no man will be called upon to bear the evils of another man; about Paradise and its bliss; and about Hellfire and its torment.

Regarding the Hereafter, the Qur'an also corrected the false notion that the false gods of polytheists ill intercede for them, or that so called 'saint' will intercede for the People of the Book. Intercession will occur only by the permission of Allah (sp); it will only be on behalf of True Monotheists; and a specific instance of intercession can occur only if Allah (sp) is pleased with it.[65]

Section Two:

Removing Difficulties from People's Lives

Life is a test: Human beings are called upon to perform certain religious duties, and those that perform them achieve success in both this life and the Hereafter; those who don't perform them fail, and depending on the duty they neglect to perform, their final destination can be eternity in the Hellfire. Certain religious duties can be difficult for certain people to perform; after all, man, as Allah (sp) of course knows, is weak. Allah said:

وَخُلِقَ ٱلْإِنسَٰنُ ضَعِيفًا

"*And man was created weak*" (Qur'an 4: 28)

One of the main features of Islam is that, in it, Allah (sp) legislated laws that are meant to remove hardships and difficulties from people's lives. Some of those legislations might be seemingly difficult, but they take human ability into consideration to such a degree that believers love to apply them, and they do so with dedication and without becoming tired in the process.

Removing hardships was a function of every single Prophet (s). Allah (sp) said:

مَّا كَانَ عَلَى ٱلنَّبِىِّ مِنْ حَرَجٍ فِيمَا فَرَضَ ٱللَّهُ لَهُۥ ۖ سُنَّةَ ٱللَّهِ فِى ٱلَّذِينَ خَلَوْا۟ مِن قَبْلُ

"*There is no blame on the Prophet (s) in that which Allah has made legal for him. That has been Allah's way with those who have passed away of (the Prophets of) old.*" (Qur'an 33: 38)

This Verse means: To make matters easy for people has been Allah's way with previous Prophets as well.

Ease and leniency are two of the most salient features of Islamic Law. Allah (sp) said:

يُرِيدُ ٱللَّهُ بِكُمُ ٱلْيُسْرَ وَلَا يُرِيدُ بِكُمُ ٱلْعُسْرَ

"*Allah intends for you ease, and He does not want to make things difficult for you.*" (Qur'an 2:185)

In another Verse, Allah (sp) said:

مَا يُرِيدُ ٱللَّهُ لِيَجْعَلَ عَلَيْكُم مِّنْ حَرَجٍ

"*Allah does not want to place you in difficulty.*" (Qur'an 5: 6)

And one of the Qur'anic supplications of believers is as follows:

رَبَّنَا وَلَا تَحْمِلْ عَلَيْنَآ إِصْرًا كَمَا حَمَلْتَهُۥ عَلَى ٱلَّذِينَ مِن قَبْلِنَا رَبَّنَا وَلَا تُحَمِّلْنَا مَا لَا طَاقَةَ لَنَا بِهِۦ

---

[65] *Kaifa Nata'aamul Ma'al-Qur'an Al-Adheem* (pgs. 83-88), and *Al-Wahyee Al-Muhammadee* (pgs. 108-116).

"Our Lord! Lay not on us a burden like that which You did lay on those before us (Jews and Christians); our Lord! Put not on us a burden greater than we have strength to bear." (Qur'an 2: 286) Allah (sp) has made Islam a religion that is in harmony with the innate nature of man. And man, by his very nature, likes ease, and turns away from harshness; hence the wisdom behind the leniency of Islam's laws. Allah (sp) said:

$$يُرِيدُ ٱللَّهُ أَن يُخَفِّفَ عَنكُمْ ۚ وَخُلِقَ ٱلْإِنسَـٰنُ ضَعِيفًا$$

"Allah wishes to lighten (the burden) for you; and man was created weak." (Qur'an 4: 28)
Allah (sp) intended Islam to be a religion whose laws can be applied by all peoples of all eras; to make that possible, it was necessary to make easy for people the application of Islam's laws. The ease and leniency of Islam's laws has a great deal to do with the spread of Islam throughout the world.
Throughout the teachings of Islam, there are many instances of laws that are explicitly made easy in order to remove hardships from Muslims. And in the Qur'an, there are two kinds of Verses that deal with the issue of removing hardships from Muslims. First, Verses that promised the legislation of laws that feature the quality of making matters easy for people; for instance, Allah (sp) said:

$$وَنُيَسِّرُكَ لِلْيُسْرَىٰ$$

"And We shall make easy for you (O Muhammad (s)) the easy way (i.e., the doing of righteous deeds)." (Qur'an 87: 8)
In this Verse, Allah (sp) gave the Messenger of Allah (s) and his people glad tidings of a *Shariah* (set of religious laws) that is just, upright, and easy to follow.
And second, Verses that dealt with making specific legislations easier for people to follow, either by removing hardships in their entirety, or by lightening the burden of a given religious duty. An example of the former is mentioned in this Verse:

$$لَّيْسَ عَلَى ٱلضُّعَفَآءِ وَلَا عَلَى ٱلْمَرْضَىٰ وَلَا عَلَى ٱلَّذِينَ لَا يَجِدُونَ مَا يُنفِقُونَ حَرَجٌ إِذَا نَصَحُوا۟ لِلَّهِ وَرَسُولِهِۦ ۚ مَا عَلَى ٱلْمُحْسِنِينَ مِن سَبِيلٍ ۚ وَٱللَّهُ غَفُورٌ رَّحِيمٌ$$

"There is no blame on those who are weak or ill or who find no resources to spend in holy fighting (Jihad), if they are sincere and true (in duty) to Allah and His Messenger. No ground (of complaint) can there be against the Muhsinun (good-doers). And Allah is Oft-Forgiving, Most Merciful." (Qur'an 9: 91)
An entire group of people, because of their circumstances, are completely absolved from the responsibility of fighting in war, as long as they are sincere to Allah (sp) and His Messenger (s). And an example of the latter is found in this Verse:

$$وَإِذَا ضَرَبْتُمْ فِى ٱلْأَرْضِ فَلَيْسَ عَلَيْكُمْ جُنَاحٌ أَن تَقْصُرُوا۟ مِنَ ٱلصَّلَوٰةِ إِنْ خِفْتُمْ أَن يَفْتِنَكُمُ ٱلَّذِينَ كَفَرُوٓا۟$$

"And when you (Muslims) travel in the land, there is no sin on you if you shorten your Salat (prayer) if you fear that the disbelievers may attack you." (Qur'an 4: 101)
If people find themselves to be in the circumstances that are described in this Verse, they are not completely absolved from the duty of performing prayer; nonetheless, prayer is lightened for them: instead of performing four units for the *Zuhr* prayer, for instance, they only have to perform two. The *Shariah* is filled with examples of legislations whose main feature is removing hardships from people: If a person is ill during the month of Ramadan, he may make up his fast at a later date; if a person is traveling during Ramadan, he too may make up his fast at a later date; if a person is on the verge of starving, he may eat food that is otherwise unlawful in Islam; if a person is ill to the degree that it is difficult for him to pray standing up, he may pray sitting down; if a person does not have the means to

travel to Makkah, Hajj is not compulsory upon him; and so on from the many merciful legislations of Islam. Thus it is clear that, through His infinite Wisdom, Allah (sp) decreed laws that are in harmony with reality and that take the innately weak state of man into consideration; as such, Allah (sp) did not decree any law that man is incapable of performing. And this is from the greatness, generosity, and mercy of Allah (sp).

Section three:

Confirming the Dignity of Man and the Sanctity of Human Rights

First: Confirming the Dignity of Man

When human beings associate partners with Allah (sp) or perpetrate evil deeds, they debase themselves, lowering themselves from their original position of honor and dignity. In the Noble Qur'an, Allah (sp) reminds mankind that He has conferred honor and dignity upon them. From the very beginning of human life, Allah (sp) has conferred honor upon human beings, creating Adam (p) with His own Hand, blowing into him with His *Rooh*, and granting him and his children a degree of authority on earth. Allah (sp) honored man to such a degree that even the angels were taken aback, not understanding why man deserved such honors or why they themselves were not the recipients of those honors. Allah (sp): said:

وَإِذْ قَالَ رَبُّكَ لِلْمَلَٰٓئِكَةِ إِنِّى جَاعِلٌ فِى ٱلْأَرْضِ خَلِيفَةً قَالُوٓا۟ أَتَجْعَلُ فِيهَا مَن يُفْسِدُ فِيهَا وَيَسْفِكُ ٱلدِّمَآءَ وَنَحْنُ نُسَبِّحُ بِحَمْدِكَ وَنُقَدِّسُ لَكَ قَالَ إِنِّىٓ أَعْلَمُ مَا لَا تَعْلَمُونَ

"And (remember) when your Lord said to the angels: Verily, I am going to place (mankind) generations after generations on earth. They said: 'Will You place therein those who will make mischief therein and shed blood, while we glorify You with praises and thanks (Exalted be You above all that they associate with You as partners) and sanctify You.' He (Allah) said: I know that which you do not know." (Qur'an 2:30)

In another Verse, Allah (sp) said:

وَلَقَدْ كَرَّمْنَا بَنِىٓ ءَادَمَ وَحَمَلْنَٰهُمْ فِى ٱلْبَرِّ وَٱلْبَحْرِ وَرَزَقْنَٰهُم مِّنَ ٱلطَّيِّبَٰتِ وَفَضَّلْنَٰهُمْ عَلَىٰ كَثِيرٍ مِّمَّنْ خَلَقْنَا تَفْضِيلًا

"And indeed We have honored the Children of Adam, and We have carried them on land and sea, and have provided them with At-Tayibat (lawful good things), and have preferred them above many of those whom We have created with a marked preference." (Qur'an 17: 70)

In another Verse, Allah (sp) said:

أَلَمْ تَرَوْا۟ أَنَّ ٱللَّهَ سَخَّرَ لَكُم مَّا فِى ٱلسَّمَٰوَٰتِ وَمَا فِى ٱلْأَرْضِ وَأَسْبَغَ عَلَيْكُمْ نِعَمَهُۥ ظَٰهِرَةً وَبَاطِنَةً

"See you not (O man) that Allah has subjected for you whatsoever is in the heavens and whatsoever is in the earth, and has completed and perfected His Graces upon you, both) apparent (i.e., Islamic Monotheism, and the lawful pleasures of this world, including health, good looks, etc.) and hidden (i.e., One's Faith in Allah (of Islamic Monotheism) knowledge, wisdom, guidance for doing righteous deeds, and also the pleasures and delights of the Hereafter in Paradise, etc.)" (Qur'an 31: 20)

Having completed His Graces upon mankind, and having subjected for them whatsoever is in the heavens and whatsoever is in the earth, Allah (sp) censured those human beings who were unthankful to him – and who turned the very inanimate objects that were meant to serve their needs into false deities, whom they worshipped instead of Allah (sp). Allah (sp) said:

$$\text{وَمِنْ ءَايَـٰتِهِ ٱلَّيْلُ وَٱلنَّهَارُ وَٱلشَّمْسُ وَٱلْقَمَرُ ۚ لَا تَسْجُدُوا۟ لِلشَّمْسِ وَلَا لِلْقَمَرِ وَٱسْجُدُوا۟ لِلَّهِ ٱلَّذِى خَلَقَهُنَّ إِن كُنتُمْ إِيَّاهُ تَعْبُدُونَ}$$

"And from among His Signs are the night and the day, and the sun and the moon, Prostate not to the sun nor to the moon, but prostate to Allah Who created them, if you (really) worship Him." (Qur'an 41: 37)

Man, by his very nature, is honorable and dignified. But then instead of acting with dignity by following the commands of Allah (sp), many men lower themselves – and in essence strip themselves of their dignity – by blindly following creatures who are weak like themselves. Allah (sp) said:

$$\text{وَقَالُوا۟ رَبَّنَآ إِنَّآ أَطَعْنَا سَادَتَنَا وَكُبَرَآءَنَا فَأَضَلُّونَا ٱلسَّبِيلَا۠}$$

"And they will say: Our Lord! Verily, we obeyed our chiefs and our great ones, and they misled us from the (Right) Way." (Qur'an 33: 67)

A specific group of human beings were conferred with special honors; they were the People of the Book, and Allah (sp) blessed them by sending them Prophets, peace be upon all of them, and divinely revealed Books. Having been raised by Allah (sp) to a special status of honor and dignity, they lowered themselves to the basest of depths by disobeying their Prophets (st) by killing some of them – and later on by taking their rabbis and their monks to be their lords besides Allah (sp). Allah (sp) said:

$$\text{ٱتَّخَذُوا۟ أَحْبَارَهُمْ وَرُهْبَـٰنَهُمْ أَرْبَابًا مِّن دُونِ ٱللَّهِ وَٱلْمَسِيحَ ٱبْنَ مَرْيَمَ وَمَآ أُمِرُوٓا۟ إِلَّا لِيَعْبُدُوٓا۟ إِلَـٰهًا وَٰحِدًا}$$

"They (Jews and Christians) took their rabbis and their monks to be their lords besides Allah (by obeying them in things which they made lawful or unlawful according to their own desires without being ordered by Allah, and (they also took as their Lord) Messiah, son of Maryam (Mary), while they (Jews and Christians) were commanded in the Torah and the Injeel (Gospel) to worship none but One Ilah (God - Allah)." (Qur'an 9: 31)

They even made the claim that Jesus (p) invited people to worship him, a claim that Allah (sp) refuted in this Verse:

$$\text{مَا كَانَ لِبَشَرٍ أَن يُؤْتِيَهُ ٱللَّهُ ٱلْكِتَـٰبَ وَٱلْحُكْمَ وَٱلنُّبُوَّةَ ثُمَّ يَقُولَ لِلنَّاسِ كُونُوا۟ عِبَادًا لِّى مِن دُونِ ٱللَّهِ}$$

"It is not (possible) for any human being to whom Allah has given the Book and Al-Hukm (the knowledge and understanding of the laws of religion, etc.) and Prophethood to say to the people: Be my worshippers rather than Allah's." (Qur'an 3: 79)

Second: Confirming the Sanctity of Human Rights

Today, 'Human rights' is a slogan that is chanted by everybody; and it is championed by countries that are the greatest violators of human rights in the world. The very human rights that are extolled today were guaranteed by Islamic law over fourteen centuries ago.

In the Noble Qur'an, Allah (sp) established the right of every human being to life, as long as one does not perpetrate a crime that warrants the punishment of death. Allah (sp) said:

وَلَا تَقْتُلُوا۟ ٱلنَّفْسَ ٱلَّتِى حَرَّمَ ٱللَّهُ إِلَّا بِٱلْحَقِّ

"And kill not anyone whom Allah has forbidden, except for a just cause (according to Islamic law)." (Qur'an 6: 151).

Allah (sp) accorded every individual the right to privacy in his home; in Islam, therefore, no one has the right to enter an individual's home without his permission. Allah (sp) said:

يَـٰٓأَيُّهَا ٱلَّذِينَ ءَامَنُوا۟ لَا تَدْخُلُوا۟ بُيُوتًا غَيْرَ بُيُوتِكُمْ حَتَّىٰ تَسْتَأْنِسُوا۟ وَتُسَلِّمُوا۟ عَلَىٰٓ أَهْلِهَا ذَٰلِكُمْ خَيْرٌ لَّكُمْ لَعَلَّكُمْ تَذَكَّرُونَ (٢٧) فَإِن لَّمْ تَجِدُوا۟ فِيهَآ أَحَدًا فَلَا تَدْخُلُوهَا حَتَّىٰ يُؤْذَنَ لَكُمْ وَإِن قِيلَ لَكُمُ ٱرْجِعُوا۟ فَٱرْجِعُوا۟ هُوَ أَزْكَىٰ لَكُمْ

"O you who believe! Enter not houses other than your own, until you have asked permission and greeted those in them, that is better for you, in order that you may remember. And if you find no one therein, still, enter not until permission has been given. And if you are asked to go back, go back, for it is purer for you." (Qur'an 24: 27, 28)

Allah (sp) gave each man the right to earn lawfully derived wealth and guaranteed, through laws that protect the citizens of a Muslim country, the safety of his life and of his wealth. Allah (sp) said:

يَـٰٓأَيُّهَا ٱلَّذِينَ ءَامَنُوا۟ لَا تَأْكُلُوٓا۟ أَمْوَٰلَكُم بَيْنَكُم بِٱلْبَـٰطِلِ إِلَّآ أَن تَكُونَ تِجَـٰرَةً عَن تَرَاضٍ مِّنكُمْ وَلَا تَقْتُلُوٓا۟ أَنفُسَكُمْ إِنَّ ٱللَّهَ كَانَ بِكُمْ رَحِيمًا

"O you who believe! Eat not up your property among yourselves unjustly except it be a trade amongst you, by mutual consent. And do not kill yourselves (nor kill one another). Surely, Allah is Most Merciful to you." (Qur'an 4: 29)

Furthermore, Allah (sp) forbade slander and defamation; no one in Islam has the right to smear the character of another individual. And every individuals honor and dignity are deemed sacrosanct in Islam. Allah (sp) said:

يَـٰٓأَيُّهَا ٱلَّذِينَ ءَامَنُوا۟ لَا يَسْخَرْ قَوْمٌ مِّن قَوْمٍ عَسَىٰٓ أَن يَكُونُوا۟ خَيْرًا مِّنْهُمْ وَلَا نِسَآءٌ مِّن نِّسَآءٍ عَسَىٰٓ أَن يَكُنَّ خَيْرًا مِّنْهُنَّ وَلَا تَلْمِزُوٓا۟ أَنفُسَكُمْ وَلَا تَنَابَزُوا۟ بِٱلْأَلْقَـٰبِ

"O you who believe! Let not a group scoff at another group, it may be that the latter are better than the former, nor let (some) women scoff at other women, it may be that the latter are better than the former, nor defame one another, nor insult one another by nicknames." (Qur'an 49:11)

Allah (sp) also gave every individual, both male and female, the right to get married:

وَمِنْ ءَايَـٰتِهِۦٓ أَنْ خَلَقَ لَكُم مِّنْ أَنفُسِكُمْ أَزْوَٰجًا لِّتَسْكُنُوٓا۟ إِلَيْهَا وَجَعَلَ بَيْنَكُم مَّوَدَّةً وَرَحْمَةً إِنَّ فِى ذَٰلِكَ لَءَايَـٰتٍ لِّقَوْمٍ يَتَفَكَّرُونَ

"And among His Signs is this, that He created for you wives from among yourselves, that you may find repose in them, and He has put between you affection and mercy. Verily, in that are indeed signs for a people who reflect." (Qur'an 30: 21)

And Allah (sp) granted every person the right to produce offspring:

وَٱللَّهُ جَعَلَ لَكُم مِّنْ أَنفُسِكُمْ أَزْوَٰجًا وَجَعَلَ لَكُم مِّنْ أَزْوَٰجِكُم بَنِينَ وَحَفَدَةً

"And Allah has made for you wives of your own kind, and has made for you, from your wives, sons and grandsons." (Qur'an 16: 72)

Not only did Allah (sp) give parents the right to produce offspring, He (sp) also gave babies, even while they are in their mothers' wombs, the right to live. It is for this reason that Allah (sp) repudiated the practice of burying one's daughters alive, a practice that was rampant during the pre-Islamic days of ignorance. Allah (sp) said:

$$\text{وَلَا تَقْتُلُوٓا۟ أَوْلَٰدَكُم مِّنْ إِمْلَٰقٍ ۖ نَّحْنُ نَرْزُقُكُمْ وَإِيَّاهُمْ}$$

"Kill not your children because of poverty – We provide sustenance for you and for them." (Qur'an 6: 151)

In another Verse, Allah (sp) said:

$$\text{وَلَا تَقْتُلُوٓا۟ أَوْلَٰدَكُمْ خَشْيَةَ إِمْلَٰقٍ ۖ نَّحْنُ نَرْزُقُهُمْ وَإِيَّاكُمْ ۚ إِنَّ قَتْلَهُمْ كَانَ خِطْـًٔا كَبِيرًا}$$

"And kill not your children for fear of poverty. We provide for them and for you. Surely, the killing of them is a great sin." (Qur'an 17: 31)

And in yet another Verse, Allah (sp) said:

$$\text{وَإِذَا ٱلْمَوْءُۥدَةُ سُئِلَتْ بِأَىِّ ذَنۢبٍ قُتِلَتْ}$$

"And when the female (infant) buried alive (as the pagan Arabs used to do) shall be questioned. For what sin she was killed?" (Qur'an 81: 8, 9)

In the Noble Qur'an, Allah (sp) gave rights to every member of society, especially to the weak and poor, to whom He (sp) allotted a portion of the wealth of the rich and prosperous:

$$\text{وَٱلَّذِينَ فِىٓ أَمْوَٰلِهِمْ حَقٌّ مَّعْلُومٌ لِّلسَّآئِلِ وَٱلْمَحْرُومِ}$$

"And those in whose wealth there is a known right, for the beggar who asks, and for the unlucky who has lost his property and wealth, (and his means of living has been straitened)" (Qur'an 70: 24, 25)

In another Verse, Allah (sp) said:

$$\text{خُذْ مِنْ أَمْوَٰلِهِمْ صَدَقَةً تُطَهِّرُهُمْ وَتُزَكِّيهِم بِهَا}$$

"Take Sadaqah (alms) from their wealth in order to purify them and sanctify them with it." (Qur'an 9: 103)

And Allah (sp) gave the individuals of a society the right to live in an atmosphere that is free of evil and lewdness. As a result of having that right, individuals are charged with the duty of repudiating evil whenever they see it being perpetrated out in the open. Allah (sp) said:

$$\text{وَلَا تَرْكَنُوٓا۟ إِلَى ٱلَّذِينَ ظَلَمُوا۟ فَتَمَسَّكُمُ ٱلنَّارُ وَمَا لَكُم مِّن دُونِ ٱللَّهِ مِنْ أَوْلِيَآءَ ثُمَّ لَا تُنصَرُونَ}$$

"And incline not toward those who do wrong, lest the Fire should touch you, and you have no protectors other than Allah, nor you would then be helped." (Qur'an 11:113)

The right to live in a society in which evil is not rampant results in a duty to eradicate evil, a duty that is binding on every individual. If the members of society do not fulfill the duty of promoting good and repudiating vice, they become like the people that are mentioned in the following Verses:

لُعِنَ ٱلَّذِينَ كَفَرُواْ مِنۢ بَنِىٓ إِسْرَٰٓءِيلَ عَلَىٰ لِسَانِ دَاوُۥدَ وَعِيسَى ٱبْنِ مَرْيَمَ ذَٰلِكَ بِمَا عَصَواْ وَّكَانُواْ يَعْتَدُونَ (٧٨) كَانُواْ لَا يَتَنَاهَوْنَ عَن مُّنكَرٍ فَعَلُوهُ لَبِئْسَ مَا كَانُواْ يَفْعَلُونَ (٧٩)

"Those among the Children of Israel who disbelieved were cursed by the tongue of Dawud (David) and 'Issa (Jesus), son of Maryam (Mary). That was because they disobeyed (Allah and the Messengers) and were ever transgressing beyond bounds. They used not to forbid one another from the Munkar (wrong, evildoing, sins, polytheism, disbelief, etc.) which they committed. Vile indeed was what they used to do" (Qur'an 5: 78, 79)

Allah (sp) elevated human rights to the level of obligatory duties. Anyone can voluntarily give up his right to something, but no one can abandon an obligatory duty. Thus, in the Noble Qur'an, Allah (sp) raised human rights from the level of optional to that of sacrosanct.[66]

Section Four:

Promoting Strong Family Morals, and Doing Justice to Women

First: Promoting Strong Family Morals
One of the aims of the Qur'an is to promote the formation of righteous Muslim families; the family, after all, is the primary pillar of an upright and righteous society. Obviously, the first stage of forming a family is marriage, which Allah (sp) enumerated as being one of His signs – just as the creation of the heavens and the earth, for instance, is one of His signs. Allah (sp) said:

وَمِنْ ءَايَٰتِهِۦٓ أَنْ خَلَقَ لَكُم مِّنْ أَنفُسِكُمْ أَزْوَٰجًا لِّتَسْكُنُوٓاْ إِلَيْهَا وَجَعَلَ بَيْنَكُم مَّوَدَّةً وَرَحْمَةً إِنَّ فِى ذَٰلِكَ لَءَايَٰتٍ لِّقَوْمٍ يَتَفَكَّرُونَ

"And among His Signs is this, that He created for you wives from among yourselves, that you may find repose in them, and He has put between you affection and mercy. Verily, in that are indeed signs for a people who reflect." (Qur'an 30: 21)
In this Verse, Allah (sp) pointed out the three pillars of a sound marriage: finding repose in one's spouse, mutual affection, and reciprocal mercy. So strong is the bond of marriage that Allah (sp) termed the connection between husband and wife 'a firm and strong covenant':

وَأَخَذْنَ مِنكُم مِّيثَٰقًا غَلِيظًا

"And they have taken from you a firm and strong covenant." (Qur'an 4:21)
In the Qur'an, Allah (sp) describes the level of closeness that should exist between husband and wife:

هُنَّ لِبَاسٌ لَّكُمْ وَأَنتُمْ لِبَاسٌ لَّهُنَّ

"They are Libas (i.e. body cover, or screen, or Sakan (i.e., you enjoy the pleasure of living with her - as in Verse 7: 189) for you and you are the same for them." (Qur'an 2:187)

---

[66] *Kaifa Nata'aamal Ma'al-Qur'an Al-'Adheem* (pgs. 89-94) and *Al-Wahyee Al-Muhammadee* (pgs. 173-177).

And importantly, Allah (sp) made clear one of the main goals of marriage: producing righteous offspring. Allah (sp) said:

$$وَاللَّهُ جَعَلَ لَكُم مِّنْ أَنفُسِكُمْ أَزْوَاجًا وَجَعَلَ لَكُم مِّنْ أَزْوَاجِكُم بَنِينَ وَحَفَدَةً$$

"*And Allah has made for you wives of your own kind, and has made for you, from your wives, sons and grandsons.*" (Qur'an 16: 72)

By informing Muslims about one of the supplications of His righteous slaves, Allah (sp) instills in each Muslim a sense of what his attitudes and goals should be when he goes about the business of forming a family:

$$رَبَّنَا هَبْ لَنَا مِنْ أَزْوَاجِنَا وَذُرِّيَّاتِنَا قُرَّةَ أَعْيُنٍ وَاجْعَلْنَا لِلْمُتَّقِينَ إِمَامًا$$

"*Our Lord! Bestow on us from our wives and our offspring who will be the comfort of our eyes, and make us leaders for the Muttaqun (pious ones).*" (Qur'an 25: 74)

If husband and wife are to bond together in mutual harmony, Allah informs us, they must be of the same religion. It is for this reason that, in the Noble Qur'an, Allah (sp) forbade Muslim men from marrying disbelieving women, and Muslim women from marrying disbelieving men:

$$وَلَا تَنكِحُوا الْمُشْرِكَاتِ حَتَّىٰ يُؤْمِنَّ ۚ وَلَأَمَةٌ مُّؤْمِنَةٌ خَيْرٌ مِّن مُّشْرِكَةٍ وَلَوْ أَعْجَبَتْكُمْ ۗ وَلَا تُنكِحُوا الْمُشْرِكِينَ حَتَّىٰ يُؤْمِنُوا ۚ وَلَعَبْدٌ مُّؤْمِنٌ خَيْرٌ مِّن مُّشْرِكٍ وَلَوْ أَعْجَبَكُمْ ۗ أُولَٰئِكَ يَدْعُونَ إِلَى النَّارِ ۖ وَاللَّهُ يَدْعُو إِلَى الْجَنَّةِ وَالْمَغْفِرَةِ بِإِذْنِهِ ۖ وَيُبَيِّنُ آيَاتِهِ لِلنَّاسِ لَعَلَّهُمْ يَتَذَكَّرُونَ$$

"*And indeed a slave woman who believes is better than a (free) Mushrikah (idolatress, etc.), even though she pleases you. And give not (your daughters) in marriage to Al-Mushrikun (polytheists, pagans, disbelievers in the Oneness of Allah and in His Messenger (s)) till they believe (in Allah alone) and verily, a believing slave is better than a (free) Mushrik (idolater, etc.), even though he pleases you. Those (Al-Mushrikun) invite you to the Fire, but Allah invites (you) to Paradise and Forgiveness by His Leave, and makes His Ayat (proofs, evidences, Verses, lessons, signs, revelations, etc.) clear to mankind that they may remember.*" (Qur'an 2: 221)

Allah (sp) ended this Verse by explicitly stating the wisdom behind the prohibition: Disbelievers invite their spouses to the Hellfire, whereas a righteous believing person invites his or her spouse to Paradise and to forgiveness from his Lord.

The exception to this rule involves a marriage between a Muslim man and a woman from the People of the Book – a Jew or a Christian. This kind of marriage is permissible because a woman from the People of the Book believes in a religion that was originally revealed by Allah (sp). Although her beliefs are corrupted, and although she is in fact a disbeliever, she at least, in a general way, has faith in Allah (sp) and the Hereafter. For this reason Allah revealed the Verse:

$$وَطَعَامُ الَّذِينَ أُوتُوا الْكِتَابَ حِلٌّ لَّكُمْ وَطَعَامُكُمْ حِلٌّ لَّهُمْ ۖ وَالْمُحْصَنَاتُ مِنَ الْمُؤْمِنَاتِ وَالْمُحْصَنَاتُ مِنَ الَّذِينَ أُوتُوا الْكِتَابَ مِن قَبْلِكُمْ إِذَا آتَيْتُمُوهُنَّ أُجُورَهُنَّ مُحْصِنِينَ غَيْرَ مُسَافِحِينَ وَلَا مُتَّخِذِي أَخْدَانٍ$$

"*The food (slaughtered cattle, edible animals, etc.) of the people of the Scripture (Jews and Christians) is lawful to you and yours is lawful to them. (Lawful to you in marriage) are chaste women from the believers and chaste women from those who were given the Scripture (Jews and Christians) before your time, when you have given their due Mahr (bridle money given by the husband to his wife at the time of marriage), desiring chastity (i.e., taking them in legal wedlock) not committing illegal sexual intercourse, nor taking them as girlfriends."* (Qur'an 5: 5)

Why then, one might ask, is a Muslim man allowed to marry a Jewish or Christian woman, while a Muslim woman is not allowed to marry a Jewish or Christian man? The answer to this question requires from us that we understand a man's role in a marriage: a man is stronger than his wife, and he is the leader of his household. Now, in a marriage between a Muslim man and a Jewish or Christian woman, it is not feared that that woman's rights will be violated, since her husband acknowledges the original truthfulness of her religion and of the original version of the Book she follows. A Jewish or Christian man, on the other hand, does not acknowledge the truthfulness of his Muslim wife's religion, nor does he accept the fact that the Book she follows – the Noble Qur'an - has a divine source; furthermore, he doesn't even accept the fact that the Prophet (s) she follows was sent by Allah (sp). It is therefore likely that he will have little respect for her, that he will not treat her properly, that she will not be able to practice her religion in his presence – or, what is worse, that she will convert to his religion. Based on these reasons, it is prohibited in Islam for a Muslim woman to marry a disbelieving man, regardless of whether that man is an idol worshipper, an atheist, a Christian, a Jew, or otherwise.[67]

Second: Doing Justice to Women and Freeing Them from the Oppression of Pre-Islamic Ignorance

Among the more important aims of the Qur'an was doing justice to women and freeing them from the shackles of pre-Islamic ignorance and tyranny. For prior to the advent of Islam, women were oppressed, humiliated, slave-like in the treatment they received, and treated as mere objects. This was the condition of women not just in Arab societies, but among all of the nations of the world. Even among the People of the Book, women were not treated in an honorable manner. Then, with the advent of Islam and the revelation of the Qur'an, Allah (sp) gave women all of the rights that He (sp) gave to men. The only difference between men and women was that women were given roles and duties that were in keeping with their feminine nature. And even regarding those roles and duties, the laws of Islam still taught the importance of honoring women and showing mercy and compassion towards them.[68] With clear-cut legislations in the Qur'an, men were no longer able to wrongfully harm, misuse, or debase women. Women were given similar rights to men not as a way of compromise, but because they are just as much human beings as men are, and human beings are innately honored and dignified. And they were further treated with honor because they are the sisters, daughters, wives, and mothers of believing men, and because they are active and important members of a prosperous and righteous Muslim society.[69]

The Qur'an does Justice to Women

The Qur'an gave women all of their divinely decreed rights; in fact, one of the seven long chapters of the Qur'an was named *"The Women Chapter"*, and in it Allah (sp) affirms many important rights for womankind, rights that a woman could not even have dreamed of prior to the advent of Islam. Among the ways in which the Qur'an did justice to women and gave them their rights are the following:

1) In the pre-Islamic days of ignorance, women were deemed burdens upon a family, so whenever a daughter was born to a married couple, it was an occasion of immense sadness. It was even common for men to bury their daughters alive. After the advent of Islam, Allah (sp) revealed Verses in which He forbade the vile practiced of burying daughters alive; for instance, He (sp) said:

$$\text{وَإِذَا بُشِّرَ أَحَدُهُم بِٱلْأُنثَىٰ ظَلَّ وَجْهُهُ مُسْوَدًّا وَهُوَ كَظِيمٌ}$$

---

[67] *Kaifa Nata'aamal Ma'al-Qur'an Al-Adheem* (pgs. 89-94).
[68] *Al-Wahyee Al-Muhammadee* (pg. 216).
[69] *Al-Wahyee Al-Muhammadee* (pg. 112).

$$\text{يَتَوَارَىٰ مِنَ ٱلْقَوْمِ مِن سُوٓءِ مَا بُشِّرَ بِهِۦٓ ۚ أَيُمْسِكُهُۥ عَلَىٰ هُونٍ أَمْ يَدُسُّهُۥ فِى ٱلتُّرَابِ ۗ أَلَا سَآءَ مَا يَحْكُمُونَ}$$

"And when the news of (the birth of) a female (child) is brought to any of them, his face becomes dark, and he is filled with inward grief! He hides himself from the people because of the evil of that whereof he has been informed. Shall he keep her with dishonor or bury her in the earth? Certainly, evil is their decision." (Qur'an 16:58, 59)

But the Qur'an, as well as the sayings of the Prophet (s), went beyond that, instilling in Muslims not a sense of shame when a daughter is born to them, but a sense of pride and honor and happiness. In various AHadeeth, the Prophet (s) promised great rewards for those who properly raise daughters and instill in them Islamic values.

2) The Qur'an explicitly gave women the right to own property and, as with their male counterparts, to earn lawfully derived wealth. Allah (sp) said:

$$\text{لِّلرِّجَالِ نَصِيبٌ مِّمَّا ٱكْتَسَبُوا۟ ۖ وَلِلنِّسَآءِ نَصِيبٌ مِّمَّا ٱكْتَسَبْنَ ۚ وَسْـَٔلُوا۟ ٱللَّهَ مِن فَضْلِهِۦٓ}$$

"For men there is reward for what they have earned, (and likewise) for women there is reward for what they have earned, and ask Allah of His Bounty." (Qur'an 4:32)

3) Even regarding minor injustices that were perpetrated against women during the pre-Islamic days of ignorance, the Qur'an did justice to women and gave them what was rightfully theirs. For example, prior to the advent of Islam, men would keep good quality meat exclusively for themselves, and share poor quality meat with their female relatives. Regarding this vile practice, which they falsely ascribed to Allah (sp), Allah (sp) said:

$$\text{وَقَالُوا۟ مَا فِى بُطُونِ هَٰذِهِ ٱلْأَنْعَٰمِ خَالِصَةٌ لِّذُكُورِنَا وَمُحَرَّمٌ عَلَىٰٓ أَزْوَٰجِنَا ۖ وَإِن يَكُن مَّيْتَةً فَهُمْ فِيهِ شُرَكَآءُ ۚ سَيَجْزِيهِمْ وَصْفَهُمْ ۚ إِنَّهُۥ حَكِيمٌ عَلِيمٌ}$$

"And they say: 'What is in the bellies of such and such cattle (milk or fetus) is for our males alone, and forbidden to our females (girls and women, but if it is born dead, then all have shares therein.' He will punish them for their attribution (of such false orders to Allah). Verily, He is All-Wise, All-Knower." (Qur'an 6:139)

4) Like men, women can achieve honor with Allah (sp) when they act righteously. Allah (sp) said:

$$\text{يَٰٓأَيُّهَا ٱلنَّاسُ إِنَّا خَلَقْنَٰكُم مِّن ذَكَرٍ وَأُنثَىٰ وَجَعَلْنَٰكُمْ شُعُوبًا وَقَبَآئِلَ لِتَعَارَفُوٓا۟ ۚ إِنَّ أَكْرَمَكُمْ عِندَ ٱللَّهِ أَتْقَىٰكُمْ ۚ إِنَّ ٱللَّهَ عَلِيمٌ خَبِيرٌ}$$

"O mankind! We have created you from a male and a female, and made you into nations and tribes, that you may know one another. Verily, the most honorable of you with Allah is that (believer) who has At-Taqwa (i.e., piety, righteousness, etc.)." (Qur'an 49:13)

5) Before Allah (sp), women and men are the same, in that superiority is achieved only through piety and righteousness. So whenever a woman performs a good deed for the sake of Allah (sp), she can be certain to receive a reward for it from Allah (sp). Allah (sp) said:

$$\text{فَٱسْتَجَابَ لَهُمْ رَبُّهُمْ أَنِّى لَآ أُضِيعُ عَمَلَ عَٰمِلٍ مِّنكُم مِّن ذَكَرٍ أَوْ أُنثَىٰ ۖ بَعْضُكُم مِّنۢ بَعْضٍ}$$

"So their Lord accepted of them (their supplication and answered them, Never will I allow to be lost the work of any of you, be he male or female. You are (members) one of another," (Qur'an 3: 195)

6) The Qur'an guarantees women the right to inherit wealth from their deceased relatives:

لِّلرِّجَالِ نَصِيبٌ مِّمَّا تَرَكَ ٱلْوَٰلِدَانِ وَٱلْأَقْرَبُونَ وَلِلنِّسَآءِ نَصِيبٌ مِّمَّا تَرَكَ ٱلْوَٰلِدَانِ وَٱلْأَقْرَبُونَ مِمَّا قَلَّ مِنْهُ أَوْ كَثُرَ ۚ نَصِيبًا مَّفْرُوضًا

"There is a share for men and a share for women from what is left by parents and those nearest related, whether, the property be small or large – a legal share." (Qur'an 4: 7)

7) The Qur'an guarantees women the right to take bridle-money from their husbands; in fact, in the Qur'an, Allah (sp) commanded men to pay bridle-money to their wives; therefore, the payment of bridle-money is not optional, but compulsory:

وَءَاتُوا۟ ٱلنِّسَآءَ صَدُقَٰتِهِنَّ نِحْلَةً

"And give to the women (whom you marry) their Mahr (obligatory bridle-money given by the husband to his wife at the time of marriage) with a good heart." (Qur'an 4:4)

8) The Qur'an forbade men from wrongfully taking wealth from their wives:

يَٰٓأَيُّهَا ٱلَّذِينَ ءَامَنُوا۟ لَا يَحِلُّ لَكُمْ أَن تَرِثُوا۟ ٱلنِّسَآءَ كَرْهًا

"O you who believe! You are forbidden to inherit women against their will" (Qur'an 4:19)
And in another Verse, Allah (sp) said:

وَإِنْ أَرَدتُّمُ ٱسْتِبْدَالَ زَوْجٍ مَّكَانَ زَوْجٍ وَءَاتَيْتُمْ إِحْدَىٰهُنَّ قِنطَارًا فَلَا تَأْخُذُوا۟ مِنْهُ شَيْـًٔا ۚ أَتَأْخُذُونَهُۥ بُهْتَٰنًا وَإِثْمًا مُّبِينًا

"But if you intend to replace a wife by another and you have given one of them a Cantar (of gold, ie., a great amount) as Mahr, take not the least bit of it back, would you take it wrongfully without a right and (with) a manifest sin". (Qur'an 4: 20)

9) The Qur'an strictly forbade men from mistreating women during periods of marital strife; a husband should either keep his wife and treat her properly or set her free in a just and merciful manner. Allah (sp) said:

وَإِذَا طَلَّقْتُمُ ٱلنِّسَآءَ فَبَلَغْنَ أَجَلَهُنَّ فَأَمْسِكُوهُنَّ بِمَعْرُوفٍ أَوْ سَرِّحُوهُنَّ بِمَعْرُوفٍ ۚ وَلَا تُمْسِكُوهُنَّ ضِرَارًا لِّتَعْتَدُوا۟ ۚ وَمَن يَفْعَلْ ذَٰلِكَ فَقَدْ ظَلَمَ نَفْسَهُۥ

"And when you have divorced women and they have fulfilled the term of their prescribed period, either take them back on a reasonable basis or set them free on a reasonable basis. But do not take them back to hurt them, and whoever does that, then he has wronged himself." (Qur'an 2: 231)

10) The Qur'an exhorts men to be generous to their wives even after they become divorced; this means that he should give her a reasonable amount of money, all the while taking into consideration both his means and circumstances, and her vulnerable position as a divorced woman. Allah (sp) said:

وَلِلْمُطَلَّقَٰتِ مَتَٰعٌۢ بِٱلْمَعْرُوفِ ۖ حَقًّا عَلَى ٱلْمُتَّقِينَ

"And for divorced women, maintenance (should be provided) on reasonable (scale). This is a duty on Al-Muttaqun (the pious ones)." (Qur'an 2: 241)
And elsewhere in the Qur'an, Allah (sp) said:

$$ فَمَتِّعُوهُنَّ وَسَرِّحُوهُنَّ سَرَاحًا جَمِيلًا $$

"So give them a present, and set them free, (i.e., divorce) in a handsome manner." (Qur'an 33:49)

11) The Qur'an granted pregnant divorced women spending money. Addressing husbands who divorce their wives, Allah (sp) said:

$$ وَإِن كُنَّ أُولَاتِ حَمْلٍ فَأَنفِقُوا عَلَيْهِنَّ حَتَّىٰ يَضَعْنَ حَمْلَهُنَّ $$

"And if they are pregnant, then spend on them till they deliver." (Qur'an 65: 6)

12) Regarding a woman who breastfeeds a baby she had with her divorced husband, the Qur'an orders the husband to pay her wages for her services:

$$ فَإِنْ أَرْضَعْنَ لَكُمْ فَآتُوهُنَّ أُجُورَهُنَّ $$

"Then if they give suck to the children for you, give them their due payment." (Qur'an 65: 6)

In short, it is patently clear that no religion or religious book gives women anywhere near the quantity and quality of rights that the Qur'an gives to women. Manmade laws strip women of their dignity and either distort their nature by forcing them to assume male characteristics or turn them into mere sex objects. In the past few hundred years or so, a group of Western scholars who are known as Orientalists have dedicated their lives to studying Islamic civilization and to analyzing and passing judgment on our beliefs, practices, and ways. Without a doubt, Muslim scholars need to study, analyze, and write about Western civilization in the same way. If a group of Muslim scholars embark upon such a task, I am certain that they will disabuse anyone who believes in Western values of the false notion that the Western system of law has given women an unprecedented level of freedom, rights, and dignity. From a sociological point of view, the statistics and findings of those scholars would truly be appalling, and would, among other things, have to do with the following: The percentage of single mothers in the West who have to struggle to raise their children on their own; the percentage of young women who, in order to make a living, have to sell their bodies in one way or another; the number of women who are raped each year; and, most importantly, the percentage of Western women who suffer from extreme levels of depression. As for the Qur'an, it does more than simply give rights to women; it provides them with a chance for ultimate happiness; it raises them to a status of true honor and dignity in society: For in Islam, women, like their male counterparts, are thinking honorable beings who are fully accountable for their actions, and who will be fully rewarded in the Hereafter for their deeds.

Section Five:

Bringing Happiness to Human Beings in Both this World and the Hereafter

One of the primary aims of the Qur'an is to guide mankind to the truth. Allah (sp) said:

$$ قُلْ إِنَّ هُدَى اللَّهِ هُوَ الْهُدَىٰ $$

"Say: Verily, the Guidance of Allah (i.e. Islamic Monotheism) that is the (only) Guidance." (Qur'an 2: 120)

In every unit of Prayer that a believer performs, he asks his Lord to guide him to the Straight Path:

$$ٱهْدِنَا ٱلصِّرَٰطَ ٱلْمُسْتَقِيمَ$$

"Guide us to the Straight Way." (Qur'an 1: 6)
The point here is that, if a person follows the guidance of the Qur'an, he does not 'fall into distress and misery':

$$فَمَنِ ٱتَّبَعَ هُدَايَ فَلَا يَضِلُّ وَلَا يَشْقَىٰ$$

"Then whoever follows My Guidance shall neither go astray, nor fall into distress and misery." (Qur'an 20:123)
And the opposite of misery is happiness; therefore, a guided person is a happy person; and just as the Qur'an aims to guide people, it also aims to bless them with happiness – which is a concomitant of guidance – in both this world and the Hereafter. In fact, the concepts of guidance and happiness are juxtaposed in many Verses of the Qur'an; for example, Allah (sp) said:

$$مَنْ عَمِلَ صَٰلِحًا مِّن ذَكَرٍ أَوْ أُنثَىٰ وَهُوَ مُؤْمِنٌ فَلَنُحْيِيَنَّهُۥ حَيَوٰةً طَيِّبَةً ۖ وَلَنَجْزِيَنَّهُمْ أَجْرَهُم بِأَحْسَنِ مَا كَانُوا۟ يَعْمَلُونَ$$

"Whoever works righteousness, whether male or female, while he (or she) is a true believer (of Islamic Monotheism) verily, to him We will give a good life (in this world with respect, contentment and lawful provision), and We shall pay them certainly a reward in proportion to the best of what they used to do (i.e., Paradise in the Hereafter)." (Qur'an 16:97)
This Verse explicitly states that, if a person believes and performs good deeds – and that occurs as a result of being guided — he will achieve happiness in this world: "We will give a good life (in this world with respect, contentment and lawful provision)." Similarly, it states he will achieve ultimate happiness in the Hereafter: "And We shall pay them certainly a reward in proportion to the best of what they used to do (i.e., Paradise in the Hereafter)."

Happiness in this Life
Happiness, contrary to the false notions of most human beings, is not achieved once one gets the best things in life: the best food and drink, the most expensive clothing, an unlimited supply of cash, and beautiful wives. Happiness, it must be understood, is not equivalent to moments of fleeting pleasure; it is, rather, a sustained and long-term feeling that permeates ones soul and heart.
These days, people seek happiness in worldly possessions and pleasures. Consider, for instance, the pleasure of sexual intercourse: It is fleeting in that it goes as quickly as it comes, and, if performed in an unlawful manner, is followed by a period of guilt and remorse. Similarly, food is a momentary pleasure that, if consumed extravagantly, is followed by heartburn and other ailments. Truth be told, Non-Muslims often seek happiness in alcohol or drugs; yes, those who consume alcohol and drug users describe moments of euphoria, but those moments are followed by long periods of misery and dejection. Every worldly pleasure and enjoyment has one thing in common: it is fleeting and momentary. Happiness, on the other hand, is sustained and long-term. It is interesting to note that two of the main pleasures that human beings enjoy – sexual relations and food — are in some cases enjoyed to a greater degree by animals.
No, worldly pleasures cannot bring happiness. And the world has witnessed empirical evidence which proves that worldly prosperity, if it is not coupled with guidance, leads to misery. That evidence is the lives of men and women in today's developed nations, nations whose citizens have more and eat more than ever before. Unparalleled levels of richness are, sadly, matched by unparalleled levels of drug use, alcohol addiction, misery, and clinically diagnosed depression. Each individual citizen is searching out for happiness, but, being far away from true guidance and looking for it in the wrong

places (alcohol, illicit sex, food, cigarettes, drugs, etc.), is unable to find it. Allah (sp) informed us about their misery and warned us against becoming deluded by their ostensible prosperity:

$$\text{فَلَا تُعْجِبْكَ أَمْوَالُهُمْ وَلَا أَوْلَادُهُمْ إِنَّمَا يُرِيدُ اللَّهُ لِيُعَذِّبَهُم بِهَا فِى ٱلْحَيَوٰةِ ٱلدُّنْيَا}$$

"So let not their wealth or their children amaze you (O Muhammad), in reality Allah's Plan is to punish them with these things in the life of this world" (Qur'an 9:55)

The Qur'an teaches us that happiness in this life has nothing to do with physical and sensual pleasures, but with what is hidden in our hearts – a sustained feeling of peace, contentment, and happiness. That the yardstick of happiness is measured by the state of our hearts is a message that is given in more than one Verse of the Qur'an; for instance, Allah (sp) said:

$$\text{هُوَ ٱلَّذِىٓ أَنزَلَ ٱلسَّكِينَةَ فِى قُلُوبِ ٱلْمُؤْمِنِينَ لِيَزْدَادُوٓا۟ إِيمَٰنًا مَّعَ إِيمَٰنِهِمْ}$$

"He it is Who sent down As-Sakinah (calmness and tranquility) into the hearts of the believers, that they may grow more in faith along with their (present) faith." (Qur'an 48: 4)

And in another Verse, Allah (sp) said:

$$\text{أَلَا بِذِكْرِ ٱللَّهِ تَطْمَئِنُّ ٱلْقُلُوبُ}$$

"Verily, in the remembrance of Allah do hearts find rest." (Qur'an 13:28)

Verily, we ask Allah (sp), the Almighty, to make us among those who are blessed with happiness both in this life and in the Hereafter; and to make us among those who are described in the Saying of Allah (sp):

$$\text{وَأَمَّا ٱلَّذِينَ سُعِدُوا۟ فَفِى ٱلْجَنَّةِ خَٰلِدِينَ فِيهَا مَا دَامَتِ ٱلسَّمَٰوَٰتُ وَٱلْأَرْضُ إِلَّا مَا شَآءَ رَبُّكَ عَطَآءً غَيْرَ مَجْذُوذٍ}$$

"And those who are blessed and made happy, they will be in Paradise, abiding therein for all the time that the heavens and the earth endure, except as your Lord will, a gift without an end." (Qur'an 11: 108)

The preceding was a brief discussion of five of the Qur'an's aims; in fact, there are many others. Here is a summary of some of the more important aims of the Qur'an (some I haven't mentioned yet and others are taken from the preceding discussion):

1) **Correcting People's Beliefs:** The Qur'an achieves this aim by guiding people to the realities of this universe, and to truths about its Creator, its beginning, its end, and much of what happens in between.
2) **Teaching People how to Worship Allah (sp):** This aim is achieved by teaching human beings how to purify and nourish their souls through the sincere performance of prayer, fasting, and other acts of worship.
3) **Promoting Good Manners:** The Qur'an accomplishes this aim by encouraging people to adopt noble characteristics and by warning them not to take on evil and base ones.
4) **Promoting the Development of a Righteous Society:** The Qur'an achieves this aim by instructing Muslims to do the following:
   - Become united, erasing all forms of allegiance that are not based on religion, such as allegiance that is based on tribal ties or nationalism:

$$\text{وَإِنَّ هَٰذِهِۦٓ أُمَّتُكُمْ أُمَّةً وَٰحِدَةً وَأَنَا۠ رَبُّكُمْ فَٱتَّقُونِ}$$

"And verily! This your religion (of Islamic Monotheism) is one religion, and I am your Lord, so keep your duty to Me." (Qur'an 23:52)

- Realize that all human beings are the same; they are all of the same family, sharing the same father (Adam (p)) and the same mother (Hawwaa (sh)); no race of people is better than another race; instead, superiority is achieved only through merit – ones level of piety and righteousness.
- Treat one another equally, with the understanding that everyone is equal before Allah (sp) and therefore everyone – regardless of race, gender, age, or status – should be treated equally before the law; and there are no exceptions to this rule.

5) **Promote the Formation of a Just Society:** The Qur'an achieves this aim by pointing out the virtues of being just and trustworthy; by promoting mutual love and mercy in society; by discouraging people from adopting evil characteristics, such as treachery, lying, untrustworthiness, cheating, and so on.
6) **Establishing an Economically Prosperous Muslim Society:** The Qur'an achieves this aim by calling upon Muslims to be neither miserly nor extravagant in their spending ways, but instead moderate and reasonable. Also, the Qur'an commands Muslims to spend their wealth on noble causes and to give each person what is rightfully his.
7) **Guaranteeing the Well-Being of Women:** The Qur'an accomplishes this aim by conferring honor upon women and by guaranteeing all of the rights that she deserves as an individual, as a citizen, and as a Muslim.
8) **Making Muslims Militarily Capable of Taking on their Enemies:** The Qur'an aims to protect Muslims from external threats and to promote the spread of Islam throughout the world. These aims can be achieved only if Muslims are militarily capable of defeating their enemies. Therefore, the Qur'an calls upon Muslims to be prepared for war as a nation, to fight for the betterment of mankind and upon Sound principles, to be merciful in war, and to honor the treaties they enact with other nations.
9) **Waging War against Slavery:** The Qur'an promoted an end to slavery in many ways, the most important of which was promising a great reward to those who free slaves. Allah (sp) even declared that the act of freeing a slave atones for various sins.
10) **Giving People the Freedom to Make Decisions for Themselves:** The Qur'an accomplishes this aim by making it forbidden to force people to believe in Islam. Allah (sp): said:

"There is no compulsion in religion." (Qur'an 2:256)
And elsewhere in the Qur'an, Allah (sp) said:

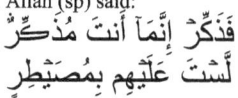

"So remind them (O Muhammad), you are only one who reminds, You are not a dictator over them." (Qur'an 88: 21, 22)

PART 2

The Greatness of the Qur'an's Legislations

This Part Consists of Three Sections:

Section One: The Comprehensiveness of the Qur'an's Legislations
Section Two: The Permanent and Lasting Applicability of the Qur'an's Legislations
Section Three: The Justice of the Qur'an's Legislations

Introduction

The Qur'an is a rich treasure of knowledge that deals not only with beliefs, such as faith in Islamic Monotheism, or with lessons that we can learn from past nations; but also with laws and legislations that cover every aspect of human life. Such laws aim to refine the manners of individuals, implement justice among the members of society, and improve the dealings that take place among the members of society.

In the Noble Qur'an, Muslims are commanded to perform a variety of deeds, some of which have to do with basic acts of worship, such as prayer and supplication; others, with societal or economic issues; and so on. All such compulsory deeds are considered to be acts of worship and, after faith in Allah (sp), combine to form the foundation of Islam. The Qur'an consists of 6236 Verses that deal with acts of worship, beliefs, dealings among individuals, relations among nations, the rules of sound governance in a Muslim country, the principles of justice within a society, the rights of individuals within a society

– in short, everything that has to do with forming the character of a Muslim, as well as everything that pertains to forming an upright and just Muslim society. The Qur'an consists of just legislations that deal with all aspects of life. Allah (sp) said:

$$وَكُلَّ شَىْءٍ فَصَّلْنَاهُ تَفْصِيلاً$$

"And We have explained everything (in detail) with full explanation." (Qur'an and 17:12)
And elsewhere in the Qur'an, Allah (sp) said:

$$وَنَزَّلْنَا عَلَيْكَ ٱلْكِتَابَ تِبْيَانًا لِّكُلِّ شَىْءٍ$$

"And We have sent down to you the Book (Qur'an) as an exposition of everything." (Qur'an 16: 89)
Among the Verses that deal with economic issues is the following:

$$وَلَا تُؤْتُوا۟ ٱلسُّفَهَآءَ أَمْوَٰلَكُمُ ٱلَّتِى جَعَلَ ٱللَّهُ لَكُمْ قِيَٰمًا وَٱرْزُقُوهُمْ فِيهَا وَٱكْسُوهُمْ وَقُولُوا۟ لَهُمْ قَوْلًا مَّعْرُوفًا$$

"And give not unto the foolish your property which Allah has made a means of support for you, but feed and clothe them therewith, and speak to them words of kindness and justice" (Qur'an 4: 5).
One of Verses that deals with family and marriage law is the following:

$$وَٱلْوَٰلِدَٰتُ يُرْضِعْنَ أَوْلَٰدَهُنَّ حَوْلَيْنِ كَامِلَيْنِ ۖ لِمَنْ أَرَادَ أَن يُتِمَّ ٱلرَّضَاعَةَ ۚ وَعَلَى ٱلْمَوْلُودِ لَهُۥ رِزْقُهُنَّ وَكِسْوَتُهُنَّ بِٱلْمَعْرُوفِ ۚ لَا تُكَلَّفُ نَفْسٌ إِلَّا وُسْعَهَا ۚ لَا تُضَآرَّ وَٰلِدَةٌۢ بِوَلَدِهَا وَلَا مَوْلُودٌ لَّهُۥ بِوَلَدِهِۦ ۚ وَعَلَى ٱلْوَارِثِ مِثْلُ ذَٰلِكَ ۗ فَإِنْ أَرَادَا فِصَالًا عَن تَرَاضٍ$$

مِّنْهُمَا وَتَشَاوُرٍ فَلَا جُنَاحَ عَلَيْهِمَا ۗ وَإِنْ أَرَدتُّمْ أَن تَسْتَرْضِعُوٓا۟ أَوْلَٰدَكُمْ فَلَا جُنَاحَ عَلَيْكُمْ إِذَا سَلَّمْتُم مَّآ ءَاتَيْتُم بِٱلْمَعْرُوفِ ۗ وَٱتَّقُوا۟ ٱللَّهَ وَٱعْلَمُوٓا۟ أَنَّ ٱللَّهَ بِمَا تَعْمَلُونَ بَصِيرٌ

"The mothers shall give suck to their children for two whole years, (that is) for those (parents) who desire to complete the term of suckling, but the father of the child shall bear the cost of the mother's food and clothing on a reasonable basis. No person shall have a burden laid on him greater than he can bear. No mother shall be treated unfairly on account of her child, nor father on account of his child. And on the (father's) heir is incumbent the like of that (which was incumbent on the father). If they both decide on weaning, by mutual consent, and after due consultation, there is no sin on them. And if you decide on a foster suckling-mother for your children, there is no sin on you, provided you pay (the mother) what you agreed (to give her) on reasonable basis. And fear Allah and know that Allah is All-Seer of what you do" (Qur'an 2; 233)

The following is an example of a Verse that deals with inheritance law:

لِّلرِّجَالِ نَصِيبٌ مِّمَّا تَرَكَ ٱلْوَٰلِدَانِ وَٱلْأَقْرَبُونَ وَلِلنِّسَآءِ نَصِيبٌ مِّمَّا تَرَكَ ٱلْوَٰلِدَانِ وَٱلْأَقْرَبُونَ مِمَّا قَلَّ مِنْهُ أَوْ كَثُرَ ۚ نَصِيبًا مَّفْرُوضًا

"There is a share for men and a share for women from what is left by parents and those nearest related, whether, the property be small or large -a legal share." (Qur'an 4: 7)

The following is an example of a Verse that explains criminal law in Islam:

وَكَتَبْنَا عَلَيْهِمْ فِيهَآ أَنَّ ٱلنَّفْسَ بِٱلنَّفْسِ وَٱلْعَيْنَ بِٱلْعَيْنِ وَٱلْأَنفَ بِٱلْأَنفِ وَٱلْأُذُنَ بِٱلْأُذُنِ وَٱلسِّنَّ بِٱلسِّنِّ وَٱلْجُرُوحَ قِصَاصٌ ۚ فَمَن تَصَدَّقَ بِهِۦ فَهُوَ كَفَّارَةٌ لَّهُۥ ۚ وَمَن لَّمْ يَحْكُم بِمَآ أَنزَلَ ٱللَّهُ فَأُو۟لَٰٓئِكَ هُمُ ٱلظَّٰلِمُونَ

"And We ordained therein for them: 'Life for life, eye for eye, nose for nose, ear for ear, tooth for tooth, and wounds equal for equal.' But if anyone remits the retaliation by way of charity, it shall be for him an expiation. And whosoever does not judge by that which Allah has revealed, such are the Zalimun (polytheists and wrongdoers - of a lesser degree)." (Qur'an 5: 45)

The following is an example of the Verses that discuss capital punishment:

وَٱلَّذِينَ يَرْمُونَ ٱلْمُحْصَنَٰتِ ثُمَّ لَمْ يَأْتُوا۟ بِأَرْبَعَةِ شُهَدَآءَ فَٱجْلِدُوهُمْ ثَمَٰنِينَ جَلْدَةً وَلَا تَقْبَلُوا۟ لَهُمْ شَهَٰدَةً أَبَدًا ۚ وَأُو۟لَٰٓئِكَ هُمُ ٱلْفَٰسِقُونَ

"And those who accuse chaste women, and produce not four witnesses, flog them with eighty stripes, and reject their testimony forever; they indeed are the Fasiqun (liars, rebellious, disobedient to Allah)." (Qur'an 24:4)

Two examples of Verses that deal with relations among Nations are the following:

وَإِن جَنَحُوا۟ لِلسَّلْمِ فَٱجْنَحْ لَهَا وَتَوَكَّلْ عَلَى ٱللَّهِ ۚ إِنَّهُۥ هُوَ ٱلسَّمِيعُ ٱلْعَلِيمُ

"But if they incline to peace, you also incline to it, and (put your) trust in Allah. Verily, he is the All-Hearer, the All-Knower." (Qur'an 8: 61)

وَإِمَّا تَخَافَنَّ مِن قَوْمٍ خِيَانَةً فَٱنۢبِذْ إِلَيْهِمْ عَلَىٰ سَوَآءٍ ۚ إِنَّ ٱللَّهَ لَا يُحِبُّ ٱلْخَآئِنِينَ

"If you (O Muhammad (s)) fear treachery from any people throw back (their covenant) to them (so as to be) on equal terms (that there will be no more covenant between you and them. Certainly Allah likes not the treacherous." (Qur'an 8:58)

The following is one of the Verses that call upon Muslims to defend their lands:

وَقَٰتِلُواْ فِى سَبِيلِ ٱللَّهِ ٱلَّذِينَ يُقَٰتِلُونَكُمْ وَلَا تَعْتَدُوٓاْ إِنَّ ٱللَّهَ لَا يُحِبُّ ٱلْمُعْتَدِينَ

"And fight in the Way of Allah those who fight you, but transgress not the limits. Truly, Allah likes not the transgressors." (Qur'an 2:190) This Verse is the first one that was revealed in connection with Jihad, but it was supplemented by another (9:36).

The following are examples of Verses that discuss judicial law:

إِنَّ ٱللَّهَ يَأْمُرُكُمْ أَن تُؤَدُّواْ ٱلْأَمَٰنَٰتِ إِلَىٰٓ أَهْلِهَا وَإِذَا حَكَمْتُم بَيْنَ ٱلنَّاسِ أَن تَحْكُمُواْ بِٱلْعَدْلِ إِنَّ ٱللَّهَ نِعِمَّا يَعِظُكُم بِهِۦٓ إِنَّ ٱللَّهَ كَانَ سَمِيعًۢا بَصِيرًا
يَٰٓأَيُّهَا ٱلَّذِينَ ءَامَنُوٓاْ أَطِيعُواْ ٱللَّهَ وَأَطِيعُواْ ٱلرَّسُولَ وَأُوْلِى ٱلْأَمْرِ مِنكُمْ فَإِن تَنَٰزَعْتُمْ فِى شَىْءٍ فَرُدُّوهُ إِلَى ٱللَّهِ وَٱلرَّسُولِ إِن كُنتُمْ تُؤْمِنُونَ بِٱللَّهِ وَٱلْيَوْمِ ٱلْءَاخِرِ ذَٰلِكَ خَيْرٌ وَأَحْسَنُ تَأْوِيلًا

"Verily! Allah commands that you should render back the trusts to those, to whom they are due; and that when you judge between men, you judge with justice. Verily, how excellent is the teaching which He (Allah) gives you! Truly, Allah is Ever All-Hearer, All-Seer. O you who believe! Obey Allah and obey the Messenger (Muhammad (s)), and those of you (Muslims) who are in authority. (And) if you differ in anything amongst yourselves, refer it to Allah and His Messenger, if you believe in Allah and in the Last Day. That is better and more suitable for final determination." (Qur'an 4: 58, 59)

The Superiority of Qur'anic Legislations
It was from the divine wisdom of Allah (sp) that the Qur'an was revealed thirteen centuries after the establishment of Roman law, which, around the time of the advent of Islam, was applied in many lands. Roman law benefited from periodic revisions that were made by philosophers, scholars, and men of law. Roman law was, in short, detailed and well-developed. In this regard, Roman law resembled the Arabic language, which was also well-developed by the time the Prophet (s) was sent with the Qur'an. And just as the Qur'an, as a miracle of Arabic expression, challenged poets and language experts to produce something similar to it, it also, as a miracle of laws and legislations, issued a challenge to philosophers, men of law, and experts of all systems of codified law.

Any just and unbiased researcher will appreciate the vast difference between the superior code of law that is detailed in the Qur'an and all other inferior systems of law. Qur'anic law does not have any weak points; it is in harmony with the inherent nature of man; it is completely just; it comprehensively deals with all spheres of life; and it can just as appropriately be applied today as it was over fourteen centuries ago. It is for this reason that, for Muslims, the Qur'an is not only a book of prayers, supplications, and spiritual nourishment – although it is all of these things as well – but is also a Book of divinely revealed laws that govern every aspect of their lives. The Qur'an is a reminder of how Islam was applied by the Prophet (s) and his Companions (rp). And if the laws of the Qur'an are not applied today, the thought of applying Qur'anic law one day in the future imbues Muslims with a profound sense of hope.[70]

Section one:

---

[70] *Diraasaat Islaamiyyah Fil'Ilaaqaat Al-Ijtimaa'iyyah Wad-Dauliyyah* by Dr. Muhammad 'Abdullah Darraaz (pg. 31).

The Comprehensiveness of the Qur'an's Legislations

Among the more salient features of the Noble Qur'an are its comprehensiveness and its perfection. As for the latter quality, Allah (sp) said:

$$\text{ٱلْيَوْمَ أَكْمَلْتُ لَكُمْ دِينَكُمْ وَأَتْمَمْتُ عَلَيْكُمْ نِعْمَتِى وَرَضِيتُ لَكُمُ ٱلْإِسْلَـٰمَ دِينًا}$$

"This day, I have perfected your religion for you, completed My Favor upon you, and have chosen for you Islam as your religion." (Qur'an 5:3)

The former quality is a natural accompaniment of the Qur'an's perfection: One of the reasons why the Qur'an is perfect is that it comprehensively serves the needs of mankind. For every occurrence – in all places and all times – there is an Islamic ruling that applies to it. The comprehensive nature of Islam's laws is specific to the message with which Prophet Muhammad (s) was sent. All previously revealed laws were, at least in some ways, specific; for instance, one of the most detailed set of revealed laws was the one that was revealed to Moses and it was meant not comprehensively for all of mankind, but specifically for the Children of Israel. Furthermore, no one claimed that those set of laws possessed the qualities of perfection and comprehensiveness.

The Qur'an does not deal exclusively with man's worldly needs, nor does it deal solely with his religious duties; rather, it comprehensively takes care of both. Likewise, the Qur'an does not take the narrow and unbalanced approach of taking care of the needs of the individual while ignoring the needs of the community, or vice-versa; instead, the Qur'an strikes a perfect balance by comprehensively taking into consideration the needs of both the individual and the community. The individual is a part or a limb, while the community is the whole or the body. Also, the Qur'an does not focus on the importance of the body to the exclusion of the soul, or vice-versa, but instead comprehensively focuses on the important role that each one of them plays. Similarly, the Qur'an does not take into consideration the mind while ignoring emotions, or vice-versa, but rather it comprehensively takes both into consideration. In short, Islamic Law is complete, perfect, comprehensive – and magnificent. In every respect, it strikes a perfect balance. The following Verse is an instance of the Qur'an striking a perfect balance between man's religious duties and his worldly needs:

$$\text{وَٱبْتَغِ فِيمَآ ءَاتَىٰكَ ٱللَّهُ ٱلدَّارَ ٱلْـَٔاخِرَةَ وَلَا تَنسَ نَصِيبَكَ مِنَ ٱلدُّنْيَا}$$

"But seek, with that (wealth) which Allah has bestowed on you, the home of the Hereafter, and forget not your portion of legal enjoyment in this world." (Qur'an 28:77)

Qataadah said, "Here is the meaning of this Verse: Do not lose out on your share of this world; instead, seek out your share of lawful enjoyment and set worldly goals for yourself."[71]

In this context, it is important to note that the Shariah does not consist of a set of dry laws or an arbitrary list of dos and don'ts; to the contrary, it calls out to our minds, our hearts, and our emotions, stimulating into life faith that otherwise lies dormant deep within our souls. The Qur'an achieves this effect with the use of such phrases as, "If you are truly believers", or, "So that perhaps you might fear (Allah (sp))," or, "So that perhaps you might remember and take heed." In his sayings, the Prophet (s) was similarly able to awaken dormant faith in the hearts of Muslims by using such phrases as, "Whoever believes in Allah (sp) and the Last Day..."

Manmade laws, on the other hand, are dry and, in many ways, consist of an arbitrary list of dos and don'ts. Manmade laws deal with the surface of problems, while ignoring their underlying reasons and causes; and, while ignoring faith (*Eemaan*) and the spiritual needs of man, they focus wholly on worldly benefits and harms. In short, manmade laws deal with the problems of any given community in an ineffective and shortsighted manner, whereas Allah's laws comprehensively take man's overall

---

[71] *Tafseer Al-Qurtubi* (13/326).

condition into consideration.[72] Allah's laws strike a perfect balance between achieving benefits for this world and for the Hereafter. No one knows more about what benefits human beings than their Creator, Allah (sp); it is therefore only fitting that we should follow His laws, which are meant for our benefit. Allah (sp) said:

$$\text{أَلَا يَعْلَمُ مَنْ خَلَقَ وَهُوَ ٱللَّطِيفُ ٱلْخَبِيرُ}$$

"Should not He Who has created know? And He is the Most Kind and Courteous (to His slaves) All-Aware (of everything)." (Qur'an 67: 14)

Manmade laws not only focus on worldly benefits to the exclusion of benefits of the Hereafter; but they also – regardless of which system of manmade laws one might refer to — strike a pathetically weak and inadequate balance between the needs of the individual and the needs of the community. A capitalist, Western society, for instance, gives the individual an inordinate amount of rights, and meanwhile ignores the rights and needs of the community; conversely, a communist society focuses too much on the rights of the community and too little on the rights of individuals. Other manmade systems of law are little better.

As I have hitherto pointed out, the Qur'an is comprehensive in more than one way; the most salient ways in which it is comprehensive are as follows:

1) **Comprehensive of all eras:** The Qur'an's laws and legislations have been compulsory to follow from the time the Prophet (s) was sent to mankind, and they will remain that way until the end of this world. Therefore, there will never come a time on this earth – not now and not later – when it will be permissible for human beings to follow any set of laws other than Islamic Law.

2) **Comprehensive of all places:** The laws of Islam are applicable not only in the desert lands of Arabia, but also in all of the plains, mountains, jungles, forests, valleys, rivers, seas, and oceans of the earth. There is not a spot on earth on which it is permissible to avoid applying Islamic Law. Allah (sp) said:

$$\text{إِن كُلُّ مَن فِى ٱلسَّمَٰوَٰتِ وَٱلْأَرْضِ إِلَّا ءَاتِى ٱلرَّحْمَٰنِ عَبْدًا}$$

"There is none in the heavens and earth but comes unto the Most Beneficent (Allah) as a slave." (Qur'an 19: 93)

3) **Comprehensive of all human beings:** It is obligatory for all human beings of all races and colors to follow the laws of Islam. Islamic law is meant as much for the Arabs of the Arabian Peninsula as it is for the inhabitants of Iceland, Europe, Africa, or anywhere else on earth; in fact, the message of Islam was meant not only for all human beings, but for jinns as well. Allah (sp) said:

$$\text{وَمَا خَلَقْتُ ٱلْجِنَّ وَٱلْإِنسَ إِلَّا لِيَعْبُدُونِ}$$

"And I (Allah (sp)) created not the jinns and humans except they should worship Me (Alone)." (Qur'an 51:56)

And in another Verse, Allah (sp) said:

$$\text{قُلْ يَٰٓأَيُّهَا ٱلنَّاسُ إِنِّى رَسُولُ ٱللَّهِ إِلَيْكُمْ جَمِيعًا}$$

"Say (O Muhammad (s)): Verily, I am sent to you all as the Messenger of Allah." (Qur'an 7:158).

4) **Comprehensive in the topics it covers:** Islamic law deals with all things, and with all aspects of life; in fact, it even deals with laws that relate to animals and to the dead. In short, for every

---

[72] *Min Mazaayaa At-Tashree' Al-Islaamee* by Muhammad bin Naasir As-Sahyibaanee, and *Majallah Al-Jaami'ah Al-Islaamiyyah Bil-Madeenah Al-Nabawiyyah* (number 61, Muharram, 1404 H. pg. 74).

occurrence, for every problem, and for every situation there is an appropriate ruling in Islam. Allah (sp) said:

$$\text{مَّا فَرَّطْنَا فِى ٱلْكِتَٰبِ مِن شَىْءٍ}$$

"We have neglected nothing in the Book." (Qur'an 6:38)

Section Two:

The Permanent and Lasting Applicability of the Qur'an's Legislations

As long as there is life on this earth, the laws of the Qur'an remain not only applicable, but completely appropriate and fitting as well. Such is the amazing nature of the Qur'an's laws that they require neither changes nor amendments.
One of the reasons why the Qur'an's laws are so timeless is that they are flexible; and yet, at the same time, their foundations are strong and firmly-established. In this way the Qur'an resembles a tree whose roots are firmly established in the ground and whose branches move flexibly with the wind.
In both the Qur'an and Sunnah, there are many proofs that establish the timeless nature of Islam's laws. I will suffice here by mentioning only two of those proofs. First, in Chapter *As-Saff*, Allah (sp) said:

$$\text{هُوَ ٱلَّذِىٓ أَرْسَلَ رَسُولَهُۥ بِٱلْهُدَىٰ وَدِينِ ٱلْحَقِّ لِيُظْهِرَهُۥ عَلَى ٱلدِّينِ كُلِّهِۦ وَلَوْ كَرِهَ ٱلْمُشْرِكُونَ}$$

"He it is Who has sent His Messenger (Muhammad (s)) with guidance and the religion of truth (Islamic Monotheism) to make it victorious over all (other) religions even though the Mushrikun (polytheists, pagans, idolaters, and disbelievers in the Oneness of Allah and in His Messenger Muhammad (s)) hate (it)." (Qur'an 61: 9)
In this Verse, Allah (sp) explained the purpose of sending Prophet Muhammad (s) to mankind, but He (sp) did not specify any time limit to the applicability of the Prophet's message, which indicates that it is a timeless message that must be followed until the Day of Resurrection.
And second, Allah (sp) said:

$$\text{إِنَّا نَحْنُ نَزَّلْنَا ٱلذِّكْرَ وَإِنَّا لَهُۥ لَحَٰفِظُونَ}$$

"Verily We: It is We Who have sent down the Dhikr (i.e., the Qur'an) and surely, We will guard it (from corruption)." (Qur'an 15: 9)
The Qur'an's laws and legislations are safeguarded in two ways. The first, as is indicated in the abovementioned Verse, involves direct protection from Allah (sp): Allah (sp) guaranteed to preserve the Qur'an until the end of time. The Second safeguard requires an effort on the part of Muslims, in that they can help preserve the Qur'an if they apply its teachings on a continual basis until the end of time. It is only logical, after all, that as long as a group of people continue to apply a system of law, that system will become neither lost nor forgotten.
That the Qur'an's laws are eternal can be attributed to a number of its qualities, among which are the following:
1) Islamic Law is based on pure and complete justice. The One Who created this world and human beings – be He exalted – best knows how to establish justice on earth; hence our dire need to follow His Shariah.

2) Islamic Law is not tainted by the ignorance, desires, biases, and extreme views of weak, created beings. The opposite holds true for all laws that are the handiwork of human beings. After all, human beings, by dint of their inherent weaknesses, ignorance, biases, desires, ambitions, and lusts, are incapable of creating a system of law that is truly just and fair. It matters not whether the founder of a system of law is an individual, a group of people, or generations of legal scholars: manmade laws will inevitably be inadequate, unjust, and tainted by human weaknesses; that is why every generation looks to amend previously legislated laws and sometimes to even form a completely new system of laws.

3) Islamic Law is in harmony with the laws of the universe since its legislator is the Creator of this universe and all that is in it. When Allah (sp) decrees a law for human beings, He does so with the knowledge that they are a part of the universe He (sp) created, and with the knowledge of what their primary role is in that universe. A follower of Islamic Law, therefore, is in harmony with nature and the universe; conversely, a person who does not follow Islamic Law is at odds with the universe around him, and is a rebel amidst a universe that is otherwise harmonious.

4) Islamic Law is the only system of law on earth that emancipates man from slavery to other human beings. As a follower of Islamic Law, a Muslim is a slave only to Allah (sp); followers of all other systems of law take other human beings as deities, by agreeing to obey them instead of Allah (sp). Muslims submit themselves not to the laws of men, but to the laws of the One True God, Allah (sp); as such, they abandon slavery to created beings in favor of slavery to the Lord of all created beings.

5) Islamic Law, since it came from Allah (sp), the Creator of the universe and of all created beings, is founded upon complete knowledge of man's needs, his inner secrets, and the secrets of the universe in which he lives. All other systems of law have been thought up by men who are no better than me or you: They have limited knowledge of the true nature of man and therefore, in their legislations, decree laws that deal with problems at a very superficial level.

6) Islamic Law strengthens the bonds of brotherhood between all races of men. Under the shade of Islamic Law – as opposed to all other systems of law – racial differences as well as differences in societal status vanish. A community of Muslims is like a single individual, for each of its members shares a common sense of purpose in life and a common set of goals. Allah (sp) said:

$$إِذْ كُنتُمْ أَعْدَاءً فَأَلَّفَ بَيْنَ قُلُوبِكُمْ فَأَصْبَحْتُم بِنِعْمَتِهِ إِخْوَانًا$$

"For you were enemies one to another but He joined your hearts together, so that, by His Grace, you became brethren (in Islamic faith)" (Qur'an 3: 103)

Section Three:

The Justice of the Qur'an's Legislations

Under the shade of Islamic Law, all people are equal. Islamic Law focuses not at all on the outward, physical features of human beings, but on their insides – on their spiritual worth. As equals in society, each individual – be he white, black, or brown; rich or poor – is treated in a fair and just manner. Allah (sp) said:

$$إِنَّ ٱللَّهَ يَأْمُرُكُمْ أَن تُؤَدُّوا۟ ٱلْأَمَٰنَٰتِ إِلَىٰٓ أَهْلِهَا وَإِذَا حَكَمْتُم بَيْنَ ٱلنَّاسِ أَن تَحْكُمُوا۟ بِٱلْعَدْلِ$$

"Verily Allah commands that you should render back the trusts to those, to whom they are due; and that when you judge between men, you judge with justice." (Qur'an 4: 58)

In this Verse, Allah (sp) orders us to be just not only with people of a certain complexion, nor only with the rich and prosperous members of society, but with everyone. Justice means to give each person what is rightfully his; to remove wrongful aggression and oppression from society; to remove oppression from the weak and oppressed; and, in general, to organize the affairs of society's members in a way that looks after their collective (as well as individual) needs.[73]

To be sure, justice is one of the most salient features of Islamic Law. Allah (sp) said:

إِنَّ ٱللَّهَ يَأْمُرُ بِٱلْعَدْلِ وَٱلْإِحْسَٰنِ وَإِيتَآئِ ذِى ٱلْقُرْبَىٰ وَيَنْهَىٰ عَنِ ٱلْفَحْشَآءِ وَٱلْمُنكَرِ وَٱلْبَغْىِ يَعِظُكُمْ لَعَلَّكُمْ تَذَكَّرُونَ

"Verily, Allah enjoins Al-Adl (i.e., justice and worshiping none but Allah Alone – Islamic Monotheism) and Al-Ihsan (i.e., to be patient in performing your duties to Allah, totally for Allah's sake and in accordance with the Sunnah (legal ways) of the Prophet (s) in a perfect manner), and giving (help) to kith and kin (i.e., all that Allah has ordered you to give them, e.g., wealth, visiting, looking after them, or any other kind of help, etc.); and forbids Al-Fahsha (i.e., all evil deeds, e.g., illegal sexual acts, disobedience of parents, polytheism, to tell lies, to give false witness, to kill a life without right, etc.), and Al-Munkar (i.e., all that is prohibited by Islamic law; polytheism of every kind, disbelief and every kind of evil deeds, etc.), and Al-Baghy (i.e., all kinds of oppression), He admonishes you, that you may take heed." (Qur'an 16:90)

In his famous book of Tafseer, Al-Qurtubee wrote, "This Verse lists the most important rulings in Islam; in essence, it summarizes all of the religion and all of Islamic Law."[74]

The Noble Qur'an Exhorts Muslims to Act Justly

In more than one Verse of the Noble Qur'an, Allah (sp) declares His love for those of His slaves who are just in their dealings and judgments. For example, Allah (sp) said:

وَإِنْ حَكَمْتَ فَٱحْكُم بَيْنَهُم بِٱلْقِسْطِ إِنَّ ٱللَّهَ يُحِبُّ ٱلْمُقْسِطِينَ

"And if you judge, judge with justice between them. Verily, Allah loves those who act justly." (Qur'an 5: 42) In another Verse, Allah said:

فَأَصْلِحُوا۟ بَيْنَهُمَا بِٱلْعَدْلِ وَأَقْسِطُوٓا۟ إِنَّ ٱللَّهَ يُحِبُّ ٱلْمُقْسِطِينَ

"Then make reconciliation between them justly, and be equitable. Verily! Allah loves those who are equitable." (Qur'an 49:9)

And in yet another Verse, Allah (sp) said:

لَّا يَنْهَىٰكُمُ ٱللَّهُ عَنِ ٱلَّذِينَ لَمْ يُقَٰتِلُوكُمْ فِى ٱلدِّينِ وَلَمْ يُخْرِجُوكُم مِّن دِيَٰرِكُمْ أَن تَبَرُّوهُمْ وَتُقْسِطُوٓا۟ إِلَيْهِمْ إِنَّ ٱللَّهَ يُحِبُّ ٱلْمُقْسِطِينَ

"Allah does not forbid you to deal justly and kindly with those who fought not against you on account of religion and did not drive you out of your homes. Verily, Allah loves those who deal with equity." (Qur'an 60: 8)

In certain Verses of the Qur'an, Allah (sp) uses the word "balance" or "scale" (in English, it is interesting to note, the word scale is used in the expression, the scales of justice) as a term for justice; for instance, in Verse 7 of Chapter *Ar-Rahmaan*, Allah (sp) said:

---

[73] *At-Tahreer Wat-Tanweer* (4/162).
[74] *Al-Jaam'i Li-Ahkaam Al-Qur'an* (5/285).

$$\text{وَٱلسَّمَآءَ رَفَعَهَا وَوَضَعَ ٱلْمِيزَانَ}$$

"And the heaven He has raised high, and He has set up the Balance." (Qur'an 55: 7)
"Balance" means justice; in the Verses that follow, the word balance" is used twice more:

$$\text{أَلَّا تَطْغَوْا۟ فِى ٱلْمِيزَانِ}$$
$$\text{وَأَقِيمُوا۟ ٱلْوَزْنَ بِٱلْقِسْطِ وَلَا تُخْسِرُوا۟ ٱلْمِيزَانَ}$$

"In order that you may not transgress (due) balance. And observe the weight with equity and do not make the balance deficient." (Qur'an 55: 8, 9)

The overall meaning of these Verses is as follows: Just as Allah (sp) has created the heavens and the earth by the truth and with justice, so you too should be just in all of your actions; for if you do so, all things will be based upon truth and justice (i.e., not just Allah's creation of the universe, but also the actions and interactions of men.[75]

The aforementioned Verses discuss the blessing of man's creation, the blessing of revelation, the submission of all that is in the universe to Allah (sp), and the forming of the universe upon truth and justice. Having discussed these matters, the Verses then go on to order human beings to act justly. A similar pattern can be discerned in the following sequence of Verses:

$$\text{ٱلرَّحْمَٰنُ (١) عَلَّمَ ٱلْقُرْءَانَ (٢) خَلَقَ ٱلْإِنسَٰنَ (٣) عَلَّمَهُ ٱلْبَيَانَ (٤) ٱلشَّمْسُ وَٱلْقَمَرُ بِحُسْبَانٍ (٥) وَٱلنَّجْمُ وَٱلشَّجَرُ يَسْجُدَانِ (٦) وَٱلسَّمَآءَ رَفَعَهَا وَوَضَعَ ٱلْمِيزَانَ (٧) أَلَّا تَطْغَوْا۟ فِى ٱلْمِيزَانِ (٨) وَأَقِيمُوا۟ ٱلْوَزْنَ بِٱلْقِسْطِ وَلَا تُخْسِرُوا۟ ٱلْمِيزَانَ (٩)}$$

"The Most Beneficent (Allah)! Has taught (you mankind) the Qur'an (by His Mercy). He created man. He taught him eloquent speech. The Sun and the moon run on their fixed courses (exactly) calculated with measured out stages for each (for reckoning, etc.). And the herb (or stars) and the trees - both prostrate. And the heaven He has raised high, and He has set up the Balance. In order that you may not transgress (due) balance. And observe the weight with equity and do not make the balance deficient." (Qur'an 55: 1 – 9)

In the Noble Qur'an, the concept of justice has a profoundly spiritual meaning. It is not merely a set of laws that are transcribed on scrolls and then stored away on shelves. Nay, indeed: justice in the Qur'an is a virtue that must be applied and that, as the preceding Verses indicate, is a salient feature of the very creation of the universe and all that is in it. The Qur'an elevated the quality of justice to the degree that, in the following Verse, it is juxtaposed with the all important belief of Islamic Monotheism (Tawheed). Allah (sp) said:

$$\text{شَهِدَ ٱللَّهُ أَنَّهُۥ لَآ إِلَٰهَ إِلَّا هُوَ وَٱلْمَلَٰٓئِكَةُ وَأُو۟لُوا۟ ٱلْعِلْمِ قَآئِمًۢا بِٱلْقِسْطِ لَآ إِلَٰهَ إِلَّا هُوَ ٱلْعَزِيزُ ٱلْحَكِيمُ}$$

"Allah bears witness that La ilaha illa Huwa (none has the right to be worshipped but He), and the Angels, and those having knowledge (also give this witness); (He is always) maintaining His creation in justice. La ilaha illa Huwa (none has the right to be worshiped but He), the All-Mighty, the All-Wise." (Qur'an 3:18)

---

[75] Tafseer Ibn Katheer (7/495).

In this Verse, we find testimony from Allah (sp), the Angels, Prophets (st) and the people of knowledge that none has the right to be worshipped but Allah (sp) and that Allah (sp) always maintains His creation with justice.[76]

Just as justice and Islamic Monotheism are juxtaposed in the previous Verse, oppression (or doing wrong) is juxtaposed with polytheism (Shirk) in this Verse:

$$إِنَّ ٱلشِّرْكَ لَظُلْمٌ عَظِيمٌ$$

"Verily! Joining others in worship with Allah is a great Zulm (wrong) indeed." (Qur'an 31: 13)

Nothing is more beloved to Allah (sp) than justice; conversely, nothing is more detested by Him than wrongdoing and oppression. For this reason, Allah (sp), before making it prohibited for his slaves, made wrongdoing and oppression forbidden for Himself. In a Qudsee Hadeeth, the Prophet (s) related that Allah (sp) said: *"O my slaves! Verily, I have made wrongdoing and oppression forbidden upon Myself,[77] and I have made it forbidden upon you among yourselves, so do not wrong or oppress one another."*[78]

That Allah (sp) made oppression forbidden upon Himself is confirmed in this Verse:

$$وَمَا أَنَا بِظَلَّامٍ لِّلْعَبِيدِ$$

"And I am not unjust (to the least) to the slaves." (Qur'an 50: 29)

And in another Verse, Allah (sp) said:

$$وَمَا ٱللَّهُ يُرِيدُ ظُلْمًا لِّلْعَٰلَمِينَ$$

"And Allah wills no injustice to the 'Alamin (mankind and jinns)." (Qur'an 3: 108)

In yet another Verse, Allah (sp) said:

$$وَمَا ٱللَّهُ يُرِيدُ ظُلْمًا لِّلْعِبَادِ$$

"And Allah wills no injustice for (His) slaves." (Qur'an 40: 31)

And in yet another Verse, Allah (sp) said:

$$إِنَّ ٱللَّهَ لَا يَظْلِمُ ٱلنَّاسَ شَيْئًا$$

"Truly! Allah wrongs not mankind in aught." (Qur'an 10: 44)

And Allah (sp) also said:

$$إِنَّ ٱللَّهَ لَا يَظْلِمُ مِثْقَالَ ذَرَّةٍ$$

"Surely! Allah wrongs not even of the weight of an atom (or a small ant)." (Qur'an 4: 40)

Since Allah (sp) made wrongdoing forbidden upon Himself, and since Allah is not in the least unjust to His slaves, it follows that everything He (sp) legislated and decreed is nothing other than pure justice and fairness. For their part, men, if they want to achieve success for both this life and the Hereafter, are left with only one logical choice: To believe in and apply the divinely revealed laws of

---

[76] *Tafseer Al-Jalaalain* (pg. 67).
[77] As for Allah's Saying, "I have made wrongdoing and oppression forbidden upon Myself", the people of knowledge say it means: Far above am I from oppressing (others) and doing wrong. *Saheeh Muslim with the commentary of An-Nawawee* (16/348).
[78] Related by Muslim (4/1994).

Allah (sp). Having made wrongdoing and oppression forbidden, Allah (sp) ordered mankind to act justly. Allah (sp) said:

$$\text{لَقَدْ أَرْسَلْنَا رُسُلَنَا بِالْبَيِّنَاتِ وَأَنزَلْنَا مَعَهُمُ الْكِتَابَ وَالْمِيزَانَ لِيَقُومَ النَّاسُ بِالْقِسْطِ}$$

"Indeed We have sent Our Messengers with clear proofs, and revealed with them the Scripture and the Balance (justice) that mankind may keep up justice." (Qur'an 57:25)

The Different Spheres of Justice

In the Noble Qur'an, Allah (sp) ordered the Messenger of Allah (s) as well as all believers to act justly; as for the former, Allah (sp) said:

$$\text{وَأُمِرْتُ لِأَعْدِلَ بَيْنَكُمْ}$$

"And I am commanded to do justice among you." (Qur'an 42: 15)
And in regard to the latter, Allah said:

$$\text{اعْدِلُوا هُوَ أَقْرَبُ لِلتَّقْوَى}$$

"Be just; that is nearer to piety." (Qur'an 5: 8)

Justice in Islam is not limited to certain actions; it pervades all aspects of human life. And so, in the Noble Qur'an, Allah (sp) ordered Muslims to be just always and in all of the different spheres of their lives. When they speak, they must speak in a just, upright, and fair manner:

$$\text{وَإِذَا قُلْتُمْ فَاعْدِلُوا وَلَوْ كَانَ ذَا قُرْبَى}$$

"And whenever you give your word (i.e., judge between men or give evidence, etc.), say the truth even if a near relative is concerned." (Qur'an 6: 152)
When they act, they must act justly:

$$\text{يَا أَيُّهَا الَّذِينَ آمَنُوا كُونُوا قَوَّامِينَ بِالْقِسْطِ شُهَدَاءَ لِلَّهِ وَلَوْ عَلَى أَنفُسِكُمْ أَوِ الْوَالِدَيْنِ وَالْأَقْرَبِينَ}$$

"O you who believe! Stand out firmly for justice, as witnesses to Allah, even though it be against yourselves, or your parents, or your kin." (Qur'an 4:135)
In their family dealings they must act justly and equitably:

$$\text{وَإِنْ خِفْتُمْ شِقَاقَ بَيْنِهِمَا فَابْعَثُوا حَكَمًا مِّنْ أَهْلِهِ وَحَكَمًا مِّنْ أَهْلِهَا إِن يُرِيدَا إِصْلَاحًا يُوَفِّقِ اللَّهُ بَيْنَهُمَا}$$

"If you fear a breach between them twain (the man and his wife), appointed (two) arbitrators, one from his family and the other from hers; if they both wish for peace, Allah will cause their reconciliation." (Qur'an 4: 35)
They must be honest and just in their financial dealings:

$$\text{وَلْيَكْتُب بَّيْنَكُمْ كَاتِبٌ بِالْعَدْلِ}$$

"Let a scribe write it down in justice between you." (Qur'an 2: 282)

$$\text{فَلْيُمْلِلْ وَلِيُّهُ بِالْعَدْلِ}$$

"Then let his guardian dictate in justice." (Qur'an 2: 282)
They must act justly in all matters that are of a judicial nature:

$$\text{وَأَشْهِدُوا ذَوَيْ عَدْلٍ مِّنكُمْ وَأَقِيمُوا الشَّهَادَةَ لِلَّهِ}$$

"And take for witness two just persons from among you (Muslims). And establish the witness for Allah." (Qur'an 65: 2)
Even in matters of worship – such as when one intentionally kills an animal that is forbidden to him because of the inviolability of the Sanctuary of Makkah - they must act justly:

$$\text{وَمَن قَتَلَهُ مِنكُم مُّتَعَمِّدًا فَجَزَاءٌ مِّثْلُ مَا قَتَلَ مِنَ النَّعَمِ يَحْكُمُ بِهِ ذَوَا عَدْلٍ مِّنكُمْ}$$

"And whosoever of you kills it intentionally, the penalty is an offering, brought to the Ka'bah, of an edible animal (i.e., sheep, goat, cow, etc.) equivalent to the one he killed, as adjudged by two just men among you." (Qur'an 5: 95)
They must act justly not only in their outward dealings, but also in the choices they make deep down in their hearts:

$$\text{وَلَا يَجْرِمَنَّكُمْ شَنَآنُ قَوْمٍ عَلَىٰ أَلَّا تَعْدِلُوا اعْدِلُوا هُوَ أَقْرَبُ لِلتَّقْوَىٰ}$$

"And let not the enmity and hatred of others make you avoid justice. Be just; that is nearer to piety." (Qur'an 5: 8)
When they act as rulers or judges, they most certainly must be just and fair:

$$\text{وَإِذَا حَكَمْتُم بَيْنَ النَّاسِ أَن تَحْكُمُوا بِالْعَدْلِ}$$

"And that when you judge between men, you judge with justice." (Qur'an 4: 58)
Even with their enemies they are commanded to act justly:

$$\text{وَقَاتِلُوهُمْ حَتَّىٰ لَا تَكُونَ فِتْنَةٌ وَيَكُونَ الدِّينُ لِلَّهِ فَإِنِ انتَهَوْا فَلَا عُدْوَانَ إِلَّا عَلَى الظَّالِمِينَ}$$

"And fight them until there is no more Fitnah (disbelief and worshiping of others along with Allah) and (all and every kind of) worship is for Allah (Alone). But if they cease, let there be no transgression except against Az-Zalimun (the polytheists, and wrongdoers, etc.)." (Qur'an 2:193)
And they are commanded to act justly with all of their Muslim brothers, with those among them who are noble and righteous, as well as with those among them who are evil-doers:

$$\text{فَقَاتِلُوا الَّتِي تَبْغِي حَتَّىٰ تَفِيءَ إِلَىٰ أَمْرِ اللَّهِ فَإِن فَاءَتْ فَأَصْلِحُوا بَيْنَهُمَا بِالْعَدْلِ وَأَقْسِطُوا إِنَّ اللَّهَ يُحِبُّ الْمُقْسِطِينَ}$$

"Then fight you (all) against the one that which rebels till it complies with the Command of Allah; then if it complies, then make reconciliation between them justly, and the equitable. Verily! Allah loves those who are equitable." (Qur'an 49: 9).
What we have discussed hitherto underscores the importance of justice; that being the case, we should not be surprised to learn that the command to act justly is part of the Covenant that Allah (sp) made with His slaves:

$$\text{وَأَوْفُوا۟ ٱلْكَيْلَ وَٱلْمِيزَانَ بِٱلْقِسْطِ ۖ لَا نُكَلِّفُ نَفْسًا إِلَّا وُسْعَهَا ۖ وَإِذَا قُلْتُمْ فَٱعْدِلُوا۟ وَلَوْ كَانَ ذَا قُرْبَىٰ ۖ وَبِعَهْدِ ٱللَّهِ أَوْفُوا۟ ۚ ذَٰلِكُمْ وَصَّىٰكُم بِهِۦ لَعَلَّكُمْ تَذَكَّرُونَ}$$

"And give full measure and full weight with justice. We burden not any person, but that which he can bear. And whenever you give your word (i.e., judge between men or give evidence, etc.), say the truth even if a near relative is concerned, and fulfill the Covenant of Allah, This He commands you, that you may remember." (Qur'an 6: 152).

True justice means that each person in society is given the rights he deserves; for this reason, many texts from the Qur'an and Sunnah explain in detail the rights of every individual – such as the rights of a father, mother, son, wife, husband, leader, and each citizen of the Muslim nation. A master is not the only one who is given rights in Islam; his slave is given an ample amount of rights as well.

That each individual Muslim receives the rights he deserves is perhaps most clearly noticeable in the Islamic laws of inheritance. Every relative gets his fair share of the deceased's estate: The father has a share, the mother has a share, as do sons, daughters, brothers, and sisters; and, when warranted, even extended family members can receive a share of the deceased's estate.

As for the penal code in Islamic Law, individual criminals receive a just punishment that fits the crime. Allah (sp) said:

$$\text{وَجَزَٰٓؤُا۟ سَيِّئَةٍ سَيِّئَةٌ مِّثْلُهَا}$$

"The recompense for an evil is an evil like thereof." (Qur'an 42: 40)
And in another Verse, Allah (sp): said:

$$\text{وَإِنْ عَاقَبْتُمْ فَعَاقِبُوا۟ بِمِثْلِ مَا عُوقِبْتُم بِهِۦ}$$

"And if you punish (your enemy, O you believers in the Oneness of Allah), then punish them with the like of that with which you were afflicted." (Qur'an 16: 126)

In summary, as long as we believe that the laws of Islam have been revealed by Allah (sp), and as long as we have faith in the fact that justice is one of Allah's attributes, we must consequently believe with certainty that the laws of Islam are perfect and just. Furthermore, we must have complete faith in the fact that justice is the dominant feature of Qur'anic legislations and laws.[79]

The concept of justice in the Qur'an is not limited to the goings on of this world; instead, it extends to what will happen in the Hereafter. In this world, human beings are charged with the duty of establishing justice on earth. In the Hereafter, however, Allah (sp) will take it upon Himself to be the sole distributor of justice, rewarding His obedient slaves with Paradise, and punishing His disbelieving slaves with the Hellfire. Allah (sp) said:

$$\text{وَقُلْ ءَامَنتُ بِمَآ أَنزَلَ ٱللَّهُ مِن كِتَٰبٍ ۖ وَأُمِرْتُ لِأَعْدِلَ بَيْنَكُمُ ۖ ٱللَّهُ رَبُّنَا وَرَبُّكُمْ لَنَآ أَعْمَٰلُنَا وَلَكُمْ أَعْمَٰلُكُمْ}$$

"But say: I believe in whatsoever Allah has sent down of the Book (all the holy Books, this Qur'an and the Books of the old from the Torah, or the Injeel (Gospel) or the Pages of Ibrahim (Abraham)) and I am commanded to do justice among you, Allah is our Lord and your Lord. For us our deeds and for you your deeds." (Qur'an 42: 15)

In these Verses we see how justice is strongly linked to both this world and the Hereafter. In the middle of the Verse, the Prophet (s) declares his responsibility to be just in his dealings among men, particularly regarding his duty to convey the message of Islam to them as well as situations wherein he is called upon to mediate their disputes. Then, in the end of the Verse, we are reminded of the fact that justice will be meted out to human beings in the Hereafter: Each person will be rewarded or punished

---

[79] *Min Mazaayaa At-Tashree' Al-Islaamee* (pg. 69, 70).

for his deeds, and each person will neither benefit from the good deeds of others nor be harmed by their misdeeds.

The Differences Between Justice in Islamic Law and Other Systems of Law

Manmade laws are at best superficial attempts at implementing justice. They deal only with the surface of problems and not with their root causes. This is a natural consequence of man not being fully acquainted with his own nature, never mind the nature of the universe's laws. Furthermore, manmade laws ignore issues such as faith in Allah (sp) and the Hereafter. Islamic Law, on the other hand, comes from Allah (sp), the Lord, Creator, and Sustainer of the universe. He (sp) best knows the nature of man, what is in his best interests, and the laws of the universe; hence He (sp) alone can decree a system of laws that is truly and completely just. In Islamic Law, individual Muslims act not merely out of a fear of being punished in this life for their crimes; their motives are much more profound and nuanced. They hold themselves accountable, fearing what will happen to them in the Hereafter as a result of their actions. Furthermore, they act out of a desire to be admitted into Paradise and to be saved from the Hellfire. Hollow Manmade laws do not have anywhere the same effect on individual citizens; under a system of manmade laws, the best members of society act based on the dictates of their consciences; under any given circumstances, they, in order to satisfy their consciences, do what they think is right. Everyone else tries to get away with as much as possible, abstaining from criminal acts only out of a fear of being punished by the authorities.

In Islam, Allah (sp) orders individual citizens to be just in all aspects of their lives:

يَٰٓأَيُّهَا ٱلَّذِينَ ءَامَنُوا۟ كُونُوا۟ قَوَّٰمِينَ بِٱلْقِسْطِ شُهَدَآءَ لِلَّهِ وَلَوْ عَلَىٰٓ أَنفُسِكُمْ أَوِ ٱلْوَٰلِدَيْنِ وَٱلْأَقْرَبِينَ

"O you who believe! Stand out firmly for justice, as witnesses to Allah, even though it be against yourselves, or your parents, or your kin." (Qur'an 4:135)

In this Verse, Allah (sp) uses the word *Qawwaameena* instead of *Qaaimeenah*. Had Allah (sp) used the latter, the Verse would have meant: "Stand out firmly for justice (which is the translation mentioned above; this goes to show that translations cannot give a true and complete rendering of the original Arabic of the Qur'an. But the Verse contains the former *Qawwaameenah* – which means more than "stand out firmly"; it means, with an added degree of emphasis, "Stand out firmly over and over again."

In Islamic Law, Muslims must be just even when dealing with those whom they hate:

وَلَا يَجْرِمَنَّكُمْ شَنَـَٔانُ قَوْمٍ عَلَىٰٓ أَلَّا تَعْدِلُوا۟

"And let not the enmity and hatred of others make you avoid justice. Be just: that is nearer to piety." (Qur'an 5: 8)

One of the main features of Islamic Law is the permanence and fixedness of its laws. What was the truth yesterday is the truth today, which is why the laws of Islam have been applicable from the time of the Prophet (s), and will continue to be applicable until the end of this world. Manmade laws, on the other hand, are constantly changing. Because of their arbitrary nature, manmade laws deem lawful a practice one year, and forbid it the next. One hundred years ago, for instance, the death penalty was in effect in England. In recent years, many Western countries have abolished the death penalty for many crimes, giving the excuse that the death penalty is an unjust and extreme form of punishment. What this means is that, by their own admission, they ruled over one another in the past in an unjust and oppressive manner. Such is the nature of manmade laws: Because it consists of falsehood, it always changes, whereas the foundations of the divinely revealed laws of Islam are permanent and fixed.

Testimonies from Islam's Enemies

Even during the lifetime of the Prophet (s), some of the staunchest of Islam's enemies bore witness to the justness of Islam's laws. The Prophet (s) and his Companions (rp), it should be remembered, lived in close proximity to communities from the People of the Book. In more than one instance, disputing

Jews or Christians, not being satisfied with the laws of their own religion, went to the Prophet (s), asking him to mediate their disputes based upon Islamic Law.

The justness of Islamic Law has caught the attention of many contemporary Christian thinkers and scholars. Here are just a few examples of what prominent Western figures have said about Islamic Law:

1) The eminent historian Gustav Laubon said, "The truth is that the Nations of this world have not seen conquerors that have been more forgiving and lenient than Arabs; nor have they encountered a religion that is more forgiving and merciful than that of the Arabs."[80]

2) The famous scholar Robertson said, "It is only the Muslims that have managed to combine a strong level of zeal for their religion with a spirit of forgiveness and justice towards the followers of other religions. Despite their great enthusiasm for spreading their religion, they, based on their own religious leave alone those who do not desire to embrace Islam."[81]

3) Maishod said, "The very Qur'an that has commanded its followers to perform Jihad is very forgiving towards the followers of other religions. For instance, it has exempted priests, monks, and their servants from the obligation of paying taxes. And Muhammad (s) forbade the killing of monks because of their dedication to acts of worship. And contrary to how the crusaders later slaughtered Muslims and barbarously burned Jews alive, Umar bin Al-Khattaab (r), upon entering Jerusalem, did not harm its Christian inhabitants in the least."[82]

4) Elsewhere in his book, Gustav Laubon wrote, "Unequivocally and sincerely, Arabs believe in and apply the principle of equality (among all members of society). True, equality is a principle that is championed in Europe, but it is championed with words and not actions. Conversely, equality is a principle that is deeply ingrained (for religious reasons) in the hearts of the people of the East. There is no precedent among Muslim societies of the class disparities (and struggles) that led to major upheavals in Western societies. The same class struggles continue to be waged today. In the East, however, it is not uncommon for a servant to marry the daughter of his master, or for mere laborers to climb the ladder of success until they became prosperous and highly-respected members of society."[83]

5) Dr. Will Durant expressed a similar degree of amazement at the degree to which the principle of equality is given importance in Qur'anic Law: "In Muslim societies, slaves were allowed to get married, and, if their children showed a basic level of intelligence, they would learn (under the tutelage of a master or teacher). One would probably be surprised upon learning of the number of children of slaves that later became eminent scholars or rulers. The most famous example of slaves becoming leaders after they embraced Islam is the history of the *Mamaaleek* of Egypt."[84]

PART 3

The Magnificence of the Qur'an Stories

This Part Consists of Two Sections:
Section One: Instances of Magnificence in the Qur'an's Stories

---

[80] *Hadaaratul-Arab* by Gustav Laubon, and translated by 'Aadil Zu'aitar (pg. 605).
[81] *Hadaaratul-Arab* by Gustav Laubon, and translated by 'Aadil Zu'aitar (pg. 127).
[82] *Hadaaratul-Arab* by Gustav Laubon, and translated by 'Aadil Zu'aitar (pg.127).
[83] *Hadaaratul-Arab* by Gustav Laubon, and translated by 'Aadil Zu'aitar (pg. 391).
[84] *Qissah Al-Hadaarah* by Dr. Durant, and translated by Zakee Najeeb Mahmood (3/112, 113); and *Al-Hukm Wat-Tahaakum Fee Khitaab Al-Wahyee* (1/415,417,419,422,423).

Section Two: The Magnificence of the Aims and Purposes of the Qur'an's Stories

Introduction

The relating of stories is one of the key ways in which the Qur'an seeks to further the spiritual development of Muslims. The stories of the Qur'an are historically true, providing us with a summary of the experiences of past nations and peoples. We learn about how they lived, what they did, and what reward they received from Allah (sp) for their actions. We learn not just about Prophets (st) and righteous people, but also about polytheists and evildoers, as well as about the consequences of their actions. In short, the Qur'an's stories teach us about certain universal laws that govern the fate of nations and peoples. So, for instance, if we, as a nation, want to avoid the fate that befell nations of the past, we must avoid committing the same mistakes that they made.

The Noble Qur'an provides us with vivid descriptions of the lives of various historical individuals and peoples. It is up to us, then, to contemplate their lives and to benefit from the myriad of lessons that their stories contain. We should emulate those historical figures who strove patiently to uphold the truth and who, in spite of the hardships they temporarily endured, achieved ultimate success: Forgiveness from Allah (sp) and Paradise. Conversely, we should avoid imitating those who turned away from Allah (sp); and consequently were made to suffer miserable lives, and, what is worse, were doomed to an eternity in the Hellfire. Allah (sp) said:

لَقَدْ كَانَ فِى قَصَصِهِمْ عِبْرَةٌ لِّأُولِى ٱلْأَلْبَـٰبِ ۗ مَا كَانَ حَدِيثًا يُفْتَرَىٰ وَلَـٰكِن تَصْدِيقَ ٱلَّذِى بَيْنَ يَدَيْهِ وَتَفْصِيلَ كُلِّ شَىْءٍ وَهُدًى وَرَحْمَةً لِّقَوْمٍ يُؤْمِنُونَ

"Indeed in their stories, there is a lesson for men of understanding. It (the Qur'an) is not a forged statement but a confirmation of Allah's existing Books (the Torah, the Injeel (Gospel) and other Scriptures of Allah (sp)) and a detailed explanation of everything and a guide and a Mercy for the people who believe." (Qur'an 12:111)

It is a tremendous blessing from Allah (sp) that the stories of past nations remain preserved for us in the Noble Qur'an. The Quran's description of the lives of past peoples remains pure and uncorrupted, unlike the stories found in the Torah and the Injeel (The Gospel), which have been corrupted and distorted and altered. The stories of the Qur'an, like the rest of the Qur'an, will remain preserved and unchanged as long as there is life on earth, and as long as the sun sets and rises. Allah said:

إِنَّا نَحْنُ نَزَّلْنَا ٱلذِّكْرَ وَإِنَّا لَهُ لَحَـٰفِظُونَ

"Verily We: It is We Who have sent down the Dhikr (i.e., the Qur'an) and surely, We will guard it (from corruption)." (Qur'an 15: 9)

Section One:

Instances of Magnificence in the Qur'an's Stories

The stories of the Qur'an differ from the stories of men in a variety of ways. Like the rest of the Qur'an, Verses that contain in them stories of past nations are miraculously wrought – with impeccably eloquent speech and profoundly wise lessons. Here are some of the main features of the superiority and magnificence of the Qur'an's stories:

1) Their Divine Source

The Qur'anic Verses that contain in them stories are like any other part of the Qur'an. Therefore, everything we have hitherto discussed about the miraculous nature of the Qur'an applies to those of the Qur'an's Verses that discuss the histories of past peoples. Furthermore, like the rest of the Qur'an, Verses that discuss the histories of past peoples have been revealed by Allah (sp) to Prophet Muhammad (s). They are the words of Allah (sp) alone, and the sole contribution the Prophet (s) made to those Verses was conveying them to people in the exact same form and manner in which they were revealed to him. Allah (sp) mentioned this reality in the beginning and end of certain stories; for instance, in Chapter *Hood*, He (sp) said:

تِلْكَ مِنْ أَنۢبَآءِ ٱلْغَيْبِ نُوحِيهَآ إِلَيْكَ ۖ مَا كُنتَ تَعْلَمُهَآ أَنتَ وَلَا قَوْمُكَ مِن قَبْلِ هَـٰذَا

"This is of the news out of the unseen which We reveal unto you (O Muhammad (s)), neither you nor your people knew them before this." (Qur'an 11:49)

2) Their Exact Correspondence with what Actually Took Place Historically

All of the stories that are found in the Noble Qur'an are completely true; everything that is described in any given story actually took place at one point in time in history. Every detail and every nuance of each story is precise and accurate.

Qur'anic stories are superior to the stories and narrations of men in many ways, but in one major way in particular. If you or I witness an event and then relate it to others, we can simply mention the things we saw and heard; our stories will be limited to what outwardly happened, and that is all. If we try to relate the thoughts of the people that were involved in the incident, we will most likely have to rely on conjecture or our imagination. As for the incidents that are recorded in the Qur'an, Allah (sp) witnessed everything about them. He (sp), being the All-Seer and the All-Hearer, not only knows with complete precision the events that occurred, but also knows – given that He (sp) knows everything that is in the hearts of men – what all of the participants of those events were thinking deep down in their hearts.

A further difference between the Qur'an's stories and the stories of men revolves around the meaning of the word "story". If a human being says, "Let me tell you a story, he could either be referring to a true occurrence or to something that his imagination conjured up and that has no basis on an actual event in reality. As for the stories of the Qur'an, they are all one-hundred percent true, a fact that is made clear in the following two Verses of the Qur'an:

إِنَّ هَـٰذَا لَهُوَ ٱلْقَصَصُ ٱلْحَقُّ

"Verily! This is the true narrative about the story of 'Iesa (Jesus)" (Qur'an 3: 62)

لَقَدْ كَانَ فِى قَصَصِهِمْ عِبْرَةٌ لِّأُو۟لِى ٱلْأَلْبَـٰبِ ۗ مَا كَانَ حَدِيثًا يُفْتَرَىٰ وَلَـٰكِن تَصْدِيقَ ٱلَّذِى بَيْنَ يَدَيْهِ وَتَفْصِيلَ كُلِّ شَىْءٍ وَهُدًى وَرَحْمَةً لِّقَوْمٍ يُؤْمِنُونَ

"Indeed in their stories, there is a lesson for men of understanding. It (the Qur'an) is not a forged statement but a confirmation of Allah's existing Books and a detailed explanation of everything and a guide and a Mercy for the people who believe." (Qur'an 12:111)

Not even Jews or Christians were able to deny the authenticity and truthfulness of the Qur'an's stories, many of which were known, either in part or in their entirety, to the People of the Book. The Jews of Al-Madeenah were determined to disprove any part of the Qur'an, particularly those parts that contained stories, but they failed to find any mistake in them. In fact, on one occasion, they asked the Prophet (s) about Dhil-Qarnain, whose story they knew since it was found in their scriptures. In answer to their question, Allah (sp) revealed Dhil-Qarnain's story to the Prophet (s) with such precise and true details that the Jews of Al-Madeenah could find no mistake in it whatsoever. Allah (sp) began the Verses that contained Dhil-Qarnain's story with His saying:

وَيَسْتَلُونَكَ عَن ذِى ٱلْقَرْنَيْنِ

"And they ask you about Dhul-Qarnain." (Qur'an 18: 83)

In the Noble Qur'an, Allah (sp) related not just any set of stories, but those stories that imparted important and profound lessons; in short, He (sp) related only "the best of stories":

نَحْنُ نَقُصُّ عَلَيْكَ أَحْسَنَ ٱلْقَصَصِ بِمَآ أَوْحَيْنَآ إِلَيْكَ هَٰذَا ٱلْقُرْءَانَ وَإِن كُنتَ مِن قَبْلِهِۦ لَمِنَ ٱلْغَٰفِلِينَ

"We relate unto you (Muhammad (s)) the best of stories through Our Revelations unto you, of this Qur'an. And before this (i.e., before the coming of Divine Inspiration to you), you were among those who knew nothing about it (the Qur'an)." (Qur'an 12:3)

3) Mentioning the Key Parts of Stories

The stories of the Qur'an are not always mentioned in their entirety; rather, a key part of a story is often mentioned all by itself. This methodology of storytelling is unique and has a powerful effect on the reader, for he is exposed, in an eloquent manner, to the part of a story that contains in it important lessons and morals. So, for instance, the beginning of the story of Adam (p) is mentioned in one part of the Qur'an; its middle elsewhere; and its ending elsewhere. When an entire story is relevant and full of lessons, such as is the case regarding the story of Yusuf (p), Allah (sp) relates it in its entirety. At other times, Allah (sp) relates only that part of a story that has to do with a Messenger's duty to convey his message, as is the case with the Qur'anic stories of Noah (p) and Hood (p). In short, what part of a story Allah (sp) relates in the Noble Qur'an depends on the morals and lessons He (sp) wants to impart in a given set of Verses.

4) Telling the Same Story in a Variety of Ways, or in Other Words, Repetition

Repetition, repetition, repetition: Man is in dire need of constant repetition and reminders if he wants to remain steadfast upon the truth. And since one of the aims of the Qur'an is to guide believers to remain steadfast upon the truth, Allah (sp) repeats various stories, relating them in more than one part of the Qur'an.

Without a doubt, the path to spiritual development is fraught with difficulties and temptations. One can follow the truth his entire life, only to fall into the trap of sin and temptation during the latter years of his life (may Allah protect us from such an ending). For this reason, and because man is forgetful by nature, every Muslim needs to be reminded of his duties on a continual basis; otherwise, a lifetime of efforts can be wasted in a moment of lust or anger or ignorance.

Therefore, repetition is a valuable tool in the process of maintaining spiritual wellness and purification of the soul. If one repeats something over and over again, it becomes second nature to him. One of the primary goals of the Qur'an is to guide human beings and to nurture their spiritual development; it is only logical, therefore, that many lessons, teachings, and even stories are repeated over and over again throughout the Noble Qur'an.[85]

Section Two:

The Magnificence of the Aims and Purposes of the Qur'an's Stories

The purpose behind the Qur'an's stories is not simply to explain certain historical events; nor is it merely the idea of enlightening us about how the people of past nations lived; nor is it merely to console or amuse us. In fact, we cannot correctly assert that there is one true purpose behind the stories of the Qur'an, for there are many, and each of them revolves around the overall goal of instilling people with faith and then cementing it into their hearts.

Since, given the scope of this work, I cannot discuss each purpose behind the stories of the Qur'an, I will briefly discuss the most important ones. My aim here is to show the reader that the stories of the Qur'an were not chosen randomly, but instead were chosen for reasons of great import, such as those that follow:

1) To Establish the Oneness of Allah (sp), and to Order Human Beings to Worship Him Alone

Most of the Qur'an's stories have a great deal to do with the missions of past Prophets and Messengers (st), each of whom invited his people to worship none save Allah (sp), without associating any partner with Him. Even though they all had the same goal, they, depending upon their situation, relied on different approaches to invite their people to embrace Islam. The Qur'anic stories that describe the doings of Prophets and Messengers (st) focus on their efforts to invite their people to worship the One True God, Allah (sp), and to convince them to turn away from all forms of polytheism and idolatry.

There are many proofs from the Qur'an which establish the fact that all Prophets and Messengers (st) invited their people to embrace *Tawheed* (true Islamic Monotheism). For example, there is the story of Ibraaheem (p), which describes how he went about explaining *Tawheed* to his father:

وَإِذْ قَالَ إِبْرَاهِيمُ لِأَبِيهِ ءَازَرَ أَتَتَّخِذُ أَصْنَامًا ءَالِهَةً إِنِّى أَرَىٰكَ وَقَوْمَكَ فِى ضَلَـٰلٍ مُّبِينٍ

"And (remember) when Ibraheem (Abraham) said to his father Azar: Do you take idols as aliha (gods)? Verily, I see you and your people in manifest error." (Qur'an 6:74)

To the Saying of Allah (sp):

إِنِّى وَجَّهْتُ وَجْهِىَ لِلَّذِى فَطَرَ ٱلسَّمَـٰوَٰتِ وَٱلْأَرْضَ حَنِيفًا وَمَآ أَنَا۠ مِنَ ٱلْمُشْرِكِينَ

"Verily, I have turned my face towards Him Who has created the heavens and the earth Hanifa (Islamic Monotheism, i.e., worshiping none but Allah Alone) and I am not of Al-Mushrikun." (Qur'an 6: 79)

In Chapter *Al-Baqarah*, Allah (sp) relates to us how Ya'qub (p) made sure his children would be worshippers of the One True God, Allah (sp):

---

[85] *Ma'aalim Al-Qissah Fil-Qur'an Al-Adheem* (pgs. 118-120).

أَمْ كُنتُمْ شُهَدَاءَ إِذْ حَضَرَ يَعْقُوبَ ٱلْمَوْتُ إِذْ قَالَ لِبَنِيهِ مَا تَعْبُدُونَ مِنْ بَعْدِى قَالُوا۟ نَعْبُدُ إِلَـٰهَكَ وَإِلَـٰهَ ءَابَآئِكَ إِبْرَٰهِـۧمَ وَإِسْمَـٰعِيلَ وَإِسْحَـٰقَ إِلَـٰهًا وَٰحِدًا وَنَحْنُ لَهُۥ مُسْلِمُونَ

"Or were you witnesses when death approached Ya'qub (Jacob)? When he said unto his sons, 'What will you worship after me?' They said, 'We shall worship your Ilah (God – Allah) the Ilah (God) of your fathers, Ibrahim (Abraham), Ismail (Ishmael, Ishaque, Isaac), One Ilah (God), and to Him we submit (in Islam)." (Qur'an 2: 133)

In various parts of Chapter *Al-A'raaf*, Allah (sp) relates to us what Noah, Hood, Saaleh, and Shuaib (st) said to their people when they invited them to embrace Islam:

لَقَدْ أَرْسَلْنَا نُوحًا إِلَىٰ قَوْمِهِۦ فَقَالَ يَـٰقَوْمِ ٱعْبُدُوا۟ ٱللَّهَ مَا لَكُم مِّنْ إِلَـٰهٍ غَيْرُهُۥ

"Indeed, We sent Nuh (Noah) to his people and he said, 'O my people! Worship Allah! You have no other Ilah (God) but Him (none has the right to be worshiped but Allah).'" (Qur'an 7:59)

وَإِلَىٰ عَادٍ أَخَاهُمْ هُودًا قَالَ يَـٰقَوْمِ ٱعْبُدُوا۟ ٱللَّهَ مَا لَكُم مِّنْ إِلَـٰهٍ غَيْرُهُۥ

"And to 'Ad (people, We sent) their brother Hud. He said: 'O my people! Worship Allah! You have no other Ilah (God) but Him (none has the right to be worshiped but Allah).'" (Qur'an 7: 65)

وَإِلَىٰ ثَمُودَ أَخَاهُمْ صَـٰلِحًا قَالَ يَـٰقَوْمِ ٱعْبُدُوا۟ ٱللَّهَ مَا لَكُم مِّنْ إِلَـٰهٍ غَيْرُهُۥ

"And to Thamud (people, We sent) their brother Salih (Saleh). He said: 'O my people! Worship Allah! You have no other Ilah (God) but Him (none has the right to be worshiped but Allah).'" (Qur'an 7: 73)

وَإِلَىٰ مَدْيَنَ أَخَاهُمْ شُعَيْبًا قَالَ يَـٰقَوْمِ ٱعْبُدُوا۟ ٱللَّهَ مَا لَكُم مِّنْ إِلَـٰهٍ غَيْرُهُۥ

"And to (the people of) Madyan (Midian), (We sent) their brother Shu'aib. He said: 'O my people! Worship Allah! You have no other Ilah (God) but Him (none has the right to be worshiped but Allah).'" (Qur'an 7: 85)

The theme of *Tawheed* (Islamic Monotheism) is further discussed in the story of Sulaimaan (p):

أَلَّا يَسْجُدُوا۟ لِلَّهِ ٱلَّذِى يُخْرِجُ ٱلْخَبْءَ فِى ٱلسَّمَـٰوَٰتِ وَٱلْأَرْضِ وَيَعْلَمُ مَا تُخْفُونَ وَمَا تُعْلِنُونَ
ٱللَّهُ لَا إِلَـٰهَ إِلَّا هُوَ رَبُّ ٱلْعَرْشِ ٱلْعَظِيمِ

"(As-Shaitan (Satan) has barred them from Allah's Way) so that they do not worship (prostrate before) Allah; Who brings to light what is hidden in the heavens and the earth, and knows what you conceal and what you reveal. Allah, La ilaha illa Huwa (none has the right to be worshiped but He), the Lord of the Supreme Throne" (Qur'an 27:25, 26)

Tawheed is also discussed in the story of Moosa (p):

إِنَّنِىٓ أَنَا ٱللَّهُ لَآ إِلَـٰهَ إِلَّآ أَنَا۠ فَٱعْبُدْنِى وَأَقِمِ ٱلصَّلَوٰةَ لِذِكْرِى

"Verily! I am Allah! La ilaha illa Ana (none has the right to be worshiped but I), so worship Me, and perform As-Salat (Iqamat-as-Salat) for My Remembrance." (Qur'an 20:14)

And in Chapter *Yusuf*, we are informed of how Yusuf (p), even while in prison, invited others to embrace Islam:

$$\text{قَالَ لَا يَأْتِيكُمَا طَعَامٌ تُرْزَقَانِهِ إِلَّا نَبَّأْتُكُمَا بِتَأْوِيلِهِ قَبْلَ أَن يَأْتِيَكُمَا ذَالِكُمَا مِمَّا عَلَّمَنِي رَبِّي إِنِّي تَرَكْتُ مِلَّةَ قَوْمٍ لَّا يُؤْمِنُونَ بِاللَّهِ وَهُم بِالْآخِرَةِ هُمْ كَافِرُونَ}$$

"He said: No food will come to you (in wakefulness or in dream) as your provision, but I will inform (in wakefulness) its interpretation before it (the food) comes. This is of that which my Lord has taught me. Verily, I have abandoned the religion of a people that believe not in Allah and are disbelievers in the Hereafter (i.e., the Kananium of Egypt who were polytheists and used to worship sun and other false deities)." (Qur'an 12:37)

To the Saying of Allah (sp):

$$\text{إِنِ الْحُكْمُ إِلَّا لِلَّهِ أَمَرَ أَلَّا تَعْبُدُوا إِلَّا إِيَّاهُ ذَالِكَ الدِّينُ الْقَيِّمُ وَلَكِنَّ أَكْثَرَ النَّاسِ لَا يَعْلَمُونَ}$$

"The command (or the judgment) is for none but Allah. He has commanded that you worship none but Him (i.e., His Monotheism, that is the (true) straight religion), but most men know not." (Qur'an 12:40)

Yusuf (p) made it clear in the abovementioned Verses that he was not inventing a new religion, but was instead following the religion of his fathers and forefathers, who were all guided by Allah (sp) to the truth and to true beliefs. The aforementioned Verses teach us that all Prophets and Messengers (p) invited their people to embrace *Tawheed* (Islamic Monotheism); but they also show us how individuals among them resorted to unique approaches to achieve their overall goal. Noah (p), the Qur'an informs us, feared that, if his people disobeyed him and acted contrary to Allah's command, they would face a severe torment from Allah (sp). Hood (p) demanded from his people that they fear Allah (sp), since they had no true God but Him (sp). Saleh (p) told his people that he came to them with a clear sign – the camel of Allah (sp) – and that they should leave it alone, allowing it to graze freely on Allah's earth. He ordered them not to harm it, fearing for them a painful punishment if they disobeyed him. The different approaches of the Prophets (st) resulted in different ways that people expressed their disbelief. The people of Noah (p), for example, accused him of being in manifest error. The people of Hood (p) accused him of being foolish and a liar. And the people of Saleh (p) expressed their doubts about him being sent to them by Allah (sp).[86]

2) Confirming the Truthfulness of the Prophet's Mission (s)

The stories of the Qur'an discuss events of the unseen world, since past events are part of the unseen world for everyone other than those who were alive when they transpired. Therefore, the Qur'an describes much that neither the Prophet (s) nor his people knew about. After relating the story of Noah (p) Allah (sp) made the same point clear when He (sp) said:

$$\text{تِلْكَ مِنْ أَنبَاءِ الْغَيْبِ نُوحِيهَا إِلَيْكَ مَا كُنتَ تَعْلَمُهَا أَنتَ وَلَا قَوْمُكَ مِن قَبْلِ هَذَا فَاصْبِرْ إِنَّ الْعَاقِبَةَ لِلْمُتَّقِينَ}$$

"This is of the news of the unseen which We reveal unto you (O Muhammad (s)), neither you nor your people knew them before this. So be patient. Surely, the (good) end is for the Muttaqun (pious ones)." (Qur'an 11:49)

And following the story of Moosa (p) Allah (sp) said:

---

[86] *Diraasaat Qur'aaniyyah* (pg. 25).

$$وَمَا كُنتَ بِجَانِبِ ٱلْغَرْبِىِّ إِذْ قَضَيْنَآ إِلَىٰ مُوسَى ٱلْأَمْرَ وَمَا كُنتَ مِنَ ٱلشَّٰهِدِينَ$$

"And you (O Muhammad (s)) were not on the western side (of the Mount), when We made clear to Moosa (Moses) the commandment, and you were not among those present."
To the Saying of Allah (sp):

$$وَمَا كُنتَ بِجَانِبِ ٱلطُّورِ إِذْ نَادَيْنَا$$

"And you (O Muhammad (s)) were not at the side of the Tur (Mount) when We did call." (Qur'an 28: 44 and 46)

Add to that the fact that the Prophet (s) was illiterate, having never read a book or studied under the tutelage of a teacher. Yet in spite of all of that, historical events are described in a great amount of detail in the Qur'an. Great detail in storytelling is usually accompanied by mistakes and contradictions, and yet the Qur'an's stories contain not a single mistake or contradiction. All of this clearly shows us that the stories of the Qur'an were revealed by Allah (sp), thus proving the truthfulness of the Prophet's mission.[87] Thus it is clear that one of the aims of the Qur'an's stories is to provide us with clear proofs that the Qur'an was revealed to the Prophet (s) by Allah (sp). Allah (sp) said:

$$إِنَّآ أَنزَلْنَٰهُ قُرْءَٰنًا عَرَبِيًّا لَّعَلَّكُمْ تَعْقِلُونَ$$
$$نَحْنُ نَقُصُّ عَلَيْكَ أَحْسَنَ ٱلْقَصَصِ بِمَآ أَوْحَيْنَآ إِلَيْكَ هَٰذَا ٱلْقُرْءَانَ وَإِن كُنتَ مِن قَبْلِهِۦ لَمِنَ ٱلْغَٰفِلِينَ$$

"Verily, We have sent it down as an Arabic Qur'an in order that you may understand. We relate unto you (Muhammad (s)) the best of stories through Our Revelations unto you, of this Qur'an. And before this (i.e., before the coming of Divine Inspiration to you), you were among those who knew nothing about it (the Qur'an)." (Qur'an 12: 2, 3)
In Chapter Aal-Imraan, Allah (sp) said:

$$ذَٰلِكَ مِنْ أَنۢبَآءِ ٱلْغَيْبِ نُوحِيهِ إِلَيْكَ وَمَا كُنتَ لَدَيْهِمْ إِذْ يُلْقُونَ أَقْلَٰمَهُمْ أَيُّهُمْ يَكْفُلُ مَرْيَمَ وَمَا كُنتَ لَدَيْهِمْ إِذْ يَخْتَصِمُونَ$$

"This is a part of the news of the Ghaib (unseen, i.e., the news of the past nations of which you have no knowledge) which We inspire you with (O Muhammad (s)), You were not with them, when they cast lots with their pens as to which of them should be charged with the care of Muryum (Mary); nor were you with them when they disputed." (Qur'an 3:44)
And in Chapter Ash-Shu'araa, Allah (sp) said:

$$وَإِنَّهُۥ لَتَنزِيلُ رَبِّ ٱلْعَٰلَمِينَ (١٩٢) نَزَلَ بِهِ ٱلرُّوحُ ٱلْأَمِينُ (١٩٣) عَلَىٰ قَلْبِكَ لِتَكُونَ مِنَ ٱلْمُنذِرِينَ (١٩٤)$$

"And truly, this (the Qur'an) is a revelation from the Lord of the 'Alamin (mankind, jinns, and all that exists), which the trustworthy Ruh (Jibreel, Gabriel) has brought down; upon your heart (O Muhammad (s)) that you may be (one) of the warners." (Qur'an 26; 192-194)

3) Establishing the Reality of Resurrection After Death

---

[87] *Tafseer AtTabaree* (14/140).

The stories of the Qur'an contain important lessons about a variety of issues. An oft-repeated lesson of the Qur'an's stories involves confirming the reality of life after death, as well as of being rewarded for one's actions after death. A clear example of this is the story of Ibraheem (p), which is related to us towards the end of Chapter Al-*Baqarah*:

$$\text{أَلَمْ تَرَ إِلَى ٱلَّذِى حَاجَّ إِبْرَاهِۦمَ فِى رَبِّهِۦٓ أَنْ ءَاتَىٰهُ ٱللَّهُ ٱلْمُلْكَ إِذْ قَالَ إِبْرَاهِۦمُ رَبِّىَ ٱلَّذِى يُحْىِۦ وَيُمِيتُ}$$

"Have you not looked at him who disputed with Ibraheem (Abraham) about his Lord (Allah) because Allah had given him the kingdom? When Ibraheem (Abraham) said (to him): 'My Lord (Allah) is He Who gives life and causes death.'"

To the Saying of Allah (sp):

$$\text{قَالَ فَخُذْ أَرْبَعَةً مِّنَ ٱلطَّيْرِ فَصُرْهُنَّ إِلَيْكَ ثُمَّ ٱجْعَلْ عَلَىٰ كُلِّ جَبَلٍ مِّنْهُنَّ جُزْءًا ثُمَّ ٱدْعُهُنَّ يَأْتِينَكَ سَعْيًا وَٱعْلَمْ أَنَّ ٱللَّهَ عَزِيزٌ حَكِيمٌ}$$

"He said: 'Take four birds, then cause them to incline towards you (then slaughter them, cut them into pieces), and then put a portion of them on every hill, and call them, they will come to you in haste. And know that Allah is All-Mighty, All-Wise.'" (Qur'an 2; 258 and 260)

And in Chapter *Noah*, Allah (sp) related that Noah (p) said:

$$\text{يَغْفِرْ لَكُم مِّن ذُنُوبِكُمْ وَيُؤَخِّرْكُمْ إِلَىٰٓ أَجَلٍ مُّسَمًّى إِنَّ أَجَلَ ٱللَّهِ إِذَا جَآءَ لَا يُؤَخَّرُ لَوْ كُنتُمْ تَعْلَمُونَ}$$

"He (Allah) will forgive you of your sins and respite you to an appointed term. Verily, the term of Allah when it comes, cannot be delayed, if you but knew.'" (Qur'an 71: 4)

4) Strengthening the Faith and Resolve of the Prophet (s) and of True Believers

Without a doubt, one of the primary purposes of the Qur'an's stories is strengthening the faith and resolve of believers during periods of hardship. The Prophet (s) and his Companions (rp) faced persecution at the hands of the Quraish. Derision, ridicule, as well as mental and physical torture were meted out to Muslims on a daily basis. And yet as much as certain Companions (rp) suffered, some Muslims who came before them suffered just as much or more. And so, in order to console the Prophet's Companions (rp), Allah (sp) related stories about the hardships that were suffered by Muslims of previous nations. Such stories were meant for the Prophet (s) as well. For he was not the only Prophet who faced persecution at the hands of his people; there were many Prophets (st) before him who faced similar circumstances; some of them were even killed by their own people. Qur'anic stories that related their ordeals had the effect of consoling the Prophet (s). The stories of past Prophets (st) and believers taught an important lesson to the Prophet (s) and his Companions (rp): In the end, truth always overcomes falsehood. Allah (sp) said:

$$\text{وَكُلًّا نَّقُصُّ عَلَيْكَ مِنْ أَنۢبَآءِ ٱلرُّسُلِ مَا نُثَبِّتُ بِهِۦ فُؤَادَكَ وَجَآءَكَ فِى هَٰذِهِ ٱلْحَقُّ وَمَوْعِظَةٌ وَذِكْرَىٰ لِلْمُؤْمِنِينَ}$$

"And all that We relate to you (O Muhammad (s)) of the news of the Messengers is in order that We may make strong and firm your heart thereby. And in this (Chapter of the Qur'an) has come to you the truth, as well as an admonition and a reminder for the believers." (Qur'an 11: 120)

The Prophet (s) was informed of the fact that some Prophets (st) worked day and night to convince their people to embrace Islam, and yet in spite of their valiant efforts, their people remained intransigently committed to following evil. Such was certainly the case regarding Noah (p) and his people, a point that is made amply clear in the following Verses:

قَالَ رَبِّ إِنِّى دَعَوْتُ قَوْمِى لَيْلاً وَنَهَارًا (٥) فَلَمْ يَزِدْهُمْ دُعَآءِىٓ إِلَّا فِرَارًا (٦) وَإِنِّى كُلَّمَا دَعَوْتُهُمْ لِتَغْفِرَ لَهُمْ جَعَلُوٓاْ أَصَـٰبِعَهُمْ فِىٓ ءَاذَانِهِمْ وَٱسْتَغْشَوْاْ ثِيَابَهُمْ وَأَصَرُّواْ وَٱسْتَكْبَرُواْ ٱسْتِكْبَارًا (٧)

"He said: O my Lord! Verily, I have called my people night and day (i.e., secretly and openly to accept the doctrine of Islamic Monotheism), but all my calling added nothing but to (their) flight (from the truth). And verily! Every time I called unto them that You might forgive them, they thrust their fingers into their ears, covered themselves up with their garments, and persisted (in their refusal), and magnified themselves in pride." (Qur'an and 71: 5-7)

Later on in Chapter *Noah*, Allah (sp) said:

قَالَ نُوحٌ رَّبِّ إِنَّهُمْ عَصَوْنِى وَٱتَّبَعُواْ مَن لَّمْ يَزِدْهُ مَالُهُۥ وَوَلَدُهُۥٓ إِلَّا خَسَارًا

"Nuh (Noah) said: 'My Lord! They have disobeyed me, and followed one whose wealth and children give him no increase but only loss.'" (Qur'an 71: 21)

5) Teaching Muslims Important Lessons about Prophets (st) and about the People to Whom They were Sent

The lessons of the Qur'an are clear. But to make their application in everyday life easier to understand, they are given life through the characters and personages of past nations. Thus we are not only told about the importance of being patient and of conveying the message of Islam to others, we are told about how Prophets and Messengers (st) did those very things. Conversely, we are not only prohibited from perpetrating acts of disbelief, we are informed about how certain peoples from the past were guilty of those crimes, and we are further informed about the consequences they suffered as a result of their crimes. Allah (sp) said:

لَقَدْ كَانَ فِى قَصَصِهِمْ عِبْرَةٌ لِّأُوْلِى ٱلْأَلْبَـٰبِ

"Indeed in their stories, there is a lesson for men of understanding." (Qur'an 12:111)
And in another Verse, Allah (sp) said:

وَلَقَدْ كُذِّبَتْ رُسُلٌ مِّن قَبْلِكَ فَصَبَرُواْ عَلَىٰ مَا كُذِّبُواْ وَأُوذُواْ حَتَّىٰٓ أَتَىٰهُمْ نَصْرُنَا وَلَا مُبَدِّلَ لِكَلِمَـٰتِ ٱللَّهِ وَلَقَدْ جَآءَكَ مِن نَّبَإِى۟ ٱلْمُرْسَلِينَ

"Verily, many Messengers were denied before you (O Muhammad (s)), but with patience they bore the denial, and they were hurt, till Our Help reached them, and none can alter the Words (Decisions) of Allah. Surely there has reached you the information (news) about the Messengers (before you)." (Qur'an :34)

6) Pointing Out the End Destinations of the People of Past Nations

Most people from past nations disbelieved in the Prophets (st) that were sent to them. What is more, they answered their Prophets' invitations with evil and slanderous words, and sometimes even with violence. For instance, the people of Noah (p) said:

إِنَّا لَنَرَىٰكَ فِى ضَلَـٰلٍ مُّبِينٍ

"Verily, we see you in plain error." (Qur'an 7: 60)
The people of Hood (p) said:

$$\text{إِنَّا لَنَرَاكَ فِى سَفَاهَةٍ وَإِنَّا لَنَظُنُّكَ مِنَ ٱلْكَاذِبِينَ}$$

"Verily, we see you in foolishness, and verily, we think you are one of the liars." (Qur'an 7: 66)
The people of Saleh (p) said to his followers:

$$\text{إِنَّا بِٱلَّذِىٓ ءَامَنتُم بِهِۦ كَافِرُونَ}$$

"Verily, we disbelieve in that which you believe in" (Qur'an 7: 76).

The people of Loot (p) said:

$$\text{أَخْرِجُوهُم مِّن قَرْيَتِكُمْ إِنَّهُمْ أُنَاسٌ يَتَطَهَّرُونَ}$$

"Drive them out of your town; these are indeed men who want to be pure (from sins)!" (Qur'an 7:82)
The people of Shu'aib (p) said:

$$\text{نُخْرِجَنَّكَ يَـٰشُعَيْبُ وَٱلَّذِينَ ءَامَنُوا۟ مَعَكَ مِن قَرْيَتِنَآ أَوْ لَتَعُودُنَّ فِى مِلَّتِنَا}$$

"We shall certainly drive you out, O Shu'aib, and those who have believed with you from our town, or else you (all) shall return to our religion." (Qur'an 7: 88)
And the people of Fir'aun said about Moosa (p):

$$\text{إِنَّ هَـٰذَا لَسَـٰحِرٌ عَلِيمٌ}$$

"This is indeed a well-versed sorcerer." (Qur'an 7: 109)
The peoples of these nations, as a result of their disbelief and rejection of their Prophets (st) were destroyed and were doomed to eternal damnation in the Hellfire. Allah (sp) said:

$$\text{أَلَمْ يَرَوْا۟ كَمْ أَهْلَكْنَا مِن قَبْلِهِم مِّن قَرْنٍ مَّكَّنَّـٰهُمْ فِى ٱلْأَرْضِ مَا لَمْ نُمَكِّن لَّكُمْ وَأَرْسَلْنَا ٱلسَّمَآءَ عَلَيْهِم مِّدْرَارًا وَجَعَلْنَا ٱلْأَنْهَـٰرَ تَجْرِى مِن تَحْتِهِمْ فَأَهْلَكْنَـٰهُم بِذُنُوبِهِمْ وَأَنشَأْنَا مِنۢ بَعْدِهِمْ قَرْنًا ءَاخَرِينَ}$$

"Have they not seen how many a generation before them. We have destroyed whom We had established on the earth such as We have not established you? And We poured out on them rain from the sky in abundance, and made the rivers flow under them. Yet We destroyed them for their sins, and created after them other generations." (Qur'an 6: 6)
In another Verse, Allah (sp) said:

$$\text{أَوَلَمْ يَسِيرُوا۟ فِى ٱلْأَرْضِ فَيَنظُرُوا۟ كَيْفَ كَانَ عَـٰقِبَةُ ٱلَّذِينَ مِن قَبْلِهِمْ كَانُوٓا۟ أَشَدَّ مِنْهُمْ قُوَّةً وَأَثَارُوا۟ ٱلْأَرْضَ وَعَمَرُوهَآ أَكْثَرَ مِمَّا عَمَرُوهَا وَجَآءَتْهُمْ رُسُلُهُم بِٱلْبَيِّنَـٰتِ فَمَا كَانَ ٱللَّهُ لِيَظْلِمَهُمْ وَلَـٰكِن كَانُوٓا۟ أَنفُسَهُمْ يَظْلِمُونَ}$$

"Do they not travel in the land, and see what was the end of those before them? They were superior to them in strength, and they tilled the earth and populated it in greater numbers than these (pagans) have done, and there came to them their Messengers with clear proofs. Surely, Allah wronged them not, but they used to wrong themselves." (Qur'an 30: 9)

As Muslims, we should read the Qur'an's stories of past nations as they should be read: with trembling hearts and with an appreciation of the fact that, if we want to avoid a similar fate and a similar awful destination, we must avoid making the same mistakes that the disbelievers of past nations made when they were alive.

In the Noble Qur'an, Allah (sp) informs us not only about what happened to disbelievers, but also about the honor He bestowed upon the Prophets (st), Messengers (st) and righteous believers who faced oppression at their hands.

Allah (sp) said:

إِنَّا لَنَنصُرُ رُسُلَنَا وَٱلَّذِينَ ءَامَنُواْ فِى ٱلْحَيَوٰةِ ٱلدُّنْيَا وَيَوْمَ يَقُومُ ٱلْأَشْهَٰدُ

"Verily, We will indeed make victorious Our Messengers and those who believe (in the Oneness of Allah – Islamic Monotheism) in this world's life and on the Day when the witnesses will stand forth (i.e. Day of Resurrection)" (Qur'an 40:51)

And in Chapter *Al-An'aam*, Allah (sp) said:

وَلَقَدْ كُذِّبَتْ رُسُلٌ مِّن قَبْلِكَ فَصَبَرُواْ عَلَىٰ مَا كُذِّبُواْ وَأُوذُواْ حَتَّىٰ أَتَىٰهُمْ نَصْرُنَا وَلَا مُبَدِّلَ لِكَلِمَٰتِ ٱللَّهِ وَلَقَدْ جَآءَكَ مِن نَّبَإِىْ ٱلْمُرْسَلِينَ

"Verily, (many) Messengers were denied before you (O Muhammad (s)), but with patience they bore the denial, and they were hurt, till Our Help reached them, and none can alter the Words (Decisions) of Allah. Surely there has reached you the information (news) about the Messengers (before you)." (Qur'an 6:34)

7) Providing Spiritual Development for Believers

With the aim of guiding Muslims, the Qur'an contains important teachings and commands that run the gamut from sound beliefs to noble manners and honest dealings. Faith in Allah (sp), faith in Resurrection and the Day of Judgment, faith in the Prophets (st) and Messengers (st), being patient in the face of persecution at the hands of disbelievers – these are only some important issues that are discussed in the Noble Qur'an.

Such issues are given life when we hear about them being applied by righteous people from the past. Thus we are encouraged to improve as Muslims when we hear about the strong faith of Ibraaheem (p) the patience of Yusuf (p), the determination of Moosa (p), the consistency and steadfastness of Noah (p), and so on.

It is one thing to be told that we should remain steadfast upon our religion, no matter what hardships we face, and no matter what the difficulties we encounter. It is an altogether different matter to not only be told that, but also to be informed about the story of the magicians who believed in Moosa (p). After they proclaimed their true faith, Fir'aun sentenced them to death by crucifixion. Having spent some time in Fir'aun's good favor, they simply had to take back their words, and Fir'aun would have forgiven them. But instead they remained steadfast upon their faith, in spite of their sure knowledge that Fir'aun would make good on his threats and that they would suffer a great deal of physical torment at his hands before they died.

From the story of the people of the cave, we see the importance of remaining firm upon *Tawheed* (Islamic Monotheism). In the story of Ibraaheem and Ismaa'eel (st), we learn the importance of patience, of being dutiful towards one's parents, and of obeying Allah's commands. Allah (sp) said:

فَبَشَّرْنَٰهُ بِغُلَٰمٍ حَلِيمٍ (١٠١) فَلَمَّا بَلَغَ مَعَهُ ٱلسَّعْىَ قَالَ يَٰبُنَىَّ إِنِّى أَرَىٰ فِى ٱلْمَنَامِ أَنِّى أَذْبَحُكَ فَٱنظُرْ مَاذَا تَرَىٰ قَالَ يَٰأَبَتِ ٱفْعَلْ مَا تُؤْمَرُ سَتَجِدُنِى إِن شَآءَ ٱللَّهُ مِنَ ٱلصَّٰبِرِينَ

(١٠٢) فَلَمَّآ أَسۡلَمَا وَتَلَّهُۥ لِلۡجَبِينِ (١٠٣) وَنَٰدَيۡنَٰهُ أَن يَٰٓإِبۡرَٰهِيمُ (١٠٤) قَدۡ صَدَّقۡتَ ٱلرُّءۡيَآۚ إِنَّا كَذَٰلِكَ نَجۡزِي ٱلۡمُحۡسِنِينَ (١٠٥)

"So We gave him the glad tidings of a forbearing boy. And, when he (his son) was old enough to walk with him, he said: 'O my son! I have seen in a dream that I am slaughtering you (offer you in sacrifice to Allah (sp)), so look what you think!' He said: 'O my father! Do that which you are commanded, In shaa Allah (if Allah will), you shall find me of As-Sabirin (the patient ones, etc.)'. Then, when they had both submitted themselves (to the Will of Allah), and he had laid him prostrate on his forehead (or on the side of his forehead for slaughtering); and We called out to him: 'O Abraham! You have fulfilled the dream (vision)!' Verily! Thus do We reward the Muhsinun (good-doers)." (Qur'an 37: 101-105)

In the story of Luqmaan (p) and his son, we learn a number of important morals and lessons, which are related to us in the form of Luqmaan (p) advising his son:

وَلَقَدۡ ءَاتَيۡنَا لُقۡمَٰنَ ٱلۡحِكۡمَةَ أَنِ ٱشۡكُرۡ لِلَّهِۚ وَمَن يَشۡكُرۡ فَإِنَّمَا يَشۡكُرُ لِنَفۡسِهِۦۖ وَمَن كَفَرَ فَإِنَّ ٱللَّهَ غَنِيٌّ حَمِيدٞ (١٢) وَإِذۡ قَالَ لُقۡمَٰنُ لِٱبۡنِهِۦ وَهُوَ يَعِظُهُۥ يَٰبُنَيَّ لَا تُشۡرِكۡ بِٱللَّهِۖ إِنَّ ٱلشِّرۡكَ لَظُلۡمٌ عَظِيمٞ (١٣) وَوَصَّيۡنَا ٱلۡإِنسَٰنَ بِوَٰلِدَيۡهِ حَمَلَتۡهُ أُمُّهُۥ وَهۡنًا عَلَىٰ وَهۡنٖ وَفِصَٰلُهُۥ فِي عَامَيۡنِ أَنِ ٱشۡكُرۡ لِي وَلِوَٰلِدَيۡكَ إِلَيَّ ٱلۡمَصِيرُ (١٤) وَإِن جَٰهَدَاكَ عَلَىٰٓ أَن تُشۡرِكَ بِي مَا لَيۡسَ لَكَ بِهِۦ عِلۡمٞ فَلَا تُطِعۡهُمَاۖ وَصَاحِبۡهُمَا فِي ٱلدُّنۡيَا مَعۡرُوفٗاۖ وَٱتَّبِعۡ سَبِيلَ مَنۡ أَنَابَ إِلَيَّۚ ثُمَّ إِلَيَّ مَرۡجِعُكُمۡ فَأُنَبِّئُكُم بِمَا كُنتُمۡ تَعۡمَلُونَ (١٥) يَٰبُنَيَّ إِنَّهَآ إِن تَكُ مِثۡقَالَ حَبَّةٖ مِّنۡ خَرۡدَلٖ فَتَكُن فِي صَخۡرَةٍ أَوۡ فِي ٱلسَّمَٰوَٰتِ أَوۡ فِي ٱلۡأَرۡضِ يَأۡتِ بِهَا ٱللَّهُۚ إِنَّ ٱللَّهَ لَطِيفٌ خَبِيرٞ (١٦) يَٰبُنَيَّ أَقِمِ ٱلصَّلَوٰةَ وَأۡمُرۡ بِٱلۡمَعۡرُوفِ وَٱنۡهَ عَنِ ٱلۡمُنكَرِ وَٱصۡبِرۡ عَلَىٰ مَآ أَصَابَكَۖ إِنَّ ذَٰلِكَ مِنۡ عَزۡمِ ٱلۡأُمُورِ (١٧) وَلَا تُصَعِّرۡ خَدَّكَ لِلنَّاسِ وَلَا تَمۡشِ فِي ٱلۡأَرۡضِ مَرَحًاۖ إِنَّ ٱللَّهَ لَا يُحِبُّ كُلَّ مُخۡتَالٖ فَخُورٖ (١٨) وَٱقۡصِدۡ فِي مَشۡيِكَ وَٱغۡضُضۡ مِن صَوۡتِكَۚ إِنَّ أَنكَرَ ٱلۡأَصۡوَٰتِ لَصَوۡتُ ٱلۡحَمِيرِ (١٩)

"And indeed We bestowed upon Luqman Al-Hikmah (wisdom and religious understanding, etc.) saying: 'Give thanks to Allah', and whoever gives thanks, he gives thanks for (the good of) his own self. And whoever is unthankful, then verily, Allah is All-Rich (free of all wants), Worthy of all praise. And (remember) when Luqman said to his son when he was advising him: 'O my son! Join not in worship others with Allah. Verily! Joining others in worship with Allah is a great Zulm (wrong) indeed. And We have enjoined on man (to be dutiful and good) to his parents. His mother bore him in weakness and hardship upon weakness and hardship, and his weaning is in two years – give thanks to Me and to your parents – unto Me is the final destination. But if they (both) strive with you to make you join in worship with Me others that of which you have no knowledge, then obey them not, but behave with them in the world kindly, and follow the path of him who turns to Me in repentance and in obedience. Then to Me will be your return, and I shall tell you what you used to do, 'O my son! If it be (anything) equal to the weight of a grain of mustard seed, and though it be in a rock, or in the heavens or in the earth, Allah will bring it forth. Verily, Allah is Subtle (in bringing out that grain), Well-Aware (of its place). O my son! Aqimis-Salat (perform As-Salat), enjoin (people) for Al-Maruf (Islamic Monotheism and all that is good), and forbid (people) from Al-Munkar (i.e., disbelief in the Oneness of Allah, polytheism of all kinds and all that is evil and bad), and bear with patience whatever befall you. Verily! These are some of the important commandments ordered by Allah with no exemption. And turn not your face away from men with pride, nor walk in insolence through the earth. Verily, Allah likes not each arrogant boaster. And be moderate (or show no insolence) in your walking, and lower your voice. Verily, the harshest of all voices is the voice (the braying) of ass.'" (Qur'an 31: 12 – 19)

In Chapter *Maryam*, we are reminded about the truthfulness of Prophet Ibraaheem (p), which has the effect of encouraging us to be truthful in our everyday lives:

$$\text{وَاذْكُرْ فِى ٱلْكِتَٰبِ إِبْرَٰهِيمَ ۚ إِنَّهُۥ كَانَ صِدِّيقًا نَّبِيًّا}$$

"And mention in the Book (the Qur'an) Ibraheem (Abraham). Verily! He was a man of truth, a Prophet." (Qur'an 19:41)

Later on in the same chapter, we are informed about the noble qualities of Moosa (p):

$$\text{وَاذْكُرْ فِى ٱلْكِتَٰبِ مُوسَىٰٓ ۚ إِنَّهُۥ كَانَ مُخْلَصًا وَكَانَ رَسُولًا نَّبِيًّا}$$

"And mention in the Book (this Qur'an) Moosa (Moses). Verily! He was chosen and he was a Messenger (and) a Prophet." (Qur'an 19:51)

In the Noble Qur'an, and in the Sunnah of the Prophet (s), we are encouraged to be trustworthy and loyal in our dealings with others. Loyalty here means repaying kindness with kindness. The qualities of trustworthiness and loyalty are practically manifested in the story of Yusuf (p), who remembered all too well the kindness that his master, Al-Azeez, showed to him, and who wanted to repay that kindness not with betrayal but with a show of loyalty and thankfulness):

$$\text{قَالَ مَعَاذَ ٱللَّهِ ۖ إِنَّهُۥ رَبِّىٓ أَحْسَنَ مَثْوَاىَ ۖ إِنَّهُۥ لَا يُفْلِحُ ٱلظَّٰلِمُونَ}$$

"He said: 'I seek refuge in Allah (or Allah forbid)! Truly, he (your husband) is my master. He made my stay agreeable! (So I will never betray him). Verily, the Zalimun (wrong and evildoers) will never be successful." (Qur'an 12:23)

And after his innocence was established, Yusuf (p) explained that, all along, he wanted to prove to Al-Azeez that he did not betray him:

$$\text{ذَٰلِكَ لِيَعْلَمَ أَنِّى لَمْ أَخُنْهُ بِٱلْغَيْبِ وَأَنَّ ٱللَّهَ لَا يَهْدِى كَيْدَ ٱلْخَآئِنِينَ}$$

"Then Yusuf (Joseph) said: 'I asked for this inquiry in order that he (Al-Aziz) may know that I betrayed him not in secret. And, verily! Allah guides not the plot of the betrayers.'" (Qur'an 12:52)

And we learn about the importance of a number of noble qualities in the story of Shu'aib (p):

$$\text{قَالَ يَٰقَوْمِ ٱعْبُدُوا۟ ٱللَّهَ مَا لَكُم مِّنْ إِلَٰهٍ غَيْرُهُۥ ۖ قَدْ جَآءَتْكُم بَيِّنَةٌ مِّن رَّبِّكُمْ ۖ فَأَوْفُوا۟ ٱلْكَيْلَ وَٱلْمِيزَانَ وَلَا تَبْخَسُوا۟ ٱلنَّاسَ أَشْيَآءَهُمْ وَلَا تُفْسِدُوا۟ فِى ٱلْأَرْضِ بَعْدَ إِصْلَٰحِهَا ۚ ذَٰلِكُمْ خَيْرٌ لَّكُمْ إِن كُنتُم مُّؤْمِنِينَ}$$

"He said: 'O my people! Worship Allah! You have no other Ilah (God) but Him. La ilaha ill-Allah (none has the right to be worshiped but Allah).Verily, a clear proof (sign) from your Lord has come unto you; so give full measure and full weight and wrong not men in their things, and do not mischief on the earth after it has been set in order, that will be better for you, if you are believers.'" (Qur'an 7: 85)

The reader would do well to notice the order in which Shu'aib (p) invited his people to the truth. He began by inviting them to what was most important, having correct beliefs (regarding the Oneness of Allah – Islamic Monotheism); and only after he invited them to believe in *Tawheed* (Islamic Monotheism) did he move on to other matters, such as being honest in the buying and selling of goods.

8) Promoting Justice and Righteousness in Society, and Forbidding the Spread of Corruption and Evildoing

Upon contemplating the stories of the Qur'an, one finds that two of their aims are to promote justice in society and to forbid all forms of corruption – such as murder, unfair business practices, hoarding wealth in a manner that hurts the poor and weak members of society, and so on. In Chapter *Al-Araaf*, we are informed of how Shu'aib (p) would impress upon his people the importance of establishing a just society and of eradicating all forms of corruption:

$$\text{وَإِلَىٰ مَدْيَنَ أَخَاهُمْ شُعَيْبًا ۗ قَالَ يَٰقَوْمِ ٱعْبُدُوا۟ ٱللَّهَ مَا لَكُم مِّنْ إِلَٰهٍ غَيْرُهُۥ ۖ قَدْ جَآءَتْكُم بَيِّنَةٌ مِّن رَّبِّكُمْ ۖ فَأَوْفُوا۟ ٱلْكَيْلَ وَٱلْمِيزَانَ وَلَا تَبْخَسُوا۟ ٱلنَّاسَ أَشْيَآءَهُمْ وَلَا تُفْسِدُوا۟ فِى ٱلْأَرْضِ بَعْدَ إِصْلَٰحِهَا ۚ ذَٰلِكُمْ خَيْرٌ لَّكُمْ إِن كُنتُم مُّؤْمِنِينَ}$$

"And to (the people of) Madyan (Midian), (We sent) their brother Shu'aib. "He said: 'O my people! Worship Allah! You have no other Ilah (God) but Him. La ilaha ill-Allah (none has the right to be worshiped but Allah). Verily, a clear proof (sign) from your Lord has come unto you; so give full measure and full weight and wrong not men in their things, and do not mischief on the earth after it has been set in order, that will be better for you, if you are believers.'" (Qur'an 7: 85)

In other Verses, Allah (sp) highlights the importance of this issue by pointing out the consequences of both righteousness and moral decay on human beings. In this regard, the stories of the two sons of Adam (p), the two owners of gardens, and the flood of the Ma'rib dam come to mind. As for the first of those stories, Allah (sp) said:

$$\text{وَٱتْلُ عَلَيْهِمْ نَبَأَ ٱبْنَىْ ءَادَمَ بِٱلْحَقِّ إِذْ قَرَّبَا قُرْبَانًا فَتُقُبِّلَ مِنْ أَحَدِهِمَا وَلَمْ يُتَقَبَّلْ مِنَ ٱلْءَاخَرِ قَالَ لَأَقْتُلَنَّكَ ۖ قَالَ إِنَّمَا يَتَقَبَّلُ ٱللَّهُ مِنَ ٱلْمُتَّقِينَ (٢٧) لَئِنۢ بَسَطتَ إِلَىَّ يَدَكَ لِتَقْتُلَنِى مَآ أَنَا۠ بِبَاسِطٍ يَدِىَ إِلَيْكَ لِأَقْتُلَكَ ۖ إِنِّىٓ أَخَافُ ٱللَّهَ رَبَّ ٱلْعَٰلَمِينَ (٢٨) إِنِّىٓ أُرِيدُ أَن تَبُوٓأَ بِإِثْمِى وَإِثْمِكَ فَتَكُونَ مِنْ أَصْحَٰبِ ٱلنَّارِ ۚ وَذَٰلِكَ جَزَٰٓؤُا۟ ٱلظَّٰلِمِينَ (٢٩) فَطَوَّعَتْ لَهُۥ نَفْسُهُۥ قَتْلَ أَخِيهِ فَقَتَلَهُۥ فَأَصْبَحَ مِنَ ٱلْخَٰسِرِينَ (٣٠) فَبَعَثَ ٱللَّهُ غُرَابًا يَبْحَثُ فِى ٱلْأَرْضِ لِيُرِيَهُۥ كَيْفَ يُوَٰرِى سَوْءَةَ أَخِيهِ ۚ قَالَ يَٰوَيْلَتَىٰٓ أَعَجَزْتُ أَنْ أَكُونَ مِثْلَ هَٰذَا ٱلْغُرَابِ فَأُوَٰرِىَ سَوْءَةَ أَخِى ۖ فَأَصْبَحَ مِنَ ٱلنَّٰدِمِينَ (٣١) مِنْ أَجْلِ ذَٰلِكَ كَتَبْنَا عَلَىٰ بَنِىٓ إِسْرَٰٓءِيلَ أَنَّهُۥ مَن قَتَلَ نَفْسًۢا بِغَيْرِ نَفْسٍ أَوْ فَسَادٍ فِى ٱلْأَرْضِ فَكَأَنَّمَا قَتَلَ ٱلنَّاسَ جَمِيعًا وَمَنْ أَحْيَاهَا فَكَأَنَّمَآ أَحْيَا ٱلنَّاسَ جَمِيعًا ۚ وَلَقَدْ جَآءَتْهُمْ رُسُلُنَا بِٱلْبَيِّنَٰتِ ثُمَّ إِنَّ كَثِيرًا مِّنْهُم بَعْدَ ذَٰلِكَ فِى ٱلْأَرْضِ لَمُسْرِفُونَ (٣٢)}$$

"And (O Muhammad (s)) recite to them (the Jews) the story of the two sons of Adam (Habil and Qabil) in truth; when each offered a sacrifice (to Allah, it was accepted from the one but not from the other. The latter said to the former: 'I will surely kill you.' The former said: 'Verily, Allah accepts only from those who are Al-Muttaqun (the pious ones). If you do stretch your hand against me to kill me, I shall never stretch my hand against you to kill you, for I fear Allah; the Lord of the 'Alamin (mankind, jinns, and all that exists). Verily, I intend to let you draw my sin on yourself as well as yours, then you will be one of the dwellers of the Fire, and that is the recompense of the Zalimun (polytheists and wrong-doers).' So the Nafs (self) of the other (latter one) encouraged him and made fair-seeming to him the murder of his brother; he murdered him and became one of the losers. Then Allah sent a crow who scratched the ground to show him to hide the dead body of his brother. He (the murderer) said: 'Woe to me! Am I not even able to be as this crow and to hide the dead body of my brother?' Then he became one of those who regretted. Because of that We ordained for the Children of Israel that if anyone killed a person not in retaliation of murder, or (and) to spread mischief in the land – it would be as if he killed all mankind, and if anyone saved a life, it would be as if he saved the life of all mankind. And indeed, there came to them Our messengers with clear proofs, evidences, and signs, even then after that many of them continued to exceed the limits (e.g., by doing oppression unjustly and exceeding beyond the limits set by Allah by committing the major sins) in the land!" (Qur'an 5: 27-32)

In regard to the story of the two men who owned gardens, Allah (sp) is said:

وَٱضْرِبْ لَهُم مَّثَلاً رَّجُلَيْنِ جَعَلْنَا لِأَحَدِهِمَا جَنَّتَيْنِ مِنْ أَعْنَابٍ وَحَفَفْنَاهُمَا بِنَخْلٍ وَجَعَلْنَا بَيْنَهُمَا زَرْعًا (٣٢) كِلْتَا ٱلْجَنَّتَيْنِ ءَاتَتْ أُكُلَهَا وَلَمْ تَظْلِم مِّنْهُ شَيْئًا وَفَجَّرْنَا خِلَٰلَهُمَا نَهَرًا (٣٣) وَكَانَ لَهُ ثَمَرٌ فَقَالَ لِصَٰحِبِهِ وَهُوَ يُحَاوِرُهُ أَنَا أَكْثَرُ مِنكَ مَالًا وَأَعَزُّ نَفَرًا (٣٤) وَدَخَلَ جَنَّتَهُ وَهُوَ ظَالِمٌ لِنَفْسِهِ قَالَ مَا أَظُنُّ أَن تَبِيدَ هَٰذِهِ أَبَدًا (٣٥) وَمَا أَظُنُّ ٱلسَّاعَةَ قَائِمَةً وَلَئِن رُّدِدتُّ إِلَىٰ رَبِّي لَأَجِدَنَّ خَيْرًا مِّنْهَا مُنقَلَبًا (٣٦) قَالَ لَهُ صَاحِبُهُ وَهُوَ يُحَاوِرُهُ أَكَفَرْتَ بِٱلَّذِي خَلَقَكَ مِن تُرَابٍ ثُمَّ مِن نُّطْفَةٍ ثُمَّ سَوَّىٰكَ رَجُلًا (٣٧) لَّٰكِنَّا۠ هُوَ ٱللَّهُ رَبِّي وَلَا أُشْرِكُ بِرَبِّي أَحَدًا (٣٨) وَلَوْلَا إِذْ دَخَلْتَ جَنَّتَكَ قُلْتَ مَا شَاءَ ٱللَّهُ لَا قُوَّةَ إِلَّا بِٱللَّهِ إِن تَرَنِ أَنَا۠ أَقَلَّ مِنكَ مَالًا وَوَلَدًا (٣٩) فَعَسَىٰ رَبِّي أَن يُؤْتِيَنِ خَيْرًا مِّن جَنَّتِكَ وَيُرْسِلَ عَلَيْهَا حُسْبَانًا مِّنَ ٱلسَّمَاءِ فَتُصْبِحَ صَعِيدًا زَلَقًا (٤٠) أَوْ يُصْبِحَ مَاؤُهَا غَوْرًا فَلَن تَسْتَطِيعَ لَهُ طَلَبًا (٤١) وَأُحِيطَ بِثَمَرِهِ فَأَصْبَحَ يُقَلِّبُ كَفَّيْهِ عَلَىٰ مَا أَنفَقَ فِيهَا وَهِيَ خَاوِيَةٌ عَلَىٰ عُرُوشِهَا وَيَقُولُ يَٰلَيْتَنِي لَمْ أُشْرِكْ بِرَبِّي أَحَدًا (٤٢)

"And put forward to them the example of two men; unto one of them We had given two Gardens of grapes, and We had surrounded both with date palms; and had put between them green crops (cultivated fields etc.). Each of those two Gardens brought forth its produce, and failed not in the least therein, and We caused a river to gush forth in the midst of them. And he had property (or fruit) and he said to his companion, in the course of mutual talk: 'I am more than you in wealth and stronger in respect of men.' And he went into his garden while in a state (of pride and disbelief) unjust to himself. He said: 'I think not that this will ever perish. And I think not the Hour will ever come, and if indeed I am brought back to my Lord (on the Day of Resurrection), I surely shall find better than this when I return to Him.' His companion said to him, during the talk with him: 'Do you disbelieve in Him Who created you out of dust (i.e., your father Adam, then out of Nutfah (mixed semen drops of male and female discharge), then fashioned you into a man? But as for my part, I (believe) that He is Allah, my Lord and none shall I associate as partner with my Lord. It was better for you to say, when you entered your garden: 'That which Allah wills (will come to pass)! There is no power but with Allah'. 'If you see me less than you in wealth, and children, it may be that my Lord will give me something better than your garden, and will send on it Husban (forment, bolt, etc.) from the sky, then it will be a slippery earth. Or the water thereof (of the Gardens) becomes deep-sunken (underground) so that you will never be able to seek it.' So his fruits were encircled (with a ruin). And he remained clapping his hands with sorrow over what he had spent upon it, while it was all destroyed on its trellises, he could only say: 'Would I had ascribed no partners to my Lord'" (Qur'an 18: 32-42)

And the evil consequences of corruption are further illustrated in the following Verses, which discuss the breaking of the Ma'rib dam and the destructive flood that ensued:

لَقَدْ كَانَ لِسَبَإٍ فِي مَسْكَنِهِمْ ءَايَةٌ جَنَّتَانِ عَن يَمِينٍ وَشِمَالٍ كُلُوا مِن رِّزْقِ رَبِّكُمْ وَٱشْكُرُوا لَهُ بَلْدَةٌ طَيِّبَةٌ وَرَبٌّ غَفُورٌ (١٥) فَأَعْرَضُوا فَأَرْسَلْنَا عَلَيْهِمْ سَيْلَ ٱلْعَرِمِ وَبَدَّلْنَاهُم بِجَنَّتَيْهِمْ جَنَّتَيْنِ ذَوَاتَيْ أُكُلٍ خَمْطٍ وَأَثْلٍ وَشَيْءٍ مِّن سِدْرٍ قَلِيلٍ (١٦) ذَٰلِكَ

$$\text{جَزَيْنَـٰهُم بِمَا كَفَرُوا۟ۖ وَهَلْ نُجَـٰزِىٓ إِلَّا ٱلْكَفُورَ (١٧) وَجَعَلْنَا بَيْنَهُمْ وَبَيْنَ ٱلْقُرَى ٱلَّتِى بَـٰرَكْنَا فِيهَا قُرًۭى ظَـٰهِرَةًۭ وَقَدَّرْنَا فِيهَا ٱلسَّيْرَۖ سِيرُوا۟ فِيهَا لَيَالِىَ وَأَيَّامًا ءَامِنِينَ (١٨) فَقَالُوا۟ رَبَّنَا بَـٰعِدْ بَيْنَ أَسْفَارِنَا وَظَلَمُوٓا۟ أَنفُسَهُمْ فَجَعَلْنَـٰهُمْ أَحَادِيثَ وَمَزَّقْنَـٰهُمْ كُلَّ مُمَزَّقٍۚ إِنَّ فِى ذَٰلِكَ لَـَٔايَـٰتٍۢ لِّكُلِّ صَبَّارٍۢ شَكُورٍۢ (١٩)}$$

"Indeed there was for Saba' (Sheba) a sign in their dwelling place - two gardens, on the right hand and on the left (and it was said to them) 'Eat of the provision of your Lord, and be grateful to Him, a fair land and an Oft-Forgiving Lord.' But they turned away (from the obedience of Allah), so We sent against them Sail Al-'Arim (flood released from the dam), and We converted their two gardens into gardens producing bitter bad fruit, and tamarisks, and some few lote-trees. Like this We requited them because they were ungrateful disbelievers. And never do We requite in such a way except those who are ungrateful, disbelievers). And We placed between them and the towns which We had blessed, towns easy to be seen, and We made the stages (of journey) between them easy (saying): 'Travel in them safely both by night and day.' But they said: 'Our Lord! Make the stages between our journey longer!' And they wronged themselves, so We made them as tales (in the land), and We dispersed them all, totally. Verily, in this are indeed signs for every steadfast grateful (person)." (Qur'an 34: 15-19)

9) Reminding Muslims About Their Eternal Struggle Against Their Most Despised and Dangerous of Foes: Shaitaan (the Devil)

As Muslims, we are reminded about our continual enmity with *Shaitaan* (the Devil) through Verses that discuss how he constantly strives to turn us away from the Straight Path. That enmity, however, is given a sense of physical palpability in the story of our forefather Adam (p) and of his having been deceived by *Shaitaan*, a story that, because of its importance, is repeated throughout the Noble Qur'an. By being reminded of how our father was deceived by *Shaitaan*, we are made to better appreciate Shaitaan's hatred for all of Adam's descendants and the danger that he constantly poses to us in every moment of our lives.

10) Helping Muslims Overcome Hopelessness and Depression

We can overcome a sense of hopelessness with patience and a positive attitude. This very message is given life in many stories of the Qur'an. In such stories, a righteous person is made to suffer hardships that would, in many circumstances, lead people down the path of hopelessness and misery. But that righteous person is saved from going down that path because he is patient, and because he maintains a positive attitude and, more importantly, good thoughts about Allah (sp). This lesson is repeated over and over again in the story of Yusuf (p), for instance, Allah (sp) said:

$$\text{وَجَآءُو عَلَىٰ قَمِيصِهِۦ بِدَمٍۢ كَذِبٍۢۚ قَالَ بَلْ سَوَّلَتْ لَكُمْ أَنفُسُكُمْ أَمْرًۭاۖ فَصَبْرٌۭ جَمِيلٌۭۖ وَٱللَّهُ ٱلْمُسْتَعَانُ عَلَىٰ مَا تَصِفُونَ}$$

"And they brought his shirt stained with false blood. He said: 'Nay, but your own selves have made up a tale. So (for me) patience is most fitting. And it is Allah (Alone) Whose help can be sought against that which you assert.'" (Qur'an 12:18)

Then, in Verse number 64 of Chapter *Yusuf*, we are informed about the positive attitude of Ya'qub (p):

$$\text{قَالَ هَلْ ءَامَنُكُمْ عَلَيْهِ إِلَّا كَمَآ أَمِنتُكُمْ عَلَىٰٓ أَخِيهِ مِن قَبْلُۖ فَٱللَّهُ خَيْرٌ حَـٰفِظًۭاۖ وَهُوَ أَرْحَمُ ٱلرَّٰحِمِينَ}$$

"He said: 'Can I entrust him to you except as I entrusted his brother (Yusuf/Joseph) to you aforetime? But Allah is the Best to guard, and He is the Most Merciful of those who show mercy.'" (Qur'an 12: 64)

A number of Verses later, Ya'qub (p) reacts to bad news with an amazing display of patience and faith in Allah's help:

$$\text{قَالَ بَلْ سَوَّلَتْ لَكُمْ أَنفُسُكُمْ أَمْرًا ۖ فَصَبْرٌ جَمِيلٌ ۖ عَسَى ٱللَّهُ أَن يَأْتِيَنِى بِهِمْ جَمِيعًا ۚ إِنَّهُۥ هُوَ ٱلْعَلِيمُ ٱلْحَكِيمُ}$$

"He (Ya'qub (Jacob)) said: 'Nay, but your own selves have beguiled you into something. So patience is most fitting (for me). May be Allah will bring them (back) all to me. Truly He! Only He is All-Knowing, All-Wise.'" (Qur'an 12: 83)

And in the following Verse, Ya'qub (p) makes clear why he always remains patient and positive, explaining that the only people who despair of Allah's Mercy are those who disbelieve:

$$\text{يَٰبَنِىَّ ٱذْهَبُوا۟ فَتَحَسَّسُوا۟ مِن يُوسُفَ وَأَخِيهِ وَلَا تَا۟يْـَٔسُوا۟ مِن رَّوْحِ ٱللَّهِ ۖ إِنَّهُۥ لَا يَا۟يْـَٔسُ مِن رَّوْحِ ٱللَّهِ إِلَّا ٱلْقَوْمُ ٱلْكَٰفِرُونَ}$$

"O my sons! Go you and enquire about Yusuf (Joseph) and his brother, and never give up hope of Allah's Mercy. Certainly no one despairs of Allah's Mercy, except the people who disbelieve." (Qur'an 12:87)

11) Pointing Out Allah's Ability to Make Miracles Occur

Without a doubt, Allah (sp) is the greatest, and is able to do all things. These are beliefs that we are innately born with, and that we are informed about throughout the Noble Qur'an. Various stories of the Qur'an highlight Allah's greatness and almightiness by pointing out instances of miracles that Allah (sp) willed to occur on earth. Such miracles include the creation of Adam (p), the miraculous birth of Jesus (p), and the way in which a bird was brought to life for the benefit of Ibraaheem (p). The miracles we are informed about in the Qur'an instill us with the knowledge that Allah (sp) has control over all things,

that He knows all things, and that He (sp) is able to do all things. That knowledge, in turn, leads to calmness and to a deeper level of faith – hopefully to the point that we realize that we should place our complete trust in Allah (sp) and depend upon His help in all of our affairs.

The following Verses provide a few examples of the miracles that are related to us in the Noble Qur'an:

$$\text{أَوْ كَٱلَّذِى مَرَّ عَلَىٰ قَرْيَةٍ وَهِىَ خَاوِيَةٌ عَلَىٰ عُرُوشِهَا قَالَ أَنَّىٰ يُحْىِۦ هَٰذِهِ ٱللَّهُ بَعْدَ مَوْتِهَا ۖ فَأَمَاتَهُ ٱللَّهُ مِا۟ئَةَ عَامٍ ثُمَّ بَعَثَهُۥ ۖ قَالَ كَمْ لَبِثْتَ ۖ قَالَ لَبِثْتُ يَوْمًا أَوْ بَعْضَ يَوْمٍ ۖ قَالَ بَل لَّبِثْتَ مِا۟ئَةَ عَامٍ فَٱنظُرْ إِلَىٰ طَعَامِكَ وَشَرَابِكَ لَمْ يَتَسَنَّهْ ۖ وَٱنظُرْ إِلَىٰ حِمَارِكَ وَلِنَجْعَلَكَ ءَايَةً لِّلنَّاسِ ۖ وَٱنظُرْ إِلَى ٱلْعِظَامِ كَيْفَ نُنشِزُهَا ثُمَّ نَكْسُوهَا لَحْمًا ۚ فَلَمَّا تَبَيَّنَ لَهُۥ قَالَ أَعْلَمُ أَنَّ ٱللَّهَ عَلَىٰ كُلِّ شَىْءٍ قَدِيرٌ (٢٥٩) وَإِذْ قَالَ إِبْرَٰهِـۧمُ رَبِّ أَرِنِى كَيْفَ تُحْىِ ٱلْمَوْتَىٰ ۖ قَالَ أَوَلَمْ تُؤْمِن ۖ قَالَ بَلَىٰ وَلَٰكِن لِّيَطْمَئِنَّ قَلْبِى ۖ قَالَ فَخُذْ أَرْبَعَةً مِّنَ ٱلطَّيْرِ فَصُرْهُنَّ إِلَيْكَ ثُمَّ ٱجْعَلْ عَلَىٰ كُلِّ جَبَلٍ مِّنْهُنَّ جُزْءًا ثُمَّ ٱدْعُهُنَّ يَأْتِينَكَ سَعْيًا ۚ وَٱعْلَمْ أَنَّ ٱللَّهَ عَزِيزٌ حَكِيمٌ (٢٦٠)}$$

"Or like the one who passed by a town and it had tumbled over its roofs. He said: 'Oh! How will Allah ever bring it to life after its death?' So Allah caused him to die for a hundred years, and then raised him up (again). He said: 'How long did you remain (dead)?' He (the man) said: 'Perhaps I remained (dead) a day or part of a day'. He said: 'Nay, you have remained (dead) for a hundred years, look at your food and your drink, they show no change; and look at your donkey! And thus We have made of you a sign for the people. Look at the bones, how We bring them together and clothe them with flesh.' When this was clearly shown to him, he said, 'I know (now) that Allah is Able to do all things.' And (remember) when Ibrahim (Abraham) said, 'My Lord! Show me how You give life to the dead.' He (Allah) said: 'Do you not believe?' He Ibraheem (Abraham)] said: 'Yes (I believe), but to be stronger in faith.' He said: 'Take four birds, then cause them to incline towards you (then slaughter them, cut them into pieces), and then put a portion of them on every hill, and call them, they will come to you in haste. And know that Allah is All-Mighty, All-Wise." (Qur'an 2: 259, 260)

12) Pointing Out the Favors with which Allah (sp) Blessed Prophets (st) and Others Among His Righteous Servants

Another aim of the Qur'an is to show Muslims how Allah (sp) has showered his obedient slaves with rewards and blessings. The obedient slaves I am referring to here are Prophets (st) and righteous people from past nations. That the Qur'an mentions instances of how they were blessed and rewarded has a positive effect on believers. How so? Well, when a believer reads about a Prophet (p) who was rewarded for his good works, he is made to understand, through a practical example, that Allah (sp) rewards his obedient slaves, and bestows upon them honors and blessings both in this life and in the Hereafter. Without a doubt, this motivates a believer to remain steadfast upon the truth. Examples of how Allah (sp) blessed righteous people from the past abound in the Noble Qur'an. For instance, in the following Verses, Allah (sp) informs us of how He (sp) gave Sulaiman (p) special powers:

وَوَرِثَ سُلَيْمَٰنُ دَاوُۥدَ ۖ وَقَالَ يَٰٓأَيُّهَا ٱلنَّاسُ عُلِّمْنَا مَنطِقَ ٱلطَّيْرِ وَأُوتِينَا مِن كُلِّ شَىْءٍ ۖ إِنَّ هَٰذَا لَهُوَ ٱلْفَضْلُ ٱلْمُبِينُ

"And Sulaiman (Solomon) inherited (and knowledge of) Dawud (David). He said: 'O mankind! We have been taught the language of birds, and on us have been bestowed all things. This, verily, is an evident grace (from Allah)." (Qur'an 27:16)

The following Verses also discuss the special powers with which Allah (sp) blessed Sulaiman (p):

وَلِسُلَيْمَٰنَ ٱلرِّيحَ غُدُوُّهَا شَهْرٌ وَرَوَاحُهَا شَهْرٌ ۖ وَأَسَلْنَا لَهُۥ عَيْنَ ٱلْقِطْرِ ۖ وَمِنَ ٱلْجِنِّ مَن يَعْمَلُ بَيْنَ يَدَيْهِ بِإِذْنِ رَبِّهِۦ ۖ وَمَن يَزِغْ مِنْهُمْ عَنْ أَمْرِنَا نُذِقْهُ مِنْ عَذَابِ ٱلسَّعِيرِ

"And to Solomon (We subjected) the wind, its morning (stride from sunrise till mid-noon) was a month's (journey), and its afternoon (stride from the midday decline of the sun to sunset) was a months (journey, i.e., in one day he could travel two months' journey). And We caused a fount of (molten) brass to flow for him, and there were jinns that worked in front of him, by the Leave of his Lord, and whosoever of them turned aside from Our Command, We shall cause him to taste of the torment of the blazing Fire." (Qur'an 34:12)

And in Chapter *Al-Anbiyaa*, Allah (sp) said:

وَلِسُلَيْمَٰنَ ٱلرِّيحَ عَاصِفَةً تَجْرِى بِأَمْرِهِۦٓ إِلَى ٱلْأَرْضِ ٱلَّتِى بَٰرَكْنَا فِيهَا

"And to Sulaiman (Solomon), (We subjected) the wind strongly raging, running by his command towards the land which We had blessed." (Qur'an 21:81)

In the following Verses, Allah (sp) informs us about how He blessed David (p):

$$\text{وَلَقَدْ ءَاتَيْنَا دَاوُۥدَ مِنَّا فَضْلًا ۖ يَـٰجِبَالُ أَوِّبِى مَعَهُۥ وَٱلطَّيْرَ ۖ وَأَلَنَّا لَهُ ٱلْحَدِيدَ (١٠) أَنِ ٱعْمَلْ سَـٰبِغَـٰتٍ وَقَدِّرْ فِى ٱلسَّرْدِ ۖ وَٱعْمَلُوا۟ صَـٰلِحًا ۖ إِنِّى بِمَا تَعْمَلُونَ بَصِيرٌ (١١)}$$

"And indeed We bestowed grace on David from Us (saying): 'O you mountains. Glorify (Allah) with him! And you birds (also)! And We made the iron soft for him.' Saying: 'Make you perfect coats of mail, balancing well the rings of chain armor, and work you (men) righteousness. Truly, I am All-Seer of what you do.'" (Qur'an 34:10, 11)

And in Chapter *Al-Anbiya*, Allah (sp) further discussed David (p), saying:

$$\text{وَعَلَّمْنَـٰهُ صَنْعَةَ لَبُوسٍ لَّكُمْ لِتُحْصِنَكُم مِّنۢ بَأْسِكُمْ ۖ فَهَلْ أَنتُمْ شَـٰكِرُونَ}$$

"And We taught him the making of metal coats of mail (for battles), to protect you in your fighting. Are you then grateful?" (Qur'an 21:80)

In Chapter *As-Saaffaat*, Allah (sp) mentions one of the favors He (sp) bestowed upon Ibraaheem (p):

$$\text{فَبَشَّرْنَـٰهُ بِغُلَـٰمٍ حَلِيمٍ}$$

"So We gave him the glad tidings of a forbearing boy." (Qur'an 37: 101)

And later on in the same Chapter, Allah (sp) discusses the glad tidings He (sp) gave to Ibraaheem (p) of another child, Ishaaq (p):

$$\text{وَبَشَّرْنَـٰهُ بِإِسْحَـٰقَ نَبِيًّا مِّنَ ٱلصَّـٰلِحِينَ}$$

"And We gave him the glad tidings of Ishaque (Isaac) – a Prophet from the righteous." (Qur'an 37: 112)

When Fir'aun and his army were on the verge of capturing Moosa (p) and his people, Allah (sp) saved the latter group, instructing Moosa (p) to strike the sea with his stick, and causing it to part:

$$\text{فَأَوْحَيْنَا إِلَىٰ مُوسَىٰٓ أَنِ ٱضْرِب بِّعَصَاكَ ٱلْبَحْرَ ۖ فَٱنفَلَقَ فَكَانَ كُلُّ فِرْقٍ كَٱلطَّوْدِ ٱلْعَظِيمِ (٦٣) وَأَزْلَفْنَا ثَمَّ ٱلْءَاخَرِينَ (٦٤) وَأَنجَيْنَا مُوسَىٰ وَمَن مَّعَهُۥٓ أَجْمَعِينَ (٦٥) ثُمَّ أَغْرَقْنَا ٱلْءَاخَرِينَ (٦٦)}$$

"Then We inspired Moosa (Moses) (saying): 'Strike the sea with your stick!' And it parted, and each separate part (of that sea water) became like the huge, firm mass of a mountain. Then We brought near the others (Fir'aun's (Pharoah) party) to that place. And We saved Moosa (Moses) and all those with him. Then We drowned the others." (Qur'an 26: 63-66)

And Allah (sp) saved Ismaa'eel (p) by replacing him with a ram:

$$\text{وَفَدَيْنَـٰهُ بِذِبْحٍ عَظِيمٍ}$$

"And We ransomed him with a great sacrifice (i.e., a ram)." (Qur'an 37: 107)

After Yunus (p) was swallowed by a large fish, Allah (sp) saved him, expelling him from the fish's belly, taking him to the safety of shore, causing a plant of gourd to grow over him, and guiding his people to embrace Islam:

$$\text{وَإِنَّ يُونُسَ لَمِنَ ٱلْمُرْسَلِينَ (١٣٩) إِذْ أَبَقَ إِلَى ٱلْفُلْكِ ٱلْمَشْحُونِ (١٤٠) فَسَاهَمَ فَكَانَ مِنَ ٱلْمُدْحَضِينَ (١٤١) فَٱلْتَقَمَهُ ٱلْحُوتُ وَهُوَ مُلِيمٌ (١٤٢) فَلَوْلَآ أَنَّهُۥ كَانَ مِنَ}$$

ٱلْمُسَبِّحِينَ (١٤٣) لَلَبِثَ فِى بَطْنِهِۦٓ إِلَىٰ يَوْمِ يُبْعَثُونَ (١٤٤) ۞ فَنَبَذْنَـٰهُ بِٱلْعَرَآءِ وَهُوَ سَقِيمٌ (١٤٥) وَأَنۢبَتْنَا عَلَيْهِ شَجَرَةً مِّن يَقْطِينٍ (١٤٦) وَأَرْسَلْنَـٰهُ إِلَىٰ مِا۟ئَةِ أَلْفٍ أَوْ يَزِيدُونَ (١٤٧) فَـَٔامَنُوا۟ فَمَتَّعْنَـٰهُمْ إِلَىٰ حِينٍ (١٤٨)

"And verily, Yunus (Jonah) was one of the Messengers. When he ran to the laden ship, he (agreed to) cast lots, and he was among the losers, then a (big) fish swallowed him and he had done an act worthy of blame. Had he not been of them who glorify Allah, he would have indeed remained inside its belly (the fish) till the Day of Resurrection. But We cast him forth on the naked shore while he was sick, and We caused a plant of gourd to grow over him. And We sent him to 100,000 (people) or even more. And they believed; so We gave them enjoyment for a while." (Qur'an 37: 139-148)

And Allah (sp) blessed Jesus (p) by causing many miracles to occur at his hands; some of those miracles are described in this Verse:

أَنِّىٓ أَخْلُقُ لَكُم مِّنَ ٱلطِّينِ كَهَيْـَٔةِ ٱلطَّيْرِ فَأَنفُخُ فِيهِ فَيَكُونُ طَيْرًۢا بِإِذْنِ ٱللَّهِ ۖ وَأُبْرِئُ ٱلْأَكْمَهَ وَٱلْأَبْرَصَ وَأُحْىِ ٱلْمَوْتَىٰ بِإِذْنِ ٱللَّهِ ۖ وَأُنَبِّئُكُم بِمَا تَأْكُلُونَ وَمَا تَدَّخِرُونَ فِى بُيُوتِكُمْ ۚ إِنَّ فِى ذَٰلِكَ لَـَٔايَةً لَّكُمْ إِن كُنتُم مُّؤْمِنِينَ

"That I design for you out of clay, as it were, the figure of a bird, and breathe into it, and it becomes a bird by Allah's Leave; and I heal him who was born blind, and the leper, and I bring the dead to life by Allah's Leave. And I inform you of what you eat, and what you store in your houses. Surely, therein is a sign for you, if you believe." (Qur'an 3:49)

And when people accused Maryam (sh) of perpetrating a lewd and vile act, Allah (sp) established her innocence in a manner that was nothing short of a miracle:

قَالَتْ رَبِّ أَنَّىٰ يَكُونُ لِى وَلَدٌ وَلَمْ يَمْسَسْنِى بَشَرٌ ۖ قَالَ كَذَٰلِكِ ٱللَّهُ يَخْلُقُ مَا يَشَآءُ ۚ إِذَا قَضَىٰٓ أَمْرًا فَإِنَّمَا يَقُولُ لَهُۥ كُن فَيَكُونُ

"She said: 'O my Lord! How shall I have a son when no man has touched me.' He said: 'So (it will be) for Allah creates what He wills. When he has decreed something, He says to it only: 'Be!' – and it is.'" (Qur'an 3: 47)

يَـٰٓأُخْتَ هَـٰرُونَ مَا كَانَ أَبُوكِ ٱمْرَأَ سَوْءٍ وَمَا كَانَتْ أُمُّكِ بَغِيًّا (٢٨) فَأَشَارَتْ إِلَيْهِ ۖ قَالُوا۟ كَيْفَ نُكَلِّمُ مَن كَانَ فِى ٱلْمَهْدِ صَبِيًّا (٢٩) قَالَ إِنِّى عَبْدُ ٱللَّهِ ءَاتَىٰنِىَ ٱلْكِتَـٰبَ وَجَعَلَنِى نَبِيًّا (٣٠) وَجَعَلَنِى مُبَارَكًا أَيْنَ مَا كُنتُ وَأَوْصَىٰنِى بِٱلصَّلَوٰةِ وَٱلزَّكَوٰةِ مَا دُمْتُ حَيًّا (٣١) وَبَرًّۢا بِوَٰلِدَتِى وَلَمْ يَجْعَلْنِى جَبَّارًا شَقِيًّا (٣٢)

"O sister (i.e., the like) of Harun (Aaron) (not the brother of Musa (Moses), but he was another pious man at the same time of Maryam (Mary))! Your father was not a man who used to commit adultery, nor your mother was an unchaste woman.' Then she pointed to him. They said: 'How can we talk to one who is a child in the cradle' 'He (Iesa) (Jesus) said: 'Verily! I am a slave of Allah, He has given me the Scripture and made me a Prophet; and He has made me blessed wheresoever I be, and has enjoined on me Salat (prayer), and Zakat, as long as I live; and dutiful to my mother, and made me not arrogant, unblest.'" (Qur'an 19: 28-32)

In Chapter *Aal-Imraan*, Allah (sp) described how He cured Zakariyyah's wife, and blessed them both with a righteous child, Yahya (p):

هُنَالِكَ دَعَا زَكَرِيَّا رَبَّهُ ۖ قَالَ رَبِّ هَبْ لِى مِن لَّدُنكَ ذُرِّيَّةً طَيِّبَةً ۖ إِنَّكَ سَمِيعُ ٱلدُّعَآءِ فَنَادَتْهُ ٱلْمَلَٰٓئِكَةُ وَهُوَ قَآئِمٌ يُصَلِّى فِى ٱلْمِحْرَابِ أَنَّ ٱللَّهَ يُبَشِّرُكَ بِيَحْيَىٰ مُصَدِّقًۢا بِكَلِمَةٍ مِّنَ ٱللَّهِ وَسَيِّدًا وَحَصُورًا وَنَبِيًّا مِّنَ ٱلصَّٰلِحِينَ

"At that time Zakariya (Zechariah) invoked his Lord, saying: 'O my Lord! Grant me from You, a good offspring. You are indeed the All-Hearer of invocation.' Then the angels called him, while he was standing in prayer in Al-Mihrab (a praying place or a private room), (Saying): 'Allah gives you glad tidings of Yahya (John, confirming (believing in) the word from Allah (i.e., the creation of Iesa (Jesus)), the Word from Allah ('Be!' - and he was!), noble, keeping away from sexual relations with women, a Prophet, from among the righteous." (Qur'an 3: 38, 39)

فَٱسْتَجَبْنَا لَهُۥ وَوَهَبْنَا لَهُۥ يَحْيَىٰ وَأَصْلَحْنَا لَهُۥ زَوْجَهُۥٓ ۚ إِنَّهُمْ كَانُوا۟ يُسَٰرِعُونَ فِى ٱلْخَيْرَٰتِ وَيَدْعُونَنَا رَغَبًا وَرَهَبًا ۖ وَكَانُوا۟ لَنَا خَٰشِعِينَ

"So We answered his call, and We bestowed upon him Yahya (John), and cured his wife (to bear a child) for him. Verily, they used to hasten on to do good deeds and they used to call on Us with hope and fear, and used to humble themselves before Us." (Qur'an 21:90)

PART 3
The Greatness of the Qur'an's Influence

This Part Consists of Three Sections:

Section One: The Importance of Inviting Others to Islam with the Qur'an

Section Two: Applying the Principle of Inviting Others to Islam with the Qur'an

Section Three: Examples of How the Qur'an has Influenced Modern-Day Figures to Embrace Islam

Introduction

Century after century, the Qur'an has continued to have a profound and powerful impact on the hearts of people. Over 14 centuries ago, the Arabs of the Arabian Peninsula underwent a complete metamorphosis, one that saw them go from ignorance to knowledge, from polytheism to pure Islamic Monotheism, from division and chaos to unity and harmony. They then poured out of Arabia, flowing with the irresistible force of a flood to neighboring lands, spreading Islam to other peoples, and bringing down the two major empires of that era. Muslims uprooted polytheism and oppression, and spread in their place the seeds of Islamic Monotheism, truth, and justice. As a result, people entered into the religion of Allah (sp) in throngs. This tremendous early success for the Muslim nation can be attributed to many things; without a doubt, however, credit for that success should go first and foremost to the Noble Qur'an and to the powerful effect it has on the hearts of people.

From the moment they heard it for the first time, Arabs were captivated by the Qur'an, and here I am referring equally to those who embraced Islam and to those upon whose hearts Allah (sp) placed a dark cover, those who refused to embrace the truth – a miserable group that consisted of the likes of Al-Waleed bin Al-Mugheerah. So long as a person is humble and has an open mind, he will be greatly moved by the Qur'an when he recites it or hears it being recited. But the Arabs were more than stubborn; they were intransigent:

$$قَوْمٌ خَصِمُونَ$$

"A quarrelsome people." (Qur'an 43:58)
They are again described as being quarrelsome in this Verse:

$$وَتُنذِرَ بِهِۦ قَوْمًا لُّدًّا$$

"And warn with it the Ludda (most quarrelsome) people." (Qur'an. 19.97)
As a result of their intransigence, they began to raise doubts about the Qur'an, though deep down in their hearts they knew that it was the absolute truth from their Lord; their sole purpose was to deride the Qur'an, and to thus turn people away from it.

Based on what I have hitherto mentioned, we should rely heavily on the Qur'an when we invite others to Islam. Sadly, however, many Muslims, even those who are specialized in the field of Islamic propagation, fail to mention Verses of the Qur'an when they address an audience of non-Muslims. In their speeches, they will say much that comes to their minds, while citing very few Verses of the Qur'an, if any. To be sure, such an approach is wrong. Throughout history, it has been the words of Allah (sp) and not the words of men, that have captivated the hearts of billions and motivated them to embrace Islam. That being said, I should point out that I am not advocating an approach to Islamic propagation which involves recitation of the Qur'an's Verses and nothing else. To the contrary, a Muslim who is active in the field of Islamic propagation should mention Verses of the Qur'an, but at the same time he should explain those Verses, clarify the main teachings and beliefs of Islam, provide examples to his audience, mention stories whenever appropriate, put forward sound and logical arguments, and so on. Therefore, when inviting others to Islam, a Muslim should follow the guidance and methodology of the Messenger of Allah (s), which can be summarized in the saying of Allah (sp):

$$وَأَنزَلْنَا إِلَيْكَ ٱلذِّكْرَ لِتُبَيِّنَ لِلنَّاسِ مَا نُزِّلَ إِلَيْهِمْ وَلَعَلَّهُمْ يَتَفَكَّرُونَ$$

"And We have also sent down unto you (O Muhammad (s)) the reminder and the advice (the Qur'an), that you may explain clearly to men what is sent down to them, and that they may give thought." (Qur'an 16:44)

Section 1
The Importance of Inviting Others to Islam with the Qur'an

Introduction

Allah (sp) sent His Messenger (s) to mankind on an important mission: To convey to them the message of Islam. To help him complete his mission, Allah (sp) provided him (s) with a Book, the Noble Qur'an, and ordered him to rely on it and to use it for the purpose of achieving his mission. Within the Noble Qur'an itself, Allah (sp) commanded the Prophet (s) to invite people to Islam with the Qur'an. What this entailed was reciting the Qur'an to the people, explaining it to them, and applying its teachings. The following are some of the Qur'an's Verses that command or encourage the Prophet (s) to invite people to Islam with the Qur'an.

1) Allah (sp) said:

وَأُوحِيَ إِلَيَّ هَذَا ٱلْقُرْءَانُ لِأُنذِرَكُم بِهِۦ وَمَنۢ بَلَغَ

"This Qur'an has been revealed to me that I may therewith warn you and whomsoever it may reach." (Qur'an 6:19)
In this Verse, Allah (sp) informs us that He revealed the Qur'an in order to benefit human beings and make right their affairs. In it is a stern warning for all people until the Day of Resurrection. For this reason, Mujaahid (may Allah have mercy on him) said, "Every part of the Qur'an invites (to goodness) and warns (against evil)." After he said this, he recited the Verse, "That I may therewith warn you and whomsoever it may reach".

2) Allah (sp) said:

كِتَابٌ أُنزِلَ إِلَيْكَ فَلَا يَكُن فِى صَدْرِكَ حَرَجٌ مِّنْهُ لِتُنذِرَ بِهِۦ وَذِكْرَىٰ لِلْمُؤْمِنِينَ

"(This is the) Book (the Qur'an) sent down unto you (O Muhammad (s)), so let not your breast be narrow therefrom, that you warn thereby, and a reminder unto the believers." (Qur'an 7: 2)
Here, two functions of the Qur'an are mentioned: First, it should be used to warn disbelievers, and second, it should be used to remind believers. Furthermore, in this Verse, Allah (sp) instructs believers that they should not feel skeptical or doubtful about using the Qur'an to invite people to Islam; it is, after all, Allah's speech, and falsehood cannot come anywhere near it. Therefore, a Muslim should be at peace with the principle of using the Qur'an to invite others to Islam, and in doing so, he should not fear the reproach or blame of his audience.[88]

3) Allah (sp) said:

وَقُرْءَانًا فَرَقْنَاهُ لِتَقْرَأَهُۥ عَلَى ٱلنَّاسِ عَلَىٰ مُكْثٍ وَنَزَّلْنَاهُ تَنزِيلًا

"And (it is) a Qur'an which We have divided (into parts), in order that you might recite it to men at intervals. And We have revealed it by stages." (Qur'an 17: 106)

---

[88] *Tafseer At-Tabaree* (12/297), *Tafseer Al-Qurtubee* (7/160, 161), *Tafseer As-Sadee* (pgs. 245, 246), and to *Fee Dhilaal Al-Qur'an* (3/1254-1259).

To make it easier for the people to absorb the Qur'an's teachings in a slow yet timely manner, Allah (sp) revealed the Qur'an to His Messenger (s) in parts, over a span of 23 years. In a similar vein, a Muslim who invites others to Islam should proceed with slow and measured steps, giving time for his audience to absorb one lesson before moving on to the next.

4) Allah (sp) said:

$$قُلْ إِنَّمَآ أُنذِرُكُم بِٱلْوَحْىِ ۚ وَلَا يَسْمَعُ ٱلصُّمُّ ٱلدُّعَآءَ إِذَا مَا يُنذَرُونَ$$

"Say (O Muhammad (s)): 'I warn you only by the revelation (from Allah and not by the opinion of the religious scholars and others). But the deaf (who follow the religious scholars and others blindly) will not hear the call, even) when they are warned .)" (Qur'an 21: 45) (i.e., one should follow only the Qur'an and the Sunnah (legal ways, orders, acts of worship, statements of Prophet Muhammad (s), as the Companions of the Prophet did) The meaning of this Verse is as follows: 'O Muhammad , warn all people and invite them with the Grand Qur'an, which is revealed to you by your Lord. If they answer your invitation, then they do so for the benefit of their own selves. And if they don't, then that is because the voice of the Qur'an does not reach hearts that are unwilling to be guided. Due to their unwillingness to hear the voice of the Qur'an, it is as if they are deaf[89]. Deaf people do not benefit from the voices that surround them; similarly, disbelievers do not benefit from the Qur'an when they hear it being recited.

5) Allah (sp) said:

$$فَلَا تُطِعِ ٱلْكَٰفِرِينَ وَجَٰهِدْهُم بِهِۦ جِهَادًا كَبِيرًا$$

"So obey not to the disbelievers, but strive against them (by preaching) with the utmost endeavor, with it (the Qur'an)." (Qur'an 25:52)
In this Verse, Allah (sp) informs us that inviting others to Islam with the Qur'an is a form of *Jihad* – of struggling in the way of Allah (sp); of this there is no doubt, since He (sp) explicitly used the name *Jihad* to describe the act of inviting others to Islam with the Qur'an. Here, Allah (sp) honors those who strive to bring others into the fold of Islam, describing their efforts not simply as a struggle, but as a struggle that is carried out with the "utmost endeavor (or the utmost, or highest form of, struggle)." Muslim preachers engage in this struggle not just with disbelievers, but with sinning Muslims as well. This is because, if it is a high priority to use the Qur'an to invite disbelievers to Islam, it is certainly an even higher priority to use Verses of the Qur'an to invite sinning Muslims to repent and to return to the truth.

6) Allah (sp) said:

$$وَمَا كَانَ رَبُّكَ مُهْلِكَ ٱلْقُرَىٰ حَتَّىٰ يَبْعَثَ فِىٓ أُمِّهَا رَسُولًا يَتْلُوا۟ عَلَيْهِمْ ءَايَٰتِنَا ۚ وَمَا كُنَّا مُهْلِكِى ٱلْقُرَىٰٓ إِلَّا وَأَهْلُهَا ظَٰلِمُونَ$$

"And never will your Lord destroy the towns (populations) until He sends to their mother town a Messenger reciting to them Our Verses. And never would We destroy the towns unless the people thereof are Zalimun (polytheists, wrong-doers, disbelievers in the Oneness of Allah, oppressors and tyrants)." (Qur'an 28:59)
This Verse clearly points to the importance of preaching with the Qur'an, for in it, Allah (sp) states that listening to Verses of the Qur'an can directly prevent calamities that result in the destruction of an entire group of disbelievers. The Qur'an acts as a decisive proof (for or) against them once they listen

---

[89] *Tafseer Al-Qurtubee* (11/292), *Tafseer Ibn Katheer* (3/181), and *Tafseer As-Sadee* (pg. 473).

to it and decide to either believe in it or reject it.[90] Similar in meaning to the abovementioned Verse is the Saying of Allah (sp):

$$\text{وَإِنْ أَحَدٌ مِّنَ ٱلْمُشْرِكِينَ ٱسْتَجَارَكَ فَأَجِرْهُ حَتَّىٰ يَسْمَعَ كَلَٰمَ ٱللَّهِ ثُمَّ أَبْلِغْهُ مَأْمَنَهُۥ ۚ ذَٰلِكَ بِأَنَّهُمْ قَوْمٌ لَّا يَعْلَمُونَ}$$

"And if anyone of the Mushrikun (polytheists, idolaters, pagans, disbelievers in the Oneness of Allah) seeks your protection then grant him protection, so that he may hear the Word of Allah (the Qur'an), and then escort him to where he can be secure, that is because they are men who know not." (Qur'an 9: 6)

This Verse means: "Wait until he listens to the Qur'an and has a chance to contemplate its meanings, for then a decisive proof will have been established either for or against him. If he embraces Islam, then he automatically will begin to enjoy all of the rights that other citizens of the Muslim nation enjoy. And if he refuses, then he should be sent back to where he can be secure or to his homeland. Then, if doing so is desirable and appropriate, you may fight against him by declaring war upon him."[91]

A person should be able to determine the truthfulness of Islam just by listening to the Qur'an, which is why so many people throughout history have simply had to listen to a few Verses of the Qur'an before deciding to become Muslims. By its very nature, the Qur'an reaches the inner depths of man's soul like no other speech can. After all, had not the Qur'an been so powerful in its influence on those who listen to it, it would not have been the final and decisive factor that dictates the fate of a polytheist who seeks the protection of Muslims.

7) Allah (sp) said:

$$\text{فَذَكِّرْ بِٱلْقُرْءَانِ مَن يَخَافُ وَعِيدِ}$$

"But warn by the Qur'an, him who fears My Threat." (Qur'an 50: 45)

As this Verse suggests, the Qur'an should be used to warn people because it has the effect of awakening people from a state of slumber and heedlessness. A man might spend years thinking only about gratifying his worldly desires, but then wakes up with a start and becomes afraid upon hearing about the fate of disbelievers in the Hereafter or about the punishment of the Hellfire. For all of the above-mentioned reasons, every Muslim should realize that the Qur'an is his greatest weapon in his struggle to influence others and invite them to the truth.

Section 2

Applying the Principle of Inviting Others to Islam with the Qur'an

---

[90] *Tafseer Al-Qurtubee* (13/301-303), *Tafseer Ibn Katheer* (3/397), and *Tafseer As-Sa'dee* (pg. 571).
[91] *Tafseer Al-Qaasimee*, a book that is also known by the title *Mahaasin At-Ta'weel* (4/90).

Introduction

Allah (sp) commanded the Prophet (s) to invite people to Islam with the Noble Qur'an, and that is exactly what he did. He used the Qur'an as a tool for spreading Islam with his speech, his actions, and his overall demeanor. When the Mother of the Believers Aishah (rh) was asked about the character of the Prophet (s), she said: "Verily, the character of the Prophet of Allah (s) was (simply put) the Qur'an."[92]

Or in other words, the Prophet (s) was a practical manifestation of the Qur'an in all of his affairs: he followed all of the commands of the Qur'an, he adopted all of the characteristics that are extolled in the Qur'an, he learned from the morals and stories of the Qur'an, and he recited the Qur'an in a beautiful manner. In short, it was as if Aishah (rh) said that the Prophet (s) was a walking, talking version of the Qur'an.

In fact, the Prophet (s) made it clear that the Qur'an is the primary reason why he will have so many followers on the Day of Resurrection; moreover, he proclaimed that the Qur'an is the greatest miracle that Allah (sp) has ever given to any of his Prophets (st). In a Hadeeth that is related both in Bukhaaree and Muslim, the Messenger of Allah (sp) said: "Without exception, every single Prophet has been given something (i.e., a miracle) that leaves man with no logical choice except to believe (therefore, those who disbelieve act contrary to the dictates of logic, and instead follow their whims and desires). And that which I have been given is revelation that Allah has inspired to me. And verily, I hope to have more followers than any other Prophet on the Day of Resurrection."[93]

Some of the Main Differences between the Miracle of the Noble Qur'an and the Miracles that other Prophets (st) came with

1) The miracle of the Qur'an can be witnessed by the people of all generations until the Day of Resurrection, whereas the miracles of other Prophets (st) had limited witnesses and were momentary in nature. Any given miracle that occurred at their hands, such as the healing of the blind, ended as soon as it had finished taking place, and was witnessed in a direct way only by those who were there when it happened. Because we are informed about them in the Qur'an, we know about specific miracles that occurred at the hands of past Prophets (st) but because we neither saw nor heard those miracles occur, we are not direct witnesses to them. As for the Noble Qur'an, anybody who reads it with his eyes or listens to it with his ears is a direct witness to its grandeur.

2) The Qur'an consists of a number of miracles, which have to do with its style, its eloquence, its flow, its organization, and the information it gives about the unseen world – the past and future; other beings that exist in the universe, such as jinns and angels; Paradise and the Hellfire; and so on. In every era, a new miracle of the Qur'an manifests itself or is discovered. So, for instance, from the Qur'an and the Sunnah of the Prophet (s), the Companions (rp) learned that Jesus (p) was not crucified on a cross, but was instead raised to the heavens, and that he will one day return to Earth. In this case, the Qur'an provides information about the unseen world. When that information is confirmed through direct experience – i.e., when Jesus actually returns to the earth – a miracle of the Qur'an will be confirmed, i.e., the fact that it gave correct information about the unseen world: That Jesus (p) was not crucified, but was instead raised to the heavens. Therefore, it will be the people of a later generation (or perhaps even the people of this generation, and not the Companions (rp) of the Messenger of Allah (s), who will be direct witnesses of that miracle. Such is not the case for the miracles of other Prophets (st) for the direct witnesses of those miracles consisted of a very limited audience – of those who were alive and present to witness those miracles when they occurred.

---

[92] *Muslim* (746).
[93] *Bukhaaree* (4981) and *Muslim* (152).

3) The miracles of past Prophets (st) were of a sensual nature, in that they were witnessed in a physical way or by the senses. One saw the splitting of the sea, a rod turning into a snake, or a blind man being healed. The miracle of the Qur'an, on the other hand, is witnessed not so much by the senses as it is by the mind. Therefore, the Qur'an has a greater impact on human beings than do other miracles. A person who witnesses a miracle with his eyes sees something amazing, but the experience lasts only a few minutes and then is over with. But a person who witnesses the miracle of the Qur'an witnesses it with his mind within himself, and as a result, the experience of that miracle is continual in that it repeats itself in his mind every time he attempts to recall or contemplate it.[94]

To be sure, the Messenger of Allah (s) was charismatic, awe-inspiring in his demeanor, as well as eloquent and influential in his speech. Yet in spite of all those qualities, he still needed to rely on the Qur'an when he wanted to invite others to Islam. Then what about us today? We, who do not possess the same qualities, or who possess them to only a small degree, are in dire need of using the Qur'an as a tool to fulfill our duty to spread the message of Islam to the rest of mankind. Those who are specialized in the field of Islamic propagation should realize that, in influencing others to embrace Islam, their best asset is not their eloquence, their charm, their personality, or their charisma; rather, it is the Noble Qur'an, which is an eternal miracle that can be witnessed by all.

Examples of How the Prophet (s) Would Use the Qur'an to Invite People to Islam

First: Preaching Islam to the Delegations that came during the Hajj Season
Ibn Abbaas (r2) reported that 'Alee bin Abee Taalib (r) said, "When Allah (sp) commanded His Messenger (s) to present himself to Arab tribes, he went out (to meet them, and both Abu Bakr As-Siddeeq (r) and I accompanied him. Upon reaching a gathering of Arabs... Mafrooq bin 'Amr (one of the people that was seated in the gathering) said (to the Prophet (s)), 'To what do you invite us, O brother of Quraish?' The Messenger of Allah (s) (instead of answering him with his own words) recited the Verse:

قُلْ تَعَالَوْاْ أَتْلُ مَا حَرَّمَ رَبُّكُمْ عَلَيْكُمْ أَلَّا تُشْرِكُواْ بِهِ شَيْئًا وَبِٱلْوَٰلِدَيْنِ إِحْسَٰنًا وَلَا تَقْتُلُوٓاْ أَوْلَٰدَكُم مِّنْ إِمْلَٰقٍ نَّحْنُ نَرْزُقُكُمْ وَإِيَّاهُمْ وَلَا تَقْرَبُواْ ٱلْفَوَٰحِشَ مَا ظَهَرَ مِنْهَا وَمَا بَطَنَ وَلَا تَقْتُلُواْ ٱلنَّفْسَ ٱلَّتِى حَرَّمَ ٱللَّهُ إِلَّا بِٱلْحَقِّ ذَٰلِكُمْ وَصَّىٰكُم بِهِۦ لَعَلَّكُمْ تَعْقِلُونَ

"Say (O Muhammad (s)): 'Come, I will recite what your Lord has prohibited you from: Join not anything in worship with Him; be good and dutiful to your parents; kill not your children because of poverty – We provide sustenance for you and for them; come not near to Al-Fawahish (Shameful sins, illegal sexual intercourse, etc.) whether committed openly or secretly, and kill not anyone whom Allah has forbidden, except for a just cause (according to Islamic law). This He has commanded you that you may understand.'" (Qur'an 6:151)

Mafrooq then asked, "And to what else do you invite (people to follow), O brother of Quraish?" In response to this question, the Messenger of Allah (s) recited this Verse:

إِنَّ ٱللَّهَ يَأْمُرُ بِٱلْعَدْلِ وَٱلْإِحْسَٰنِ وَإِيتَآئِ ذِى ٱلْقُرْبَىٰ وَيَنْهَىٰ عَنِ ٱلْفَحْشَآءِ وَٱلْمُنكَرِ وَٱلْبَغْىِ يَعِظُكُمْ لَعَلَّكُمْ تَذَكَّرُونَ

"Verily, Allah enjoins Al-Adl (i.e., justice and worshipping none but Allah Alone – Islamic Monotheism) and Al-Ihsan (i.e., to be patient in performing your duties to Allah, totally for Allah's sake and in accordance with the Sunnah (legal ways) of the Prophet in a perfect manner), and giving

---

[94] *Fathul-Baaree Sharh Saheeh Al-Bukhaaree* by Ibn Hajr (9/9, 10).

(help) to kith and kin (i.e., all that Allah has ordered you to give them, i.e., wealth, visiting, looking after them, or any other kind of help, etc.); and forbids Al-Fahsha (i.e., all evil deeds, i.e., illegal sexual acts, disobedience of parents, polytheism, to tell lies, to give false witness, to kill a life without right, etc.), and Al-Munkar (i.e., all that is prohibited by Islamic law; polytheism of every kind, disbelief and every kind of evil deeds, etc.) and Al-Baghy (i.e., all kinds of oppression). He admonishes you, that you may take heed." (Qur'an 16:90)

Without having heard a single word of the Prophet (s), and having heard only a few Verses of the Qur'an, Mafrooq said, "O brother of Quraish, you have invited us to the noblest of manners and to the best of deeds."[95]

When the Prophet (s) invited Mafrooq's people to embrace Islam, and when Mafrooq asked the Prophet (s) questions about Islam, the Prophet (s) relied on the best asset he had with him: not his own words, but the words of Allah (sp). By choosing to answer Mafrooq's questions with Verses of the Qur'an, the Prophet (s) was reaching out to the inner depths of his heart, helping to establish a direct link between him and Allah (sp). The desired effect was achieved, for Mafrooq was greatly moved by the Verses that were being recited to him; he was so impressed, in fact, that he said, "O brother of Quraish, you have invited us to the noblest of manners and to the best of deeds."

Second: Traveling to See People and Inviting them with the Qur'an

Khaalid Al-'Udwaanee (r) related that he saw the Messenger of Allah (s) in the eastern part of Thaqeef, and he noticed that he was standing over a bow or a stick. This took place when the Messenger of Allah (s) went to the people of Thaqeef, seeking their aid and support. Years later, Khaalid (r) thought about that day; he remembered that the Prophet (s) was addressing the people of Thaqeef and inviting them to embrace Islam. What Khaalid (r) remembered in particular was how he had heard the Prophet (s) reciting the entire chapter of *At-Taariq*, which begins with the Verse:

$$وَٱلسَّمَآءِ وَٱلطَّارِقِ$$

"By the heaven, and At-Tariq (the night-comer, i.e., the bright star)" (Qur'an 86: 1)

Upon recalling that occurrence, Khaalid (r), who by now was a Muslim, said, "I had these Verses memorized even during the days of pre-Islamic ignorance, when I was still a polytheist. I then recited them again after I became a Muslim. (Years ago, when I first heard the Prophet (s) reciting these Verses) the people of Thaqeef called me and asked me, 'What did you hear from this man?' I recited the Verses to them. In their company was someone from the Quraish who said, 'We know our companion (i.e., Prophet Muhammad (s)) better than anyone else. Had we known that what he says is the truth, we would have followed him.'"[96]

From this story, we see how the Prophet (s) would go to people of different tribes and invite them to embrace Islam by reciting Verses of the Qur'an to them. Due to the profound effect that the Verses of the Qur'an have on a person's heart, the noble Companion Khaalid Al-'Udwaanee (r) took special notice of the chapter that he heard the Prophet (s) recite, having memorized it even while he was still a polytheist.

Third: Inviting Kings and Rulers with the Qur'an

1) In regard to her migration to Abyssinia, Umm Salamah (rh) recalled that An-Najjaashee, the king of that country, asked, "Do you have something from that which he (i.e., your Prophet (s) came with?" When he asked this question, he was surrounded by his priests, who had their scrolls spread out before them, and who were eager to hear what their visitors had to say. Jafar bin Abu Taalib (r) replied, "Yes", after which he forthwith proceeded to recite the beginning of Chapter *Maryam*. The effect Jafar's recitation had on An-Najjaashee and his priests was

---

[95] Related by Ibn Hibbaan in *Ath-Thiqaat* (180-88) and by Al-Baihaqee in *Dalaa'il An-Nubuwwah* (2422). And in his judgment of this Hadeeth's authenticity, Ibn Hajar said, Its chain is *Hasan* (i.e., good or acceptable). *Fathul-Baaree* (7/220).

[96] Related by Ahmad in *Al-Musnad* (4/335). The author of *Fathur-Rabbaanee* wrote, 'Its chain is good.' (20/243).

truly amazing. They were all moved so much by Jafar's recitation of the Qur'an that they cried until both their beards and their scrolls became soaked in tears.[97]

2) There is an authentic narration that contains the text of a letter that the Prophet (s) sent with Daihyah Al-Kalbee (r) to Haraql, the Emperor of Rome. The letter was sent after the Treaty of Al-Hudaibiyyah, and its text ran as follows:

"In the Name of Allah, the Most Beneficent, the Most Merciful. This is from Muhammad bin Abdullah, the Messenger of Allah, to Haraql, the leader of Rome: Peace be upon he who follows true guidance. To proceed: Verily, I invite you by the invitation of Islam. Submit and embrace Islam. If you do so, you will achieve safety and Allah will give you your reward twice (one interpretation of this phrase is that the first reward was for embracing Islam, and the second was for setting an example for his people to embrace Islam). And if you turn away, then upon you is the sin of Al-'Areesiyyeen (this word literally means, farmers; here, it means, the citizens of your country)."

And:

يَٰٓأَهْلَ ٱلْكِتَٰبِ تَعَالَوْاْ إِلَىٰ كَلِمَةٍ سَوَآءٍ بَيْنَنَا وَبَيْنَكُمْ أَلَّا نَعْبُدَ إِلَّا ٱللَّهَ وَلَا نُشْرِكَ بِهِۦ شَيْـًٔا وَلَا يَتَّخِذَ بَعْضُنَا بَعْضًا أَرْبَابًا مِّن دُونِ ٱللَّهِ فَإِن تَوَلَّوْاْ فَقُولُواْ ٱشْهَدُواْ بِأَنَّا مُسْلِمُونَ

"O people of the Scripture (Jews and Christians): Come to a word that is just between us and you, that we worship none but Allah, and that we associate no partners with Him, and that none of us shall take others as lords besides Allah. Then, if they turn away, say: "Bear witness that we are Muslims." (Qur'an 3:64).[98]

Anyone who hears the Qur'an is necessarily moved by it, a reality that applies to both Muslims and non-Muslims. The only difference is that some non-Muslims deny the effect that the Qur'an has on them, or that they are so far away from the truth that they are deaf in their spirits, souls, and hearts, and are thus unable to truly hear it.

Likewise, the Qur'an has a powerful impact on the hearts of all categories of people –the common masses, the poor, the rich, and kings. Consider how An-Najjaashee and his priests, who were the most honored members of their country, reacted to Jafar's recitation of the Qur'an: They did not shed merely a few tears but instead cried so much that their beards and scrolls became soaked in tears.

Fourth: The Qur'an's Influence on the Hearts of the Enemies of Islam

The powerful impact that the Qur'an has on the hearts of Islam's enemies is undeniable; this holds especially true for the leaders of the Quraish, who, because of their profound knowledge of the Arabic language and of Arab poetry, were best able to appreciate the eloquence and miraculous wording of the Qur'an.

Jaabir bin Abdullah (sp) said, "One day, the Quraish gathered together and said (to one another), 'Choose that man among you who has the most knowledge regarding magic, soothsaying, and poetry. And then let that man go to the one (i.e., the Prophet (s)) who has divided our ranks...and found fault with our religion. Let the one we choose speak to him and see what he says in reply.'" The leaders of the Quraish chose 'Utbah bin Rabee'ah, who went to the Prophet (s) and spoke to him for a long time; even though 'Utbah spoke without pause for a long time, the Prophet (s) did not interrupt him, but instead let him continue until he was done. Finally, when 'Utbah ended his long speech, the Prophet (s) politely asked him, "Are you finished, O son of Abul-Waleed?" 'Utbah said, "Yes".Then the Prophet (s) said, "In the Name of Allah, the Most Beneficent, the Most Merciful", after which he proceeded to recite the following Verses:

---

[97] Related by Ahmad in *Al-Musnad* (1/201). Commenting on the narrators of this Hadeeth, Al-Haithamee wrote in *Al-Majma'*, "Narration firsthand from the narrator who comes before him in the chain."
[98] Sahih Bukhaaree (4553).

$$\text{حم (١) تَنزِيلٌ مِّنَ ٱلرَّحْمَـٰنِ ٱلرَّحِيمِ (٢) كِتَـٰبٌ فُصِّلَتْ ءَايَـٰتُهُ قُرْءَانًا عَرَبِيًّا لِّقَوْمٍ يَعْلَمُونَ (٣) بَشِيرًا وَنَذِيرًا فَأَعْرَضَ أَكْثَرُهُمْ فَهُمْ لَا يَسْمَعُونَ (٤) وَقَالُوا۟ قُلُوبُنَا فِىٓ أَكِنَّةٍ مِّمَّا تَدْعُونَآ إِلَيْهِ وَفِىٓ ءَاذَانِنَا وَقْرٌ وَمِنۢ بَيْنِنَا وَبَيْنِكَ حِجَابٌ فَٱعْمَلْ إِنَّنَا عَـٰمِلُونَ (٥)}$$

"Ha.Mim (these letters are one of the miracles of the Qur'an, and none but Allah (Alone) knows their meanings.). A revelation from Allah, the Most Beneficent, the Most Merciful. A Book whereof the Verses are explained in detail; - A Qur'an in Arabic for people who know. Giving glad tidings of Paradise to the one who believes in the Oneness of Allah (i.e., Islamic Monotheism) and fears Allah much (abstain from all kinds of sins and evil deeds) and loves Allah much (performing all kinds of good deeds which He has ordained), and warning (of punishment in the Hell Fire to the one who disbelieves in the Oneness of Allah), but most of them turn away, so they listen not. And they say: "Our hearts are under coverings (screened) from that to which you invite us, and in our ears is deafness and between us and you is a screen, so work you (on your way); verily, we are working (on our way)." (Qur'an 41: 1-5)

The Prophet (s) continued to recite Chapter *Fussilat* until he reached Verse number 13, which is the Saying of Allah (sp):

$$\text{فَإِنْ أَعْرَضُوا۟ فَقُلْ أَنذَرْتُكُمْ صَـٰعِقَةً مِّثْلَ صَـٰعِقَةِ عَادٍ وَثَمُودَ}$$

"But if they turn away, then say (O Muhammad): 'I have warned you of as-Sa'iqah (a destructive awful cry, torment, hit, a thunderbolt) like the Sa'iqah which overtook 'Ad and Thamud (people)." (Qur'an 41: 13)

'Utbah, who by this time was overwhelmed by the captivating flow and cadence and meanings of the said Verses, put his hand over the Prophet's mouth and pleaded with him to stop, which, considering the meaning of Verse number 13, indicates that 'Utbah was terrified by the warning he was hearing. 'Utbah, losing his swagger and his sense of confidence, returned with a defeated comportment to his companions. Seeing him approach, the leaders of the Quraish said to one another, "We swear by Allah, Abul-Waleed has returned to you with a face (or expression) that is different from the one he had when he went away (from us to see the Prophet (s) a short while ago)."

Truly, 'Utbah was, albeit momentarily, changed; the effect that the Quran's Verses had on him had still not worn off when he returned to his fellow tribal leaders. And so among the things he said to them was the following: "O people of the Quraish, obey me, and let me decide on our present course of action. Let this man do what he is doing, and leave him alone. For by Allah, the speech he recited to me will be a matter of great importance in the world (i.e., many people will believe in it)." This was certainly sound advice; sadly, however, the other leaders of the Quraish responded, "By Allah, he has put a spell on you with his tongue, O Abul-Waleed!"[99]

Such was the effect that the Qur'an had on Islam's enemies. In fact, they became so terrified by the Qur'an's warnings that they became constantly preoccupied by and obsessed with the Qur'an. Having heard it once, they yearned to listen to it again. Fearing that they would embrace Islam if they listened to it over and over again, they set limits upon themselves, forbidding one another, in the strongest of terms, from listening to the Prophet (s) recite the Qur'an or from even sitting with him. On a similar note, they would forbid visiting tribes from either listening to or meeting with the Prophet (s).

One might ask, if the Qur'an had such a tremendous influence on Quraish's leaders, why did they not embrace Islam? The answer to this question is simple: It was their pride and stubbornness that prevented them from embracing Islam; otherwise, deep down in their hearts they knew that the Qur'an was truly the speech of their Lord, Allah (sp). Understanding the effect that the Qur'an would have on

---

[99] *Dalaa'il An-Nubuwwah* (2/220-222) and *Musnad Abu Ya'la* (3/350). According to another narration, the man who heard Chapter *Fussilat* from the Prophet (s) in this story, and who consequently reacted in the manner that is described above, was not 'Utbah but Al-Waleed bin Al-Mugheerah; refer to *Tafseer At-Tabaree* (28/155-157).

them if they would continue to be exposed to it over and over again, they forbade one another from listening to it. Allah (sp) said:

$$\text{وَقَالَ ٱلَّذِينَ كَفَرُوا۟ لَا تَسْمَعُوا۟ لِهَٰذَا ٱلْقُرْءَانِ وَٱلْغَوْا۟ فِيهِ لَعَلَّكُمْ تَغْلِبُونَ}$$

"And those who disbelieve say: 'Listen not to this Qur'an, and make noise in the midst of its (recitation) that you may overcome.'" (Qur'an 41: 26)
Had they not experienced the Qur'an's effect on their hearts, they would not have warned one another not to listen to its recitation. Indeed, the fact is that the Qur'an did have a strong and powerful effect on their hearts, but they refused to acknowledge the truthfulness of the Qur'an because they were a proud and arrogant people.

Fifth: Reminding People during Sermons and Lectures
Umm Hishaam bint Haarithah bin An-No'maan (r2) said: "Our oven and the oven of the Messenger of Allah (s) was the same for two years or at least for one year and some part of the next year. As for (the Verse) *'Qaf. By the Glorious Qur'an'*, I heard it being recited on the tongue of the Messenger of Allah (s); he would recite it every Friday when he stood on the pulpit which is when he would deliver a sermon to the people."[100]
When I say that we should use the Qur'an to invite others to Islam, I am referring not only to non-Muslim audiences, but to Muslim audiences as well. There are preachers who sometimes ramble on for more than half-an hour without mentioning a single Verse from the Noble Qur'an. To be sure, such speeches are, as eloquent as some of them may be, at the very least deficient. Scholars and preachers should strive to intersperse their speeches with Verses of the Qur'an, when they do that, their speeches become more blessed, and they get a more positive response from their audience. To be sure, a preacher should explain in simple language the teachings of Islam; a sermon, especially in these times, should not consist of a recitation of various Verses of the Qur'an without an explanation of their meanings. And so a preacher's speeches should strike a balance between mentioning Verses of the Qur'an and explaining their meanings.

Sixth: Reciting the Qur'an in a Melodious yet Fearful Tone, and Reciting Those Verses that are Especially Known for their Effect on the Hearts of People
Jaabir bin Mut'im (r) said, "One day, during Maghrib prayer, I heard the Messenger of Allah (s) recite from Chapter *At-Toor*:

$$\text{أَمْ خُلِقُوا۟ مِنْ غَيْرِ شَىْءٍ أَمْ هُمُ ٱلْخَٰلِقُونَ (٣٥) أَمْ خَلَقُوا۟ ٱلسَّمَٰوَٰتِ وَٱلْأَرْضَ ۚ بَل لَّا يُوقِنُونَ (٣٦) أَمْ عِندَهُمْ خَزَآئِنُ رَبِّكَ أَمْ هُمُ ٱلْمُصَيْطِرُونَ (٣٧)}$$

"Were they created by nothing, or were they themselves the creators? Or did they create the heavens and the earth? Nay, but they have firm Belief. Or are with them the treasures of your Lord? Or are they the tyrants with the authority to do as they like?" (Qur'an 52: 35-37)
When he (s) reached this part of the Verse, my heart almost flew away (so moved was I by his recitation)".[101]
This was certainly not an exaggeration on the part of Jubair (r). And why should the Qur'an not have the effect that Jubair (r) described; after all, in another Verse of the Qur'an (a point that we have hitherto discussed), we learn that if the strongest and firmest of mountains were to be given life, and were the Qur'an to descend upon it, it would, as a result of becoming terrified, fall down to the ground and break apart into pieces.

---

[100] *Saheeh Muslim* (873).
[101] *Saheeh Bukhaaree* (4854).

Section 3

Examples of How the Qur'an has Influenced Modern-Day Figures to Embrace Islam

Introduction

The Qur'an has always had a profound impact on people. Even during the times we live in - a period during which most people have a weak understanding of the Arabic language or don't understand Arabic at all and have to rely on translations of the meanings of the Qur'an - many people still continue to be amazed by the Qur'an to the degree that they decide to change their lives and enter into the fold of Islam.

Even if a person does not speak Arabic, there is much that the modern-day non-Muslim has to appreciate in the Noble Qur'an. For one thing, people of other religions, particularly Jews and Christians, rely on Scriptures that have been distorted and changed. A Jew or a Christian who is fair and honest cannot help but be impressed by the fact that the wording of the Qur'an, a Book that is more than 600 pages (in a recent printing of the Qur'an), has not changed even a single iota over the last 14 centuries. Other non-Muslims, even if they do not speak Arabic, are impressed by what has in these days become known as the scientific miracles of the Qur'an. We are living in an age of unprecedented scientific and technological knowledge, and much of the knowledge that mankind has gained in the past century is either mentioned directly or alluded to in the Noble Qur'an. This reality has prompted the authoring of many books that deal exclusively with the scientific miracles of the Qur'an. Another category of non-Muslims, those that are of Arab origin, are still able to appreciate the majestic and miraculous rhythm, tone, flow, and eloquence of the Noble Qur'an. And yet other non-Muslims delve into the meanings of the Qur'an and are captivated by its spirituality and its just and wonderful teachings.

Based on all of the things there are to admire about the Qur'an, one would think that entire populations would be racing to be the first to enter into the fold of Islam. Although that has happened in the past, today, even though thousands of people are entering into the fold of Islam on a monthly or yearly basis (and Allah (sp) best knows what the statistics are regarding this issue), we do not see entire nations of people becoming Muslims at the same time. It is usually individuals who, having undertaken a spiritual journey, decide all on their own to enter into the fold of Islam. These days, theoretically at least, a great deal of emphasis is placed on the individual – his right to think as he wants, and his right to live as he wants. That being the case, it is important to understand that, vis-à-vis Islam, individual non-Muslims can, in a general way, be divided into two categories. The first consists of those who have a sincere desire to be unbiased in their judgments; such people try their best to do away with any preconceived notions they might have about Islam. Even when such people do not embrace Islam, they at least are fair in pointing out the many good qualities they find in Islam and in the holy book of Islam, the Noble Qur'an. The second category consists of individuals – and sadly they are in the majority these days – who, whether they admit it or not, are not as much interested in the truth as they are in upholding their previously held beliefs, the beliefs of their forefathers and of their community. Such people are highly prejudiced in nature, and they feel a sense of superiority over people of all other faiths as well as a sense of contempt for anything that is deemed foreign, and these days the worst kind of foreign in their minds is anything that is associated with the East or with the Middle East.

In this chapter, we are of course concerned with the sayings of the former category. For a Muslim, it is always a cause for an increase in faith to hear about praise of Islam from a non-Muslim or from a Muslim who has just recently entered into the fold of Islam. It is important to note that what such people say does not establish the rules or principles of our religion, but instead confirms rules and principles that are already established. Or in other words, we do not rely on them to learn about the truth, but instead we listen to them in order to increase our faith and to confirm what we already believe to be true.[102]

The sayings that I quote in this section come from people who have become Muslims. They uttered the quotes that follow either while they were still non-Muslims or after they entered into the fold of Islam.

1) A Christian missionary whose name is now Ibraaheem Khaleel Ahmad

While still a non-Muslim, Ibraaheem delved deeply into the teachings of Islam, and his preferred subject of study was the Noble Qur'an. Each person, based on his background, previous knowledge, or preferred field of study, approaches the study of the Noble Qur'an with a specific mindset. As for Ibraaheem, he was interested, more than anything else, in the scientific miracles of the Qur'an; those alone, he felt, confirmed the truthfulness and divine source of the Qur'an. Having officially embraced Islam in the year 1380 H (1987 CE), Ibraaheem was once quoted as having said, "I believe with certainty that had I been an existentialist – that is, someone who doesn't believe that this universe has a creator and that doesn't believe in any divinely revealed messages – and had a group of people come to me and spoken to me about the vast array of modern knowledge that is mentioned in the Qur'an (centuries before that knowledge came to the attention of mankind), that alone would have made me believe in the Almighty Lord, the Creator of the heavens and the earth. And that alone would have been sufficient for me to make me not associate any partners with Him in worship."[103]

On another occasion, Ibraaheem said something that is very uplifting for Muslims, particularly for those Muslims who feel inferior because of the scientific and technological advances that have been made by the peoples of other nations. He said, "A Muslim should feel honored and proud because of the Qur'an, for it is like water: in it is life for anyone who drinks from it."[104]

And on yet another occasion, he said, "The Noble Qur'an is a forerunner in all of the fields of modern-day knowledge, whether it is medicine, astronomy, geography, geology, law, sociology, or history. In fact, it is because of our present-day knowledge that we are truly able to appreciate and recognize the knowledge that is discussed first (not in any scientific journal but) in the Noble Qur'an."[105]

2) Dr. Jareenee

Upon being asked for the reason why he embraced Islam, Dr. Jareenee said, "I studied very closely all of the Verses of the Qur'an that had anything to do with the fields of medicine and science, subjects that I studied from a very young age and that I knew very well. I concluded that the Verses I studied corresponded exactly with our modern-day knowledge of those subjects, and so I embraced Islam. My decision was further based on the fact that I believed with certainty that Muhammad (s), more than a thousand years ago, came with the plain truth; and he came at a time when there were no teachers of the subjects I mentioned earlier. In fact, were the specialists of every branch of modern-day knowledge to study those Verses of the Qur'an that pertain to their fields of study – which is basically what I did – they would, without a doubt, embrace Islam, so long as they possessed an adequate degree of intelligence and lacked ulterior motives."[106]

3) Etienne Dinet

It is truly amazing to see how some people, who do not even speak a word of the Arabic language, have been greatly influenced and moved by the Noble Qur'an. One such person was the French orientalist Etienne Dinet, who announced his entry into the fold of Islam and said, "It has been easy for believers of every era... to appreciate the miracle of the Qur'an simply by hearing it being recited; this miracle alone (i.e., the beauty of the Qur'an being recited) sufficiently explains the great success Islam has had in spreading throughout the earth. Europeans do not understand why Islam has spread so

---

[102] *Ad-Da'wah Ilallah Bil-Qur'an Al-Kareem* by Dr. Khaalid Al-Quraishee (pgs. 311-313).
[103] *Qaaloo 'Anil-Islam* (pg. 49).
[104] *Bil-Qur'an Aslama Haa'oolaa* (pgs. 131-136).
[105] *Muhammad Fit-Tauraah Wal-Injeel Wal-Qur'an* (pgs. 47, 48).
[106] *Bil-Qur'an Aslama Haaoolaa* (pg. 76).

far and so wide for the simple fact that they are ignorant of the Qur'an; or perhaps they are only acquainted with it through weak translations that do not precisely convey the Qur'an's meanings."[107]
On another occasion, he said, "If, through its style and through the beauty of its meanings, the Qur'an has had such a powerful effect on scholars who are wholly unconnected with Arabs and Muslims, then imagine the effect it has on the Arabs of Al-Hijaaz. After all, the Qur'an was revealed in their beautiful language."[108]

4) John Batiste Ahuneemo

A former priest, John Batiste said, "I embraced Islam when I attended a debate that took place between two scholars, one of whom was a Muslim, and the other a Christian. During the course of that debate, I became convinced of the truthfulness of Chapter *Maryam* (from the Noble Qur'an) and of another Chapter as well. And I became convinced that Islam is the one true religion."[109] It is important to note here that the Muslim debater that John referred to did his job well, presenting, during the course of the debate, not just his own words, but the words of Allah (sp) as well. He understood that his best chance of appealing to his audience involved reciting passages from the Book of Allah.

5) Dr. Ahmad Naseem Sosa

Prior to his entry into the fold of Islam, Dr. Ahmad was a Jew. Explaining his decision to become a Muslim, Dr. Ahmad said, "I became inclined to embrace Islam when I began to study the Noble Qur'an. The very first time I read the noble Qur'an, I felt a great and profound love for it, and I greatly enjoyed hearing its Verses being recited."[110]
He also said, "If a person truly understands the reality and spirituality of the religion of Islam, I do not think that there is anything that can have a greater effect on his emotions than him hearing the Qur'an being recited. By simply hearing the recitation of the Qur'an, one feels the one has entered into a realm that abounds with spirituality."[111]
We have hitherto discussed the effect that the meanings of the Qur'an have on the hearts of people. But we should not also forget the effect that a simple recitation of the Qur'an has on people who don't even understand the Arabic language, never mind those who do understand it. The noble Qur'an contains in it important teachings, laws, legislations, parables, etc. Even though that is the case, its words have been ordered in such a manner that Verses of the Qur'an are not meant to be read as other books are read, but instead are meant to be recited in a melodious tone. When it is recited in a beautiful manner, it reaches the most inner depths of people's hearts, even if those people do not speak a word of Arabic. Like Dr. Ahmad, many people who have embraced Islam have attributed their newfound faith to having heard someone's recitation of the Qur'an.

6) Cat Stevens, Who Changed His Name to Yusuf Islam

In recent years, certain famous and wealthy Westerners have embraced Islam, which is certainly a positive development considering how the masses of people in the West look up to celebrities. Famous converts have come from a variety of fields; some are famous athletes, others are singers, others are politicians, and yet others are actors. Perhaps one of the most famous converts over the last 30 years is the famous singer Cat Stevens, who, upon embracing Islam, changed his name to Yusuf Islam.
"A very famous and popular singer, Cat Stevens lived the ideal life according to Western standards. He was rich, he was famous, and he could basically have anything he wanted. And yet he knew there was something missing. Upon hearing the Qur'an for the first time, he realized what it was that he was missing, and he came to realize that the pleasures he enjoyed in this life did not come anywhere near the happiness and pleasure he felt when he listened to the Noble Qur'an."

---

[107] *Qaaloo 'Anil-Islam* (pgs. 63, 64) and *Al-Islam Fil'Aql Al-'Aalamee* (pgs. 197, 198).
[108] *Qaaloo 'Anil-Islam* (pg. 64).
[109] *Bil-Qur'an Aslama Haaoolaa* (pg. 89).
[110] *Qaaloo 'Anil-Islam* (pg. 70).
[111] *Fee Tareeqee Ilal-Islam* (1/183, 184).

Not only did Yusuf embrace Islam, but he also became famous once again; this time, not for his singing, but for his full-time efforts in spreading the message of Islam to others. Yusuf was once quoted as having said, "During that period of my life (i.e., before he embraced Islam), I felt as if I had achieved everything; after all, I achieved for myself success, fame, wealth, women... and basically everything. But in reality I was like a monkey, jumping from one tree to another (moving about without a definite sense of purpose). I do not recall ever having been satisfied or content with what I had (even though I had so much). But then when I heard the Qur'an being recited, I knew that it confirmed everything I believed deep down in my heart, and it confirmed everything I knew to be true."[112]

7) Fansai Montai

Fansai once said, "Verily, the example of a so-called Arab Islamic way of thinking that is far removed from the influence of the Qur'an, is that of a man whose entire supply of blood has been drained from his body."[113]

8) Hony

Hony was a women who loved philosophy. It became her field of study in university, and after a few years of hard work, she graduated and was awarded a degree. As she studied the different philosophies and religions of the world, she came across the Noble Qur'an. Describing her personal experience with the Qur'an, she later said, "As much as I try, I cannot describe in words the effect that the Qur'an has had on my heart. No sooner did I finish reading the third Chapter of the Qur'an, than I found myself prostrating on the ground and worshipping the Creator of this universe. And that was the first prayer that I performed as a Muslim."[114]

9) 'Aamir 'Alee Daawood

Before he became a Muslim, 'Aamir was a Christian who was a native of India. Describing his experience with the Qur'an, he said, "I once picked up a copy of an English translation of the meanings of the Qur'an. I knew that it was the holy Book of Muslims, and so, out of a feeling of curiosity, I began to read it and contemplate its meanings. I soon found myself to be wholly engrossed in the study of the Qur'an, and I was amazed to see how quickly it answered an important question that had been on my mind for a long time: 'What is the purpose behind life?' I found the answer to that question in the first few pages of the Noble Qur'an, or, more particularly, Verses 30 to 39 of Chapter *Al-Baqarah*. In these Verses, the reality and purpose of life is explained very clearly and can be appreciated by anyone who is fair and unbiased. The Verses not only explain the purpose of life, but also achieve that end in a convincing manner by informing us about the story of how mankind was first created."[115]

10) Brown and the Secrets of the Deep Ocean

A man named Brown, desiring to learn more about the religion of Islam, began with a casual reading of the Qur'an. But what began as a leisurely reading ended with a heightened sense of interest when he reached this Verse:

---

[112] *Qaaloo 'Anil-Islam* (pg. 68) and *Bil-Qur'an Aslama Haaoolaa* (pages. 91-93).
[113] *Rijaal Wa Nisaa Aslamoo* (5/50, 51).
[114] *Rijaal Wa Nisaa Aslamoo* (1/59, 60).
[115] *Rijaal Wa Nisaa Aslamoo* (8/109).

$$\text{أَوْ كَظُلُمَاتٍ فِي بَحْرٍ لُّجِّيٍّ يَغْشَاهُ مَوْجٌ مِّن فَوْقِهِ مَوْجٌ مِّن فَوْقِهِ سَحَابٌ ۚ ظُلُمَاتٌ بَعْضُهَا فَوْقَ بَعْضٍ إِذَا أَخْرَجَ يَدَهُ لَمْ يَكَدْ يَرَاهَا ۗ وَمَن لَّمْ يَجْعَلِ اللَّهُ لَهُ نُورًا فَمَا لَهُ مِن نُورٍ}$$

"Or (the state of a disbeliever) is like the darkness in a vast deep sea, overwhelmed with a great wave topped by a great wave, topped by dark clouds, darkness, one above another, if a man stretches out his hand, he can hardly see it! And he for whom Allah has not appointed light, for him there is no light." (Qur'an 24: 40)

A Muslim who already knows about the scientific miracles of the Qur'an can refer to one of the recently authored books on the topic, and thus point out a number of modern-day discoveries that are in harmony with specific Verses of the Qur'an. Through his own reading, and without the aid of a reference book, Brown came across one of those miracles and understood its implications. The abovementioned Verse discusses the darkness at the bottom of the ocean and the various layers of darkness that are above it. This is information that mankind has only recently learned about, as a result of manned and unmanned vessels that have plunged deep down into oceans and have reached levels of the ocean that are completely dark; before the level of complete darkness, the vessels went through a series of layers that were of varying degrees of darkness.

Brown wondered with amazement how a man who lived in the desert of Arabia could have had such accurate information about oceans. And so he approached a Muslim Indian scholar and asked him, "Did your Prophet Muhammad (s) ever travel by sea?" "No," the Muslim scholar replied. "Then who taught him so much about oceans?" The Muslim scholar replied with a question, "And what do you hope to get as a response to your question?" Brown said, "I read in the book of Islam a Verse that is so profound and accurate in its meaning that only a person who has vast knowledge of the oceans could have said it." Brown proceeded to recite the Verse, after which he said, "If Muhammad (s) did not travel by sea, if he did not learn about oceans from a knowledgeable scholar or sea-traveler, if he didn't study in a university, and if he was illiterate, then who is it that taught him this accurate and correct information? The only answer that comes to me is that he received revelation from the Creator of the universe. And so, indeed, I bear witness that none has the right to be worshipped but Allah and that Muhammad (s) is the Messenger of Allah (sp)."[116]

11) A German Scholar

In Chapter *Al-Qiyaamah*, Allah (sp) said:

$$\text{أَيَحْسَبُ الْإِنسَانُ أَلَّن نَّجْمَعَ عِظَامَهُ (٣) بَلَىٰ قَادِرِينَ عَلَىٰ أَن نُّسَوِّيَ بَنَانَهُ (٤)}$$

"Does man (a disbeliever) think that We shall not assemble his bones? Yes, We are Able to put together in perfect order the tips of his fingers." (Qur'an 75: 3, 4)

This Verse clearly alludes to fingerprints. The author of *Tafseer Al-Jawaahir 'Anir-Rahhaalah Mahmood Saamee* related the story of a German scholar who was blessed with Allah's mercy, and who embraced Islam and announced his change of religion in front of a group of scholars. When he was asked why he had decided to embrace Islam, he said, "It was this Verse that convinced me to do so: *"We are Able to put together in perfect order the tips of his fingers."* (Qur'an 75:4)

Neither Europeans nor Arabs knew about fingerprints until the recent past. That it was discussed in the Qur'an (more than fourteen centuries ago) proves that it is not the speech of man, but is instead the speech of Allah."[117]

Notice in many of the abovementioned quotes how specific individuals decided to embrace Islam based on just one of the Qur'an's miracles that came to their attention. The fact is that no human being

---

[116] *Bil-Islam Aslama Haaoolaa* (pg. 130) and *Tafseer Al-Jawaahir by Tantaawee Jauharee* (24/309).
[117] *Ma'a Kitaabullah* by Ahmad Abdur-Raheem As-Saayaih; and *Majallah AlJaamiah Al-Islaamiyyah* (Issue number 40, Rabee'ul Awwal, 1398 H, pgs. 23-27).

knows about all of its miracles, for they are many, and each one of them, on its own, sufficiently proves the truthfulness of the Qur'an.

CHAPTER 2

The Greatness of the Qur'an Virtues

This Chapter Consists of Three Parts:

Part One: The Greatness of the Qur'an's Overall Superior Qualities
Part Two: The Greatness of the Qur'an's Specific Superior Qualities
Part Three: The Rights of the Qur'an Over Muslims

Part 1

The Greatness of the Qur'an's Overall Superior Qualities

This part consists of nine sections:

Section One: The Qur'an is Allah's Revealed Speech
Section Two: The Qur'an is an Honor for Arabs in Particular, and for the Muslim Nation in General
Section Three: The Qur'an Guides to that which is Most Upright
Section Four: The Qur'an is a Blessed Book
Section Five: The Qur'an Contains in it an Explanation of All Things
Section Six: The Qur'an is Allah's Favor and a Cause of Happiness for His Slaves
Section Seven: The Qur'an is Guidance, Mercy, and Glad Tidings for Muslims
Section Eight: The Qur'an is Light
Section Nine: The Qur'an is Life for those Who Believe in It

Section One:

The Qur'an is Allah's Revealed Speech

In the following pages, we will be looking at the virtues or superior qualities of the Qur'an - the qualities that set it apart from other books. Without a doubt, one of the most important qualities of the Qur'an is that it is the speech of the All-Knowing, the All-Wise – Allah (sp). Allah (sp) said:

وَإِنْ أَحَدٌ مِّنَ ٱلْمُشْرِكِينَ ٱسْتَجَارَكَ فَأَجِرْهُ حَتَّىٰ يَسْمَعَ كَلَٰمَ ٱللَّهِ

"*And if anyone of the Mushrikun (polytheists, idolaters, pagans, disbelievers in the Oneness of Allah) seeks your protection then grant him protection, so that he may hear the Word of Allah (the Qur'an)*" (Qur'an 9: 6)

This Verse proves that the Qur'an that we recite and that is written within the covers of copies of the Qur'an is Allah's speech, not figuratively, but literally. It also proves that the Qur'an was revealed from Allah (sp). What this means is that Allah (sp) spoke the Qur'an, that Jibreel (p) heard it from Him, and that Jibreel (p) then descended with it and conveyed it to the Messenger of Allah (s) just as it was
conveyed to him from Allah (sp).[118]

Because the Qur'an is the speech of the Lord of all that exists, another one of its superior qualities is that it was not created. The Qur'an is the speech of the One Who has no equal, no rival, and no one that is similar to Him.

And since the Qur'an is Allah's speech, its words are weighty and of great import, and are thus not easy to bear, which is why Allah (sp) informed us that, were the firmest of mountains to be given life, and were the Qur'an to descend upon it, it would have, as a result of being terrified, fallen down and broken into pieces. Allah (sp) said:

لَوْ أَنزَلْنَا هَٰذَا ٱلْقُرْءَانَ عَلَىٰ جَبَلٍ لَّرَأَيْتَهُۥ خَٰشِعًا مُّتَصَدِّعًا مِّنْ خَشْيَةِ ٱللَّهِ

"*Had We sent down this Qur'an on a mountain, you would surely have seen it humbling itself and rending asunder by the fear of Allah.*" (Qur'an 59: 21)

To be sure, the strength of men's hearts do not come anywhere near the strength of mountains. Nonetheless, mountains cannot bear the message of the Qur'an, whereas Allah (sp), through His infinite wisdom and mercy, has given human being some ability to do just that: to bear the message of the Qur'an and to apply its teachings.[119]

Section Two:

The Qur'an is an Honor for Arabs in Particular, and for the Muslim Nation in General

There is no need to sugarcoat the situation of Arabs prior to the advent of Islam; for the simple fact is that they lived in a state of complete ignorance and darkness. Corruption was widespread, and everything about their lives – their beliefs, their worship, their dealings among themselves, and their system of governance – could be described as reprehensible, ridiculous, or wicked. Then Allah (sp) sent to them the Prophet (s), who came to them with the Noble Qur'an, which drastically changed their

---

[118] *Sharh Al-'Aqeedah Al-Waasitiyyah* by Muhammad Khaleel Harraas (pgs. 153, 154).
[119] *At-Tidhkaar Fee Afdalil-Adhkaar* (pg. 45).

lives. Once a people that were despised and known for their ignorance, Arabs, through their adherence to the
Qur'an, were raised to a level of honor, dignity, and power. They became the best of nations, and leaders of all other nations.

The Qur'an is a blessing for all Muslims in general, but it is particularly so for Arabs. With the emergence of two powerful empires – the Roman and Persian Empires – Arabs were alive on borrowed time, and were ripe for subjugation or assimilation at the hands of either the Romans or the Persians. Empires, by their very nature, need to expand, or at least they need the members of conquered nations to do their dirty work for them – fighting wars, working as slaves, and so on. Already, some of the Arabs of Ash-Sham (Syria and surrounding regions – the Levant) had become Christians, and were virtually assimilated into the Roman Empire. If it was not going to be subjugation or assimilation, Arabs were ripe for extinction. They had very little to offer the outside world; they were not exactly concerned with the goings on of the world; and they were tribal in nature: They even drew distinctions among themselves, with the members of one tribe considering the members of other tribes as being foreigners. They were ready, if not for complete extinction, then for at least a degree of extinction: the kind that involves living in remote areas with the members of one's tribe, contributing nothing to mankind, and having virtually no impact on the world at large – like the tribes that, even today, are discovered deep within the jungles of the world.

But the Qur'an saved them, helping to preserve their identity, their culture, and their language. The Qur'an was the main reason why the Arabic language spread to Asia, Africa, Europe (Andalusia), and elsewhere throughout the world. Arabic became one of the most important and widely-spoken languages on the world stage, since every Muslim, all over the world, felt, and still continues to feel, that Arabic is his language. Every Muslim feels that way because Arabic is the language of the Qur'an. There are three Verses which prove that the Qur'an should be a cause of pride and honor for Arabs in particular, and for Muslims in general:

1) Allah (sp) said:

وَإِنَّهُ لَذِكْرٌ لَّكَ وَلِقَوْمِكَ ۖ وَسَوْفَ تُسْـَٔلُونَ

"And verily, this (the Qur'an) is indeed a Reminder for you (O Muhammad (s)) and your people (Quraish people, or your followers) and you will be questioned (about it)." (Qur'an 43:44)

There are two possible interpretations of this Verse. According to the proponents of the first interpretation, the Qur'an is a reminder for the Prophet (s) and for his people; according to the second interpretation, the Qur'an is a source of honor for the Prophet (s) and for his people. The latter, regardless of whether or not it is the correct interpretation of the Verse, conveys a true meaning. How so? Well, because of the Qur'an, billions of Muslims throughout history have sent prayers and salutations upon the Prophet (s), and they will continue to do so until Allah (sp) inherits the earth and that which is on it. As for the Prophet's people, prior to the advent of Islam they were considered a nonentity in the world. If the people of other nations did mention them, they spoke of them in a scornful and disparaging manner. But once the Qur'an was revealed to the Prophet (s), Arabs took a leading role on the world stage, and they continued to do so in the centuries that followed.

2) Allah (sp) said:

لَقَدْ أَنزَلْنَآ إِلَيْكُمْ كِتَٰبًا فِيهِ ذِكْرُكُمْ ۖ أَفَلَا تَعْقِلُونَ

"Indeed, We have sent down for you (O Mankind) a Book, (the Qur'an) in which there is Dhikrukum (your Reminder or an honor for you, i.e., honor for the one who follows the teaching of the Qur'an and acts on its orders). Will you not then understand?" (Qur'an 21:10)

As the translator pointed out within parentheses, the meaning of this Verse is as follows:

If you obey the commands of the Qur'an and avoid perpetrating its prohibitions, your status will be raised, and the Qur'an will be a source of honor for you.[120]

Technological knowledge, scientific knowledge, domestically produced products – Arabs had none of these things to offer to the world. The one thing they had to contribute to mankind was the one thing that was more valuable than everything else combined: The religion of Islam. Mankind came to know Arabs due to their religion, their Book, their beliefs, and their manners.[121]

3) Allah (sp) said:

$$ص ۚ وَٱلْقُرْءَانِ ذِى ٱلذِّكْرِ$$

"Sad. By the Qur'an full of reminding." (Qur'an 38: 1)

Contrary to the interpretation of Dhil-Dhikr in the abovementioned translation – full of reminding – As-Sa'dee (may Allah have mercy on him) said that it means, "Possessor of great honor and distinction." Added to that overall meaning, As-Sa'dee (may Allah have mercy on him) stated, is the fact that the Qur'an is a reminder for human beings, providing them with all of the knowledge they need in this life, in terms of both their beliefs and the laws by which they must abide.[122]

Section Three:

The Qur'an guides to that which is Most Upright

In Chapter *Al-Israa* of the Noble Qur'an, Allah (sp) said:

$$إِنَّ هَٰذَا ٱلْقُرْءَانَ يَهْدِى لِلَّتِى هِىَ أَقْوَمُ$$

"Verily, this Qur'an guides to that which is most just and right". (Qur'an 17: 9)

In this Verse, Allah (sp) informs us that the Noble Qur'an, which is the greatest of all revealed Books and the most comprehensive in terms of the knowledge it contains, "guides to that which is most just and right." Or in other words, it guides mankind to the path that is the straightest, the most upright, and the most correct.

In a general way, this Verse states that the Qur'an guides mankind to the most upright and just of paths. But were we to go into specifics, by mentioning examples of how the Qur'an achieves that aim, we would have to mention every Verse of the Qur'an, since the Qur'an, in its entirety, guides mankind to what is best for them regarding both this world and the Hereafter.[123] If one wants to know the best and most upright way of treating any issue – whether it has to do with beliefs, manners, deeds, politics, work, acts of worship, etc. – one simply has to go to the Qur'an to find his answer.

Section Four:

The Qur'an is a Blessed Book

---

[120] *Tafseer as-Sa'dee* (3/269).
[121] *Tafseer as-Sa'dee* (3/269).
[122] *Tafseer as-Sa'dee* (4/279).
[123] *Adwaa al-Bayaan* (3/372).

In four different Verses, Allah (sp) described the Qur'an as being blessed:

1) Allah (sp) said:

$$\text{وَهَـٰذَا كِتَـٰبٌ أَنزَلْنَـٰهُ مُبَارَكٌ مُّصَدِّقُ ٱلَّذِى بَيْنَ يَدَيْهِ}$$

"And this (the Qur'an) is a blessed Book which We have sent down, confirming (the revelations) which came before it." (Qur'an 6:92)

2) Allah (sp) said:

$$\text{وَهَـٰذَا كِتَـٰبٌ أَنزَلْنَـٰهُ مُبَارَكٌ فَٱتَّبِعُوهُ وَٱتَّقُوا۟ لَعَلَّكُمْ تُرْحَمُونَ}$$

"And this is a blessed Book (the Qur'an) which We have sent down, so follow it and fear Allah (i.e., do not disobey His Orders), that you may receive mercy (i.e., saved from the torment of Hell)." (Qur'an 6: 155)

3) Allah (sp) said:

$$\text{وَهَـٰذَا ذِكْرٌ مُّبَارَكٌ أَنزَلْنَـٰهُ أَفَأَنتُمْ لَهُ مُنكِرُونَ}$$

"And this is a blessed Reminder (the Qur'an) which We have sent down, will you then (dare to) deny it?" (Qur'an 21:50)

4) Allah (sp) said:

$$\text{كِتَـٰبٌ أَنزَلْنَـٰهُ إِلَيْكَ مُبَارَكٌ لِّيَدَّبَّرُوٓا۟ ءَايَـٰتِهِۦ وَلِيَتَذَكَّرَ أُو۟لُوا۟ ٱلْأَلْبَـٰبِ}$$

"(This is) a Book (the Qur'an) which We have sent down to you, full of blessings that they may ponder over its Verses, and that men of understanding may remember." (Qur'an 38:29)

Something that is blessed is not only something whose goodness is confirmed to be present, but also something whose goodness is perpetual and plentiful. Such is certainly the case regarding the Noble Qur'an.[124]

Regardless of any other consideration, the Qur'an is blessed because it is Allah's speech, because its carrier was Jibreel (p), and because its destination was the heart of the Prophet (s). It is furthermore blessed because of its contents. Compared to the large and multiple volume works that have been authored by many men throughout history, the Qur'an is small in size – just over six-hundred pages in its most recent print. And yet each one of its Verses conveys a quantity and quality of meaning that are not found in scores of pages of any book that a human being has authored.

In short, the Qur'an is blessed in every way possible: Its recitation is blessed; its knowledge is blessed; its meanings are blessed; the effect it has on people's hearts is blessed; its goals and aims are blessed; and so on.[125]

Without a doubt, the Qur'an is more blessed than any other divinely revealed Book. If we were to compare the Qur'an to the Torah, for instance, we would find that the Qur'an is small in size. Nonetheless, it is, by dint of its blessedness, more comprehensive in terms of the meanings it conveys. Every day, the Qur'an gives something new, for its wonders never run out. When a group of people read the same Verse of the Qur'an, one of them understands one meaning, and another comes out with another beautiful meaning, which, though different, is equally correct. This quality of the Qur'an –

---

[124] *At-Tabarruk Wa-Anwaa'uhu wa ahkaamuhu* by Dr. Naasir 'Abdur-Rahmaan Al-Judai' (pgs. 45, 46).
[125] *Fee Dhilaal Al-Qur'an* (2/1147), and *Lataa'if Al-Qur'aaniyyah* by Dr. Salaah Abdul-Fattaah Al-Khaalidee (pgs. 15, 16).

that many meanings can be derived from few of its words – is proof that its speaker is Allah (sp), the All-Wise. What I have mentioned here thus far is the meaning of the Saying of Allah (sp):

$$كِتَابٌ أَنزَلْنَاهُ إِلَيْكَ مُبَارَكٌ$$

"(This is) a Book (the Qur'an) which We have sent down to you, full of blessings." (Qur'an 38:29)
Every divinely-revealed book that has come before the blessed Qur'an was meant for a specific period of time, and for a specific nation of people. As for the Qur'an, it addresses the needs of all of mankind, and its Verses provide appropriate legislations for the needs of people of all eras, which it will continue to do until the Day of Resurrection.

Section Five:

The Qur'an Contains in it an Explanation of All Things

Allah (sp) said:

$$وَنَزَّلْنَا عَلَيْكَ الْكِتَابَ تِبْيَانًا لِّكُلِّ شَيْءٍ$$

"And We have sent down to you the Book (the Qur'an) as an exposition of everything." (Qur'an 16: 89)
Ibn Masood (r) said, "Each field of knowledge, as well as each and every thing, has been explained to us in the Noble Qur'an."[126] What this means is that, either explicitly, implicitly, or by way of allusion or suggestion, the Qur'an comprehensively deals with every worldly field of knowledge. Up until this day, as has been attested to by a score of scientists and doctors and scholars, newly discovered knowledge is found to be mentioned, hinted at, or alluded to in the Noble Qur'an – whose revelation preceded the actual discovery by more than 1400 years. It is for this reason that we find a number of Western specialists either praising Islam and the Qur'an or going all the way and entering into the fold of Islam.

Section Six:

The Qur'an is Allah's Favor and a Cause of Happiness for His Slaves

Allah (sp) said:

$$قُلْ بِفَضْلِ اللَّهِ وَبِرَحْمَتِهِ فَبِذَٰلِكَ فَلْيَفْرَحُوا هُوَ خَيْرٌ مِّمَّا يَجْمَعُونَ$$

"Say:' In the Bounty of Allah, and in His Mercy (i.e., Islam and the Qur'an) – therein let them rejoice.' That is better than what (the wealth) they amass." (Qur'an 10:58)
Commenting on this Verse, Abu Sa'eed Al-Khudree (r) said, "The Bounty of Allah (sp) is the Qur'an, and His Mercy is making you (O Muslims) its followers."

---

[126] *Tafseer Ibn Katheer* (4/601).

In the abovementioned Verse, Allah (sp) made it clear that following the guidance of the Qur'an is better than worldly pleasures and possessions, as well as all of the other temporary enjoyments of this world. The Companions (rp) understood this Verse correctly, and they applied its meanings as well, for they were not deceived by the fleeting pleasures of this world.

There are many examples of the Companions' disdain for worldly things and their longing for the Hereafter, but given the limited scope of this work, I will mention just one, and it is directly relevant to the abovementioned Verse. When war booty arrived in Al-Madeenah from Iraq, Umar (r), and a freed slave of his went out to check the inventory of the booty. Umar (r) began by counting the number of camels that had arrived, and there were a great many indeed. Impressed by the quantity of goods that had arrived and that could be used to help his fellow Muslims, Umar (r) said, "All praise is for Allah, the Exalted." His former slave, as if to interpret the abovementioned Verse, said, "This, by Allah, is the Bounty of Allah and His Mercy." Umar (r) responded, "You have lied. This (wealth) is not what is meant in (the beginning of) Allah's Saying: *"Say: 'In the Bounty of Allah, and in His Mercy; therein let them rejoice'. That is better than what (the wealth) they amass."* (Qur'an: 10:58)

"That is better than what (the wealth) they amass." Rather, this wealth is that which they amass (in the said Verse)."[127]

It is not wealth or material well-being of any sort that determines the true status of people in this world, never mind their status in the Hereafter. In fact, worldly things and possessions very frequently are the main causes of misery and depression for people in this world, and of eternal punishment in the Hereafter. In these days of unprecedented wealth, one does not, especially in the West, have to look hard to find instances of wealth and misery being the two main features of people's lives.

Section Seven:

The Qur'an is Guidance, Mercy, and Glad Tidings for Muslims

In Chapter *An-Nahl*, Allah (sp) said that the Noble Qur'an is:

وَهُدًى وَرَحْمَةٌ وَبُشْرَىٰ لِلْمُسْلِمِينَ

"A guidance, a mercy, and glad tidings for those who have submitted themselves (to Allah as Muslims)." (Qur'an 16:89)

It is important to note here that the Qur'an is guidance, a mercy, and glad tidings for Muslims only. It is guidance in that it informs Muslims about correct beliefs, thus saving them from false and misguided beliefs. It is a mercy because it leads to happiness in both this world and the Hereafter. And it is glad tidings in that it informs Muslims about the good they will receive in this life, as well as the blessed and joy-filled existence that awaits them in the Hereafter. These three qualities are for Muslims only; as for others, they have turned away from the Qur'an and deprived themselves of its fruits. The noble scholar Ash-Shinquitee (m) asserted this point when he said, "This Verse clearly implies that the qualities it mentions are not for non-Muslims."[128] This implied meaning is mentioned explicitly elsewhere in the Qur'an; for instance, Allah (sp) said:

قُلْ هُوَ لِلَّذِينَ ءَامَنُوا۟ هُدًى وَشِفَآءٌ وَٱلَّذِينَ لَا يُؤْمِنُونَ فِىٓ ءَاذَانِهِمْ وَقْرٌ وَهُوَ عَلَيْهِمْ عَمًى

"Say: 'It is for those who believe a guide and a healing. And as for those who disbelieve, there is heaviness (deafness) in their ears, and it (the Qur'an) is blindness for them.'" (Qur'an 41:44)

And in another Verse, Allah (sp) said:

---

[127] *Tafseer Ibn Katheer* (4/289).
[128] *Adwaa Al-Bayaan* (3/315).

$$وَنُنَزِّلُ مِنَ ٱلْقُرْءَانِ مَا هُوَ شِفَآءٌ وَرَحْمَةٌ لِّلْمُؤْمِنِينَ وَلَا يَزِيدُ ٱلظَّٰلِمِينَ إِلَّا خَسَارًا$$

"And We send down from the Qur'an that which is a healing and a mercy to those who believe (in Islamic Monotheism and act on it), and it increases the Zalimun (polytheists and wrongdoers) nothing but loss." (Qur'an 17: 82)

Section Eight:

The Qur'an is Light

Allah (sp) said:

$$يَٰٓأَيُّهَا ٱلنَّاسُ قَدْ جَآءَكُم بُرْهَٰنٌ مِّن رَّبِّكُمْ وَأَنزَلْنَآ إِلَيْكُمْ نُورًا مُّبِينًا$$

"O mankind! Verily, there has come to you a convincing proof (Prophet Muhammad (s)) from your Lord and We sent down to you a manifest light (this Qur'an)." (Qur'an 4: 174)

Elsewhere in the Qur'an, Allah (sp) said:

$$كِتَٰبٌ أَنزَلْنَٰهُ إِلَيْكَ لِتُخْرِجَ ٱلنَّاسَ مِنَ ٱلظُّلُمَٰتِ إِلَى ٱلنُّورِ بِإِذْنِ رَبِّهِمْ إِلَىٰ صِرَٰطِ ٱلْعَزِيزِ ٱلْحَمِيدِ$$

"(This is) a Book which We have revealed unto you (O Muhammad) in order that you might lead mankind out of darkness (of disbelief and polytheism) into light (of belief in the Oneness of Allah and Islamic Monotheism) by their Lord's Leave to the Path of the All-Mighty, the Owner of all Praise." (Qur'an 14:1)

The Qur'an is "light" because it illuminates the truth and drowns out the darkness of ignorance, disbelief, polytheism, sin, and corrupt manners. The Qur'an is light, and the purpose for which it was revealed is to remove people from the darkness of disbelief and ignorance and to bring them to the light of *Tawheed* (Islamic Monotheism). Had darkness reigned supreme throughout the earth, and had the light of the truth remained hidden and forgotten, life on earth would be plagued by complete and unmitigated corruption, violence, chaos, and evil.

In order to save people from darkness and misguidance, Allah (sp) has sent to them a clear Book, one that benefits them both in this life and in the Hereafter. Allah (sp) said:

$$يَٰٓأَهْلَ ٱلْكِتَٰبِ قَدْ جَآءَكُمْ رَسُولُنَا يُبَيِّنُ لَكُمْ كَثِيرًا مِّمَّا كُنتُمْ تُخْفُونَ مِنَ ٱلْكِتَٰبِ وَيَعْفُواْ عَن كَثِيرٍ قَدْ جَآءَكُم مِّنَ ٱللَّهِ نُورٌ وَكِتَٰبٌ مُّبِينٌ (١٥) يَهْدِى بِهِ ٱللَّهُ مَنِ ٱتَّبَعَ رِضْوَٰنَهُۥ سُبُلَ ٱلسَّلَٰمِ وَيُخْرِجُهُم مِّنَ ٱلظُّلُمَٰتِ إِلَى ٱلنُّورِ بِإِذْنِهِۦ وَيَهْدِيهِمْ إِلَىٰ صِرَٰطٍ مُّسْتَقِيمٍ (١٦)$$

"Indeed, there has come to you from Allah a light (Prophet Muhammad (s)) and a plain Book (this Qur'an. Wherewith Allah guides all those who seek His Good Pleasure to ways of peace, and He brings them out of darkness by His Will unto light and guides them to a Straight Way (Islamic Monotheism)." (Qur'an 5:15, 16)

Section Nine:

The Qur'an is Life for those Who Believe in It

Allah (sp) said:

$$يَٰٓأَيُّهَا ٱلَّذِينَ ءَامَنُوا۟ ٱسْتَجِيبُوا۟ لِلَّهِ وَلِلرَّسُولِ إِذَا دَعَاكُمْ لِمَا يُحْيِيكُمْ$$

"O you who believe! Answer Allah (by obeying Him) and (His) Messenger when he calls you to that which will give you life." (Qur'an 8: 24)

A fruitful life can be achieved only by those who obey Allah (sp) and His Messenger (s); all others are not truly alive. They might be alive in the sense that animals are alive: they eat, they sleep, they satisfy their carnal desires, and that is about it. But having no relationship with their Creator, they lead pointless lives; to the degree that it is as if they are dead.

Qataadah (may Allah have mercy on him) said, "(The saying of Allah (sp)) 'That which gives you life' refers to the Qur'an. In it is life...safety, and protection for both this world and the Hereafter." The truly good life, therefore, is the life of one who obeys Allah (sp) and His Messenger (s) both outwardly and inwardly. Those who fulfill this description are truly alive, even if they have died. Others are truly dead, even if they are still physically alive. Allah (sp) said:

$$أَوَمَن كَانَ مَيْتًا فَأَحْيَيْنَٰهُ وَجَعَلْنَا لَهُۥ نُورًا يَمْشِى بِهِۦ فِى ٱلنَّاسِ كَمَن مَّثَلُهُۥ فِى ٱلظُّلُمَٰتِ لَيْسَ بِخَارِجٍ مِّنْهَا$$

"Is he who was dead (without faith by ignorance and disbelief) and We gave him life (by knowledge and faith) and set for him a light (of Belief) whereby he can walk amongst men, like him who is in the darkness (of disbelief polytheism and hypocrisy) from which he can never come out" (Qur'an 6: 122)

Even among those who, by obeying Allah (sp), are truly living, there are degrees of being alive. The one who is most completely alive among them is the one who best obeys the commands of the Qur'an. Others among them are alive to the degree that they do the same, and they lose out on a truly complete and fruitful life to the degree that they are negligent regarding the Qur'an's commands.[129]

This section is titled "The Greatness of the Qur'an's Virtues", but truth be told, as much as one tries to be comprehensive, no human being can truly grasp the many virtues and superior qualities of the Qur'an. Even supposing that a human being had the ability to do just that, and supposing that he wanted to record that knowledge in print, all of the paper on earth would not be enough for him to complete his task. Long before he would have finished enumerating the Qur'an's superior qualities, he would have run out of both paper and ink. It is therefore sufficient here for us to enumerate the ones we grasp, and to appreciate the fact that there are many others that we do not grasp or that we do not fully appreciate.[130]

---

[129] *Al-Fawaaid* (pg. 88).
[130] *Khasaais Al-Qur'an Al-Kareem* (pgs. 124, 125).

PART 2

The Greatness of the Qur'an's Specific Superior Qualities

This Part Consists of Five Sections:
Section One: The Virtues of Listening to the Qur'an
Section Two: The Virtues of Learning the Qur'an and of Teaching it to Others
Section Three: The Virtues of Reciting the Qur'an
Section Four: The Virtues of Memorizing the Qur'an
Section Five: The Virtues of Applying the Teachings of the Qur'an

Section 1

The Virtues of Listening to the Qur'an

Three issues are Discussed in this Section:
First: Listening to the Qur'an Results in Being the Recipient of Allah's Mercy
Second: Listening to the Qur'an Leads to Guidance for Both Human Beings and Jinns
Third: Listening to the Qur'an Results in a Heart that is Submissive and Spiritually Strong and in Eyes that Shed Tears (Out of the Fear of Allah (sp))

Introduction

Every Muslim knows that reciting the Qur'an is an act of worship, but many Muslims seem to be unaware of the virtues of listening to the Qur'an. It is a well-known fact from the biography of the Messenger of Allah (s) that he loved to hear the Qur'an being recited by others. On one occasion, he ordered Abdullah bin Masood (r) to recite the Qur'an so that he could listen to him. When Abdullah (r) complied, the Prophet (s) became fully engrossed in his recitation, being moved to the point that his noble eyes began to shed tears. Based on this incident (as well as on other proofs as well, scholars agree that it is recommended in Islam to ask someone who has a beautiful voice and who reads the Qur'an well, to recite the Qur'an. In fact, making such requests is a habit that was common among the righteous Muslims of the early generations of Islam. Without a doubt, a sincere, heartfelt, and skillful recitation of the Qur'an promotes the ability of an audience to both contemplate and understand the meanings of the Qur'an.
The virtues of listening to the Qur'an are many; in the following pages, I will focus on some of the more important ones.

First:

Listening to the Qur'an Results in Being the Recipient of Allah's Mercy

Allah (sp) said:

$$وَإِذَا قُرِئَ ٱلْقُرْءَانُ فَٱسْتَمِعُوا۟ لَهُۥ وَأَنصِتُوا۟ لَعَلَّكُمْ تُرْحَمُونَ$$

"So, when the Qur'an is recited, listen to it, and be silent that you may receive mercy" (i.e., during the compulsory congregational prayers when the Imam (of a mosque) is leading the prayer (except Surat Al-Fatiha, and also when he is delivering the Friday prayer Khutbah. (*Tafsir At-Tabari* Vol.9, Pg. 162-164). (Qur'an 7: 204)

Here, Allah (sp) orders His slaves to listen to the Qur'an and to remain silent during its recitation. The implied meaning here is that they should contemplate and apply the Qur'an's teachings, for doing so leads to receiving Allah's mercy. The famous scholar Al-Laith (m) said, "Mercy comes no sooner to anyone than to a person who listens to the Qur'an." Al-Laith based his statement on the saying of Allah (sp): "So, when the Qur'an is recited, listen to it, and be silent that you may receive mercy".

The exact translation of the end of this Verse is, "So that perhaps you may receive mercy." The translator of the abovementioned Verses likely left out the word 'perhaps' because when Allah (sp) makes a promise with the word perhaps, it means that He (sp), being All-Generous and Most-Merciful, has made that promise binding upon himself.[131] So the meaning is not, "so that perhaps you may receive mercy," but instead, "as a result of obeying these commands, you will receive mercy".

When someone chooses not to listen to the Qur'an, he hurts himself in an unimaginable way. People who listen to the Qur'an in order to benefit thereby reap fruits that are truly wonderful, such as gaining a feeling of closeness to Allah (sp); experiencing moments of spiritual elation; feeling happy and content; and being at peace - all of which are the truly precious enjoyments of this life.

The Prophet (s) informed us that, when people gather together to study the Qur'an and to listen to its recitation, they benefit a great deal in the process. For instance, it is related in Muslim that the Prophet (s) said: *"Whenever a group of people gather in the house from the houses of Allah (sp), in order to recite the Book of Allah and to study it among themselves, peace descends upon them, mercy envelops them, the angels surround them – and Allah mentions them to those that are with Him"* (Muslim 2699).

Second:

Listening to the Qur'an Leads to Guidance for Both Human Beings and Jinns

Allah (sp) made it very clear that the Noble Qur'an is a source of guidance in both this world and the Hereafter. Hence if someone adheres to it, by reciting it, listening to it, contemplating its meanings, and applying its commands, he will neither go astray nor become miserable. Allah (sp) said:

$$إِنَّ هَٰذَا ٱلْقُرْءَانَ يَهْدِى لِلَّتِى هِىَ أَقْوَمُ$$

"Verily, this Qur'an guides to that which is most just and right." (Qur'an 17: 9)

The Qur'an gave glad tidings specifically to those who listen to the Qur'an, promising them true guidance, and describing them with the qualities of wisdom and intelligence. Allah (sp) said:

---

[131] *Tafseer Al-Qurtubee* (1/23).

$$\text{فَبَشِّرْ عِبَادِ (١٧) ٱلَّذِينَ يَسْتَمِعُونَ ٱلْقَوْلَ فَيَتَّبِعُونَ أَحْسَنَهُ أُوْلَٰٓئِكَ ٱلَّذِينَ هَدَىٰهُمُ ٱللَّهُ وَأُوْلَٰٓئِكَ هُمْ أُوْلُواْ ٱلْأَلْبَٰبِ (١٨)}$$

"So announce the good news to My slaves, those who listen to the Word good advice (La ilaha illallah none has the right to be worshipped but Allah (sp) and Islamic Monotheism, etc.) and follow the best thereof (i.e., worship Allah Alone, repent to Him and avoid Taghut, etc.) those are (the ones) whom Allah has guided and those are men of understanding" (like Zaid bin Amr bin Nufail, Salman Al-Farisi and Abu Dhar Al-Ghifari) *Tafsir Al-Qurtubi*, Vol. 12, Pg. 244. (Qur'an 39: 17, 18)

In this Verse, Allah (sp) speaks of those who listen to the "Word," or to the "Speech." Without a doubt, the best "Word" or "Speech" is that of Allah (sp), and then that of His Messenger (s). Allah (sp) said:

$$\text{ٱللَّهُ نَزَّلَ أَحْسَنَ ٱلْحَدِيثِ كِتَٰبًا مُّتَشَٰبِهًا}$$

"Allah has sent down the best statement, a Book (this Qur'an), its parts resembling each other in goodness and truth" (Qur'an 39:23)

Those that listen to the Qur'an and follow its teachings are the ones that Allah (sp) has guided to the best of deeds and manners, and they are the people of understanding.

The Qur'an can result in guidance not just for believers, but for disbelievers as well:

$$\text{وَإِنْ أَحَدٌ مِّنَ ٱلْمُشْرِكِينَ ٱسْتَجَارَكَ فَأَجِرْهُ حَتَّىٰ يَسْمَعَ كَلَٰمَ ٱللَّهِ}$$

"And if anyone of the Mushrikun (polytheists, idolaters, pagans, disbelievers in the Oneness of Allah) seeks your protection then grant him protection, so that he may hear the Word of Allah (the Qur'an)" (Qur'an 9: 6)

What is more, Allah (sp) made the Qur'an a cause of guidance for jinns as well:

$$\text{قُلْ أُوحِيَ إِلَيَّ أَنَّهُ ٱسْتَمَعَ نَفَرٌ مِّنَ ٱلْجِنِّ فَقَالُوٓاْ إِنَّا سَمِعْنَا قُرْءَانًا عَجَبًا (١) يَهْدِىٓ إِلَى ٱلرُّشْدِ فَـَٔامَنَّا بِهِۦ وَلَن نُّشْرِكَ بِرَبِّنَآ أَحَدًا (٢)}$$

"Say (O Muhammad (s)): 'It has been revealed to me that a group (from three to ten in number) of jinns listened (to this Qur'an). They said: 'Verily! We have heard a wonderful Recital (this Qur'an). It guides to the Right Path, and we have believed therein, and we shall never join (in worship) anything with our Lord (Allah).''" (Qur'an 72; 1, 2)

Allah (sp) wanted good to befall the group of jinns that are described in this Verse, and so he willed for them to go to His Messenger (s), so that they could hear the Noble Qur'an from him, and so that He (sp) could complete his favor upon them. Those jinns, having become guided themselves, returned as warners to their fellow jinns. The chain of events that led to their guidance began with them listening to the Qur'an. They said to one another, "Listen in silence; they did so, and as they listened quietly to the Prophet's recitation of the Qur'an, they contemplated its meanings; as a result, the trueness of the Qur'an's Verses reached the inner depths of their hearts. Allah (sp) said:

$$\text{وَإِذْ صَرَفْنَآ إِلَيْكَ نَفَرًا مِّنَ ٱلْجِنِّ يَسْتَمِعُونَ ٱلْقُرْءَانَ فَلَمَّا حَضَرُوهُ قَالُوٓاْ أَنصِتُواْ فَلَمَّا قُضِىَ وَلَّوْاْ إِلَىٰ قَوْمِهِم مُّنذِرِينَ (٢٩) قَالُواْ يَٰقَوْمَنَآ إِنَّا سَمِعْنَا كِتَٰبًا أُنزِلَ مِنۢ بَعْدِ مُوسَىٰ مُصَدِّقًا لِّمَا بَيْنَ يَدَيْهِ يَهْدِىٓ إِلَى ٱلْحَقِّ وَإِلَىٰ طَرِيقٍ مُّسْتَقِيمٍ (٣٠)}$$

"And (remember) when We sent towards you (Muhammad) Nafran (three to ten persons) of the jinns, (quietly) listening to the Qur'an, when they stood in the presence thereof, they said: 'Listen in silence'

And when it was finished, they returned to their people, as warners. They said: 'O our people! Verily! We have heard a Book (this Qur'an) sent down after Musa (Moses), confirming what came before it, it guides to the truth and to a Straight Path' (i.e., Islam)." (Qur'an 46: 29, 30)

Third:

Listening to the Qur'an Results in a Heart that is Submissive and Spiritually Strong, and in Eyes that Shed Tears (Out of the Fear of Allah (sp))

When a believer contemplates the meanings of the Qur'an, his heart begins to shake, being fearful of Allah (sp), and his eyes begin to shed tears. His mental state heightens as he becomes more conscious of his Lord. And he oscillates between a state of hope and a feeling of fearfulness; he is hopeful of Allah's rewards and, more importantly, of Allah (sp) being pleased with him, and he is fearful of Allah's anger and punishment.

A believer reaches such a state not just when he recites the Qur'an, but also when he hears someone else reciting it to him. We know this to be true based on the Sunnah of the Prophet (s). Abdullah bin Masood (r) reported that the Messenger of Allah (s)once said to him, "Recite (the Qur'an) to me." Not being able to believe what he had just heard, for the honor that was being bestowed upon him was indeed great, Abdullah (r) said, 'Shall I recite it to you, when to you it has descended!'

'Verily, I desire to hear it from someone other than myself," the Prophet (s) replied. Abdullah (r) then began reciting Chapter *An-Nisaa*, until he reached the Verse:

فَكَيْفَ إِذَا جِئْنَا مِن كُلِّ أُمَّةٍ بِشَهِيدٍ وَجِئْنَا بِكَ عَلَىٰ هَـٰٓؤُلَآءِ شَهِيدًا

"How (will it be) then, when We bring from each nation a witness and We bring you (O Muhammad (s)) as a witness against these people?" (Qur'an 4:41)

The Prophet (s) then said to him, "Stop", at which point Abdullah (r) looked up and saw tears flowing from the noble eyes of the Prophet (s).[132] Scholars have raised the question, why did the Prophet (s), who knew the Qur'an better than any of his Companions (rp), ask Abdullah bin Masood to recite it for him? In response to this question, Ibn Battaal (m) said, "It is possible that he wanted to hear it from someone else in order to establish a precedent: To make it an act of Sunnah for one to hear the Qur'an from another person." On the other hand, it is possible that the Prophet (s) wanted another vantage point – that of a listener as opposed to that of a reciter – from which he could contemplate the meanings of the Qur'an. This latter possibility is quite probably true, because a person who listens to the Qur'an is in a better position to contemplate the meanings of the Qur'an than is a person who recites it: The listeners mind is unoccupied by other tasks, and is able to focus wholly on the meanings of the Qur'an, whereas the reciter must, in addition to contemplating the Qur'an's meanings, focus on the task of reciting the Qur'an and making sure he is following the rules of *Tajweed* (of reciting the Qur'an in a proper manner, in terms of pronunciation of letters, elongation of vowels, etc.).[133] Whatever the case, one thing is for certain: the abovementioned Hadeeth illustrates the Prophet's humbleness in his dealings with his followers.[134]

As Imam An-Nawawee pointed out, the Hadeeth proves that it is recommended to cry sincerely upon hearing Verses of the Qur'an, doing so, we are informed in the Qur'an, was the Sunnah (i.e., way or practice) of all Prophets (st):

---

[132] Al-Bukhaaree (5055).
[133] Fathul-Baaree Sharh Saheeh Al-Bukhaaree (9/117).
[134] *Saheeh Muslim*, with *Sharh of An-Nawawee* (6/329).

$$\text{أُولَٰئِكَ ٱلَّذِينَ أَنْعَمَ ٱللَّهُ عَلَيْهِم مِّنَ ٱلنَّبِيِّينَ مِن ذُرِّيَّةِ ءَادَمَ وَمِمَّنْ حَمَلْنَا مَعَ نُوحٍ وَمِن ذُرِّيَّةِ إِبْرَاهِيمَ وَإِسْرَائِيلَ وَمِمَّنْ هَدَيْنَا وَٱجْتَبَيْنَا ۚ إِذَا تُتْلَىٰ عَلَيْهِمْ ءَايَاتُ ٱلرَّحْمَٰنِ خَرُّوا۟ سُجَّدًا وَبُكِيًّا}$$

"Those were they unto whom Allah bestowed His Grace from among the Prophets, of the offspring of Adam, and of those whom We carried (in the ship) with Nuh (Noah), and of the offspring of Ibrahim (Abraham) and Israel – and from among those whom We guided and chose. When the Verses of the Most Beneficent (Allah) were recited unto them, they fell down prostrating and weeping." (Qur'an 19:58)

The people of knowledge, who are the inheritors of the Prophets (st), similarly are moved to the point of crying and of feeling an increase of faith when they hear the Qur'an, a reality that we are informed about in the following Verses:

$$\text{قُلْ ءَامِنُوا۟ بِهِ أَوْ لَا تُؤْمِنُوٓا۟ ۚ إِنَّ ٱلَّذِينَ أُوتُوا۟ ٱلْعِلْمَ مِن قَبْلِهِ إِذَا يُتْلَىٰ عَلَيْهِمْ يَخِرُّونَ لِلْأَذْقَانِ سُجَّدًا (١٠٧) وَيَقُولُونَ سُبْحَٰنَ رَبِّنَآ إِن كَانَ وَعْدُ رَبِّنَا لَمَفْعُولًا (١٠٨) وَيَخِرُّونَ لِلْأَذْقَانِ يَبْكُونَ وَيَزِيدُهُمْ خُشُوعًا (١٠٩)}$$

"Verily! Those who were given knowledge before it (the Jews and the Christians like Abdullah bin Salam and Salman Al-Farisi), when it is recited to them, fall down on their faces in humble prostration. And they say: 'Glory be to our Lord! Truly, the Promise of our Lord must be fulfilled.' And they fall down on their faces weeping and it adds to their humility." (Qur'an 17: 107-109)

Discussing the meaning of these Verses, Al-Qurtubee (m) said, "This is a very favorable description with which Scholars are praised. In fact, every person of knowledge, and even every person who has gained a degree of knowledge, should strive to reach the level that is described in these Verses, a level in which one, while listening to the Qur'an, feels moved, humbled, and fearful all at once."[135]

Section 2

The Virtues of Learning the Qur'an and of Teaching it to Others

In This Section Five Issues are Discussed:
First: Both the Qur'an's Teacher and Student are Similar in a Way to Angels and Messengers (st)
Second: The Best of People are Those Who Learn the Qur'an and Teach it to Others
Third: Learning the Qur'an and Teaching it are Better than all of the Treasures of the World
Fourth: Whoever Teaches a Verse (of the Qur'an) will continue to have Its Reward, as Long as It Continues to be Recited
Fifth: The Reward of Teaching the Qur'an to One's Children

---

[135] *Al-Jaami' Li-Ahkaam Al-Qur'an* (10/347, 348); refer also to *Tafseer Al-Baidaawee* (3/481) and to Ibn Katheer (5/134).

Introduction

In Islam, teaching knowledge is recommended; in fact, it is considered to be one of the best acts of worship that a Muslim can perform. In a Hadeeth that is related in Muslim, the Prophet (s) said: *"Whoever invites (others) to guidance will receive a reward that is similar to the rewards that will be given to those who follow him, and yet that will not result in their losing out on any part of their rewards in the least."*[136]

Perhaps the most wonderful aspect of teaching is that it endows one with a second life. We all die, and for the most part, our deeds come to an end, but there are three exceptions to that rule, and one of them involves knowledge by which people benefit after one dies. So, for instance, if you teach a child how to pray, you will continue to receive rewards as long as he prays, even for the prayers he performs after you die. Abu Hurairah (r) reported that the Messenger of Allah (s) said: *"When a person dies his deeds are cut off from him except from three (exceptions); perpetual charity (i.e., charity that continues to benefit people even after the giver dies), knowledge that continues to benefit people; and a righteous son who supplicates for him (i.e., for the person who has died)."*[137]

After he mentioned this Hadeeth, Imam Ibn Al-Qayyim (m) wrote, "This Hadeeth is one of the strongest proofs of the lofty status of knowledge (in Islam) and of the greatness of its fruits. The reward of knowledge continues to accrue for a man even after he dies, so long as people continue to benefit from the knowledge he imparted. Therefore, even after such a man dies, it is as if he continues to be alive.... In fact, considering that others' deeds come to an end when they die, it is as if he is being given a second life."[138]

To be sure, one cannot understate the importance of teaching knowledge in Islam. And yet it is important to understand that not all knowledge is the same: some branches of knowledge are more important than others. That being the case, there is no doubt that the best and most superior field of study is the Book of Allah (sp). Therefore, a person who learns and teaches the Qur'an is better than someone who learns and teaches any other subject or field of study.

The pious Muslims from the early generations of Islam strove to learn the Qur'an and to teach it to others. It is from the blessings of Allah (sp), and then by dint of the efforts of our pious predecessors, that so much knowledge about the Qur'an has been passed down throughout the generations and remains preserved in books. Their role-model in this regard – as well as in every aspect of their lives – was none other than the Messenger of Allah (s), to whom the Qur'an was revealed. From the early days of his mission – when he would teach the Qur'an in the house of Al-Arqam bin Abee Arqam – the Prophet (s) would either teach the Qur'an directly to his Companions (rp) or appoint certain Companions (rp) to teach others what they knew of the Qur'an.

In discussing the virtues of learning and of teaching the Qur'an, I will focus on the following five issues.

First:

Both the Qur'an's Teacher and Student are Similar in a Way to Angels (sp) and Messengers (st)

---

[136] Muslim (2674).
[137] Muslim (1631).
[138] *Miftaah Daar As-Sa'aadah* (1/175).

Who would not want to be likened to Angels and Messengers (st). But that is exactly the honor one receives for teaching and learning the Qur'an. The likeness stems from the fact that, originally, when the Qur'an was first being revealed, there was a teacher and a student, the former being the Angel Jibreel (p), and the latter being the Prophet (s).

Second:

The Best of People are Those Who Learn the Qur'an and Teach it to Others

Learning and teaching the Qur'an are two of the best of deeds that one can perform, and are a source of honor for a person both in this life and in the Hereafter. There are numerous Hadeeth narrations that exhort Muslims to both learn and teach the Qur'an, perhaps none of them being more well-known to Muslims than the following narration: Uthmaan bin Affaan (r) reported that the Prophet (s) said: *"The best you is he who learns the Qur'an and teaches it (to others)."* [139]
In this Hadeeth it is made patently clear that, after the Prophets and Messengers (st), the best people are not those who are the richest or wealthiest members of society, but instead those who both learn and teach the Qur'an. The Hadeeth describes true and sincere followers of the Prophet (s), who strive to learn the Qur'an and to purify themselves in the process, and who also strive to teach the Qur'an to others and invite them to study it.

What is Meant by Learning and Teaching the Qur'an

One would do well to ask the question, does learning and teaching the Qur'an refer to students who learn how to recite the letters and words of the Qur'an at the hands of a skilled reciter, or to students who learn the meanings of the Qur'an from a Shaikh who is conducting a study circle. Actually, it refers to all of the above – to both learning how to recite the letters and words of the Qur'an, and to learning about the meanings of the Qur'an – although the latter kind of learning is superior to the former. After all, the chief goal of studying the Qur'an is to learn its meanings; learning to recite it properly is a means to that end. And, as is usually the case, the end is more important than the means.[140]
The Muslims of the early generations of Islam understood the importance of learning and teaching the Qur'an; in fact, a great many of them dedicating their lives to those ends. Of the many scholars who did just that, I will mention the examples of a representative few. Saad bin Ubaidah said, "Abu Abdur-Rahmaan taught others the Qur'an from the time of Uthmaan's caliphate until the rule of Al-Hajjaaj." The very same Abu Abdur-Rahmaan, whose full name is Abu Abdur-Rahmaan Abdullah bin Habeeb As-Sullamee, taught the Qur'an to people in the Masjid of Kufa for forty years, a job he began during the caliphate of Uthmaan, and which he continued to perform until the days of Al-Hajjaaj. At the end of his life, he referred to Uthmaan's Hadeeth – "The best among you is he who learns the Qur'an and teaches it" – saying, "And that is what made me sit here (as a teacher of the Qur'an for so many years)."[141]
Imam Naafai bin Abdur-Rahmaan bin Abu Nuaim Al-Madanee (m), one of the famous Seven "Recitors", was blessed with a long life. What did he do for the more than average number of years he spent on earth? The answer to this question is truly impressive: He spent more than seventy years of his life teaching the Qur'an to others.
Imam Abu Mansoor Al-Khayyaat Al-Baghdaadee (m) had a number of students who went on to become famous reciters in their own right. Imam Adh-Dhahabee (m) said about him, "He taught the Book of Allah for a long time, and entire nations of people (i.e., a great many people) studied under

---

[139] *Bukhaaree* (5027).
[140] *Miftaah Daar As-Sa'aadah* (1/74).
[141] *Fathul-Baaree Sharh Saheeh Al-Bukhaaree* (9/97).

his tutelage."[142] Imam Abu Mansoor was generous, kind, and patient; for a long time, he taught blind people the Qur'an for the sake of Allah (sp); as if that was not enough, he would also provide for their financial needs. It is related that he taught the Qur'an to more than seventy blind students, a feat that bespeaks a very kind and giving heart.[143]

Third:

Learning the Qur'an and Teaching it are Better than all of the Treasures of the World

Uqbah bin Aamir (r) said, "Once, while we were in As-Suffah (the back portion of the Prophet's Masjid, which functioned as a temporary abode for poor Muslims), the Messenger of Allah (s) came out and said: "Who among you would love to go out every morning to Buthaan or to Al-Aqeeq, and to come back from that place with two high-humped camels, without being guilty of a sin or of the crime of breaking off ties of relations?"
Here, the Prophet (s) mentioned camels in particular because, among the Arabs of that era, camels were very expensive and were owned only by those who were wealthy. And the statement "without being guilty of a sin..." means: "Who among you would like to go to either of the two said places and return with camels that, though you got them for free, were procured in an Islamically lawful manner?" Uqbah (r) went on to relate, "We answered, O Messenger of Allah! We would love to do that!" He (s) said: *"Then shall not one of you go at the beginning of the day to the Masjid and learn or recite two Verses of the Book of Allah - the Possessor of Might and Majesty, for doing so is better for him than for him to have two camels. And (reciting) three (Verses) is better for him than having three (camels, and four is better for him than having four camels..."*[144]
In this Hadeeth, the Prophet (s) informed us that, while it is a good deed to recite the Qur'an in one's home or elsewhere, it is even a better deed to recite it in the Masjid. This is because the Masjid is a place where the Qur'an should be taught, and also because the Masjid, being a place of peace and calmness, is especially conducive to freeing one's mind of foreign thoughts and to contemplating the meanings of the Qur'an.
In another Hadeeth, the Prophet (s) equated the reward of learning and teaching knowledge with the reward one receives for performing Hajj (pilgrimage to Makkah). In a Hadeeth that At-Tabaraanee (m) related in *Al-Kabeer*, the Prophet (s) said: *"Whoever goes at the beginning of the day to the Masjid, intending thereby nothing save the act of learning something good or teaching it, receives a reward that is similar to the one that is given to a Haaj (a person who performs the greater pilgrimage to Makkah), a Haaj that has completely (and correctly) performed his pilgrimage."*[145]
What specific kind of good knowledge one should learn or teach is not specified in this Hadeeth, so the stipulated reward applies to Tafseer, Islamic Jurisprudence, Tajweed (learning to recite the Qur'an properly), and all other branches of Islamic knowledge; without a doubt, however, the most superior of those subjects is the Book of Allah (sp).
In yet another Hadeeth, the Prophet (s) informed us that a person who studies good and beneficial knowledge is, in terms of ranking, like a person who fights in the way of Allah (sp). The Prophet (s) said: *"Whoever comes to this Masjid of mine, having come for no reason other than to teach something good or to learn something good, is, in terms of his ranking, like one who fights in the way*

---

[142] *Siyar Alaam An-Nubalaa* (19/222).
[143] *Siyar Alaam AnNubalaa* (19/223).
[144] *Muslim* (803).
[145] At-Tabaraanee in *Al-Kabeer* (8/94). In his grading of this Hadeeth, Al-Albaanee said in *Saheeh At-Targheeb Wat-Tarheeb* (1145), This (Hadeeth) is *Hasan Saheeh*.

of Allah. And whoever comes for another purpose is like a man who stares at someone else's possessions."[146]

It is very fitting for a student or teacher of the Qur'an to be likened to a person who fights in the way of Allah (sp), for, like the latter, the former engages in a struggle, a struggle to overcome their desires, a struggle against the Shaitaan (the Devil), a struggle to be patient, a struggle to consistently attend circles of knowledge, and a struggle to forsake the world and its pleasures.

Fourth:

Whoever Teaches a Verse (of the Qur'an) will have Its Reward, as Long as It Continues to be Recited

There are two kinds of good deeds that a person can perform: One involves an act of worship, such as two units of prayer, whereby the worshipper benefits no one save himself. And the second involves a good deed whose benefit extends beyond the doer of the good deed; so, for example, if a person gives charity to the poor and needy, he is performing a good deed of the latter kind: He is benefiting not only himself (by gaining rewards for the Hereafter), but others as well.

To be sure, the latter kind of good deed is superior to the former. Among the good deeds of the latter category is teaching beneficial knowledge to others. Abu Hurairah (r) reported that the Messenger of Allah (s) said: *"Verily, among the deeds and righteous acts that reach a person after he dies is knowledge that he taught or spread (while he was alive)."*[147]

Teaching the Qur'an falls within the intended meaning of the following Hadeeth: *"Whoever guides to that which is good receives a reward that is similar to the one that is received by the doer of that good (i.e., by the one who did the good as a result of having been guided to do so at the hands of the first person.)"*[148]

Nonetheless, an even more specific proof of the reward of teaching the Qur'an, even if it is only a single Verse, is confirmed in the following Hadeeth, in which the Messenger of Allah (s) said: *"Whoever teaches (a person or a group of persons) a Verse from the Book of Allah – the Possessor of Might and Majesty – will have the reward for having done so as long as it is recited."*[149]

The stamp one leaves on this world after one dies – in terms of one's good deeds – is referred to, in the following Verse, as one's 'traces', a trace literally meaning a remnant, sign, or vestige:

$$\text{وَنَكْتُبُ مَا قَدَّمُوا۟ وَءَاثَـٰرَهُمْ}$$

"We record that which they send before (them), and their traces" (their footsteps and walking on the earth with their legs to the mosques for the five compulsory congregational prayers, Jihad (holy fighting in Allah's Cause) and all other good and evil they did, and that which they leave behind) (Qur'an 36:12)

"That which they send before (them)" refers to the good deeds that Muslims perform before they die. With this wording, deeds are likened to things that a person sends ahead to the Hereafter, just as a traveler sends his things ahead of him to his intended destination.[150] The wording at the end of the Verse likens good deeds to physical traces or vestiges left behind by a person after he dies: The

---

[146] Ibn Maajah (227). And in *Saheeh Ibn Maajah* (186), Al-Albaanee declared this Hadeeth to be authentic.
[147] Related by Ibn Maajah (242), and Al-Albaanee declared it to be *Hasan* (acceptable) in *Saheeh Ibn Maajah* (198).
[148] Muslim (1893).
[149] In *As-Silsilah As-Saheehah*, Al-Albaanee ruled that this Hadeeth is authentic (1335).
[150] *At-Tahreer Wat-Tanweer* (22/204).

physical traces or vestiges of a person who has died are, for instance, the house and property and family he left behind. The traces or vestiges of his deeds, for which he will be rewarded, are the continued application of the good things he taught to others while he was alive.

Fifth:

The Reward of Teaching the Qur'an to One's Children

Today, many Muslims send their children to a *Qaaree* so that they can be taught the Qur'an. While such a practice is laudable, parents should also spend some time teaching their children – which of course involves learning first - since the duty of educating children rests squarely on the shoulders of parents. At least initially, a child, before being sent to a teacher, should be taught part of the Qur'an by his or her parents. In order for them to gain an appreciation of the Qur'an, children must be made to see the dominant role the Qur'an has on their household. Parents create a wrong impression on their children when, in the home, they are allowed to play and watch television all day, while they recite the Qur'an only when they go to study under the tutelage of a *Qaaree*. In such situations, a child will come to think that religion is for the Masjid only, while home is a place for worldly pleasures and pursuits.

For these reasons, it is encouraged in Islam for parents to teach their children the Qur'an; in fact, that is what our pious predecessors from the early generations of Islam would do with their children. The reward for teaching one's children the Qur'an is great indeed, and is proportionate to the effort, patience, and hardship that is involved in teaching children, whose minds frequently wander and who need constant attention.

Buraidah bin Al-Husaib (r) said that, one day, he was with the Messenger of Allah (s) when he heard him say: *"Verily, the Qur'an will meet its companion (i.e., the person who recited it and followed its teachings) on the Day of Resurrection. The Qur'an will meet him when his grave will split apart for him, and will be like a man whose face has lost his color. The Qur'an will say to him, 'Do you recognize me?' He will say, 'I do not recognize you.' The Qur'an will say, 'I am your companion, the Qur'an, which (because you were preoccupied with me) caused you to go thirsty during the middle of the day (when it is hottest outside), and made you lose Sleep at night (i.e., because you were busy reciting me)...' Then he will be given a kingdom in his right hand, and eternal life in his left; and a crown of dignity will be placed on his head. As for his parents, they will be attired in two robes.... And they will ask, 'What has made us deserving of being attired in these?' It will be said to them, 'For teaching your child the Qur'an.' Then it will be said to him, 'Recite and rise up through the levels and rooms of Paradise.' He will continue to ascend as long as he continues to recite, regardless of whether he recites quickly or slowly, carefully enunciating each letter."*[151]

A similar narration, with a similar wording is related in At-Tabaraanee's *Al-Ausat*.[152] In it, the Prophet (s) said, "His parents will be attired in two robes, robes that are more valuable than the earth and all that is in it. They will say, 'O our Lord! Why are we given these (i.e., what good deed have we performed to deserve these)?' It will be said to them, 'For teaching your child the Qur'an...'"

The parents described in this Hadeeth will be bewildered on the Day of Resurrection, not being able to understand why such expensive robes are being given to them. They will not be able to think of any deed they had performed in this life that could make them deserving of so much goodness. At this point of the Hadeeth, one might be led to believe that they are being rewarded for having performed countless prayers, for having sacrificed their lives for the sake of their religion, for having given all of

---

[151] Ahmad in *Al-Musnad* (5/348); the scholars who wrote a commentary of Imam Ahmad's Musnad have said regarding this Hadeeth, "Its chain is *Hasan* (acceptable)." (38/42).
[152] At-Tabaraanee in *Al-Ausat* (6/51); also, Al-Albaanee included this Hadeeth in his work *As-Silsilah As-Saheehah* (2829).

their wealth away in charity, or for any other deed that, among human beings, is at once rare and remarkable. But it was none of those deeds that made them deserving of the priceless robes; rather, it was the simple act of teaching their child the Qur'an. Without a doubt, if all parents contemplated this Hadeeth and understood its implications, more and more of them would sacrifice their time, their money, and their energy to make sure that their children were adequately taught the Noble Qur'an.[153]

Section 3
The Virtues of Reciting the Qur'an

In this Section Three Issues are Discussed:
First: Reciting the Qur'an is a Profitable Undertaking
Second: As a Result of Reciting the Qur'an, Tranquility, Mercy, and the Angels Descend
Third: To Recite the Qur'an, Regardless of One's Ability as a Reciter, is a Good Deed

Introduction

The Messenger of Allah (s) would read the Noble Qur'an a great deal. Through his actions, he made it clear that one should avail of any opportunity to read the Qur'an. He would read it standing up, sitting down, or lying down; while in a state of purity and in a state of minor impurity, while walking and riding; and in virtually every other situation or position he found himself to be in.

While there were no cars or trains or planes during the lifetime of the Prophet (s), there were horses and camels. People would spend days and even weeks on a camel, riding from one city to another. The Prophet (s) would avail of such long periods of free time to recite the Qur'an; for instance, Abdullah bin Mughaffal (r) said, "On the Day of the Makkah Conquest, I saw the Messenger of Allah (s); he was on his riding animal, and he was reciting Chapter *Al-Fath*."[154] Therefore, the act of reciting the Qur'an while riding on a means of conveyance is from the Sunnah of the Prophet (s); in fact, it is a Sunnah that we should strive to revive. Many of us spend long hours traveling by plane, by train, or by car; and while the average journey these days does not take weeks, it can nonetheless take a few hours and sometimes even a few days. When we find ourselves on such a journey, we should, in accordance with the Sunnah of the Prophet (s), make a concerted effort to dedicate at least a part of the journey to reciting the Noble Qur'an.

The Messenger of Allah (s) would exhort his Companions (rp) to recite the Qur'an while they were traveling by road; incidentally, many Verses of the Qur'an were revealed to the Prophet (s) while he was traveling from one place to another. Then he would continue to recite those Verses throughout the course of the remainder of his journey.

There is hardly an occasion during which it is deemed inappropriate to recite the Qur'an. Those rare occasions during which we should not recite the Qur'an have been made clear to us in the Sunnah of the Prophet (s). So, for instance, we are forbidden from reciting the Qur'an while we are in the bowing position during Prayer, when we perform prostration and during other parts of the Prayer - except

---

[153] *Anwaar Al-Qur'an* by Mustafa Al-Himsee (pgs. 181, 182).
[154] *Bukhaaree* (5034).

when we are standing up. Also, it is a detested act to recite the Qur'an while one is sitting down to urinate or defecate. And if one is sleepy or dizzy or drowsy to the point that one does not know what one is saying, one should not recite the Qur'an. And finally, during the Friday Sermon anyone who can hear the Imam speaking should not recite the Qur'an.[155] The point here is that the Prophet (s) would exhort his Companions (rp) to recite the Qur'an as much as possible, for he wanted the Qur'an to play a dominant role in every part of their lives.[156]

As is the case regarding listening to the Qur'an, the virtues of reciting the Qur'an are numerous and blessed. Were Muslims to know the virtues and rewards of reciting the Qur'an, they would carry the Qur'an with them everywhere they went, reciting it both by day and by night. Regarding the virtues of reciting the Qur'an, I will focus on three key issues.

First:

Reciting the Qur'an is a Profitable Undertaking

Allah (sp) said:

إِنَّ ٱلَّذِينَ يَتْلُونَ كِتَٰبَ ٱللَّهِ وَأَقَامُوا۟ ٱلصَّلَوٰةَ وَأَنفَقُوا۟ مِمَّا رَزَقْنَٰهُمْ سِرًّا وَعَلَانِيَةً يَرْجُونَ تِجَٰرَةً لَّن تَبُورَ (٢٩) لِيُوَفِّيَهُمْ أُجُورَهُمْ وَيَزِيدَهُم مِّن فَضْلِهِۦٓ إِنَّهُۥ غَفُورٌ شَكُورٌ (٣٠)

"Verily, those who recite the Book of Allah (this Qur'an) and perform As-Salat, and spend (in charity) out of what We have provided for them, secretly and openly, hope for a (sure) trade-gain that will never perish. That He may pay them their wages in full, and give them (even) more, out of His Grace. Verily! He is Oft-Forgiving, Most Ready to appreciate (good deeds and to recompense)." (Qur'an 35: 29, 30)

In these Verses, Allah (sp) praises those who recite the Qur'an. These Verses are so clear in their praise that Imam Al-Qurtubee (m) said regarding one of them (either Verse 29 or 30), "This Verse is the Verse of reciters (of the Qur'an), and is intended for those among them who both have knowledge (of the Qur'an) and apply that knowledge in practice."[157] As Imam Al-Qurtubee (m) stated, Allah (sp) praised reciters of the Qur'an for consistently reciting it, for studying its meanings, and for applying its teachings.[158]

Furthermore, in the abovementioned Verses, Allah (sp) likened the act of reciting the Qur'an to business – more specifically, to a very profitable business. When Allah (sp) says that He will reward people for doing a good deed, and when He (sp) does not state the amount of that reward, it means that He (sp) will give them a great deal, for He (sp) is All-Generous. Consider a mere created human being who is the king of a land. If he promises an undisclosed amount of money as a reward, he will give more than people expect him to give if he is generous. Allah is the Most Generous, so imagine the reward a reciter of the Qur'an will receive, given that Allah (sp) has said:

لِيُوَفِّيَهُمْ أُجُورَهُمْ وَيَزِيدَهُم مِّن فَضْلِهِۦٓ

"That He may pay them their wages in full, and give them (even) more, out of His Grace." (Qur'an 35:30)

None save Allah (sp) knows what "more" specifically means in this Verse in terms of exact quantity; but while we do not know that exact quantity, we can, based on the fact that Allah (sp) is the Most-Generous, safely say that it far surpasses what each of us can imagine.

---

[155] *At-Tibyaan Fee Aadaab Hamalatul-Qur'an* (3/1261).
[156] *Yuallimuhumul-Kitaab Al-Ta'aamul Ma'al-Qur'an Al-Kareem* (pgs. 42, 43).
[157] *Tafseer Al-Qurtubee* (14/345).
[158] *Fathul-Qadeer* (4/348) and to *Tafseer As-Sa'dee* (4/216).

Abdullah bin Masood (r) related that the Messenger of Allah (s) said: *"Whoever recites a letter from the Book of Allah receives for it a reward, and a reward (in Islam) is multiplied by ten. I do not say that Alif-Laam-Meem (which, for instance, is the beginning part of chapter Al-Baqarah) is a letter; rather, Alif is a letter, Laam is a letter, and Meem is a letter (i.e., in the calculation of rewards)."*[159]
In this Hadeeth, the Prophet (s) made it clear that, for every letter of the Qur'an that a Muslim recites, he will receive ten rewards. In Islam, the reward for a good deed is multiplied by a minimum of ten:

مَن جَآءَ بِٱلْحَسَنَةِ فَلَهُۥ عَشْرُ أَمْثَالِهَا

"Whosoever brings a good deed (Islamic Monotheism and deeds of obedience to Allah (sp) and His Messenger (s)) shall have ten times the like thereof to his credit." (Qur'an 6: 160)
But it must be pointed out that that is the minimum reward one receives; as for the maximum amount, the sky is the limit, for Allah (sp) being the Most-Generous, can give as much as He wants to whomsoever He pleases. He (sp) said:

وَٱللَّهُ يُضَٰعِفُ لِمَن يَشَآءُ وَٱللَّهُ وَٰسِعٌ عَلِيمٌ

"Allah gives manifold increase to whom He pleases. And Allah is All-Sufficient for His creatures' needs, All-Knower." (Qur'an 2:261)
Without a doubt, in terms of whether a reciter will receive the minimum amount of ten rewards for each letter or whether he will receive more, various factors come into play – such as the level of his sincerity, his degree of concentration, the manners he shows while reciting the Book of Allah, the lessons he takes away from the Verses he recites, and so on. Abu Dharr (r) reported that the Messenger of Allah (s) said: *"Allah, the Possessor of Might and Majesty, said, 'Whoever comes with a good deed will have ten times the like thereof to his credit, and I may even give more than that.'"*[160]
There are various AHadeeth that mention the rewards one receives for reading specific invocations; few of those invocations, if any, result in the rewards one receives for reciting the Qur'an. Consider the great many rewards – even if we calculate the minimum tenfold amount – one earns for reciting a page or chapter of the Qur'an.
On the Day of Resurrection, some people will be desperate for a single good deed, which is all they will need in order to make their good deeds outweigh their evil deeds. If we truly understood how desperate we will be for rewards on the Day of Resurrection, we would certainly spend more time reciting the Qur'an, and less time engaging in fruitless and frivolous activities.
Our problem, therefore, is either that we do not understand how desperate we will be for rewards on the Day of Resurrection, or that we just don't care. Perhaps we think that the Hereafter is a long way off, when it is truly near at hand. A student knows that he will be rewarded in the short-term – at the end of the semester – with a grade, which is why he spends hours, days, and weeks reading his textbook. And even after going through his assigned readings, he goes back to reread, review, and summarize what he learned; in many instances, he might memorize verbatim important parts of the textbook. And he does all of this in order to receive a good grade, so that he can achieve a degree of worldly success. He had to do all of that work because he knew that worldly success was not guaranteed for him, but rather that he had to work for it. So does he, or any of us for that matter, think that success in the Hereafter is guaranteed for him? Does he think no work is required to achieve Paradise? If he truly thinks this, he is deluding himself in the most unimaginably worst way possible.

Second:
As a Result of Reciting the Qur'an, Tranquility, Mercy, and the Angels Descend

---

[159] At-Tirmidhee (2910), and Al-Albaanee declared it to be authentic in *Saheeh Sunan At-Tirmidhee* (2327).
[160] Muslim (2687).

Abu Hurairah (r) reported that the Messenger of Allah (s) said:

"Whenever a group of people gather in a house from the houses of Allah(sp), in order to recite the Book of Allah and to study it among themselves, peace descends upon them, mercy envelops them, the angels surround them – and Allah mentions them to those that are with Him."[161]

In this Hadeeth, very specific rewards are promised to those who gather, not to eat or to pass time with conversation, but to "recite the Book of Allah and to study it among themselves." The people who attend such a gathering will be the recipients of four priceless rewards:

1) Peace and Tranquility Descend upon Them

When a person attends a gathering in which the Qur'an is recited, peace descends upon him. One would do well to ask what that "peace" means. It means that, unlike the people outside of the gathering, most of whom are filled with anxiety, sadness, fear, or worry of some sort, he is calm and at peace.[162] This is not to say that his life is problem free; to the contrary, like all other human beings, he has his share of problems in life. But when he enters the Masjid and meets with his brothers in order to recite the Book of Allah and to study its meanings, all of his worries go away and peace descends upon him.

These days, people try numerous methods to alleviate their stress and to forget their worries. Most commonly, people resort to alcohol and drugs, but, notwithstanding a short period of feeling "high", these products create more problems than they solve (in fact, they do not solve anything), and they make matters worse than better. Alcohol and drugs are used by those who try to escape their worries and troubles; in the end, however, they escape nothing, but instead dig a deeper hole of misery for themselves. Would that more and more people who are slaves of their addictions left gatherings of sin – wherein alcohol and drugs are consumed – and made their way to gatherings upon which peace descends. There they would find a permanent solution to their problems: a way to purify their hearts and souls of sins, and the achievement of a kind of peace that does not result in a hangover, but in a stronger soul that is better equipped to face the trials and tribulations of life. Without a doubt, as much as people try to find peace in drugs, alcohol, fornication, or any other means of escapism, the only way that mankind can truly find peace and tranquility is through the Noble Qur'an.[163]

2) Mercy Envelops Them

Mercy is near to the people of the Qur'an; in fact, it envelops or covers their gatherings. Within their gatherings, they do things that make them deserving of Allah's Mercy; outside of their gatherings, people, for the most part, are driven, in their actions, by the desire to increase their bank balance. Without a doubt, the former are better:

$$وَرَحْمَتُ رَبِّكَ خَيْرٌ مِّمَّا يَجْمَعُونَ$$

"But the Mercy (Paradise) of your Lord (O Muhammad (s)) is better than the (wealth of this world) which they amass." (Qur'an 43: 32)

Mercy envelops gatherings in which the Qur'an is recited and studied; this should not come as a surprise, considering the fact that the Qur'an itself is mercy; this applies to the knowledge that was revealed to past Prophets (st), for Allah (sp) said about Noah (p):

$$قَالَ يَٰقَوْمِ أَرَءَيْتُمْ إِن كُنتُ عَلَىٰ بَيِّنَةٍ مِّن رَّبِّى وَءَاتَىٰنِى رَحْمَةً مِّنْ عِندِهِۦ$$

---
[161] Muslim (2699).
[162] *Wa Rattilil-Qur'an Tarteela* (pg. 15).
[163] *Anwaar Al-Qur'an* (pgs. 107,108).

"He said: 'O my people! Tell me, if I have a clear proof from my Lord, and a Mercy has come to me from Him" (Qur'an 11:28)

"Mercy" in this Verse encompasses the blessings of prophethood, revelation, knowledge, and wisdom. The Prophet Saaleh (p) made a similar statement:

$$وَءَاتَىٰنِى مِنْهُ رَحْمَةً$$

"And there has come to me a Mercy from Him" (Qur'an 11: 63)

And regarding the Qur'an being a mercy, Allah (sp) said:

$$وَنَزَّلْنَا عَلَيْكَ ٱلْكِتَٰبَ تِبْيَٰنًا لِّكُلِّ شَىْءٍ وَهُدًى وَرَحْمَةً وَبُشْرَىٰ لِلْمُسْلِمِينَ$$

"And We have sent down to you the Book (the Qur'an) as an exposition of everything, a guidance, a mercy, and glad tidings for those who have submitted themselves (to Allah as Muslims)." (Qur'an 16: 89)

In Chapter *Al-A'raaf*, Allah (sp) said:

$$وَرَحْمَتِى وَسِعَتْ كُلَّ شَىْءٍ$$

"And My Mercy embraces all things" (Qur'an 7: 156)

If, as we are informed about in this Verse, Allah's Mercy embraces all things, it is only fitting that it should embrace the people of the Qur'an.

3) The Angels Surround Them

The Angels surround them with their wings in order to honor them, and what makes them deserving of that honor is the purpose for which they gathered. During the lifetime of the Prophet (s), the noble Companion Usaid bin Hudair (r) physically perceived the presence of Angels while he recited the Qur'an, for they drew very near to him. This occurred one night while Usaid (r) was reciting Chapter *Al-Baqarah* of the Noble Qur'an. In the middle of his recitation, he raised his head towards the sky and saw a cloud, and it appeared as if there were many lamps in it. Then the cloud, or what seemed to be a
cloud, left until he could no longer see it. When he later went to the Prophet (s) and asked him about what he had seen, the Prophet (s) said, "Do you know what that was?" Usaid (r) said, "No". The Prophet (s) said:

"Those were angels that came close (to you) because of your (beautiful) voice. Had you continued to recite, people would have seen them as well..."[164]

4) Allah (sp) Mentions Them to Those that are with Him

That "Allah (sp) mentions them to those that are with Him" means that He praises them to the Prophets and noble Angels (st) that are with Him.[165] It would be hard to think of any honor that is greater than being mentioned by Allah (sp), the Almighty. Imagine yourself – you being a weak and poor and needy slave to Allah (sp) - being mentioned by your Creator, Allah (sp). If a Muslim, or any person for that matter, knew that the president of his country praised him in front of his ministers, would not his heart swell with pride and happiness. Well – and to Allah belongs the highest example – should not one become even happier knowing that Allah (sp), the Possessor of Might and Majesty, mentioned him in the highest of gatherings?

---

[164] Bukhaaree (5018).
[165] *'Aun Al-Ma'bood Sharh Sunan Abu Daawood* (4/230).

The aforementioned rewards should be ample reason for Muslims to search out for gatherings in which the Qur'an is studied. The people of the Qur'an are truly blessed in many ways; others who turn away from gatherings of the Qur'an out of laziness or a lack of understanding truly lose out on a great deal of good.[166]

Third:

To Recite the Qur'an, Regardless of One's Ability as a Reciter, is a Good Deed

Aishah (rh) reported that the Messenger of Allah (sp) said:
"The person who is proficient in the Qur'an is with the Safarah (the Messengers or the Angels), the Kiram (those that are close to Allah), and the Bararah (those that are obedient to Allah). As for the person who reads the Qur'an, though it is difficult for him and though he stutters, he has two rewards."[167]
This Hadeeth describes two kinds of people:

1) A Person Who Recites the Qur'an Well
The abovementioned Hadeeth contains glad tidings for those who went through a process of learning and practicing until they became skilled reciters of the Qur'an. Such people pronounce each letter properly, adhere to the rules of Tajweed (the rules of reciting the Qur'an properly), and are easily able to recall the Verses and chapters they have memorized. As a result of their efforts, they are told that they belong in the company of the *Safarah*, and the commentators of this Hadeeth have said that *Safarah* refers either to the Messengers of Allah or to the Angels (st). For like Messengers and Angels, skilled reciters of the Qur'an know the Qur'an by heart, convey it to others, and remember Allah (sp) frequently.[168]

2) A Person Who Receives Two Rewards for His Recitation of the Qur'an

Such a person stutters and finds it difficult to adhere to established rules of reciting the Qur'an properly. Despite his shortcomings, he is encouraged to recite the Qur'an. And so every Muslim, regardless of his ability to recite the Qur'an, receives a great reward from Allah (sp) for reciting the Qur'an, contemplating its meanings, and applying its teachings. As for those who make an effort but still find it difficult to recite the Qur'an, they receive two rewards, one for reciting the Qur'an and the other for the effort they make to do their best to recite the Qur'an in a correct manner.
Some people might take away from this Hadeeth the understanding that a person who recites the Qur'an poorly receives more reward that does a person who recites it skillfully and beautifully. But that, as Imam An-Nawawee (m) pointed out, is simply not true: "This Hadeeth does not mean that a person who stutters while reciting the Qur'an gets more reward than does a person who recites it skillfully; in fact, the latter is not only better than the former, but he also gets more rewards – that of being in the company of the *Safarah*, and many other rewards as well. The status of being with the *Safarah* is not mentioned for any other person, so how can someone who did not take the trouble of memorizing the Qur'an, of learning to recite it properly, and of reciting it frequently ... be placed on an equal footing with someone who did all of those things?"[169]

---

[166] *Anwaar Al-Qur'an* (pg. 111), and to *Wa Rattilil-Qur'an Tarteela* (pg. 15).
[167] Muslim (798).
[168] *Saheeh Muslim* with *Sharh* of An-Nawawee (6/85), and to *Wa Rattilil-Qur'an Tarteela* (pg. 19).
[169] *Saheeh Muslim* with *Sharh* of An-Nawawee (6/326).

This is not to put down those who stutter when they recite the Qur'an; it is simply to say that a person who does not stutter is better. One must remember, after all, that a skillful reciter stuttered when he first learned the Qur'an. He then had to struggle and learn until he achieved proficiency, and until he became deserving of being likened to Messengers and Angels (st).[170]

What Muslim would want to live the rest of his life without being able to recite the Qur'an properly? In this regard, not every poor reciter is to blame. Some people have a natural stutter that they cannot overcome, and others, particularly those who are non-Arabs, find it difficult to pronounce certain letters of the Qur'an. Such people, who strive to improve but do not succeed, receive two rewards from Allah (sp), and they are not blameworthy in the least. That being said, some people use the abovementioned Hadeeth as an excuse not to learn how to recite the Qur'an. The reason for their failure to recite the Qur'an properly is not the result of being limited in their abilities, but is instead the result of laziness and not taking the time to improve. Most non-Arab Muslims find it difficult to pronounce certain Arabic letters, and yet, through practice and determination, they learn and become proficient reciters of the Qur'an. And so, yes, some people are blameworthy for stuttering while reciting the Qur'an, especially those who speak and read Arabic fluently but do not go to the trouble of learning how to recite the Qur'an; or those who studied Islam at a university level, but while they learned Islamic Jurisprudence, never bothered to learn how to recite the Qur'an properly.

Such people have not given the Qur'an its just due, and their poor recitation is a result of one of two possibilities: Either they neglected the Book of Allah at a young age, and then by the time they wanted to learn, the rules of recitation were too demanding for them to master; or they learned how to recite the Qur'an when they were young, but then they abandoned the Qur'an for many years. Their long estrangement from the Qur'an resulted in it being difficult for them to re-learn the rules of recitation. The people of the latter category, unless they repent and strive to improve themselves, are in danger of being among the people that are referred to in the following Verse:

$$وَقَالَ ٱلرَّسُولُ يَٰرَبِّ إِنَّ قَوْمِى ٱتَّخَذُوا۟ هَٰذَا ٱلْقُرْءَانَ مَهْجُورًا$$

"And the Messenger (Muhammad (s)) said: 'O my Lord! Verily, my people deserted this Qur'an (neither listened to it nor acted on its laws and orders).'" (Qur'an 25: 30)

This Verse makes it clear that a Muslim, no matter what his circumstances, should never stop reciting the Qur'an. This applies both to proficient reciters and to poor reciters who use their weakness as an excuse not to recite the Qur'an. Like everything else in life, achieving proficiency in one's recitation of the Qur'an, or at least gaining a degree of adequacy, can be achieved through practice and determination. One simply has to make a good intention and then strive to improve; if one does that, as is known by all those who have tried, Allah (sp) will make matters easy for him. After making an effort to improve one's recitation, one can either hope for success or at least the achievement of two rewards.[171]

Section 4

The Virtues of Memorizing the Qur'an

In this section, Three Issues are Discussed:
First: The High Ranking of a *Haafidh* (i.e., a Person Who has committed the Entire Qur'an to Memory)
Second: A *Haafidh* is Placed Before Others Both in this World and in the Hereafter

---

[170] *At-Tidhkaar fee Afdalil-Adhkaar* (pg. 83).
[171] *Anwaar al-Qur'an* (pgs. 93-98).

Third: The Various Virtues of Being a *Haafidh*

Introduction

In the early generations of Islam, people, for the most part, learned the Qur'an by committing it to memory. Allah (sp) said:

$$\text{بَلْ هُوَ ءَايَٰتٌۢ بَيِّنَٰتٌ فِى صُدُورِ ٱلَّذِينَ أُوتُواْ ٱلْعِلْمَ}$$

"Nay, but they, the clear Ayat are preserved in the breasts of those who have been given knowledge" (Qur'an 29: 49).
Allah (sp) blessed this nation by making the hearts of its righteous members repositories of His Noble Book; it is as if in their hearts there are layers upon layers of scrolls upon which the Qur'an is written, so accurately have they committed the Qur'an to memory.
In a Qudsee Hadeeth, the Prophet (s) related that Allah (sp) said to him (s):
"Verily, I have sent you only in order to test you and to test (others) through you. And I have revealed to you a Book that is not washed off with water. You recite it both when you are awake and when you are asleep."[172]
That the Qur'an "is not washed off with water" means that it is preserved in the hearts of men and that it cannot be wiped off, erased, or destroyed; instead, it will remain until the end of time.[173]
Many people throughout history have succeeded in memorizing the entire Qur'an; they were able to do so because Allah (sp) made His speech easy for human beings to remember. Allah (sp) said:

$$\text{وَلَقَدْ يَسَّرْنَا ٱلْقُرْءَانَ لِلذِّكْرِ فَهَلْ مِن مُّدَّكِرٍ}$$

"And We have indeed made the Qur'an easy to understand and remember, then is there any that will remember (or receive admonition)?" (Qur'an 54: 17)
Some non-Muslims might not comprehend how the Qur'an is easier to memorize than any other book, and yet most Muslims, though they might not understand the 'how' part, have experienced the ease with which the Qur'an is memorized. Some Muslims are able to read a page of the Qur'an only once or twice, and, though they are not known for any exceptional ability to retain knowledge, that is all they need to commit it to memory. This is especially the case for those who understand the Arabic language. That being said, one of the truly amazing aspects of the Qur'an being easy to memorize is the fact that a great many people who have memorized the Qur'an these days do not even speak the Arabic language. Though they do not understand more than a few words of the Qur'an, by the grace and mercy and help of Allah (sp), been able to commit all of it to memory. It is difficult to enumerate the number of Muslims that have memorized the entire Qur'an. We know there are great many of them – as has been the case throughout history – but the exact number we do not know.[174]
Imam Abul-Hasan Al-Maawardee (m) said, "One of the ways in which the Qur'an is a miracle is the ease with which it is memorized by people, regardless of the language they speak, for the Qur'an has been memorized even by a person who not only is unable to speak or understand Arabic, but also is a mute. No other divinely revealed Book is memorized to the degree that the Qur'an is memorized,

---

[172] Muslim (2865).
[173] *Saheeh Muslim* with *Sharh* of An-Nawawee (17/204).
[174] *Kaifa tatawajjahu Ilal-'Ulum Wal-Qur'an Al-Kareem Masdaruha* by Dr. Noorud-Deen 'Atr (pgs. 83, 84).

which is one of the various ways in which Allah, by His grace, has made it superior to every other Book that He has revealed."[175]

Whenever the opportunity presented itself to him, the Prophet (s) encouraged the Companions (rp) to memorize the Noble Qur'an. In fact, in various ways he treated people differently based on how much Qur'an they had committed to memory. So, for instance, he (s) would give the banner of an army to the soldier that had the most Qur'an memorized. Also, if he sent out a military unit, he would appoint as its leader the one who had the most Qur'an memorized. And most Muslims know that the Imam for prayer should be the person who knows the most Qur'an. Even when certain Companions (rp) died, the Prophet (s) treated them differently based on their knowledge of the Qur'an, for he would place first in the side compartment of a shared grave the Companion (r) who had the most Qur'an memorized.

Finally, the Prophet (s) stipulated that, if a man wanted to get married, he had to give his wife some dowry (*Mahr*), which could be in the form of gold, silver, a ring, etc. But on certain occasions, if a man did not have any wealth to give his wife-to-be, the Prophet (s) would marry him off to her based on the Qur'an he had committed to memory; or in other words, the Qur'an he had committed to memory was considered his dowry, for it was understood that he was going to teach it to her. Our discussion on memorizing the Qur'an revolves around the following three issues.

First:

First: The High Ranking of a *Haafidh* (i.e., a Person Who has committed the Entire Qur'an to Memory)

The word *Haafidh* is a well-known term to Muslims – to non-Arab and Arab Muslims alike – and it refers to someone who has committed the entire Qur'an to memory. When the believers will enter Paradise, a *Haafidh* will achieve special honors, one of them being that he will rise above others towards the higher stations of Paradise. Abdullah bin Amr (r) reported that the Messenger of Allah (s) said:

"It will be said to a person of the Qur'an, 'recite and ascend, and recite slowly, carefully enunciating each letter, just as you used to do in the world. For indeed, your station (in Paradise) will be the height you reach when you have recited your last Verse.'"[176]

This Hadeeth refers specifically to one who has memorized the Qur'an, and not to one who reads it from a copy of the Qur'an. Ibn Hajar Al-Haitamee (m) said, "The said narration refers to a person who has committed the Qur'an to memory, and not to a person who reads it from a copy of the Qur'an. This is so because people are the same when it comes to reading from a copy of the Qur'an; the question of less and more does not come into play. People do vary, however, in regard to how much Qur'an they have memorized; the differences between them are quantifiable, and so their stations in Paradise differ based on how much Qur'an they have committed to memory."[177]

We must keep in mind, however, that, in order to achieve the honor that is described in the abovementioned Hadeeth, certain conditions must be fulfilled. Al-Albaanee (m) pointed out those conditions when he said, "This Hadeeth clearly establishes the superiority of a person who has committed the entire Qur'an to memory, but still, such a person has to fulfill an important condition, namely, that he memorized the Qur'an for the sake of Allah (sp) and not for worldly gain, such as the

---

[175] *'Alaam An-Nubuwwah* (pg. 69).
[176] Abu Dawood (1464). And in *Saheeh Abu Dawood*, Al-Albanee said, *Hasan Saheeh* (1300).
[177] Al-Fataawa Al-Hadeethiyyah (pg. 156).

earning of a dinar or dirham. For it must be remembered that the Prophet (s) said: *'Most of the hypocrites from my nation are reciters (of the Qur'an).'*[178]

The people of the Qur'an are a special breed. For, as At-Teebee pointed out, 'Recitation of the Qur'an is for them what glorifying Allah is for the Angels. Nothing turns them away from the fulfilling act of reciting the Qur'an; in fact, there is nothing they enjoy more or find more fulfilling than reciting the Qur'an.'"[179]

Second:

A *Haafidh* is Placed Before Others Both in this World and in the Hereafter

1) A *Haafidh* is Most Deserving of being Chosen to Lead Others

A *Haafidh*, or even someone who is very knowledgeable of the Qur'an, deserves to be honored and placed ahead of others. Consider the story of Abdur-Rahmaan bin Abzaa Al-Khuzaa'ee (r). He was one of the youngest Companions (rp) of the Messenger of Allah (sp), and he was the *Maulaa*, or freed slave, of Naafai bin Abdul-Haarith.[180] Because he was a freed slave, AbdurRahmaan did not enjoy many of the advantages that were enjoyed by other members of society, people who had wealth, honor, status, and strong family ties. Nonetheless, he lived, by the grace and mercy of Allah (sp), not during the days of pre-Islamic ignorance, when he would have been oppressed and made to do hard labor, but during the golden years of Islam. As such, because of his qualifications, he rose to the rank of governor and ruled over an entire region, an achievement that was unheard of just a decade earlier.

'Aamir bin Waathilah reported that Naafai bin Al-Haarith met Umar bin Al-Khattaab (rp) at Usfaan. The two were well-acquainted with one another, for Umar had appointed him governor of Makkah. Umar (r) asked him, "Who did you appoint as governor of the people of Al-Waadee (during your absence)?" Naafai replied, "AbdurRahmaan Ibn Abzaa." Umar (r) asked, "And who is Ibn Abzaa?" Naafai said, "He is one of our freed slaves."

Thinking that AbdurRahmaan bin Abzaa was probably unqualified for the job, given that he had been a slave, Umar (sp) said, "You have appointed over them a freed slave?" Naafai replied, "Verily, he is a reciter of the Book of Allah (the Possessor of Might and Majesty), and he is a scholar of Islamic Inheritance Law." Amazed at how AbdurRahmaan (r) went from being a slave to the governor of Makkah, Umar (r) recalling what he once heard from the Prophet (s), exclaimed, "Lo! Indeed your Prophet (s) said: *'Verily, Allah raises people with this Book, and with it, He lowers others.'*"[181]

One cannot understate what Islam did for the poor and weak members of Arab society, for here was a man who did not have wealth, status, or a noble lineage. According to the standards of worldly people, he was probably considered to be one of the lowest ranking members of society. But according to the standards of Islam and of the Qur'an, he was one of the noblest members of society. The Quran raised him from the status of a freed slave to that of a governor. And his knowledge of the Qur'an qualified him for the job of ruling over others and acting as a judge over them. If two rich men quarreled with one another over some money, his word was final, and his judgment was binding upon them.

As for Umar (r), he only had to hear about Abdur-Rahmaan's qualifications before he began to recognize his status as a scholar of the Qur'an; furthermore, Umar (r) approved of Naafai's appointment and even pointed out why AbdurRahmaan (r) was deserving of the job:

---

[178] Ahmad in *Al-Musnad* (2/175), and the editors of *Al-Musnad* wrote, 'Its chain is authentic.' (11/213). And Al-Albaanee included this Hadeeth in his compilation *"As-Silsilah As-Saheehah."* (2/386).
[179] *Aun Al-Ma'bood* (4/237,238).
[180] *Al-Isaabah* (4/149), *At-Taqreeb* (1/472), and *Siyar 'Alaam An-Nubalaa* (3/201).
[181] Muslim (817).

'Verily, Allah raises people with this Book, and with it, He lowers others.'[182]

2) A *Haafidh* is the Most Deserving of People to Lead Others in Prayer

Abu Masood Al-Ansaaree (r) reported that the Prophet (s) said: *"Let he who has the most knowledge of the Book of Allah lead the people (in prayer)"*[183]
The high-ranking of a *Haafidh* is most clearly seen when, for instance, hundreds of people attend congregational prayer and he, by virtue of the fact that he has committed the entire Qur'an to memory, is chosen to lead them in prayer.

3) In Matters of Importance, a *Haafidh* Should be one of the First People to be Consulted

Ibn Abbaas (r2) said, *"The Qurraa (the reciters of the Qur'an, the people who had the Qur'an memorized) would be members of Umar's gathering (during his caliphate), and they were the people with whom he consulted (regarding matters of importance), regardless of whether they were old (above forty) or young."*[184]

4) A *Haafidh* is Given Precedence in Shared Graves

Jaabir bin Abdullah (r) related that, following the Battle of Uhud, the Prophet (s) decided to bury fallen Muslim soldiers in shared graves, with a ratio of two men per one grave. For each grave, the Prophet (s) had to choose which Muslim to place first in the side compartment that was dug out inside of the grave. And so for each grave, he would ask his Companions (rp), *"Which of these two learned more of the Qur'an?"*
If one of the two men was pointed out to him, he would place him first in the side compartment of the grave. And he would then say: *"I am a witness over these (men) on the Day of Resurrection."*[185]
If the Prophet (s) ranked the dead based on what they knew of the Qur'an, it is only fitting, or even more fitting, that those who are alive should be ranked based on the same criteria.

$$\text{وَفِى ذَٰلِكَ فَلْيَتَنَافَسِ ٱلْمُتَنَافِسُونَ}$$

"And for this let (all) those strive who want to strive (i.e., hasten earnestly to the obedience of Allah)." (Qur'an 83: 26)

Third:

The Various Virtues of Being a *Haafidh*

1) Being the "People of Allah"

We are all slaves unto Allah (sp), but there are some Muslims among us who are close to him: They are his *Auliyaa*, or his close obedient slaves. Then there is another category of people. They are His

---

[182] *Anwaar Al-Qur'an* (pg. 248).
[183] Muslim (673).
[184] Bukhaaree (642).
[185] Bukhaaree (1353).

"people" and His chosen, closest slaves. Anas bin Maalik (r) reported that the Messenger of Allah (s) said:
"Verily, Allah has His people among mankind."
The Prophet's Companions (rp) asked, "And who are they?" The Prophet (s) said:
"They are the people of the Qur'an. They are Allah's people, and they are the ones that are closest to Him."[186]

First, it must be understood that we cannot make comparisons to Allah (sp), for to Him belongs the highest example: He is above all of his creation, and there is nothing like unto Him. But for the purpose of understanding the implications of this Hadeeth, imagine a rich or famous man who says, "These are my people." He is referring to a select group of people he has chosen to keep close to him. To be sure, given that he is rich, he will shower them with gifts and love. What will be the case, then, when Allah (sp) chooses the people of the Qur'an to be His "people"? Imagine, given that He is the Most Generous One, the blessings He (sp) will shower upon the people of the Qur'an. As for the Hereafter, He (sp) will give them more than they could have ever hoped or asked for.

2) A *Haafidh* is Among Those Who have been Given Knowledge

In the following Verse, Allah (sp) praised those Muslims who have committed the Qur'an to memory, describing them as being people "who have been given knowledge":

$$\text{بَلْ هُوَ ءَايَـٰتٌ بَيِّنَـٰتٌ فِى صُدُورِ ٱلَّذِينَ أُوتُواْ ٱلْعِلْمَ}$$

"Nay, but they are clear Ayat are preserved in the breasts of those who have been given knowledge" (Qur'an 29:49).

Allah (sp) guaranteed to preserve the Qur'an until the end of time. And one of the ways in which He makes sure the Qur'an remains preserved is guiding many members of this nation to store the entire Qur'an in their hearts. That in itself - i.e., being a means by which the Qur'an remains preserved – is a great honor for a Muslim. Therefore, the Qur'an is preserved both on paper and in the breasts of men. Just suppose that even the slightest vowel change was mistakenly added to the Qur'an on paper, so many Muslims have memorized the Qur'an that that mistake would not be able to find a way to their hearts; furthermore, it would be quickly found out and corrected.

3) The Hellfire will not Burn Those Who have the Qur'an Memorized

Every Muslim wishes more than anything else to be saved from the torment of the Hellfire and to be admitted into the gardens of Paradise. Those that have committed the Qur'an to memory will have at least the first part of that wish fulfilled. They will be saved from the Hellfire because of what is in their breasts - the Noble Qur'an. Uqbah bin Aamir (r) reported that the Messenger of Allah (s) said:

"Had the Qur'an been in a skin container (i.e., a container made of hide or skin), the Hellfire would not be able to consume it."[187]

Or in other words: Had a skin container been given the ability to store the Qur'an, the Hellfire would not touch it based on its proximity to and contact with the blessed Qur'an. Imagine, then, a believer who takes it upon himself to memorize the Qur'an, to store it in his mind, and to constantly review and recite it. Thus what would have applied to the skin container certainly applies to him, *In Sha Allah* (Allah Willing).

---

[186] Ibn Maajah (215), and, in *Saheeh Sunan Ibn Maajah*, Al-Albaanee declared this Hadeeth to be authentic (178).
[187] Ahmad (3/155), and, in *Saheeh Al-Jaami'*, Al-Albaanee ruled that it is a *Hasan* (acceptable) narration (2/953).

Section 5

The Virtues of Applying the Teachings of the Qur'an

Introduction

To be sure, the greater goal of every Muslim vis-à-vis the Qur'an should be to apply its teachings, by obeying its commands, staying away from its prohibitions, and making it the overall blueprint of one's life on an individual, a familial, and a societal level. As much as a person recites the Qur'an, he will not receive a complete reward until he applies what he recites, by bringing the teachings of the Qur'an into the realm of practical application. Allah (sp) said:

$$ ٱلَّذِينَ ءَاتَيْنَٰهُمُ ٱلْكِتَٰبَ يَتْلُونَهُۥ حَقَّ تِلَاوَتِهِۦ $$

"Those to whom We gave the Book (or those to whom We have given the Book) recite it as it should be recited)" (Qur'an 2:121)
To "recite the Qur'an as it should be recited" means to obey its orders and follow its teachings.[188] Throughout history, no one has better applied the teachings of the Qur'an, both outwardly and inwardly, than the Prophet (s), whom Allah (sp) praised by saying about his character:

$$ وَإِنَّكَ لَعَلَىٰ خُلُقٍ عَظِيمٍ $$

"And verily, you (O Muhammad (s)) are on an exalted standard of character." (Qur'an 68: 4)
Aishah (rh) clarified the meaning of this Verse when Saad bin Hishaam bin Aamir asked her, *"O Mother of the Believers, inform me about the character of the Messenger of Allah (s)."* She said, "Do you not recite the Qur'an?" He said, "Yes." She said, "Then, verily, the character of the Prophet of Allah was the Qur'an."[189] As An-Nawawee (m) pointed out, this means that the Prophet (s) applied the teachings of the Qur'an, adopted the manners that are extolled in the Qur'an, learned from its lessons and stories, applied its laws, contemplated its meanings, and recited it as it should be recited.[190] In short, the Prophet (s) was a practical manifestation of the Qur'an. Or in other words, he was a walking, talking version of the Qur'an.
In his *Tafseer* of the abovementioned Verse, Ibn Katheer (m) said, "Applying the teachings of the Qur'an...became a part of his nature and an integral part of his character."[191]
The deeper meanings and secrets of the Qur'an are perceived only by those who apply its teachings and transform its meanings into real world application. Those meanings and secrets remain hidden to people who recite the Qur'an in a ritual manner, seeking to be blessed thereby, but not willing to learn and act; and the same goes for those who treat the study of the Qur'an as an academic endeavor, thinking that the Qur'an should be studied because, for instance, it is part of our "Arab heritage."
The reward one receives from Allah (sp) is commensurate with the degree to which one applies the Qur'an's teachings. Suppose that a man memorizes all of the laws of his country but then clearly commits a crime and shows no regard for the law. Will his knowledge of his country's laws benefit him in the least? The answer to this question is an obvious and a resounding, no. But then why do

---
[188] *Tafseer At-Tabaree* (1519).
[189] Muslim (746).
[190] *Saheeh Muslim* with *Sharh* of An-Nawawee (5/268).
[191] *Tafseer Ibn Katheer* (8/164).

some Muslims think that, in spite of their knowledge of the Qur'an, or in spite of the many Chapters of the Qur'an they have committed to memory, they can act contrary to laws of the Qur'an with impunity?

Recitation of the Qur'an and the application of its teachings must go hand in hand; otherwise – if one does the former to the exclusion of the latter – one is heading down a dark path that leads to severe torment in the Hereafter.

How does a Muslim benefit if he memorizes Chapter *An-Noor* in its entirety and consequently knows the punishment of a fornicator, but then goes right ahead and fornicates – and we seek refuge in Allah from being such a person. Will the fact that he has memorized Chapter *An-Noor* save him from being punished? This question, understood in a broader sense, is one that each one of us should contemplate. Our knowledge must be followed by action; otherwise, we put ourselves in great danger of being punished with the Hellfire.[192]

Some of us read the Tafseer of an entire section (*Juzz*) of the Qur'an in one sitting; and while studying the Tafseer is a laudable endeavor, we must learn to strike a balance between learning and applying what we learn. Consider the manner in which the Prophet's Companions (rp) studied the Qur'an: Al-Amash related from Abu Waail that Ibn Masood (r) said, "If a man among us learned ten Verses, he would not go beyond them until he knew their meanings and applied the teachings they contained."[193]

The Virtues of Applying the Qur'an's Teachings

The greatest reward awaiting a person who applies the Qur'an's teachings is Paradise. And yet, since Muslims apply the Qur'an at different levels – with some being better than others – it is only fitting that there be different levels in Paradise. Allah (sp); said:

$$وَلِكُلٍّ دَرَجَاتٌ مِّمَّا عَمِلُوا۟ وَمَا رَبُّكَ بِغَافِلٍ عَمَّا يَعْمَلُونَ$$

"For all there will be degrees (or ranks) according to what they did. And your Lord is not unaware of what they do" (Qur'an 6: 132)

Another major reward one receives for applying the Qur'an's teachings is being blessed with a good life in this world. Allah (sp) promised that reward in Verse number 97 of Chapter *An-Nahl*:

$$مَنْ عَمِلَ صَالِحًا مِّن ذَكَرٍ أَوْ أُنثَىٰ وَهُوَ مُؤْمِنٌ فَلَنُحْيِيَنَّهُۥ حَيَوٰةً طَيِّبَةً ۖ وَلَنَجْزِيَنَّهُمْ أَجْرَهُم بِأَحْسَنِ مَا كَانُوا۟ يَعْمَلُونَ$$

"Whoever works righteousness, whether male or female, while he (or she) is a true believer (of Islamic Monotheism) verily, to him We will give a good life (in this world with respect, contentment and lawful provision, and We shall pay them certainly a reward in proportion to the best of what they used to do (i.e., Paradise in the Hereafter)." (Qur'an16:97)

The rewards for applying the Qur'an's teachings are at once many and varied; some of them are given out in this world, and others, in the Hereafter. The following are just a few examples.

1) Guidance
Allah (sp) said:

$$فَبَشِّرْ عِبَادِ ٱلَّذِينَ يَسْتَمِعُونَ ٱلْقَوْلَ فَيَتَّبِعُونَ أَحْسَنَهُۥٓ ۚ أُو۟لَٰٓئِكَ ٱلَّذِينَ هَدَىٰهُمُ ٱللَّهُ ۖ وَأُو۟لَٰٓئِكَ هُمْ أُو۟لُوا۟ ٱلْأَلْبَٰبِ$$

---

[192] *Anwaar Al-Qur'an* (pg. 211).
[193] *Muqaddimah Tafseer Ibn Katheer* (1/36); the scholars who studied the Hadeeth narrations that are mentioned in Tafseer Ibn Katheer said that the chain of this narration is good.

"So announce the good news to My slaves, those who listen to the Word and follow the best thereof, those are (the ones) whom Allah has guided and those are men of understanding" (Qur'an 39: 17, 18)
In this Verse, Allah (sp) informs those who apply the Qur'an's teachings that, of all of the people on earth, they are the ones who are truly guided and are on the Straight Path that leads to Paradise. But this Verse says something more, it intimates to the people of the Qur'an that, not only are they upon true guidance, but also they will neither go astray in this world nor suffer misery or wretchedness in the Hereafter.

2) Mercy
Allah (sp) said:

وَهَٰذَا كِتَٰبٌ أَنزَلْنَٰهُ مُبَارَكٌ فَٱتَّبِعُوهُ وَٱتَّقُوا۟ لَعَلَّكُمْ تُرْحَمُونَ

"And this is a blessed Book (the Qur'an) which We have sent down. So follow it and fear Allah, (i.e., do not disobey His orders), that you may receive mercy (Qur'an 6: 155).
We all want to be the recipients of Allah's Mercy. In this Verse, we are told that the fastest and shortest way to achieve Allah's Mercy is to follow the teachings of His Book.
Allah's Saying that "you may receive mercy" is an explicit promise that Allah (sp) makes to His slaves; and yet, it also suggests an implicit warning: That, if they do not follow the teachings of the Qur'an, they will be punished both in this life and in the Hereafter.

3) Success and Happiness Both in this World and in the Hereafter
Allah (sp) said:

فَٱلَّذِينَ ءَامَنُوا۟ بِهِۦ وَعَزَّرُوهُ وَنَصَرُوهُ وَٱتَّبَعُوا۟ ٱلنُّورَ ٱلَّذِىٓ أُنزِلَ مَعَهُۥٓ ۙ أُو۟لَٰٓئِكَ هُمُ ٱلْمُفْلِحُونَ

"So those who believe in him(Muhammad (s)), honor him, help him, and follow the light (the Qur'an) which has been sent down with him, it is they who will be successful." (Qur'an 7: 157)
In this Verse, the Qur'an is likened to light, in the sense that it removes the darkness of ignorance; and only the truth can be seen in the light of the Qur'an. Also, a follower of the Qur'an is likened to a man who travels by night; if a light appears before him, he heads in its direction, knowing for certain that at the point of the light he will gain safety from the dangers that surround him in the darkness of the night. It is compulsory upon every Muslim to seek out the light of the Qur'an, to believe in it, to apply its commands, to stay away from its prohibitions, and to learn important lessons from its stories and parables. If a person stays away from the light of the Qur'an, he will wander in darkness and fall prey to sin, temptation, doubt, and even, if he strays too far, disbelief.[194]

4) Expiation of Sins and Having One's Situation in Life Improved
Allah (sp) said:

وَٱلَّذِينَ ءَامَنُوا۟ وَعَمِلُوا۟ ٱلصَّٰلِحَٰتِ وَءَامَنُوا۟ بِمَا نُزِّلَ عَلَىٰ مُحَمَّدٍ وَهُوَ ٱلْحَقُّ مِن رَّبِّهِمْ ۙ كَفَّرَ عَنْهُمْ سَيِّـَٔاتِهِمْ وَأَصْلَحَ بَالَهُمْ

"But those who believe and do righteous good deeds, and believe in that which is sent down to Muhammad (s), for it is the truth from their Lord, He will expiate from them their sins, and will make good their state." (Qur'an 47: 2)
Allah's Saying "He will expiate from them their sins" applies to both small and major sins. If, by applying the Qur'an's teachings, their sins are expiated, they will be saved from punishment both in

---
[194] *Adwaa Al-Bayaan* (7/80), and *At-Tahreer Wat-Tanweer* (8/319).

this life and in the Hereafter.[195] It is held by some scholars that He will expiate from them their sins" means that, by virtue of their faith and their good deeds, Allah (sp) will hide for them their previous disbelief and their sins, a favor that He (sp) will bestow upon them because they changed their ways and repented from their past mistakes.[196]

A second reward in this Verse is mentioned as well: Allah (sp) will make good the state or situation of people who apply the Qur'an's teachings. This means that, in this world, He (sp) will make good their affairs for them, and that, in the Hereafter, He will admit them into Paradise, wherein they will abide for eternity.[197] According to another interpretation, Allah's Saying "will make good their state" means that He (sp) will make good for them their religion, their worldly affairs, their hearts, their deeds, and every aspect of their lives.[198]

At any rate, Allah's Saying "will make good their state" seems to have broad implications; what is certain is the fact that, if Allah makes "good the state" of a person, that person will achieve inner peace, tranquility, and strong faith in Allah (sp). And the main reason for that reward is that they:

"Followed the truth from their Lord." (Qur'an 47: 3)

Part 3

The Rights of the Qur'an Over Muslims

This part consists of seven Sections:

Section One: Having Faith in the Qur'an
Section Two: Preserving and Honoring the Qur'an
Section Three: Reciting the Qur'an
Section Four: Contemplating the Verses of the Qur'an
Section Five: Applying the Qur'an's Teachings
Section Six: Having Good Manners with the Qur'an
Section Seven: Inviting Others to Learn the Qur'an

---

[195] *Tafseer As-Sa'dee* (1/784).
[196] *Al-Kashshaaf* (4/319).
[197] *Tafseer At-Tabaree* (26/39).
[198] *Tafseer As-Sa'dee* (1/784).

Section One:

Having Faith in the Qur'an

To have faith in the Noble Qur'an and all that is in it; to believe that the Qur'an is Allah's speech, which was revealed to the Messenger of Allah (s); and to have faith in the fact that, not only is the Qur'an unchanged, but also it will remain unchanged until the Day of Resurrection – these, above all else, are the rights that the Qur'an has over us. Allah (sp) said:

$$\text{يَٰٓأَيُّهَا ٱلَّذِينَ ءَامَنُوٓاْ ءَامِنُواْ بِٱللَّهِ وَرَسُولِهِۦ وَٱلْكِتَٰبِ ٱلَّذِى نَزَّلَ عَلَىٰ رَسُولِهِۦ وَٱلْكِتَٰبِ ٱلَّذِىٓ أَنزَلَ مِن قَبْلُ}$$

"O you who believe! Believe in Allah and His Messenger and the Book (the Qur'an) which He has sent down to His Messenger, and the Scripture which He sent down to those before (him)" (Qur'an 4: 136).

When a patient goes to the hospital, it is of utmost importance that he has a good rapport with his doctor and that he trusts in his skills, his education, and his ability to both diagnose an ailment and to prescribe its proper treatment. Without that trust, the patient will not take all of his doctors advice seriously, and, consequently, he will not fully benefit from his prescribed treatment. The same, albeit regarding an even more important matter, applies to a Muslim. If he wants to truly benefit from the Qur'an, he must, above all else, have faith in it, as is indicated in the following Verse:

$$\text{وَٱلَّذِينَ يُؤْمِنُونَ بِمَآ أُنزِلَ إِلَيْكَ وَمَآ أُنزِلَ مِن قَبْلِكَ}$$

"And who believe in which has been sent down (revealed) to you (Muhammad (s)) and in which were sent down before you". (Qur'an 2: 4).

$$\text{ءَامَنَ ٱلرَّسُولُ بِمَآ أُنزِلَ إِلَيْهِ مِن رَّبِّهِۦ وَٱلْمُؤْمِنُونَ}$$

"The Messenger (Muhammad (s)) believes in what has been sent down to him from his Lord, and (so do) the believers." (Qur'an 2: 285)

There are two parts to having faith in the Qur'an. The first has to do with a feeling of certainty that settles in the heart, and the second involves confirming that feeling of certainty with action. As for the former, Allah (sp) said:

$$\text{قُولُوٓاْ ءَامَنَّا بِٱللَّهِ وَمَآ أُنزِلَ إِلَيْنَا}$$

"Say (O Muslims): 'We believe in Allah and that which has been sent down to us'" (Qur'an 2:136)
And as for the latter, Allah (sp); said:

$$\text{ٱلَّذِينَ ءَاتَيْنَٰهُمُ ٱلْكِتَٰبَ يَتْلُونَهُۥ حَقَّ تِلَاوَتِهِۦٓ أُوْلَٰٓئِكَ يُؤْمِنُونَ بِهِۦ}$$

"Those to whom We gave the Book recite it (i.e., obey its orders and follow its teachings) as it should be recited (i.e., followed), they are the ones that believe therein." (Qur'an 2: 121)

Section Two:

Preserving and Honoring the Qur'an

That we preserve and honor the Qur'an are two of the most important rights that the Qur'an has over us. In fact, the order to fulfill those two rights was the gist of the Prophet's (s) last will and testament. Talhah said, "I asked Abdullah bin Abee Aufaa, 'Did the Prophet (s) leave behind a final will and testament?' He said, 'No'. Then I said, 'People have been ordered to leave behind a final will and testament, so why then did he not do so?' Abdullah said, 'In his final will and testament, he advised (us) to adhere to and follow the Book of Allah'".[199] When Abdullah bin Abee Aufaa at first said, 'No', what he meant was that the Prophet (s), in his final will and testament, did not discuss the distribution of his estate or the appointment of his *Khaleefah*; instead, he left behind one last command: That we should adhere to and follow the Qur'an. Given our modern-day understanding of wills and final testaments, some readers might be confused by the contents of the Prophet's final will and testament. This confusion should disappear when the reader understands that, in Islam, a final will and testament consists not just of the details of a person's financial standing – his outstanding debts, the amount (though it may not exceed one third of his estate) he wishes to give to charity, an inventory of his assets, etc. – but also of the final advice and counsel he leaves to his relatives and fellow Muslims that survive him. In the Prophet's final will and testament, he focused on the latter to the complete exclusion of the former.

Perhaps the reason why he limited the focus of his final testament to one issue is the fact that the Qur'an is supremely important in the lives of human beings: it, sometimes explicitly and sometimes through the deeper meanings of its Verses, contains an "explanation of all things."[200]

The Prophet (s) ordered us to adhere to and follow the Book of Allah. This means that we should honor and protect the Qur'an, by not taking it, for instance, to enemy lands; by applying its commands and staying away from its prohibitions; by reciting it frequently; by learning it; and by teaching it to others. Therefore, protecting the Qur'an is not limited to the act of placing copies of the Qur'an on shelves instead of on the floor. One honors the Qur'an by applying its teachings, and not by hanging its Verses around one's neck or on the wall of one's home.

We should respect and honor the Qur'an, and not just by kissing it or by putting it in an appropriate place; but rather respecting and honoring the Qur'an extend to other more important displays of respect - such as being fearful and contemplative while reciting the Qur'an, listening to its recitation; applying its commands; and staying away from its prohibitions.

Section Three:

Reciting the Qur'an

In many Verses of the Qur'an, Allah (sp) has ordered us to recite His Book; for instance, in Chapter *Al-Kahf*, Allah (sp) said:

وَٱتْلُ مَآ أُوحِىَ إِلَيْكَ مِن كِتَابِ رَبِّكَ لَا مُبَدِّلَ لِكَلِمَـٰتِهِۦ وَلَن تَجِدَ مِن دُونِهِۦ مُلْتَحَدًا

"*And recite what has been revealed to you (O Muhammad (s)) of the Book (the Qur'an) of your Lord (i.e., recite it, understand and follow its teachings and act on its orders and preach it to men). None can change His Words, and none will you find as a refuge other than Him.*" (Qur'an 18: 27)

---

[199] Bukhaaree (5022).
[200] *Fathul-Baaree Sharh Saheeh Al-Bukhaaree* (5/443).

Even if the wording of this Verse indicates that Allah (sp) is addressing His Messenger (s), the fact remains that, by extension, He (sp) is also addressing His Messenger's followers – a point that is confirmed by the wording of the following Verse:

$$\text{فَاقْرَءُواْ مَا تَيَسَّرَ مِنْهُ}$$

"So recite of the Qur'an as much as may be easy for you." (Qur'an 73:20)

It is important to note that "you" in this Verse is mentioned in the plural, so it is as if Allah (sp) is saying: "So all of you recite as much of the Qur'an as may be easy for you."

Based on the above, one of the rights that the Qur'an has over us is for us to recite it; in fact, elsewhere in the Qur'an, we are instructed to recite it both when we are healthy and when we are sick; when, in general, we are busy earning our livelihood, and when we have free time; when we fight in wars, and when we are living during a period of peace and safety. Allah (sp) said:

$$\text{عَلِمَ أَن سَيَكُونُ مِنكُم مَّرْضَىٰ ۙ وَءَاخَرُونَ يَضْرِبُونَ فِى ٱلْأَرْضِ يَبْتَغُونَ مِن فَضْلِ ٱللَّهِ ۙ وَءَاخَرُونَ يُقَٰتِلُونَ فِى سَبِيلِ ٱللَّهِ ۖ فَٱقْرَءُوا۟ مَا تَيَسَّرَ مِنْهُ}$$

"He knows that there will be some among you sick, others traveling through the land, seeking of Allah's Bounty, yet others fighting in Allah's Cause. So recite as much of the Qur'an as may be easy for you." (Qur'an 73:20)

Section Four:
Contemplating the Verses of the Qur'an

One is defeating the true purpose of reciting the Qur'an when one recites it many times over without paying any attention to its meanings. As such, it is better to reflect, ponder, and slowly recite a small number of Verses than it is to recite quickly – as if one is skimming over what he is reading – a great many Verses. This is because our main aims of reading the Qur'an are to understand, contemplate, and act.

If one is always reciting the Qur'an quickly, one very likely contemplates only a little, if anything at all, the Verses he comes across. Therefore, just as walking is a means of arriving at one's destination, reciting the Qur'an in a slow, deliberate manner is a necessary step towards understanding and contemplating the Qur'an's meanings.

In the following Verse, Allah (sp) censures those who do not contemplate the Qur'an's meanings:

$$\text{أَفَلَا يَتَدَبَّرُونَ ٱلْقُرْءَانَ أَمْ عَلَىٰ قُلُوبٍ أَقْفَالُهَآ}$$

"Do they not then think deeply in the Qur'an, or are their hearts locked up (from understanding it)" (Qur'an 47: 24)

A radio that plays the recitation of the Qur'an does not, because it is an inanimate object, understand any of the Verses it plays. For all effective purposes, a person becomes like that radio when he doesn't understand the Verses he recites. Without a doubt, the primary purpose of the Qur'an is not to be recited, but to be understood. Reciting the Qur'an is a means of achieving that purpose, a reality that is pointed out in various Verses of the Qur'an; for instance, Allah (sp) said:

$$\text{كَذَٰلِكَ يُبَيِّنُ ٱللَّهُ لَكُمْ ءَايَٰتِهِۦ لَعَلَّكُمْ تَعْقِلُونَ}$$

"Thus Allah makes clear His Ayat (Laws) to you, in order that you may understand." (Qur'an 2: 242)

In another Verse, Allah (sp) said:

$$كَذَٰلِكَ نُفَصِّلُ ٱلْءَايَٰتِ لِقَوْمٍ يَتَفَكَّرُونَ$$

"Thus do We explain the Ayat (proofs, evidences, Verses, lessons, signs, revelations, laws, etc.) in detail for the people who reflect." (Qur'an 10: 24)
And in yet another Verse, He (sp) said:

$$إِنَّآ أَنزَلْنَٰهُ قُرْءَٰنًا عَرَبِيًّا لَّعَلَّكُمْ تَعْقِلُونَ$$

"Verily, We have sent it down as an Arabic Qur'an in order that you may understand." (Qur'an 12:2)
If a person hears with his ears but not with his mind, or looks with his eyes but not with his heart, or speaks with his tongue without understanding the words he utters, he is, for all effective purposes, deaf, dumb, and blind. Allah (sp) said:

$$وَمِنْهُم مَّن يَنظُرُ إِلَيْكَ أَفَأَنتَ تَهْدِى ٱلْعُمْىَ وَلَوْ كَانُوا۟ لَا يُبْصِرُونَ$$

"And among them are some who look at you, but can you guide the blind, even though they see not" (Qur'an 10:43)
This Verse clearly indicates that listening to the Qur'an is not a goal in and of itself, but is instead a means to a goal. Consider the polytheists of Makkah: They would listen to the Qur'an, but then they would leave, without changing their thinking or their demeanor in the least. What is truly troubling about what I just said is that many Muslims today are no different; so, in a way, they are like the Quraish: They listen to the Qur'an everyday on the radio, but then they do not change at all; a business swindler continues to swindle, a liar continues to lie, a usurer continues to deal with usury, and an evildoer continues to practice lewd and wicked acts. And so, for some Muslims, listening to the Qur'an is nothing more than a habit or a custom. Allah (sp) censured the polytheists of Makkah, for they listened to the Qur'an without acknowledging their errors or changing their ways.[201] Allah (sp) said:

$$سَأَصْرِفُ عَنْ ءَايَٰتِىَ ٱلَّذِينَ يَتَكَبَّرُونَ فِى ٱلْأَرْضِ بِغَيْرِ ٱلْحَقِّ$$

"I shall turn away from My Ayat (Verses of the Qur'an, signs) those who behave arrogantly on the earth, without a right." (Qur'an 7:146)
In his Tafseer of this Verse, Sufyaan bin Uyainah (m) said that "I shall turn away from My Ayat" (Verses of the Qur'an)" means: "I shall take away from them their ability to understand the Qur'an."[202]

Section Five:
Applying the Qur'an's Teachings

Applying the Qur'an's teachings is like a pinnacle in relation to the other rights of the Qur'an; in fact, it is the very reason why the Qur'an was revealed:

---

[201] *Yu'allimuhul-Kitaab At-Ta'aamul Ma'al-Qur'an* (pgs. 20, 21).
[202] *Al-Itqaan fee 'Uloom Al-Qur'an* (2/480).

$$\text{وَهَٰذَا كِتَابٌ أَنزَلْنَاهُ مُبَارَكٌ فَاتَّبِعُوهُ وَاتَّقُوا لَعَلَّكُمْ تُرْحَمُونَ}$$

"And this is a blessed Book (the Qur'an) which We have sent down, so follow it and fear Allah (i.e., do not disobey His Orders), that you may receive mercy (i.e., saved from the torment of Hell)." (Qur'an 6: 155)

One of the greatest faults of the Jews was that they deemed it sufficient to listen to and recite the Torah without applying its teachings. It is because of this shortcoming that Allah (sp) likened them to donkeys:

$$\text{مَثَلُ الَّذِينَ حُمِّلُوا التَّوْرَاةَ ثُمَّ لَمْ يَحْمِلُوهَا كَمَثَلِ الْحِمَارِ يَحْمِلُ أَسْفَارًا ۚ بِئْسَ مَثَلُ الْقَوْمِ الَّذِينَ كَذَّبُوا بِآيَاتِ اللَّهِ ۚ وَاللَّهُ لَا يَهْدِي الْقَوْمَ الظَّالِمِينَ}$$

"The likeness of those who were entrusted with the (obligation of the) Taurat (Torah) (i.e., to obey its commandments and to practice its legal laws), but who subsequently failed in those (obligations), is the likeness of a donkey who carries huge burdens of books (but understands nothing from them). How bad is the example (or the likeness) of people who deny the Ayat (proofs, evidences, Verses, signs, revelations, etc.) of Allah. And Allah guides not the people who are Zalimun (polytheists, wrong-doers, disbelievers, etc.)." (Qur'an 62:5)

Jews were entrusted with the duty of applying the Torah's teachings, a duty that they failed to fulfill. Yes, they did read the Torah, but they didn't apply its laws and teachings. Their situation, therefore, was very similar to that of a donkey upon which heaps of books are loaded: as a result of carrying them, it gets tired, but it does not benefit from their contents.[203]

Commenting on the abovementioned Verse, Ibn Al-Qayyim (m) said, "Even if this example was meant for Jews, it applies equally, in terms of its implications, to those who are entrusted with the duty of applying the teachings of the Qur'an but then fail to fulfill that duty."[204]

Abu Ad-Dardaa (r) said, "Once, we were with the Prophet (s) when he fixed his gaze at the sky and then said, 'This is around the time when knowledge will be taken away quickly from the people...'"

Ziyaad bin Labeed Al-Ansaaree said, "How will it be taken away from us, when we have recited the Qur'an? And by Allah, we will continue to recite it, and we will teach it to our women and children." The Prophet (s) said, "May your mother be bereaved of you", a statement that was originally spoken as a supplication, but which then became an expression through which one proclaimed one's feeling of astonishment. He then said, "O Ziyaad, I considered you to be one of the Fuqahaa (scholars, learned men) of the inhabitants of Al-Madeenah. Here is the Torah and the Gospel with the Jews and the Christians. But of what avail are those books to them (i.e., what benefit do they gain from them when they do not apply their teachings)?"[205]

In this Hadeeth, the Messenger of Allah (s) exhorts his followers not to limit themselves to simply reciting the Qur'an; for in addition to reciting the Qur'an, they should contemplate its meanings and apply its teachings. If they limit themselves to only reciting the Qur'an, they become similar to the Jews that are described in this Verse:

$$\text{وَمِنْهُمْ أُمِّيُّونَ لَا يَعْلَمُونَ الْكِتَابَ إِلَّا أَمَانِيَّ وَإِنْ هُمْ إِلَّا يَظُنُّونَ}$$

"And there are among them (Jews) unlettered people, who know not the Book, but they trust upon false desires and they but guess." (Qur'an 2: 78)

Based on Imam Al-Qurtubee's Tafseer of this Verse, the abovementioned translation does not convey its complete meaning. Imam Al-Qurtubee (m) said that the word *Amaanee* is the plural of *Umniyyah*, and in this Verse *Umniyyah* means recitation. Therefore, the complete meaning of the first part of the Verse is as follows: And there are among them (Jews) unlettered people, who know nothing of the

---

[203] *Rooh Al-Ma'aanee* (28/95), and *Tafseer Al-Baidaawee* (5/338).
[204] *Al-Amthaal Fil-Qur'an Al-Kareem* (pg. 27).
[205] *At-Tirmidhee* (5/31) (2653), and Al-Albaanee declared it to be authentic in *Saheeh Sunan At-Tirmidhee* (2/337).

Book save its recitation.[206] Sadly, most Muslims today know nothing of the Qur'an save its recitation. The Prophet (s) warned his Companions (rp) not to imitate a people that were to come after them, a people who were going to recite the Qur'an, without it going past their throats. He (s) said:
"A people will appear in this nation, and (in regard to them) your prayers will be nothing compared to their prayers. They will recite the Qur'an, and yet it will not go beyond their throats. They will exit from the religion just as quickly as an arrow exits from a target."[207]

Section Six:

Having Good Manners with the Qur'an

First: Manners that Pertain to One's Recitation of the Qur'an.

There are two kinds of manners that pertain to one's recitation of the Qur'an:
1) Manners of the Heart, and 2) Outward Manners

Manners of the Heart

They are as follow:

1) While reciting the Qur'an, you should appreciate the greatness of the Qur'an speech, all the while recognizing the great favor Allah (sp) has bestowed upon human beings by sending down the Qur'an to them and by making it easy for them to understand.
2) As you read the Qur'an, you should, in your heart, glorify the One Who revealed the Qur'an. This is because, when you read the Qur'an, you are not reading something that has been authored by a human being; instead, you are reading the speech of the Lord of all that exists.
3) Your heart should remain focused and concentrated during your recitation of the Qur'an. A person who truly glorifies Allah (sp) and recognizes the greatness of His speech will pay attention to the Verses he recites, without becoming mentally lazy and unfocused.
4) As much as you can, contemplate the meanings of the Qur'an. This is because worship must be accompanied by at least a degree of understanding. That being the case, you should, while you are reciting the Qur'an, focus your energies on understanding the lessons, commands, and prohibitions that are mentioned in the Qur'an.
5) You should be emotionally involved in the meaning of each Verse you recite. What this means is that, as you read the Qur'an, you should be having feelings that are appropriate to the specific Verses that you are reciting. Therefore, if you are reciting a Verse that contains some of the names of Allah (sp), you should contemplate the meanings of Allah's names. While reading about the Prophets (st), you should find solace in their stories and appreciate the sacrifices they made for their religion. If you read about the disbelievers of past nations, you should feel disdain for their actions, but moreover, you should learn from their stories by not repeating their mistakes.
6) You should feel that, in each Verse of the Qur'an, Allah (sp) is addressing you specifically. Therefore, you should read each page of the Qur'an in the same manner that a slave reads a letter in which his master gives him important instructions. Imam Ibn Al-Qayyim (m) wrote, "If you want to benefit from the Qur'an, focus with your heart when you recite it or listen to it. And pay attention with the understanding that Allah (sp) is addressing you directly. For in fact, the Qur'an is Allah's message to you, which He (sp) revealed upon the tongue of His

---
[206] *Al-Jaami' Li-Ahkaam Al-Qur'an* (6/2).
[207] Bukhaaree (6931).

Messenger (s)."[208] Sadly, many Muslims today do not feel that they are the intended audience of the Qur'an. So if one comes across a command in the Qur'an, he does not look inwardly to see whether or not he obeys that command, but instead looks at others to see whether they obey that command. It is as if he feels that the people around him, and not him personally, are being addressed by the Qur'an. Such a person feels no responsibility for his own actions but at the same time reproaches others for not fulfilling their responsibilities towards the Qur'an.

7) Each Verse of the Qur'an should have an effect on you. Therefore, when you recite Verses that contain warnings about the Hellfire, you should become afraid. When you read about Paradise, you should feel hopeful and happy. When you read about the evil actions of past disbelievers, you should humble yourself and feel disdain for their lack of manners and for their false beliefs and wicked deeds.

8) While reciting the Qur'an, you should avoid doing those things that will prevent you from understanding the Qur'an. So if you know that, by focusing all of your energy on reciting the Qur'an in a beautiful manner, you will not be able to focus on the meanings of the Qur'an, you should perhaps divert some of that energy towards understanding what you are reciting. Similarly, you should, in general, turn away from sinning, since sins have a deleterious effect on one's ability to understand and contemplate the Qur'an. A heart that is filled, for instance, with love of singing and foul speech will not share a similar love for Allah's speech, and therefore will not benefit very much from reciting the Qur'an. A heart that is at peace, on the other hand, and that is not afflicted with diseases of the heart, will find peace in the remembrance of Allah (sp); the possessor of such a heart will enjoy nothing more than the time he spends listening to or reciting the Qur'an.

9) When you recite the Qur'an, you should humble yourself, know your place, and acknowledge the fact that there is neither might nor power except with Allah (sp). If you approach the Qur'an in a humble manner, recognizing the fact that you are a weak sinner who is in dire need of Allah's help and guidance, you will benefit from the Verses you recite. But if you approach the Qur'an in an arrogant manner, thinking that you are a righteous Muslim who is better than most other Muslims, you will not, because of that attitude, be able to benefit much from what you recite.

Outward Manners

Whereas manners of the heart deal with one's inner state and one's feelings, outward manners have to do with actions we see, hear, smell or feel. These manners include performing ablution before reciting the Qur'an, applying perfume, choosing a clean place to recite, wearing nice clothes, cleaning one's mouth with a *siwak*, facing the Qiblah (the Ka'bah), sitting down in a dignified position, and reciting the Qur'an according to the proper ordering of its Chapters. Also, you should cry when you recite the Qur'an; and if the Verses of the Qur'an do not move you to the point of crying, you should cry for having a hard heart.

If you begin to yawn and feel tired, you should stop reciting the Qur'an. It is compulsory for you to pause in your recitation in order to say, "All praise is for Allah (*Al-Hamdulilleh*)" after you sneeze, or in order to say, "May Allah have mercy on you" to someone who has just sneezed. But it is only recommended to stop reciting the Qur'an when one hears the *Mu'adhdhin* make the call to prayer.

As for the things that are disliked or prohibited, it is disliked in Islam for one to take the Qur'an as a means of livelihood. It is disliked for one to recite the Qur'an while the inside of his mouth is filthy and smelly. It is disliked for one to recite the Qur'an out loud in the marketplace, in coffee shops, in restaurants, or in any place of public gathering wherein it is likely that people will not listen quietly to the Qur'an but will instead continue their conversations. Also, it is disliked for one to interpret Verses of the Qur'an in such a way as to make them apply to the mundane aspects of one's life. So, when such a person receives a visitor, he might recite:

---

[208] *Al-Fawaaid* (pg. 3)

$$ \text{جِئْتَ عَلَىٰ قَدَرٍ يَـٰمُوسَىٰ} $$

"Then you came here according to the fixed term which I ordained (for you), O Mosa (Moses)!" (Qur'an 20: 40)

Or when a meal is ready, he might say:

$$ \text{كُلُوا۟ وَٱشْرَبُوا۟ هَنِيٓـًٔۢا بِمَآ أَسْلَفْتُمْ فِى ٱلْأَيَّامِ ٱلْخَالِيَةِ} $$

"Eat and drink at ease for that which you have sent on before you in days past." (Qur'an 69: 24).

To be sure, it is categorically forbidden to change the order of the wording of the Qur'an. Some people, having had the foolish notion that they were experts of the Qur'an and of the Arabic language, decided to display their talents by changing the order of the words that are found in the Opening Chapter of the Qur'an. And we seek refuge in Allah (sp) from falling into such manifest error.

Second:

General Manners Regarding Our Handling of the Qur'an

There are a number of general manners regarding our handling of the Qur'an that each one of us should be aware of; here are some of the more important ones:

1) We should not abandon or desert the Qur'an. Allah (sp) said:

$$ \text{وَقَالَ ٱلرَّسُولُ يَـٰرَبِّ إِنَّ قَوْمِى ٱتَّخَذُوا۟ هَـٰذَا ٱلْقُرْءَانَ مَهْجُورًا} $$

"And the Messenger (Muhammad (s)) will say: 'O my Lord! Verily, my people deserted this Qur'an (neither listened to it, nor acted on its laws and orders).'" (Qur'an 25:30)

The meaning of this Verse is clear: The Prophet (s) complained to his Lord about how his people, the polytheists of Makkah, abandoned the Qur'an. They abandoned it by not believing in it, and by not applying its teachings. The Prophet's complaint was a serious matter, and it should serve as a warning to anyone who abandons the Qur'an – anyone who either stops believing in it or refrains from applying its laws and teachings.[209]

Imam Ibn Al-Qayyim (m) said that "abandoning the Qur'an" is general in meaning, in that it is comprehensive of various acts – such as refraining from listening to it; abandoning the application of its laws and teachings; abstaining from considering it a final judge over our disputes and all of the affairs of our lives; refraining from contemplating its meanings; and, while seeking cures from other sources, abstaining from deeming it a cure for all of the diseases of our hearts.

Sadly, these days Muslims have abandoned the Qur'an in every way possible – and it is to Allah (sp) alone that we complain about the situation of our nation. Many Muslims literally abandon the Qur'an by not reciting it, memorizing it, or studying its meanings; meanwhile, they have all the time in the world to watch countless hours of television, and to study the lives of famous people that have no ranking with Allah (sp).

Many Muslims do not listen to the recitation of the Qur'an; for they are far too busy listening to their favorite songs. Similarly, they do not contemplate the meanings of the Qur'an, their hearts are hard, and their eyes do not shed tears. And what is worse, they do not apply the Qur'an's teachings. For many Muslims, the teachings of the Qur'an do not represent a

---

[209] *Adwaa Al-Bayaan* (6/317).

complete way of life; instead, they recite Verses of the Qur'an over graves and donate the rewards for their recitation to the dead, even though they are in dire need of those rewards themselves. Others inscribe Verses of the Qur'an on amulets, which they hang from the chests of their children; or on posters, which they hang up in their homes and offices and schools, hoping to achieve blessings thereby. They make an effort to do all of that, but they do not take the trouble to actually apply the Qur'an's teachings.

And many Muslims today do not consider the Qur'an to be the ultimate judge over their disputes; they, in acquiescence to the claims of the enemies of Islam, argue that Allah's divinely revealed laws are outdated and that manmade laws are better suited for the needs of people in this modern-day era.

If one were to visit some of the countries whose inhabitants are primarily Muslims, one would find that many people do not seek cures to their ailments through the Qur'an; instead, the general masses of people have turned to magicians, soothsayers, and charlatans - trusting in them to provide a cure to their ailments.

Can we return to the truth, and can we repent as a nation? If so, then when? Indeed we ask Allah (sp) to provide us with safety and guidance both in this world and in the Hereafter.[210]

2) We should recite the Qur'an slowly and deliberately. Allah said:

$$\text{وَقُرْءَانًا فَرَقْنَٰهُ لِتَقْرَأَهُۥ عَلَى ٱلنَّاسِ عَلَىٰ مُكْثٍ}$$

"And (it is) a Qur'an which We have divided (into parts), in order that you might recite it to men at intervals." (Qur'an 17: 106)

According to another interpretation, the meaning of the end of this Verse is not, "that you might recite it to men at intervals", but instead, "that you might recite it to men slowly and deliberately". Therefore, the reason why the Qur'an was revealed in parts was so that the Prophet (s) could recite it to his followers slowly and deliberately, giving his Companions (rp) time to understand the meanings of one part of the Qur'an before they moved on to the next set of Verses.[211]

In Chapter *Muzammal*, Allah (sp) said:

$$\text{وَرَتِّلِ ٱلْقُرْءَانَ تَرْتِيلًا}$$

"And recite the Qur'an (aloud) in a slow (pleasant tone and) style." (Qur'an 73:4)

The Prophet (s) obeyed this command, for Qataadah related that when Anas (r) was asked about how the Prophet (s) would recite the Qur'an, he (r) responded, "He would stretch out his voice (and would thus recite slowly and deliberately)." Anas (r) then recited, "In the Name of Allah, the Most Beneficent, the Most Merciful", after which he said, "He (s) would stretch out his voice when he would recite, 'In the Name of Allah'; he would stretch out his voice when he would recite, 'The Most Beneficent'; and he would stretch out his voice when he would recite, 'The Most Merciful'".[212]

Third:

Manners that Pertain to Handling Actual Copies of the Qur'an

---

[210] *Fathur-Rahmaan Fee Bayaan Hajr Al-Qur'an* by Muhammad Aal Abdul-Azeez and Mahmood Al-Mallaah (pgs. 4, 5)
[211] *At-Tahreer Wat-Tanweer* (14/181).
[212] Bukhaaree (5045, 5046)

A copy of the Qur'an, by virtue of the fact that it contains between its covers the speech of Allah (sp), is superior to every other book in existence. For that reason we must adhere to a number of manners when we handle a copy of the Qur'an; some of the more important of those manners are as follows:

1) One must be in a state of purity if one wishes to touch the Qur'an.
2) A person who transcribes Verses of the Qur'an should write in a beautiful and clear script, and he should write on quality paper.[213]
3) No one may add any words to the pages of a copy of the Qur'an, nor should one make drawings along the margins.
4) The selling of copies of the Qur'an should not be taken as a business.
5) One should not turn one's back to the Qur'an, nor should one use a copy of the Qur'an as a pillow.
6) When handing a copy of the Qur'an to someone else, or when placing it on a shelf, one should not toss it or throw it; instead, one should handle it in a respectable manner. Also, when taking it or handing it to someone else, one should not use one's left hand.
7) One should not extend one's legs in the direction of copies of the Qur'an.
8) One should not place any book above the Qur'an; likewise, one should not place papers or notes between its pages.
9) One should not carry a copy of the Qur'an when one is entering a dirty place, such as a toilet; also, one should not carry a copy of the Qur'an when one is traveling inside of enemy territory. On a similar note, one should not do anything that will likely result in the Qur'an being mishandled or debased; so, for instance, one should not make copies of the Qur'an easily accessible to children, deranged people, or disbelievers, since each of those categories of people will likely – some of them inadvertently and others on purpose – mishandle or debase the Qur'an in some way.[214]
10) One should not transcribe Verses of the Qur'an onto the ground; nor should one transcribe Verses of the Qur'an onto the walls of the Masjid. And one should not write on the front, back, or inside cover of a copy of the Qur'an, an act of impropriety and indecency that many young students are guilty of. In recent times, some of the enemies of Islam have printed Verses of the Qur'an on to underwear, shoes, and shopping bags, in an attempt to debase the Noble Qur'an. But such people would do well to contemplate the saying of Allah (sp):

وَيَمْكُرُونَ وَيَمْكُرُ ٱللَّهُ وَٱللَّهُ خَيْرُ ٱلْمَٰكِرِينَ

"They were plotting and Allah too was planning, and Allah is the Best of the planners." (Qur'an 8:30)

11) One should not use a copy of the Qur'an for any purpose other than the one for which it was revealed. Therefore, it may not be used as a paperweight in order to prevent sheets of paper from flying off with the wind. Similarly, one should not buy a copy of the Qur'an simply for the purpose of hanging it around one's neck and seeking blessings in the process. And finally, one should not handle copies of the Qur'an in any way that is considered forbidden in Islamic Law.

---

[213] *Al-Jaami' Li-Ahkaam Al-Qur'an* (1/44)
[214] *Al-Jaami LiAhkaam Al-Qur'an* (1/46, 47)

Section Seven: **Inviting Others to Learn the Qur'an**

All Muslims throughout the world, regardless of whether they are Arabs or non-Arabs, carry upon their shoulders a great responsibility – that of conveying the teachings of the Qur'an to others. Allah (sp) said:

$$وَأَنزَلْنَا إِلَيْكَ ٱلذِّكْرَ لِتُبَيِّنَ لِلنَّاسِ مَا نُزِّلَ إِلَيْهِمْ$$

"And We have also sent down unto you (O Muhammad (s)) the reminder and the advice (the Qur'an, that you may explain clearly to men what is sent down to them." (Qur'an 16:44)

Allah's command to His Prophet (s) is, by extension, His command to the people of the Muslim nation. Like the Prophet (s) did when he was alive, all Muslims must fulfill the command that is given in the abovementioned Verse. Each person, to the degree that he is able to, must convey the message of the Qur'an to others. Without a doubt, because they are specialized in the Islamic sciences and because they are able to explain the rulings of the Qur'an, scholars bear the greater brunt of that responsibility.

Allah (sp) revealed the Qur'an to His Prophet (s), so that he could warn his people first, and so that he could then warn the general masses of people. Allah (sp) said:

$$وَأُوحِيَ إِلَيَّ هَٰذَا ٱلْقُرْءَانُ لِأُنذِرَكُم بِهِۦ وَمَنۢ بَلَغَ$$

"This Qur'an has been revealed to me that I may therewith warn you and whosoever it may reach." (Qur'an 6:19)

Ar-Rabee' bin Anas (r) said, "It is a right upon every follower of the Messenger of Allah (s) to invite (others to the Qur'an) just as the Messenger of Allah (s) would invite, and to warn others (about being punished for disobeying Allah (sp)) just as the Prophet (s) would warn others".[215]

All Muslims, and not just Arabs, are members of the nation of Prophet Muhammad (s), and as such, they must all strive to convey his message to the rest of mankind. Allah (sp) said:

$$قُلْ هَٰذِهِۦ سَبِيلِي أَدْعُوٓا۟ إِلَى ٱللَّهِ عَلَىٰ بَصِيرَةٍ أَنَا۠ وَمَنِ ٱتَّبَعَنِي وَسُبْحَٰنَ ٱللَّهِ وَمَآ أَنَا۠ مِنَ ٱلْمُشْرِكِينَ$$

"Say (O Muhammad): 'This is my way; I invite unto Allah (i.e., to the Oneness of Allah – Islamic Monotheism) with sure knowledge, I and whosoever follows me (also must invite others to Allah, i.e., to the Oneness of Allah – Islamic Monotheism) with sure knowledge. And Glorified and Exalted be Allah (above all that they associate as partners with Him), And I am not of the Mushrikun (polytheists, pagans, idolaters, and disbelievers in the Oneness of Allah, those who worship others along with Allah or set up rivals or partners to Allah).'" (Qur'an 12: 108)

Therefore, it is not enough to be a good Muslim; rather, one must also strive to improve and guide others.

Even though all Muslims share the responsibility of conveying the Qur'an to the rest of mankind, Arab Muslims are especially responsible in that regard; after all, the Noble Qur'an was revealed in their language. That the Qur'an was revealed in Arabic is both an honor for Arabs and a clear indication that they are particularly responsible for the duty of conveying the Qur'an to the rest of mankind.

And yet when will Arabs wake up from their slumber and from their state of heedlessness? The situation is both serious and dangerous, and the responsibility on our shoulders is great. Considering the present-day circumstances of Muslims, we must all multiply our efforts if we hope to fulfill our

---

[215] *Tafseer Ibn Katheer* (3/279)

duty of conveying the message of the Qur'an to all of mankind. We must multiply our efforts primarily because of all of the obstacles that stand in the way of the Qur'an being conveyed to people in a clear and coherent manner.

Every Muslim individual must feel as if he is standing on the front lines of an epic battle, except his main weapons are not guns and swords, but instead the Qur'an and whatever knowledge of Islam he has with him. All Muslims – the rich, the educated, the skilled and talented, the common masses of Muslims – must come together and pool their resources, so that they can make use of all forms of modern technology to facilitate their duty of conveying the message of the Qur'an to others. This will require the opening of satellite channels, the making of television and radio programs, the purchasing of printing presses, and so on. In short, we must do everything that is in our power to make sure that the message of the Qur'an reaches out to every human being on earth, regardless of where he lives and what language he speaks. Indeed, we ask Allah (sp) to help us achieve that aim, and to make us among those who are guided themselves, and who guide others as well.[216]

Profiles of the Eminent Figures that are Mentioned in this Work

1) L. Sedillot (1808-1876): A well-known French Orientalist, Sedillot dedicated much of his life to disseminating the scholarly works of his father, Jean-Jacques Sedillot, who had died in the year 1832. L. Sedillot authored two of his own books: *A Summarized History of the Arab Peoples*, and *A General History of the Arab Peoples*. Additionally, he wrote a great many research articles for various scholarly journals. Refer to the Arabic work *Qaaloo 'Anil-Islam*, which was written by Dr. Imaad Ad-Deen Khaleel (pg. 72).

2) Cte. De Castries (1850-1927): Having been a major in the French army, De Castries lived in Northern Africa for quite some time. Among his works were a series of unpublished books on Western history (1905), *The Saudi Ashraaf* (1921), and *A Hollander's journey to the West* (1926). Refer to *Qaaloo 'Anil-Islam* (pg. 70).

3) S. Salhab: A Christian from Lebanon, Salhab became renowned for his unbiased scholarly work. He was also well-known for his efforts to create an environment of peace between Muslims and Christians in Lebanon. During the sixties, he authored many books and delivered many lectures both at Muslim and Christian gatherings, for his message, which was one of peace, was always the same. Among his authored works were *The Meeting of Christianity and Islam* (1970) and *In the Footsteps of Muhammad* (1970). Refer to *Qaaloo 'Anil-Islam* (pg. 69).

4) Sydnee Fisher: A Professor of History in Ohio University, and the author of many works that discuss the affairs of Eastern countries (most of which are inhabited by Muslims), Sydnee Fisher authored the famous work *The Middle East in the Islamic Era*. Refer to *Qaaloo 'Anil-Islam* (pg. 78).

5) L. Veccia Vaglieri: A present-day Italian scholar, L. Veccia dedicated much of her research to Islamic History, both ancient and modern; and to the Arabic Language. Some of her written works are *The Principles of the Arabic Language*, which has been printed in two volumes (1937-1941); *Islam* (1946); *A Defense of Islam* (1952); and a number of research articles that

---

[216] *Qur'aanakum, Yaa Muslimoon* (pgs. 32-37).

have been printed in various famous Orientalist magazines. Refer to *Qaaloo 'Anil-Islam* (pg. 56).

6) John Hanna (1893-1969): A Christian from Lebanon, Hanna graduated from the Faculty of Medicine in the American University. He then moved to Paris, where he specialized in obstetrics and gynecology. Later, he founded an obstetrics hospital in the city of Beirut. Among his written works were *The Story of Man*, *From Occupation to Liberation*, *My Return from Moscow*, *A Social Conscience*, and *The New Arab Reality*. Refer to *Qaaloo 'Anil-Islam* (pg. 58); to *Mo'jam Al-Mu'allifeen* (1/513); and to *Al-'Alaam* (2/145).

7) Ibraaheem Khalil Ahmad: Born in the city of Alexandria, Ibraaheem Khalil graduated with a degree in theology from the Egyptian Faculty of Divinity. And he did his graduate work in Princeton University. In his professional life, he worked both as a Professor and as a missionary priest. It was while he worked as a Professor that he studied Islam in depth, and he later openly pronounced his entry into the fold of Islam in the year 1960. Two of his authored works were *Muhammad in the Torah, the Gospel, and the Qur'an*, and *The History of the Children of Israel*. Refer to *Qaaloo 'Anil-Islam* (pg. 49).

8) Dr. Jareenee: A famous French doctor, Dr. Jareenee served as a member of the French Parliament. Refer to *Qaaloo 'Anil-Islam* (pg.76).

9) Et. Dinet (1861-1929): Educated in France, Dinet somehow became interested in Algeria; in fact, he would spend six months of every year in the city of Bou-Sa'aadah. Towards the end of his life, he openly declared his entry into the fold of Islam, and he changed his name to Naasir Ad-Deen. That was in the year 1927, and only one year later, which was the year before he died, he performed Hajj (the greater pilgrimage to Makkah). Three of his authored works were *The Life of Arabs*, *Rays from the Light of Islam*, and *The East from the Viewpoint of the West*. Refer to *Qaaloo 'Anil-Islam* (pg. 63); and to *Al-Islam Fil-'Aql Al-'Aalamee* (pg. 179).

10) John Batiste Ahuneemo: Having earned a degree in Theology, John Batiste worked as a Catholic priest for a number of years. His work as a priest ended in 1991, when, while spending some time in Ghana, he openly declared his entry into the fold of Islam. He changed his name from John to Ibraaheem, and he dedicated the next years of his life to spreading the message of Islam to the inhabitants of the Ivory Coast, Ghana, Togo, and Niger. Refer to *Qaaloo 'Anil-Islam* (pg. 89).

11) Dr. A. N. Sousa: An Iraqi researcher and engineer, Dr. Sousa was a member of the Iraqi Research Council, and he was an eminent historian of Iraqi agricultural life. Born and raised a Jew, Dr. Sousa embraced Islam as a result of being moved by the Verses of the Noble Qur'an. Having died only a few years ago, he left behind research papers that dealt with a number of branches of knowledge. Also, arguing from a historical perspective, he wrote many tracts in which he refuted the claims of the worldwide Zionist movement. Two of his more famous works are *A Detailed Study of the Histories of Arabs and Jews*, and *My Path Towards Islam*. Refer to *Qaaloo 'Anil-Islam* (pg. 70).

12) Cat Stevens: A former British singer of great renown, Cat Stevens sold, during the course of his musical career, more than one million records. After having learned about Islam from his brother, Stevens embraced Islam in the year 1976, and from that time until the present, he has spent most of his time inviting others to embrace Islam. Refer to *Qaaloo 'Anil-Islam* (pg. 68).

13) F. Montague: A Frenchman, Montague was both a scholar and a prolific traveler. He specialized in the knowledge of Islamic and Arab affairs. He spent a number of years traveling all over the world, and at least a few of those years he spent in Africa and Asia. He authored a number of works about Islam and Islamic civilization. His lifelong research on Islam

culminated in his entry into the fold of Islam in the year 1977, an event that prompted him to change his name to Al-Mansoor Billahi Ash-Shaafi'ee. Refer to *Qaaloo 'Anil-Islam* (pg. 88).

14) Ayesha Bridget Honey: Born and raised in a Christian, English family, Ayesha became enamored with the study of Philosophy; and she moved to Canada in order to complete her studies in that field. It was during her student years in a Canadian University that Ayesha learned about Islam and eventually embraced it as her religion. Later on, she became a Professor in a Nigerian University. Refer to *Qaaloo 'Anil-Islam* (pg. 88).

15) A. Ali David: David was originally from a Hindu family that was a member of the Brahman caste. In the early years of colonization, he became a Christian at the hands of the first group of missionaries that traveled to India. But his religious journey did not end there; instead, he continued to read a great deal about many religions of the world, until, finally, he gained the opportunity to study the Noble Qur'an. Shortly thereafter, he, having become convinced of the truthfulness of Islam, became a Muslim. Refer to *Qaaloo 'Anil-Islam* (pg. 59).

16) Brown: Brown was a member of the British Naval Fleet. Refer to *Qaaloo 'Anil-Islam* (pg. 128).

Content

Introduction
The importance of this book's subject
Why I chose this subject matter
My methodology in writing this research paper
INTRODUCTION
First topic: The meaning of the word "Qur'an" in Islam

Chapter 1
The Magnificence of Its Meanings, Aims and Powerful Influence

Part 1
The Magnificence of the Qur'an's Meanings

Topic 1
The Magnificence of the Noble Qur'an as Clarified by Its Verses
Section One: Allah's Praise of His Book
Section Two: The superiority of the One Who Descended with the Qur'an
Section Three: The Qur'an is Revelation from the Lord of All that Exists
Section Four: The Qur'an is Upright and Contains in it no Crookedness
Section Five: The Humbling and Fear of Mountains
Section Six: Mankind and Jinns are Challenged to Produce something that is Comparable to the Noble Qur'an

Topic 2
Manifestations of the Qur'an's Magnificence
Introduction
Section one: The Qur'an was Revealed during the Best of Times
Section two: The Qur'an was revealed in the Best and Most Comprehensive of Languages

Section three: The Ease with which the Qur'an can be Understood by all People
Section four: Allah (sp) Preserved the Qur'an
What was done to Ensure the Preservation of the Qur'an
Section five: The Universal Message of the Qur'an
Section six: The Qur'an is a Witness over previously Revealed Books
The Relationship Between "Confirmation" and "Mohayminan"
Ways in which The Qur'an is *Mohayminan* Over Previously Revealed Scriptures

Topic 3
Proofs of the Qur'an's Magnificence

Topic 4
The Grandeur of the Names and Attributes of the Qur'an
Introduction

First: The Grandeur of the Qur'an's Names
First: *Al-Furqaan*
Second: *Al-Burhaan*
Third: *Al-Haqq*
Fourth: *An-Naba Al-'Adheem*
Fifth: *Al-Balaagh*
Sixth: *Ar-Rooh*
Seventh: *Al-Mau'idhah*
Eighth: *Ash-Shifaa*
Ninth: *Ahsanul-Hadeeth*

Second: The Grandeur of the Qur'an's Attributes
First: *Al-Hakeem*
Second: *Al-Azeez*
Third: *Al-Kareem*
Fourth: *Al-Majeed*
Fifth: *Al-'Adheem*
Sixth: *Al-Basheer Wan-Nadheer*
Seventh: *Laa Ya'tihi Al-Baatil Min Baini Yadaihi Walaa Min Khalfihi* (Falsehood cannot come to it from before it or behind it)

CHAPTER 2
The Magnificence of the Qur'an's Aims, Legislations, and Stories

Part One:
The Magnificence of the Qur'an's Aims

Introduction
Section One: Correcting People's Beliefs and Outlook on Life
  1) *At-Tawheed* (Islamic Monotheism)
  2) Correcting Beliefs about Prophethood
  3) Correcting Beliefs about Faith in the Hereafter

Section Two: Removing Difficulties from People's Lives
Section Three: Confirming the Dignity of Man and the Sanctity of Human Rights
First: Confirming the Dignity of Man
Second: Confirming the Sanctity of Human Rights

Section Four: Promoting Strong Family Morals, and Doing Justice to Women
First: Promoting Strong Family Morals
Second: Doing Justice to Women and Freeing Them from the Oppression of Pre-Islamic Ignorance
The Qur'an does Justice to Women
Section Five: Bringing Happiness to Human Beings in Both this World and the Hereafter
Happiness in this Life

Part Two:
The Greatness of the Qur'an's Legislations

Introduction
The superiority of Qur'anic Legislations
Section One: The Comprehensiveness of the Qur'an's Legislations
Section Two: The Permanent and Lasting Applicability of the Qur'an's Legislations
Section Three: The Justice of the Qur'an's Legislations
The Noble Qur'an Exhorts Muslims to Act Justly
The Different Spheres of Justice
The Differences Between Justice in Islamic Law and Other Systems of Law
Testimonies from Islam's Enemies

Part Three:
The Magnificence of the Qur'an's Stories

Introduction
Section One: Instances of Magnificence in the Qur'an's Stories
1) Their Divine Source
2) Their Exact Correspondence with what Actually Took Place Historically
3) Mentioning the Key Parts of Stories
4) Telling the Same Story in a Variety of Ways, or in Other Words, Repetition
Section Two: The Magnificence of the Aims and Purposes of the Qur'an's Stories
1) To Establish the Oneness of Allah (sp), and to Order Human Beings to Worship Him Alone
2) Confirming the Truthfulness of the Prophet's Mission (s)
3) Establishing the Reality of Resurrection After Death
4) Strengthening the Faith and Resolve of the Prophet (s) and of True Believers
5) Teaching Muslims Important Lessons about Prophets (st) and about the People to Whom They were Sent
6) Pointing Out the End Destinations of the People of Past Nations
7) Providing Spiritual Development for Believers
8) Promoting Justice and Righteousness in Society, and Forbidding the Spread of Corruption and Evildoing
9) Reminding Muslims About Their Eternal Struggle Against Their Most Despised and Dangerous of Foes: Shaitaan (the Devil)
10) Helping Muslims Overcome Hopelessness and Depression
11) Pointing Out Allah's Ability to Make Miracles Occur
12) Pointing Out the Favors with which Allah (sp) Blessed Prophets (st) and Others Among His Righteous Servants

PART 3
The Greatness of the Qur'an's Influence

Introduction
Section One: The Importance of Inviting Others to Islam with the Qur'an
Introduction
Section Two: Applying the Principle of Inviting Others to Islam with the Qur'an
Introduction
Some of the Main Differences between the Miracle of the Noble Qur'an and the Miracles that other Prophets (st) came with
Examples of How the Prophet (s) Would Use the Qur'an to Invite People to Islam
First: Preaching Islam to the Delegations that came during the Hajj Season
Second: Traveling to See People and Inviting them with the Qur'an
Third: Inviting Kings and Rulers with the Qur'an
Fourth: The Qur'an's Influence on the Hearts of the Enemies of Islam
Fifth: Reminding People during Sermons and Lectures

Sixth: Reciting the Qur'an in a Melodious yet Fearful Tone, and Reciting Those Verses that are Especially Known for their Effect on the Hearts of People
Section Three: Examples of How the Qur'an has Influenced Modern-Day Figures to Embrace Islam
Introduction
1) A Christian missionary whose name is now Ibraaheem Khaleel Ahmad
2) Dr. Jareenee
3) Etienne Dinet
4) John Batiste Ahuneemo
5) Dr. Ahmad Naseem Sosa
6) Cat Stevens, Who Changed His Name to Yusuf Islam
7) Fansai Montai
8) Hony
9) 'Aamir 'Alee Daawood
10) Brown and the Secrets of the Deep Ocean
11) A German Scholar

CHAPTER 2
The Greatness of the Qur'an Virtues

Part One:
The Greatness of the Qur'an's Overall Superior Qualities

Section One: The Qur'an is Allah's Revealed Speech
Section Two: The Qur'an is an Honor for Arabs in Particular, and for the Muslim Nation in General
Section Three: The Qur'an Guides to that which is Most Upright
Section Four: The Qur'an is a Blessed Book
Section Five: The Qur'an Contains in it an Explanation of All Things
Section Six: The Qur'an is Allah's Favor and a Cause of Happiness for His Slaves
Section Seven: The Qur'an is Guidance, Mercy, and Glad Tidings for Muslims
Section Eight: The Qur'an is Light
Section Nine: The Qur'an is Life for those Who Believe in It

Part Two:
The Greatness of the Qur'an's Specific Superior Qualities

Section One: The Virtues of Listening to the Qur'an
Introduction
First: Listening to the Qur'an Results in Being the Recipient of Allah's Mercy
Second: Listening to the Qur'an Leads to Guidance for Both Human Beings and Jinns
Third: Listening to the Qur'an Results in a Heart that is Submissive and Spiritually Strong and in Eyes that Shed Tears (Out of the Fear of Allah (sp))
Section Two: The Virtues of Learning the Qur'an and of Teaching it to Others
Introduction
First: Both the Qur'an's Teacher and Student are Similar in a Way to Angels and Messengers (st)
Second: The Best of People are Those Who Learn the Qur'an and Teach it to Others
Third: Learning the Qur'an and Teaching it are Better than all of the Treasures of the World
Fourth: Whoever Teaches a Verse (of the Qur'an) will continue to have Its Reward, as Long as It Continues to be Recited
Fifth: The Reward of Teaching the Qur'an to One's Children
Section Three: The Virtues of Reciting the Qur'an
Introduction
First: Reciting the Qur'an is a Profitable Undertaking
Second: As a Result of Reciting the Qur'an, Tranquility, Mercy, and the Angels Descend
1) Peace and Tranquility Descend upon Them
2) Mercy Envelops Them
3) The Angels Surround Them
4) Allah (sp) Mentions Them to Those that are With Him
Third: To Recite the Qur'an, Regardless of One's Ability as a Reciter, is a Good Deed

1) A Person Who Recites the Qur'an Well
2) A Person Who Receives Two Rewards for His Recitation of the Qur'an
Section Four: The Virtues of Memorizing the Qur'an
Introduction
First: The High Ranking of a *Haafidh* (i.e., a Person Who has committed the Entire Qur'an to Memory)
Second: A *Haafidh* is Placed Before Others Both in this World and in the Hereafter
1) A *Haafidh* is Most Deserving of being Chosen to Lead Others
2) A *Haafidh* is the Most Deserving of People to Lead Others in Prayer
3) In Matters of Importance, a *Haafidh* Should be one of the First People to be Consulted
4) A *Haafidh* is Given Precedence in Shared Graves
Third: The Various Virtues of Being a *Haafidh*
1) Being the "People of Allah"
2) A *Haafidh* is Among Those Who have been Given Knowledge
3) The Hellfire will not Burn Those Who have the Qur'an Memorized
Section Five: The Virtues of Applying the Teachings of the Qur'an
Introduction
The Virtues of Applying the Qur'an's Teachings
1) Guidance
2) Mercy
3) Success and Happiness Both in this World and in the Hereafter
4) Expiation of Sins and Having One's Situation in Life Improved

Part Three:
The Rights of the Qur'an Over Muslims

Section One: Having Faith in the Qur'an
Section Two: Preserving and Honoring the Qur'an
Section Three: Reciting the Qur'an
Section Four: Contemplating the Verses of the Qur'an
Section Five: Applying the Qur'an's Teachings
Section Six: Having Good Manners with the Qur'an
Manners of the Heart
Outward Manners
General Manners Regarding Our Handling of the Qur'an
Manners that Pertain to Handling Actual Copies of the Qur'an
Section Seven: Inviting Others to Learn the Qur'an
Profiles of the Eminent Figures that are Mentioned in this Work

www.ingramcontent.com/pod-product-compliance
Lightning Source LLC
LaVergne TN
LVHW011941070526
838202LV00054B/4738